There has been in recent years a plethora of defenses of theism from analytical philosophers such as Plantinga, Swinburne, and Alston. Richard Gale's important book is a critical response to these writings. New versions of cosmological, ontological, and religious-experience arguments are critically evaluated, along with pragmatic arguments to justify faith on the grounds of its prudential or moral benefits. A special feature of the book is the discussion of the atheological argument, which attempts to deduce a contradiction from the theist's way of conceiving of God's nature. In considering arguments for and against the existence of God, Gale is able to say interesting things about many important philosophical concepts including explanation, time, free will, personhood, actuality, and the objectivity of experience.

On the nature and existence of God

On the nature and existence of God

RICHARD M. GALE

DEPARTMENT OF PHILOSOPHY, UNIVERSITY OF PITTSBURGH

CAMBRIDGE UNIVERSITY PRESS

Published by the Press Syndicate of the University of Cambridge
The Pitt Building, Trumpington Street, Cambridge CB2 1RP
40 West 20th Street, New York, NY 10011-4211, USA
10 Stamford Road, Oakleigh, Melbourne 3166, Australia

First published 1991
First paperback edition 1993

Printed in the United States of America

Library of Congress Cataloging-in-Publication Data
Gale, Richard M., 1932-
On the nature and existence of God / Richard M. Gale
p.   cm.
Includes bibliographical references and index.
ISBN 0-521-40300-6
1. God – Proof.   I. Title.
BT102.G324   1991
212'.1–dc20   90–19368
                                          CIP

A catalogue record for this book is available from the British Library.

ISBN 0-521-40300-6 hardback
ISBN 0-521-45723-8 paperback

For the three wonderful wild ones
Andy, Larry, and Julia

Contents

Acknowledgments

I thank the editors of the following journals for their permission to use large sections from some of my previously published articles: "William James and the Ethics of Belief," *American Philosophical Quarterly*, 17, no. 1 (1980), 1–14; "Omniscience–Immutability Arguments," *American Philosophical Quarterly*, 23, no. 4 (1986), 319–35; *Negation and Non-Being, American Philosophical Quarterly*, Monograph no. 10 (1976), pp. 78–87; "Freedom Versus Unsurpassable Greatness," *International Journal for the Philosophy of Religion*, 23 (1988), 65–75; "Lewis' Indexical Argument for World-Relative Actuality," *Dialogue*, 28 (1989), 289–304; "Freedom and the Free Will Defense," *Social Theory and Practice*, 16, no. 3 (1990).

Introduction

This book addresses the question whether there is rational justification to believe that God, as conceived of by traditional Western theism, exists. There are contemporary fideists who hold that there is no need to justify belief by appeal to arguments, since the mere fact of belief is supposed to be self-justificatory. There is no inconsistency in offering both a fideistic and an argumentative support of belief, as do some contemporaries. My concern is only with the latter part of their justification. The question, then, is whether there are any good arguments either for or against believing that God exists.

I do not pretend to answer this question, since I completely ignore inductive arguments based on design, beauty, and lawlike regularity and simplicity for the existence of God, as well as those based on evil to show the improbability of his existence. A proper discussion of these arguments is the topic for a separate book of considerable length, since it would have to deal with the applicability of Bayesian models of probability to the aggregation of the premises of all the different inductive arguments for and against God's existence. One of the valuable lessons to be learned from Richard Swinburne's *The Existence of God*, which makes out such a Bayesian case for belief, is that the issues are exceedingly complex and need to be treated by those who are steeped in probability and confirmation theory, which eliminates me.

Our question whether there are any good arguments either for or against belief takes on special importance in the light of the startling resurgence of theism within philosophy during the past thirty or so years. What might surprise some is that the three leaders of this movement, William Alston, Alvin Plantinga, and Richard Swinburne, are themselves analytical philosophers. Some mistakenly see analytic philosophy as the natural enemy of theism, no doubt because certain movements in twentieth-century analytic philosophy, such as logical atomism, logical positivism, and some versions of ordinary language philosophy, developed theories of meaning that were employed to slay the dragon of theism by showing that it did not measure up to certain minimal standards of meaningfulness. But it is a mistake to identify analytic philosophy with these movements and their dogmas.

While these movements, along with their theories of meaning, have come and gone and the criticisms of theism based on their theories of meaning have become old hat, analytic philosophy has forged new weapons in the interim that have been deployed by analytically trained philosophers on behalf of theism: for instance, rational choice theory to breathe new life into the perennial Rodney Dangerfield of philosophy, Pascal's wager; modal logic to reformulate a more powerful version of the ontological argument; language-game analysis for justifying the practice of religion and, in particular, the prima facie acceptability of existential claims based on religious experiences; and Bayesian models of probability for an inductive justification of belief. Philosophy of religion is to the core areas of philosophy – logic, scientific methodology, the philosophy of language, metaphysics, and epistemology – as Israel is to the Pentagon. The former are a proving ground for the weapons forged in the latter. Whenever there is a significant breakthrough in one of the core areas, it eventually finds a fruitful deployment in the peripheral areas, such as the philosophy of religion. And this is what we have witnessed during the past thirty years.

Because theism has found such a powerful new formulation, due to the deployment of these new analytical weapons, there is a need for a return visit from Hume's Philo. But the sceptical Philo whose spirit imbues my book is more than just a crazed Charles Bronson, who is back again and *really* angry this time, even more so than on the previous thirty-six occasions; for my philosophical version of "Death Wish XXXVII" has the positive upshot of helping us to command a more adequate conception of God – a God that will prove a worthy object of worship and obedience, even if the the case for believing in his existence is shaky. My book, therefore, has both a negative and a positive pole.

There are two very different sorts of arguments to show that belief (disbelief) is rationally justified. One is directed toward establishing the truth (falsity) of the proposition that God exists. It will be called an "epistemological argument," since it purports to supply the sort of justification that would support a claim to know that God exists (does not exist). The other, to be called a "pragmatic argument," is directed toward showing the prudential or moral benefits that result from believing (disbelieving) this proposition. Both ways of justifying the rationality of belief (disbelief) will be considered.

The epistemological arguments will be my first and foremost concern, with only the final Chapter 9 devoted to the pragmatic arguments. I am going to reverse the usual order of presentation and begin with arguments against the existence of God, with special attention to so-called atheological arguments that attempt to deduce a contradiction from the theist's conception of God, with appeal to only necessarily true additional premises. My reason for doing so is that the first order of business should be to clarify the nature of the God whose existence is in question. And that is just what these atheological arguments help us to do. They are the thought experiments that probe the internal consistency of the theist's conception of God, often with the result that the theist must go back to the drawing board and redesign the particular divine attribute(s) that is the focus of the argument. Their role in spurring consideration of the divine nature is similar to that of Zeno's paradoxes in forcing subsequent philosophers to come to grips with the nature of space and time. The idea of God in Western civilization has in fact undergone just this sort of dialectical unfolding through the successive challenges posed by different atheological arguments.

The idea of redesigning our concept of God might strike some as blasphemous. This becomes less shocking when it is realized that the concept of God that is the target of an atheological argument is that of the theologian, which is a highly theoretical concept that is as distant from the somewhat anthropomorphic concept of God in the Scriptures as is the physicist's concept of a table from that of the ordinary person. The religiously available God – the one who communes with men and intervenes in history – was metaphysicalized by the great medieval theists so that he began to have the sort of being enjoyed by a Platonic form. Our religious experiences and traditions serve as data for these metaphysical theories about God's nature, but in virtue of their underdetermining these theories, there is considerable room for conceptual maneuvering when a given theory of God's nature runs afoul of an atheological argument, just as there is when a scientific theory faces anomalous facts. The basic problem that a theological concept of God faces is that of over metaphysicalizing God so that he no longer is a person and thereby becomes religiously unavailable. This is a special instance of the problem faced by any theoretical or rational reconstruction of an ordinary concept: Which features of the ordinary concept must get retained? In Carnapian terms, the question concerns the conditions of material adequacy for the analysis of our concept of God. This will be a recurring issue in this book.

Blasphemy aside, the idea of redesigning our concept of God raises the problem of how we can keep the referent of the word "God" constant amidst these conceptual reforms, which can involve a change in either what are taken to be the essential or defining properties of God or how they are understood. There must be some answer to how this is possible, since this is in fact what has happened.

But just how is it possible? To answer this we must see how "God" refers. Some have claimed that "God" is a title that applies to an individual in virtue of his playing the role of the absolutely perfect sovereign being, which is the concept of God in traditional Western theism. If "God" is a title, it functions quite differently from the ordinary titles with which we are familiar, for instance, "the king of France," "the heavyweight champion of the world," and so on. Being God, unlike having one of these titles, is both essential to and constitutive of the essence of its possessor, that is, this individual could not exist without being God, and no other individual could be God. The champion can lose his title to another, which shows that this title is neither essential nor necessarily possessed uniquely either within a single world or across possible worlds. The character played by Marlon Brando in *On the Waterfront* said that he could have been a contender, even the champion; but it would be a violation of the meaning of God for him to have said that he could have been God or for God to say that he might have been a two-bit enforcer for the mob. No wonder there is no theological version of the king-must-die legend.

Granted that any being who is God is God in every world in which he exists and no other being is God in any world, there still remains the question of what qualifies an individual as the denotatum of "God." "God," no doubt, is a proper name, but this is not sufficiently helpful, since there are such widely divergent views of how proper names refer. On the one hand, there is the so-called descriptivist theory according to which a proper name has a sense that is expressed by some definite description or cluster of descriptions, it being both sufficient and necessary for an individual to be its denotatum that she satisfy this description or a good number of the descriptions in the cluster. In regard to successive uses of a name, the cluster theory can require that they either have enough members of the set in common or be connected by a sequence of uses of the name, adjoining members of which satisfy this condition. This would allow successive coreferential uses to have no properties in common, this paralleling the bundle theories of the identity of material objects and persons over time. On the basis of this analogy, the latter will be called the "bundle version of the cluster theory." Opposed to this is the view of proper names as purely referential, their referent being determined by various causal or historical facts connecting the referent with the user of the name. "God" does not perfectly fit either theory, but by judiciously incorporating elements of both theories, along with some language-game analysis, an adequate answer can be given to our question as to how the referent of "God" can remain constant amidst conceptual reform.

In recent years the descriptivist theory has come under fire from the likes of Kripke, Putnam, and Donnellan. The basis of their attack is to take any description (or cluster of descriptions) that is offered as constituting the sense of a name and show that we can construct a counterfactual story in which the actual referent of the name does not satisfy the description (or a sufficient number of those in the cluster). In place of this account, they suggest that typically, a name is ostensively or indexically bestowed upon an individual and subsequent users of the name pick up the referent from their predecessors in an ongoing linguistic community, with the historical chain extending all the way back to the original baptizer. This secures constancy of reference over time to this individual and allows us in the interim to revise radically our views of the essential nature of this being. It is this reliance on an ongoing linguistic community that will have a fruitful application to the case of "God," in which the linguistic community is replaced by a religious community.

The historical-causal theory of reference also applies to names of natural kinds. Consider "gold" in this connection. We begin by ostending a paradigmatic class of specimens of gold. We then turn our scientists loose to investigate the nature or essence of these specimens. As time goes by we revise our definition of what constitutes the essential properties of gold, which is what in fact happened as the alchemist's theory gave way to that of modern atomic theory. Thus, the descriptive sense a name might have at some time is not inviolable in that a later use of it can be coreferring even though it lacks this descriptive sense, due to a change in our definition of this natural kind.

If "God" were to fit this simplified historical-*cum*-indexical-reference theory, our question would be answered. But there are two reasons for doubting that it does. First, because God is a supernatural being, he seems to defy being indexically pinned down or baptized. There are no lapels to be grabbed hold of by a use of "this." Some would contend that we can ostensively pin down the name "God" by saying "this" when having or after just having a mystical or religious experience, in which "this" denotes the intentional accusative or content of the experience. This would seem to require that these experiences are cognitive and that their objective accusative is a common object of the experiences of different persons as well as of successive experiences of a single person. These are very controversial claims and must await a full discussion (and refutation) in Chapter 8.

A second disanalogy between "God" and the sort of ordinary proper names to which the historical-*cum*-indexical-reference theory applies is that whereas it is not an analytic truth or true by definition that the referent of an ordinary proper name satisfy some description (e.g., we can imagine what it would be like to discover that the person whom we baptized as "Jones" and thought to be a human being is a robot), this does not appear to be so for "God." At any time at which "God" is used, there will be some descriptive sense that it has by definition. For example, at the present time it is analytically true that God is a powerful, benevolent being that is eminently worthy of worship and obedience. To this extent, "God" is not distinguishable from a natural-kind term, which also can have at any time a descriptive sense that is definitionally determined. But they part company because some of the descriptive properties that are definitionally tied to God are *hard core* in that we would not allow a use of "God" to be coreferring with ours if these properties were not at least partially constitutive of the sense of the name. Soft-core descriptive properties, even if definitionally linked with "God," can alter over time without destroying sameness of reference. Examples of such properties are being absolutely simple, that is, admitting no distinction between essence and existence or between his properties, and being unrestrictedly omnipotent, both of which properties have come and gone as part of the sense of "God" without affecting its reference.

Examples of the hard-core descriptive properties of "God" are being a supremely great being, that is, as great as any being could possibly be, and being eminently worthy of worship and obedience. My reason for selecting these properties as hard core is that it is essential to our idea of God, to the role it plays in the form of life in which it is implicated, that God is eminently worthy of worship and obedience, and a being could occupy this exalted position only if he is a being than which there could be none greater. These are high-level, emergent properties, since an individual can have them only in virtue of the possession of other, lower-level properties, such as omnipotence, benevolence, and so on.

The connection between these emergent properties and their lower-level determiners is very loose, and thereby permits there to be considerable conceptual reform without destroying sameness of reference. First, we can change our mind as to what the latter properties are without altering reference, for instance, giving up absolute simplicity as being one of these lower-level determiners. Second, we can revise our analysis of those determiners that we take to be hard core, such as being benevolent, powerful, or providential. The manner in which we account for the lower-level determiners of the hard-core emergent properties can, and has, varied greatly over time without causing any change in reference. There is no analogue to this in respect to ordinary proper names according to the standard descriptivist theory, including the bundle version variant of the cluster theory.

Recent discussions of intentional identity can also illuminate some features of when two uses of "God" are coreferring.[1] That they are coreferring should be independent of God's existence, and this should hold even if the referrers take having necessary existence to be one of God's hard-core properties, which would not be the case if the referent of "God" had to be pinned down indexically. Jones believes that a certain witch poisoned his well, and Smith believes that the same witch killed his calf. Here is a case of intentional identity in which the existence of the referent is not required. Nor does their identity of reference require that they completely agree in their sortal characterization of their common referent. Smith could believe, pace Jones, that the poisoner of Jones's well and the killer of his calf is not a witch but a warlock or a vampire. For Smith and Jones to be coreferrers, it is not alone sufficient that Smith intend to refer to the same individual as did Jones. What he says does not settle the issue, unlike the case in which what an artist says his painting represents settles the matter. It is also necessary that there is sufficient similarity in their sortal characterizations of their common referent (e.g., they both thought of the referent as a being possessed of supernatural powers, in spite of their differences over just what sort of a supernatural being it is) and they assign a similar explanatory role to it. Were Smith to believe that some demon caused his rheumatism and Jones to believe that the same individual caused his rheumatism, only disagreeing in his taking it to be germs rather than a demon, we would not count his reference as being coreferential with Smith's. Jones might say that demons are nothing but germs, but this would be the eliminative use of "nothing but" – the one that entails that there aren't any demons. It is contrasted with the theoretical or reductive identity use of "nothing but" as in "water is nothing but a collection of H_2O molecules," which does not have any eliminative implication.

Similar considerations hold for intentional identities involving successive uses of "God." Abraham might believe that some supernatural being created the cosmos, and Isaac might believe that the same divine person communed with him. Again, their identity of reference does not require the existence of a referent. Nor is it required that they conceive of the referent in exactly the same way (e.g., Isaac might differ from Abraham in regard to what lower-level soft-core properties he takes to be essential to God or in how he understands these divine attributes), for there is both sufficient agreement in their sortal characterization of the referent and the role they assign it as the explainer of the existence of the universe and various occurrences within it, such as numinous and other types of religious experiences. In spite of their differences in how they conceive of God, they agree in thinking of God as a supernatural being who is the creator and sustainer of the universe and eminently worthy of worship and obedience. Here we see the importance of God's hard-core properties in securing coreference in successive uses of "God."

The picture presented so far is overly intellectualized, stressing only the descriptive aspects of the name, both hard and soft core. No doubt these descriptive features are an essential part of the story, but they are not alone adequate to explain how reference can remain constant amidst alterations in the soft-core descriptive sense of the name, as well as in the analyses given of the hard-core properties. It is here that we must avail ourselves of the historical-causal theory's notion of a succession of referrers within an ongoing linguistic community who pick up the reference of a name from their predecessors; only we must replace the linguistic with a religious community. The reason we think our use of "God" refers to the same God as was referred to by Abraham, Isaac, and Jacob, despite radical differences in our theories about the nature of God, is that we are members of the same ongoing historical community of believers, sharing the same form of life.[2]

What is the form of life that is implicated in our common religious language game? It has to do with our having a common historical root to our religious community, sharing similar attitudes toward the meaning and significance of life, common ethical beliefs and practices, and the subsequent people in this ongoing historical chain identifying themselves with their predecessors in this chain. For their use of "God" to be coreferring with that of their predecessors, it is not enough that they intend it to be. What they say, though relevant in this matter, is not alone decisive. They must also share this common form of life with their predecessors and think of themselves as continuing their traditions and aspirations. How we individuate our religious community will depend upon how ecumenical we want to be, which in turn will depend on a complex of political, economic, and psychological factors. Just look at the significant shift in the Catholic Church's attitude toward those they formerly took to be heathens in Third World countries. What constitutes sameness of a religious community over time is a deep issue that deserves a separate volume, just as does the problem of what constitutes sameness of a linguistic community over time for the historical-causal theory of reference. Suffice to say that a proper account of how the reference of "God" can remain constant over time despite significant conceptual revision is crucially dependent upon how we fill in the details of what makes for sameness of a religious community over time.

Hopefully, this rough sketch, combining elements of both the historical-causal and descriptivist theories, supplemented by some language-game analysis, makes intelligible how we can redesign our concept of God without change of reference and opens the way for our excursion into atheological arguments. Chapter 1 will present a broad overview of these arguments, four of which will be singled out for in-depth treatment in the following chapters.

Atheological arguments

Chapter 1

Atheology and the nature of God

In this chapter a broad overview will be given of atheological arguments, without any attempt to determine whether they ultimately succeed. The aim is to give us a feeling for these arguments and an appreciation for their positive role in bringing about important conceptual reforms in the way in which God's nature has been conceived of over time.

The aim of an atheological argument is to reveal a logical inconsistency in the theist's concept of God. Accordingly, it begins with an *initial set* of propositions each of which is accepted by the theist as a necessary conceptual truth. For example, from the initial set containing the sole premise that necessarily God is omnipotent, an attempt is made to deduce a contradiction, namely, that there is some task that an omnipotent being cannot do. Or, from the initial set containing the conceptual truth that God is benevolent in the sense of always choosing the best alternative, it is deduced that God both does and does not actualize some possible world, with appeal being made to the additional premise that necessarily there is no best of all possible worlds. In both of these atheological arguments, the initial set contains only propositions that the theist takes to be necessary truths.

It would seem that my definition of an "atheological argument" as a deduction of a contradiction from the theist's concept of God, with appeal to only necessarily true additional premises, is unduly restrictive; for some of the most important attempts to demonstrate the logical inconsistency of theism begin with an initial set of propositions that contain at least one proposition that is taken by the theist to be only contingently true, for instance, that there exists evil, created free persons, and so on. For example, the deductive argument from evil, in one of its versions, begins with an initial set containing two propositions:

1. There exists an omnipotent and benevolent God; and
2. Evil exists,

from which it is deduced that evil does not exist, with appeal being made to some extra premises that articulate conceptual truths about omnipotence and benevolence. Herein the initial set is not comprised solely of conceptual truths, the theist taking 2 to be only contingently true, and also 1, if God's existence is taken to be contingent. Similar considerations hold for the argument that deduces from the initial set comprised of

3. There exists an omniscient God; and
4. There exist free created people

the contradiction that these created free people are not really free because their actions and choices are foreknown by this omniscient God. Proposition 4 certainly is not taken by the theist to be necessary, it not being taken to be an essential property of God that he create free persons. Similarly, the argument that attempts to deduce from the initial set containing

5. There exists an immutable and omniscient God; and
6. There are temporal indexical facts, such as what time it is right now

the contradiction that this omniscient (or immutable) God is not omniscient (or immutable) contains an initial set that seems to contain at least one contingent member – 5 and/or 6.

We might call these arguments whose initial set contains at least one proposition that is taken to be only contingently true by the theist an "impure atheological argument," in contrast with the "pure atheological arguments" of my definition. This distinction turns out to be unimportant, since every successful impure atheological argument has an equally successful counterpart pure atheological argument. The former can be recast as a pure argument by possibilizing the conjunction of the propositions in its initial set. Let us suppose that the initial set of the impure argument contains the propositions p and q, in which p and/or q is taken to be only contingently true by the theist. It is possible that (p and q) is weaker than (p and q) in that it is entailed by but does not entail the latter. Therefore, if (p and q) is accepted by the theist, so must it is possible that (p and q). For example, if the theist grants that both God and evil exist, it is thereby granted that it is conceptually possible that they coexist. Now, if (p and q) entail a contradiction, so does the weaker it is possible that (p and q). Given that (p and q) entail a contradiction r, it follows that it is not possible that (p and q). If it is not possible that (p and q), it is necessary that it is not possible that (p and q), that is, it is impossible that it is possible that (p and q), given that a proposition's modal status is invariant across possible worlds. Since an impossible proposition entails every proposition, it follows that it is possible that (p and q), being impossible, entails this contradiction r. Another way of putting this point is that if (p and q) entail a contradiction, it follows that not only (p and q) is impossible but also it is possible that (p and q), given that a proposition has its modal status necessarily. Thus, the atheologian, by the trick of possibilizing the conjunction of the propositions in the initial set of an impure atheological argument, can convert it into a pure one. In the following discussion no attempt will be made to convert impure atheological arguments into pure ones, since it is obvious that this can be done by the simple expedient of possibilizing its initial set. With this in mind we can begin our survey of the atheological arguments.

Our brief overview of atheological arguments will be based upon the divine attribute against which they are directed. Some of the arguments are not directed against just one attribute but instead attempt to demonstrate a logical clash between two or more of them. As a result, there will be some arbitrariness under which divine attribute they are considered.

OMNIPOTENCE

The first divine attribute to be taken up is omnipotence. God is supposed to have this attribute, like all of his other attributes, essentially, meaning that it is logically or conceptually impossible that God exist without having this attribute. His possession of omnipotence is an example of a de re necessity, since it follows from his nature, not our way of referring to God, that he has it. This contrasts with de dicto necessity claims, the truth of which depend upon the mode of reference; for instance, it is true that it is necessary that God is omnipotent but not that Augustine's favorite individual is omnipotent, even though God is in fact Augustine's favorite individual.

Probably the most famous atheological argument is the one that deduces a contradiction from the initial set containing only the proposition that God is omnipotent. The trick in the argument is to require of an omnipotent being that he can do anything without restriction. The following is my version of the paradox of the stone, which differs from the standard version in that it is not mounted as a dilemma argument, thereby avoiding needless complications. It begins with an initial set containing only

7. It is necessary that God is omnipotent;

and then proceeds as follows:

8. It is necessary that an omnipotent being can do anything [by definition];
9. It is necessary that God can do anything [from 7 and 8];
10. It is necessary that God can create a stone so heavy that God cannot lift it [from 8 and 9];
11. It is necessary that (if God can create a stone so heavy that God cannot lift it, then it is possible that there is something God cannot do) [conceptual truth];
12. It is possible that that there is something God cannot do [from 10 and 11];

18

13. It is not necessary that God can do anything [from 12]; and

14. It is necessary that God can do anything and it is not necessary that God can do anything [from 9 and 13].

Since a contradiction has been deduced from 7, with appeal only to necessarily true additional premises, it follows that 7 is necessarily false.

There is a variant of the "stone" argument in which "commit suicide," rather than "create a stone so heavy that God cannot lift it," is substituted for "anything" in 9. If God can commit suicide, it is possible that an omnipotent being cease to exist. If you find nothing conceptually absurd about this, try an absolutely perfect being, which is what God essentially is, ceasing to exist. This, certainly, is not possible. This variant on the suicide argument is not directed exclusively at God's omnipotence but at his being essentially both omnipotent and absolutely perfect. Accordingly, we will call it the "omnipotence–perfection argument." Another mixed-bag atheological argument involving omnipotence is the "omnipotence–benevolence argument" in which "commit an immoral action" is substituted for "anything" in 9. Because God is omnipotent, he can commit an immoral action; but, since he is essentially benevolent, he cannot. Thus, one of the two properties must be jettisoned.

What is the theist to do in response to these atheological arguments? Plainly, unless we are Kierkegaards, some response is necessary, since we do not want to accept a logically inconsistent creed. There is considerable room for conceptual reform here, since the theologian's notion of God's omnipotence is a theoretical reconstruction of the biblical notion of God Almighty. From the idea of a God who is sovereign over all there is comes that of a God whose power knows no limitations, not even of a logical or conceptual sort.[1] To escape the stone and suicide arguments, a religiously acceptable restriction must be placed upon God's omnipotence. The mixed-bag arguments – the omnipotence–

perfection and omnipotence–benevolence arguments – provide the theist more latitude, since either omnipotence or the other concerned attribute can be reconceived. It is interesting to note that usually it is omnipotence that is restricted by the theist rather than perfection or benevolence, since one of God's hard-core properties is being eminently worthy of worship and obedience, and it would seem that only a being that is essentially perfect and benevolent without restriction could qualify as such, at least according to the theist's own moral pecking order. This is quite consistent with the fact that there are nontheists who worship a being solely on the basis of his power. Since they give primary importance to power, if it turns out to be the case that the devil is the most powerful being, then he is on pragmatic grounds the most appropriate object of worship. But, for the theist, he still is not *emininently* worthy of worship because of his moral imperfection.

An obvious way to neutralize the stone argument is to restrict God's omnipotence as follows:

O_1. God can do or bring about anything that is logically possible.

While the O_1 account of God's omnipotence works for the stone argument, since "creating a stone so heavy that God [an omnipotent being] cannot lift it" is contradictory, it does not work for the suicide argument, "committing suicide" being a consistent-act description. Nor does it work for the omnipotence–benevolence argument, since "committing an immoral action" describes a possible action. The problem with O_1 is that there are many things that are logically possible to do but which God cannot do since it is not logically possible that God performs these actions.

This suggests a way of further restricting O_1 so as to get around this difficulty, namely, as

O_2. God can do anything that it is logically consistent for God to do.

There are many possible actions that God, in virtue of being absolutely perfect, cannot perform, such as playing football. Only a being possessed of a body could do this, but God "ain't got nobody," since to have a body makes one subject to the possibilities of corruption and death, which certainly would disqualify one from being an absolutely perfect being. Notice that some properties are great making in a sortally relative, but not absolute fashion, such as being well coordinated, which is great making relative to an animal but not absolutely, since to have it one must be possessed of a body and thus not be absolutely perfect.

God's actions are confined to bringing things about in his own inimitable supernatural fashion by simply willing them. Thus, a more perspicuous way of rendering O_2 is as

O_3. For any proposition p, if it is logically possible that God bring it about that p, then God can bring it about that p,

in which "can bring it about" is to be understood in the full-blooded sense of having the power, ability, opportunity, and so on of bringing about the state of affairs in question. The "can" must not be understood in the weak, logical-possibility sense, for this would render O_3 vacuously tautological. Again, there are logically possible propositions, for instance, that there exists an uncreated stone (assuming that it is not necessary that God exists) that God cannot bring about, since it would be logically inconsistent for him to do so. Another example is the proposition that God exists, and this he cannot bring about even if his existence is necessary because entailed by his essence.

While O_2 and O_3 are an improvement over O_1, they still face problems. The first difficulty is a superficial technical problem that is due to the fact that a given action or state of affairs admits of alternative descriptions such that it could be logically possible under some, but not all, of them. Imagine that Igor's favorite object is the square circle. That Igor's favorite object exists and that the square circle exists report one and the same state of affairs, yet the former is logically possible and the latter is not. Therefore, it is logically possible (in the de dicto sense) that God bring it about that Igor's favorite object exists, and yet he cannot bring this about, pace O_3.

Clement Dore has suggested a way around this difficulty in which God "can perform any action such that the statement that He can perform it is logically consistent and would turn out to be logically consistent on any true description of the action."[2] Using this strategy, O_3 can be revised as

O_4. For any proposition p, if it is logically possible that God bring it about that p as well as any proposition that is coreporting with p, then God can bring it about that p,

in which two propositions are coreporting if the participial nominalizations of the sentences that express them are coreferring. The participial nominalizations of "Igor's favorite object exists" and "The square circle exists" are, respectively, "Igor's favorite object existing" and "the square circle existing"; and they are coreferring because of the identity between Igor's favorite object and the square circle.

There are more substantive objections to O_2 and O_3, however, that are not circumvented by O_4. The difficulties result from their sortal relativization of omnipotence. First, it might be objected that this makes it too easy to qualify as omnipotent. Let a *pirod* by definition be a being that can do nothing save for singing "Dixie." With no insult to the Confederacy intended, there is no doubt that this being is not omnipotent, and yet it qualifies as omnipotent in the sortally relativized sense. That a pirod cannot create a pencil does not count against its being omnipotent, since it is not logically possible that a pirod bring it about that a pencil exists, this being due to how we defined it. The response to this counterexample is that there is a world of difference between relativizing omnipotence to God – an absolutely perfect being – and a pirod. And this seems fair enough.

But there is a more serious difficulty with a sortally relativized account of God's omnipotence; it creates a paradox of perfection consisting in such a being having a lesser degree of power than that possessed by some possible nonperfect being. Let a Pinrod be a possible being who has only one of the divine perfections – omnipotence – and thereby does not qualify as an absolutely perfect being. Anything that God can do or bring about, our Pinrod can do or bring about, and then some. Not being burdened with being absolutely perfect, our Pinrod, in addition to having all of God's powers, for instance, being able to create a universe ex nihilo and perform other parlor tricks, can be possessed of a body and thereby be able to play football. Since he is not absolutely perfect, he is not barred from committing suicide. Furthermore, since he lacks benevolence, he is able to perform an immoral action. Thus, this lesser being has a greater degree of freedom than that possessed by God, an absolutely perfect being. It looks as if no one is perfect, not even an absolutely perfect being!

The great medieval theists would have had a ready response to the paradox of perfection based on the doctrine of the divine simplicity. It will be worthwhile to consider this doctrine, not only as offering a way out of this paradox, but for its own intrinsic interest. God's status as an absolutely perfect being precluded either there being any distinctions within his nature or his being dependent upon anything. The former entails that there is no distinction between God's properties: His omnipotence is identical with his omniscience, which is identical with his omnibenevolence, and so on. Were there to be any compositeness in his nature, he would face the possibility of destruction through decomposition. (Think of Plato's argument for the immortality of the soul based on the noncompositeness of the soul.)[3] The latter entails that God does not instantiate any property, for were he to do so he would be distinct from and dependent on this property, thereby violating his aseity. Since God is identical with omnipotence, as well as all his other properties, no individual could have only one of God's properties, for this property is identical with all the other divine properties; and no individual distinct from God could have any one of these properties, since then he would be identical with God. As a result, there can be no Pinrod, which eliminates this version of the paradox of perfection, as well as versions based upon any other divine attribute.

There are two different versions of the doctrine of the divine simplicity – the property and instance identity versions. When it is said that God is identical with his properties, say omnipotence, it could mean that he is identical either with the property of omnipotence itself or with his instancing of omnipotence. Both versions face formidable objections.

One objection to the property identity version is that by making God identical with an abstract property – omnipotence itself – it renders him conceptually unfit to be a personal creator of the universe. An omnipotent being can be a causal factor but not omnipotence itself, to hark back to one of Aristotle's objections to Plato's doctrine of the forms. Another objection to this version is that it has the unwanted consequence that no individual other than God could have any one of his properties, since if it were to instantiate one of these properties it would be instantiating God himself and thereby be God. But certainly individuals other than God can have some of his intrinsic or non-Cambridge properties, for instance, being a person, self-identical, an entity, and so on. Furthermore, the property of omnipotence qua property seems to be a different property than that of, say, omnibenevolence. One is being able to do anything (within some limits, such as those imposed already), the other being disposed to perform only good actions. Another way of making this point is that since "omnipotence" and "omnibenevolence" obviously differ in sense and the sense of each is the property it expresses, the properties of omnipotence and omnibenevolence are different. In case this isn't obvious to you, the following might be of some help. Since ordinary power and benevolence obviously differ, there is all the more reason to hold that increasing degrees thereof differ. And, likewise, there is all the more reason to hold that unlimited degrees thereof – omnipotence and omnibenevolence – also differ.

The instance identity version would seem more plausible, since it is by now a familiar story that two referring expressions can be coreferential though differing in sense, for instance, "the morning star" and "the evening star." Thus, it might be possible that "an instancing of omnipotence" and "an instancing of omnibenevolence" are coreferential, although differing in sense, in that God's instancing of the one property is identical with his instancing of the other. Before we consider the possibility of this being so, it must be stressed that this instance identity version of the divine simplicity violates God's absolute aseity or independence, since it conceives of God as instantiating properties and thus as dependent upon them. Still, it is interesting to consider this version, since, if it proves viable, the theist might want to go with it and accept a restricted version of God's aseity.

Eleonore Stump and Norman Kretzmann develop a version of the instance identity theory that makes use of the aforementioned sense–reference distinction:

> 'Perfect power' and 'perfect knowledge' are precise analogues for 'the morning star' and 'the evening star'; non-synonymous expressions designating quite distinct manifestations of one and the same thing.[4]

Before critically evaluating their claim, it is necessary to rework their analogy so as to eliminate two serious blunders. In the first place, "the morning star" and "the evening star," do not designate different manifestations of one and the same planet but one and the same planet via different ways it manifests itself. Second, "perfect power" and "perfect knowledge" do not refer to an instance of a property but to the property itself, and thus must be changed to "an instancing of perfect power" and "an instancing of perfect knowledge." To avoid these two difficulties we would do well to revise their claim as follows: "An instance of perfect power" and "an instance of perfect knowledge" are precise analogues for "the morning star" and "the evening star"; non-synonymous expressions designating one and the same thing via different ways in which it manifests itself.

It would seem that we have the same intuitive grounds for denying the identity of an *instance* of perfect power with an instance of perfect knowledge as we previously had for denying the identity of the *property* of omnipotence with that of omnibenevolence. Because an instance of ordinary power is obviously not identical with an instance of ordinary benevolence, there is all the more reason to hold that instances of increasing degrees thereof are not identical, and thus to deny that an instance of an unlimited degree of the one is identical with an unlimited degree of the other.

In opposition to this line of reasoning, Stump and Kretzmann offer an analogy to show how (an instance of) perfect power can be identical with (an instance of) perfect knowledge although no instance of ordinary finite power is identical with an instance of ordinary finite knowledge. The former identity "does not entail that power is identical with knowledge any more than the fact that the summit of a mountain's east slope is identical with the summit of its west slope entails the identity of the slopes."[5] This spatial analogy is most unfortunate for their purpose, since, when it is pushed, it results in a view of God's omniproperties that is the opposite of what they intend. The common summit limits each of the slopes by serving as their common point of termination. Analogously, God's (instancing of) perfect power and perfect knowledge would also represent a limitation on ordinary power and knowledge. But this is the opposite of what they mean by these divine perfections, which are supposed to be ideal or unlimited instancings of power and knowledge. "The single summit is indeed the perfection of all the slopes" and "suggests that the idea that perfect phi and perfect psi might be identical despite the plain difference between phi and psi."[6] It might be objected that I have leaned too heavily on the spatial aspect of their analogy in drawing out the absurdity that God's omnipotence, and so on, represents a limitation rather than a perfection of ordinary power. But if we are not allowed to press their analogy in this way, it has no value.

Even if the instance identity version of the doctrine of the divine simplicity could somehow be made to work, it would still not succeed in neutralizing the paradox of perfection; for it would fail to show that one could not have one of God's perfections without having all of them, as was the case with our Pinrod. Let us assume for the sake of argument that God's instancing omnipotence is identical with his instancing benevolence. This does not entail that any instancing of omnipotence is identical with some instancing of benevolence. A token identity proposition does not entail a type identity proposition. That my instancing pain on some occasion is identical with a specific firing of my C-fibers does not entail that every instancing of pain is identical with some firing of C-fibers, no less a firing of my C-fibers.

As we have already seen, the doctrine of the divine simplicity faces a dilemma in that its property identity version renders God causally impotent, and its instance identity version destroys his aseity. William Mann has attempted to grab this dilemma by both horns by identifying God's properties with his instancing of them. This identification is supposed to escape the objection that God cannot be causally efficacious because of being an abstract property; but it still faces the aseity objection based on God instancing a property. He points out that the aseity objection assumes that properties are abstract entities:

> I do not accept this assumption. Properties, I am inclined to believe, are causal powers. P is a property of an object, only if P's presence in x confers some causal power(s) on x. P and Q are the same property if and only if (1) P and Q confer the same causal powers on their objects and (2) whatever is sufficient to bring about an instance of P in an object, x, is sufficient to bring about an instance of Q in x, and vice versa.[7]

The idea is that God's power is a certain causal capacity, and this is the same causal capacity as is his benevolence, and the like.

Even if we were to grant that properties are certain sorts of causal powers, it is unclear both how this escapes the aseity objection and how it establishes that God's different properties bestow one and the same causal power(s) upon him. When Mann says that a property P's *"presence* in x confers some causal power(s) on x (my emphasis)," he seems to be distinguishing between the property of P itself and its presence in or being instanced (instantiated) by object x. His causal theory of properties does not collapse this distinction, but shows only that the property of being F is being possessed of such-and-such causal powers. There is still the distinction between the multiply instantiatable property of being possessed of such-and-such causal powers and the concrete instantiations of this property; and, thus, the aseity objection is not laid to rest. Furthermore, if he is right that an abstract property is identical with its presence in an object, then, since identicals are indiscernible and abstract properties cannot be causally efficacious, it follows that the presence of a property in an object cannot be causally efficacious. Furthermore, there are good grounds for not identifying God's instancing of one property with his instancing of another, especially if we follow Mann's account of properties as being causal powers. Omnipotence is having the causal power to bring about anything (possibly subject to some of the mentioned restrictions), while benevolence is having the causal dispositions to perform or bring about good actions. A person's instancing of one of these properties seems to bestow on him a different set of causal powers than does its instancing of the other. This certainly is true if it is limited or finite degrees of power and goodness that are in question, and all the more so if it is infinite or unlimited degrees of power and goodness – perfect power and goodness – that are in question.

Instance or token identity, of which event identity is only a special case, is a notoriously difficult and obscure issue. None of the familiar accounts of event or token identity seem to fit the instance identity version of the doctrine of the divine simplicity. Mann is invoking a modified version of the

Davidson criterion of event identity that omits the requirement of spatiotemporal coincidence (since God isn't spatiotemporal for Mann) and goes only with the requirement of
having the same causes and effects or the same causal powers and dispositions. But this, as already indicated, does not
seem to be true of God's instancing different properties.
There are different theories of theoretical or transcategoreal
identities based upon empirical correlations cum considerations of simplicity or scientific reductions of less-to-more
basic laws; but none of them could apply to God for obvious
reasons.

I have not tried to show that there could not be an acceptable version of the doctrine of the divine simplicity, only that
none of the leading contemporary accounts are adequate.
Thus, the paradox of perfection still awaits a resolution.
Maybe the best strategy for the theist is to bite the bullet and
take back the requirement that an absolutely perfect being
have every perfection to an unlimited or unsurpassable
degree. That such a being, unlike a Pinrod, cannot commit
suicide or an immoral action does not dislodge it from its
privileged place in the religious language game and form of
life that is involved in it; for it still retains its status as the
being most eminently worthy of worship and obedience and
so on. Giving up the requirement that the Deity be absolutely
simple in no way destroys the identity of the religious community over time and causes subsequent uses of "God" not
to be coreferring with earlier uses. Not only is no real harm
done, but it helps us to escape from a devastating atheological argument.

BENEVOLENCE

We have already considered one atheological argument involving God's benevolence – the mixed-bag omnipotence–
benevolence argument – and it was seen that it is better for
the theist to reconstruct omnipotence, since essential benevolence seems to be required of a being who is going to play

the distinctive role of being eminently worshipable in a way
in which being unrestrictedly omnipotent is not. God is not
someone who as a matter of contingent fact never fails
morally but a being who cannot fail because it is an essential
property of his nature that he cannot. Similar considerations
apply to the famous argument from evil, which also is a
mixed one since it appeals to God's omnipotence in addition
to his benevolence (and also his omniscience in some versions). Again, it is one of the divine perfections other than
essential benevolence that gets reconstructed. There are
other atheological arguments directed against benevolence
that concern the nature of God's benevolence rather than its
essentiality.

The point of this atheological argument, which will be
called the "benevolence–creation argument," is to force us to
examine our conception of God's benevolence. The theist,
unless she is willing to follow the dubious path of radical
multivocalism and deny any similarity or analogy between
the properties of God and other beings, will conceive of
God's goodness as being importantly similar to that of finite
beings. Thus, if the theist holds to a utilitarian conception of
the good, God will be conceived of as a utility maximizer. The
benevolence–creation argument is directed against one such
utilitarian conception of God's benevolence, the Leibnizian
version, according to which he essentially follows the principle of perfection, that is, always chooses the best alternative
available.[8] As Leibniz makes clear in his *Theodicy*, this principle enjoins God to make no choice at all when there is no
uniquely best alternative, either because there are two or
more that are equally good or for each one there is an even
better one.

The benevolence–creation argument's initial set contains

15. God is benevolent; and
16. A benevolent being always chooses in accordance with
the principle of perfection.

It then adds this necessary premiss

17. There is no world that is the best of all possible worlds.

This could be true if there were two or more worlds of commensurate value or an infinite series of increasingly good worlds, due to there being no upper bound on goodness. As Leibniz himself said in the supplement to his *Theodicy*, "The good may and does go on to infinity." We shall work with the latter case of there being no uniquely best world, since it is more intuitively obvious:

18. God does not make any choice in regard to actualizing a world [from 16 and 17];

19. God's option to actualize a world is a forced one in that if he makes no decision, it is the same as if he actually chooses not to actualize any world [necessary truth];

20. God knows that 19 is true [based on his omniscience];

21. God chooses not to actualize any world [from 17–20]; and

22. God does make a choice in regard to actualizing a world [from 21, which explicitly contradicts 18].

The reason for 20 is that if God were not aware that his choice to actualize a possible world is a forced one, it might be disputable whether his not making any choice is a choice on his part not to actualize any world. That his choice in this matter is forced results from the theist's claim that a possible world gets actualized if and only if God wills that it does, this being a special instance of his sovereignty. The theist could escape the argument by denying that this falls within the purview of God's sovereignty, but this would represent a radical departure from the traditional conception of God as almighty.

Even if the Leibnizian can find some way out of this argument, and I don't think he can,[9] there still is the problem of whether God can actualize any world other than the best of all possible worlds. If he can't, then he is a Spinozistic type creator who has no choice in the matter. And, what is even more unpalatable, it follows that the only possible world is the best of all possible worlds, on the theistic assumptions that a possible world is one that could be actualized and that a world can get actualized only through God's creative choice, this being a special case of his sovereignty.

Most theists are not touched by the creation–benevolence argument, since they have distinctly antiutilitarian moral intuitions. Rather, they conceive of God as giving greatest value to goodness of character developed through the person's own free endeavorings. Soul building is God's primary purpose in creating a world. Or they might go the Robert M. Adams route and say that when God actualizes less perfect possible persons than he could have, he is bestowing the blessing of grace on the imperfect products of his creative act; and since grace is considered a virtue by theists, God's benevolence is not impugned by his not actualizing the best persons he could. At the opposite end of the spectrum from a utilitarian concept of God's goodness is a purely formalistic one in which God's goodness consists in being morally upright, always honoring his moral duties. How God's goodness is conceived will have important repercussions for the construction of theodicies and defenses of God in the face of evil. Whether a morally exonerating excuse can be constructed for God's permitting certain types of evils will depend crucially on what constitutes his goodness. A purely formalistic conception of God's goodness makes the task of constructing a theodicy or defense easier, since it could be said that God had no moral duty to eliminate or prevent certain kinds of evils; to do so would be an act of supererogation, thus the point of the bumper sticker that said "God does exist: He just doesn't want to get involved." But most theists want to believe in a God who is more of a do-gooder than is this coldly upright "he keeps his nose clean"-type deity.

SOVEREIGNTY

A totally unrestricted version of God's sovereignty requires that everything be determined by his will, and it is subject to the same sort of atheological arguments as is a totally unrestricted version of his omnipotence. It seems to many philosophers that abstract entities, such as numbers and properties, are not the sort of things that could be created. The theist is committed to there being objective moral truths, but a similar point could be made about them. This is the point of the following "sovereignty–benevolence argument," whose initial set contains these two propositions:

23. God determines the truth-values of ethical propositions; and
24. God is essentially benevolent.

Taking God's eternality to involve beginningless and endless duration in time, that is, omnitemporality, it is deduced from 24 that

25. God is benevolent prior to his decision as to what truth-values ethical propositions will have.

But from 23 it follows that

26. Nothing is good or bad, right or wrong, prior to God's decision as to what truth-values ethical propositions will have.

But from 24 it follows that

27. God is benevolent prior to his decision as to what truth-values ethical propositions will have;

which contradicts 26.

One might try to escape this argument by conceiving of God's decisions as to what truth-values ethical propositions are to have as an abiding one that endures throughout an infinite past and future, so that there is no time prior to that at which he makes these decisions. This is not an ad hoc move, since God's immutability requires that he not change his mind from one time to another. The same result would be achieved if the theist were to conceive of God as timelessly eternal, that is, not subject to any temporal determinations or distinctions. Again, the consequence will be that there is no time at which God has not yet made his ethical decisions.

A different version of the sovereignty–benevolence argument must be deployed against these two ways of conceiving of God's ethical decisions as being immutable. An additional premise must be added to the previous initial set – that God must have a reason for any choice he makes that is based on some moral good that is realized by his choice. But this requires that there is something morally good that is prior in the order of determination or explanation, rather than time, to God's choice as to what truth-values ethical propositions will have in the sense that it helps to explain or determine God's choice in this matter. Thus, there both is and is not something that is good prior in the order of explanation or dependency to God's choice as to what is good. This, I take it, is the thrust of the argument of Plato's *Euthyphro*. And it seems right to me. Ethical propositions are not of the right categoreal sort to be made true by anyone's decision, even God's.

Another problem for God's sovereignty is whether it is consistent for him to predetermine the free actions and choices of created persons. This will be addressed at length in Chapter 4 when we take up the free will defense of God in the face of moral evil. The predestination–freedom atheological argument carries considerably more wallop than does the omniscience–freedom argument, since it is far more difficult to reconcile an act being free with God's predetermining it than with his only foreknowing it. If one is convinced by the sovereignty-benevolence and/or predestination–freedom arguments, it will be necessary to give an O_4-type account of God's sovereignty, namely, as

S. God completely and solely determines everything that it is logically consistent that an absolutely perfect being completely and solely determine.

God's sovereignty, like his omnipotence, must be relativized not just to what is logically possible but to what it is logically possible for an absolutely perfect being to do or determine.

IMMUTABILITY

God is supposed to be immutable in that he does not change over time in respect to any of his intrinsic properties, as opposed to relational properties, such as being thought about by Jones. According to the omniscience–immutability argument, which will be our concern in Chapter 3, this gets in the way of his being completely omniscient; for there are some truths that can be known only by a temporal being that continually changes its beliefs, such as what the date is. The theist can respond to this argument by limiting either God's immutability or his omniscience, as we will see in Chapter 3.

Another mixed atheological argument involving immutability is the one that will be the topic of Chapter 2 – the creation–immutability argument. God is claimed by theism to have created the world a finite number of years ago, but this seems to require that he changed his mind in the past in regard to creating the world, thereby compromising his immutability. This atheological argument, as we shall see, has played a very significant role in prodding the theologian to reexamine God's relation to creation, often with the result that God, along with his creative acts, is placed "outside" of time. This doctrine of timeless creation will figure prominently in the next chapter. The theologian is not forced to follow this path. Instead it might be denied that an absolutely perfect being must be strictly immutable. To support this it must be shown that the reasons for the immutability of a perfect being, for instance, the Aristotelian argument that a perfect being is in a state of complete actuality and thereby cannot change, are bogus.

ABSOLUTENESS

This divine property is not made explicit by traditional Western theism but is implicit in the way in which it conceives of

God's existence and actions. God's existence is absolute and in no way world relative. Likewise, each of his actions, such as his creative choice as to which world to actualize, is absolute. God actually makes only one creative choice, though he might have made others, that is, in certain possible worlds in which he exists he makes these alternative creative choices. But only one of his many possible creative choices is actual simpliciter or absolutely, just as only one among all the possible worlds is actual simpliciter. Traditional theism pictures God as being "outside" of possible worlds in that he initially contemplates them and then makes a unique and absolute choice as to which one of them is to become actualized. That one among these worlds is actual simpliciter or absolutely is due to the absoluteness of God's existence and his creative actions. If actuality, along with existence and truth, are not absolute, but only world relative, as David Lewis has argued, this fundamental tenet of traditional theism is undercut. Chapter 5 will consider an atheological argument based on the doctrine of world-relative actuality. It will be found to be wanting.

I trust that the foregoing atheological arguments have captured your fancy and that you are anxious to pursue some of them in further detail, hoping thereby to command a more adequate conception of God's nature. And we now turn to this task.

Chapter 2

The creation–immutability argument

This argument is a dramatic case in point of the thesis of Chapter 1 concerning the positive role of the atheological arguments; for Saint Augustine's famed theory of the relation between God's eternality and the temporality of the created world, which was accepted by all of the subsequent great medieval theists and became official church doctrine, was developed in response to it. Furthermore, the account of time that falls out of his theory has gained widespread acceptance down through the present day. It will be shown that this account of time itself forms the basis of an atheological argument. Had its import been understood by his Christian followers, they would have tar and feathered rather than sainted him. The notion of God's eternality then will be subject to critical scrutiny and will be shown to render him a nonperson and thereby not religiously available.

In Book 11 of his *Confessions*, in which he develops this theory of time and eternity, Augustine begins with this Manichaean formulation of the creation–immutability argument:

> Lo are they not full of their old leaven, who say to us, "What was God doing before *He made heaven and earth?*" "For if (say they) He were unemployed and wrought not, why does He not also henceforth, and for ever, as He did heretofore? For did any new motion arise in God, and a new will to make a creature, which He had never before made, how then would that be a true eternity, where there ariseth a will, which was not?"[1]

The following is an explicit mounting of this argument, with 1–3 comprising the initial set:

1. The world came into existence at some past time, say t_0;
2. The world exists at some time if and only if God wills that it does;
3. God is immutable;
4. At t_0 God wills that the world exist [from 1 and 2];
5. There are times earlier than t_0, say t_{-1}, at which the world does not exist [from 1];
6. At t_{-1} God does not will that the world exist [from 2 and 5];
7. God has a property at one time that he lacks at another [from 4 and 6];
8. God is not immutable [from 7]; and
9. God is immutable, and God is not immutable [from 3 and 8].

Augustine's initial response is the old knee slapper that prior to t_0 God was preparing the fires of hell for those who would give the creation–immutability argument (and who said that the good saint didn't have any sense of humor). But he immediately points out that this humorous excursion hardly serves to neutralize the argument (12). His first serious response is to deny that 5 follows from 1. His exact reason is not completely evident.

He asks "whence could innumerable ages pass by, which Thou madest not, Thou the Author and Creator of all ages?" and then adds that *"before heaven and earth* there was no time," since God created the world and time together (13). The negation of 5 follows from time being ontologically dependent upon God's will and God's willing that the world and time come into being together. This way out of the argument seems to permit God to create an empty time, that is, absolute times. Being all-wise, God will make sure that in any world in which he avails himself of this creative option, he does not compromise his immutability by creating the cosmos at one of these times.

Augustine, however, has another way of blocking the inference of 5 from 1. In the summation at the end of Book 11, he says, "Let them see therefore, that time cannot be without created being" (30). Earlier he had said something that also could be construed as affirming the ontological dependence of time upon a world of created beings: "If nothing passed away, time past were not; and if nothing were coming, a time to come were not; and if nothing were, time present were not" (14). Plainly, 5 is at variance with time's ontological dependency upon created beings. Time, it might be added, is still ontologically dependent upon the will of God, since, given God's sovereignty, no beings exist without his willing that they do.

Neither of these two ways out of the creation–immutability argument is satisfactory. First, they are not sufficiently perspicuous in that they leave us with an unresolved mystery concerning the manner in which God and his acts of willing are related to time. Second, a variant of the argument can be constructed that does not require 5's commitment to absolute times. It goes this way:

10. Some object, say O, within a world of objects, exists at t_1 but not at t_2;

11. An object exists at a time if and only if God wills that it does;

12. At t_1 God wills that O exist [from 10 and 11];

13. At t_2 God does not will that O exist [from 10 and 11];

7. God has a property at one time that he does not have at another [from 12 and 13];

8. God is not immutable [from 7];

3. God is immutable;

9. God is immutable and God is not immutable [from 8 and 3].

Herein there is no need to bring in absolute time. The argument is perfectly compatible with the theses that time is ontologically dependent upon both God's will and the existence of created beings.

That these two theses do not succeed in neutralizing the creation–immutability argument hardly is news to Augustine; for if he thought that they did, he would not have felt it necessary to contrast God's eternal mode of existence with the temporal mode of existence of created beings. The point of this contrast is to show that neither God nor his actions are subject to any temporal distinctions or determinations. The upshot is that these two arguments are to be rejected because in steps 4 and 6 of the first and 12 and 13 of the second, they locate God's acts of willing in time. This is Augustine's deep objection to the creation–immutability arguments. Harry Wolfson once said that if we are to contrast two things, we should know a little bit about at least one of them. Augustine sets a higher standard and thinks that we should know a good deal about both of them. It is for this reason that he undertakes an analysis of both time and eternity, though his extended analysis of time goes far beyond what is needed for the present purpose of neutralizing the creation–immutability argument. And it is this act of philosophical supererogation, as we shall see, that makes him a suitable candidate for tar and feathering. Atheological arguments are lurking everywhere!

Augustine's notion of God's eternity closely follows the notion of eternity articulated by Plotinus. An eternal being enjoys an illimitable life that admits of no distinction between earlier and later phases, or past, present, and future, even though this life is durational in some sense. This conception of eternity has a striking similarity to Whitehead's conception of an actual occasion, and even Bergson's cotton-candyish *durée*, both of which are durational but not internally structured successions. But there is a crucial disanalogy. Whereas an actual occasion bears temporal relations to other actual occasions and admits of temporal subdivision after it has become actual, God's eternality admits of neither these determinations. God's eternity is a *totum simul*, a *nunc stans*, in which all of his "years" are had at once. He exists in an eternal present – a nontemporal present because it admits of no contrast with a past and future. All of God's acts of willing occur within this eternal present and bear no temporal relations to any times or created beings and, according to the doctrine of the divine simplicity, are one and the same act. And these timeless acts of willing bring about the existence and occurrence of things in time. Thus, God timelessly wills that a certain sequence of events occur successively in time. This is a case of timeless causation in which the cause is not in time while its effects are. It is interesting to note that Augustine's doctrine of timeless causation is compatible with the created world being infinite in its past, in which case God would timelessly will that there be an infinite succession of past events. There is no problem of how God's act of will gets into the act, at what point in time it is performed. Those who think that an infinite past would preclude God's will being the cause of the world are assuming that God's creative act must occur at some time, an infinitely extended past affording no time at which he can get into the act. Both versions of the creation–immutability argument make this mistake of temporally relating God's creative act to its worldly effects.

God's eternality sharply contrasts with the temporally incomplete mode of existence of created beings. Augustine writes:

> Thy years neither come nor go; whereas ours both come and go, that they all may come. Thy years stand together, because they do not stand; nor are departing thrust out by coming years, for they pass not away; but ours shall all be, when they shall no more be. (13)

I assume that when Augustine speaks of our years as coming and going he was not using this expression in the same way my landlady at college did when she warned me that she didn't want any coming and going.

It is this coming and going – this negativity that infects temporal beings – that is of the very essence of time for Augustine. Time, he says, is composed of past, present, and future. The past and future are types of nonbeing, the past being the no longer and the future the not yet. The present alone is real, things having being only when present. But even it is shot through with a kind of negativity:

> If time present (if it is to be time) only cometh into existence, because it passeth into time past, how can we say that either

this is, whose cause of being is, that it shall not be; so, namely, that we cannot truly say that time is, but because it is tending not to be ? (14)

Unfortunately, the present turns out to be of zero duration; for if we were to impute any finite duration to it, it would be subdivisible, if only theoretically or in our imagination, and thereby consist of successive phases. But successive phases cannot be copresent, for whatever is copresent is simultaneous and thus not successive. The present thereby turns out to be a mere mathematical knife edge at which the not yet turns into the no longer.

This view, not surprisingly, is a breeding ground of paradox; for if the present is of zero duration and entities have reality only when present, it seems that it is impossible for anything to happen or come to pass, since it doesn't have enough time in which to do so.[2] Augustine considers a particular case in point – the intervals of time itself – but, as we shall see, it can be generalized to every type of temporal entity.

It would appear that it is impossible for any time to be long, that is, to be of nonzero duration, since it must be long when present but the present "hath no space." He asks, "Where then is the time which we may call long?" continuing his use of spatial metaphors by the use of "where" (21). The present does not have sufficient "space" within which to house a finite interval of time, or a finite event for that matter. It is on this ground that he finds it misleading to say, as we ordinarily do, that it *is* a long time since some event occurred. The use of the present tense makes it appear as if the entire lengthy interval of time is present as a whole. Nor is it correct even to say that it was a long time, since no interval of time can be long when past since the past is a kind of nonbeing. Rather, we ought to say that a present time was long, that is, was long when it was present, since it can be a bearer of properties only when it is present. Unfortunately, since the present is of zero duration, it is impossible that it was long.

This creates the paradox of the impossibility of measuring time; for we can measure an interval of time only when it is present, but what is present is nothing, that is, a time of zero duration. Notice that the paradox of the seeming impossibility of measuring time could equally well be directed at the act of measuring time rather than at the interval of time that is measured: An act of measuring time takes a finite time and occurs only when present, but the present "hath no space" within which to house it. No one is fast enough to measure a time in no time at all.

Augustine has a way out of this paradox, but one that, unfortunately, is an occasion for a good tar and feathering. His solution consists in questioning the assumption that in order to measure time we must measure something that has a mind-independent being *in rerum*. It was because the past and future did not enjoy such a being that time could not be measured, given the punctual nature of the present. Instead, Augustine proposes that what we measure has only a being-for-thought, an intentional inexistence to use a later phrase. What we measure is not a past interval of time itself but only what we represent through our act of recollection, namely, the intentional accusative of this act. Consciousness, while not fully able to resurrect the past and future, can bestow on them a second-class being-for-thought sort of existence. This is the only sort of being these temporal ekstacies can enjoy.

> Nor is it properly said, "there be three times, past, present, and to come:" yet perchance it might be properly said, "there be three times; a present of things past, a present of things present, and a present of things future." For these three do exist in some sort, in the soul, but otherwise do I not see them; present of things past, memory; present of things present, sight; present of things future, expectation. (20)

Not only the past and future, but even the present, is relegated to this shadowy being-for-thought type of ontological status. To be present is to be represented as present by an act of sight. As we shall shortly see, there is an outstanding problem concerning the temporality of this act of sight, as well as those of memory and expectation. They take a finite time in which to occur, but the present hath not sufficient "space" in which to house them.

The doctrine of the ideality of time is immediately put to use in explaining how we can measure time. We know that we "measure not time to come, for it is not yet; nor past, because it now is not"; thus, we must measure "times passing." We perceive things while they are passing and this leaves us with memory impressions or contents – the beings-for-thought – that can be compared with each other, one of them can be selected as a time unit and another can be estimated to contain so many of these units. This will yield a measure of time past. Augustine speaks of time as a protraction of the mind ("Time is nothing else than protraction . . . of the mind itself"; 26), meaning a mental representation of a protracted temporal interval, rather than a temporally protracted mental state or process. He gives an example of how we measure sounds. The sound, while passing, is "extended into some space of time so that it might be measured, since the present hath no space."

> Both (sounds) have sounded, have flown, passed away, are no more; and yet I measure, and confidently answer . . . that as to space of time this syllable is but single, that double. And yet I could not do this, unless they were already past and ended. It is not then themselves, which now are not, that I measure, but something in my memory, which there remains fixed. It is in thee, my mind, that I measure times.(27)

> The impression, which things as they pass by cause in thee, remains even when they are gone; this it is which, still present, I measure, not the things which pass by to make this impression. (27)

Augustine even goes so far as to say that a "long past" is "a long memory of the past" (28). The latter refers not to the length of time that the act of remembering takes but to the manner in which it represents. It is a recollecting something-as-being-long-in-time-in-comparison-with-some-shorter-time-unit.

Wherein lies the heresy of this theory of time and the manner in which it is measured? To be sure it is ultra-subjectivisitic, bestowing a mind-dependent existence on the past, present, and future; and it is no easy task to square such an idealistic theory of time with a fairly literal reading of *Genesis*. More seriously, it completely denies the reality of time, if we accept Augustine's claim that time is composed of past, present, and future. And this, as we shall see, can't be squared with essential tenets of theism. How does it wind up denying the very reality of time? It was previously claimed that Augustine's paradox of the impossibility of measuring time can be fully generalized. When it is, the result is that there are no temporal entities, and thus time itself is unreal. It is assumed by Augustine that only the present is real and moreover is of zero duration. Given, furthermore, that something is real, that is, occurs or exists, only when it is present, it results in there not being any intervals of nonzero duration; there is nothing to be measured if what is to be measured is something *in rerum*. But by the same reason it follows that there aren't any mental acts of representation, such as memories, perceptions, and expectations; for these acts, like intervals of time, require a present of nonzero duration in which to occur or exist. These acts of representing things as past, present, and future are not themselves in time. Their being consists in their being represented, but what represents them is not itself temporal. This sounds like Kant, or one legitimate way of interpreting him, according to which things are not really in time but are only represented as in time by a noumenal self whose acts are not themselves in time. Nothing really is in time!

What Augustine has in effect done is to create the following "disappearance of time argument":

14. Only the present is real;
15. The present is of zero duration;

16. Temporal entities (including intervals of time) occur or exist only when present [from 1];

17. Temporal entities require a finite time within which to occur or exist;[3]

18. No temporal entity occurs or exists [from 15–17];

19. Time is unreal [from 18].

A contemporary philosopher might try to escape this argument by espousing a B-theory of time according to which time, pace Augustine, does not consist of past, present, and future – the A-series – but only a series of events running from earlier to later – the B-series. Not only would it be unacceptably anachronistic to read a B-theory of time back into Augustine or his predecessors, but this theory, as will be argued in Chapter 3, is unacceptable in its own right because a proposition reporting an event's position in the A-series is not reducible to one that reports its position in the B-series, pace the B-theory of time.

The disappearance of time argument turns into an atheological argument when it is combined with the theist's commitment to the reality of time. If time is unreal, certain essential tenets of theism must be rejected. There really is no *past* Creation and Incarnation, nor a *future* Resurrection and Judgment Day. The very ontological distinction between the creator and his creation dissolves. Christianity and Judaism contrast sharply with mystically based religions in their view of time, for not only do they hold time to be real but important as well. In contrast to the cyclical views of time and history that were common to all archaic civilizations, Christianity and Judaism have a linear view of time in which each event is unique and imbued with significance. There are no instant replays: Each of us has only one chance to make it. These biblically based religions, certainly, cannot be reconciled with the unreality of time.

Obviously, Saint Augustine has lost his way, unwittingly giving us the premises of the disappearance of time argument, in violation of his very own theistic commitment to the reality of time. Fortunately, his solution to the creation-immutability argument, based on God being an immutably eternal being whose creative act bears no temporal relation to any worldly time or event, such as the universe's coming into existence, does not require him to go on and commit this act of philosophical hara-kiri. He just got carried away, mesmerized by surface grammatical analogies and spatial metaphors into thinking that time is something very queer indeed. It is not my purpose to find a way out of the disappearance of time argument. There must be a way out, since we know that time is real. Even a mystic should be unhappy with the argument, since the denial of time's ultimate reality, based on what is revealed through mystical experience, does not require one to have a muddled conception of what we take this mere appearance, time, to be. My purpose, instead, is to probe Augustine's account of God's eternity and manner of connection with worldly time, and, in particular, to see whether it leaves us with a religiously available God – the problem adumbrated in Chapter 1. The discussion of God's eternality will be concerned, first, with the *intrinsic* features of this eternity and, second, with its *extrinsic* relations to the temporal world. It will be found inadequate in both areas.

God's eternity is not to be confused with the sort of timeless existence enjoyed by such denizens of the Platonic heaven as numbers, properties, and propositions. While the former is like the latter in not being subject to any temporal determinations or distinctions – that is, does not not have a past, present, or future, stand in temporal relations, or endure in time – it involves more than mere timelessness. Augustine says that "in the Eternal nothing passeth," so far imputing to it nothing more than the sort of timeless existence of the aforementioned abstracta; but he then goes on to say that "the whole is present" (11). "Thy years neither come nor go. . . . Thy years stand together, because they do stand" (13). God has an illimitable life that is comprised of something like years, but, unlike ordinary temporal years that temporally succeed each other, these "years" are had all at once in a single eternal or timeless present. The same view of eternity is expressed by Boethius in the *Consolation of*

Philosophy (Book 5, Prose 6): "Eternity . . . is the complete possession all at once of illimitable life." In explaining this doctrine, Stump and Kretzmann say that it involves an "infinite duration" that is nontemporal because it involves no internal succession.[4] At other places they speak of it as an "atemporal duration."[5] Just as there is a nontemporal sort of duration, there is a nontemporal sort of presentness that is had by God, a present that has no contrast with a past and future.

The first thing that must be pointed out is that these descriptions of God's eternality, if taken literally, involve straight-out contradictions. The notion of a "timeless duration," judged by the standards of ordinary language, is a contradiction in terms. The *OED* says that "duration" is "lasting, continuance in time; the continuance or length of time; the time during which a thing, action, or state continues." It says nothing about a timeless duration. Similarly, the claim that God has all his years at once is contradictory according to our ordinary ways of using language. By definition, numerically distinct years are successive. There are other contradictions that will be explored later. Stump and Kretzmann seem oblivious to these contradictions, and thus make no effort to find some way to surmount them. And this is what I will now try to do.

While such phrases make no sense according to the logic of ordinary discourse, they do make sense when interpreted within the mystical tradition, with its grounding in unitive mystical experiences. The doctrine of the timeless or eternal present bears a striking similarity to the Zen doctrine of the eternal now according to which all times are present, there being no past or future distinct from the present moment. During the summer of 1960, I was privileged to spend an afternoon with Daisetsu Suzuki – Mr. Zen Buddhist to the West at that time – and in the course of the conversation I challenged the Zen doctrine of the eternal now with absurdity. "Present" is used without the needed contrast with "past" and "future." This causes language to idle, just as it would if we were to continue to use first-person discourse but eliminated from our language the needed contrast with second- and third-person discourse. He listened intently to this polemic and then replied that I was indeed right that the Zen doctrine of the eternal now is absurd from the standpoint of ordinary language or common sense but that, nevertheless, it is a fact!

Under fear of being swatted with a broom, I venture this analysis of what he might have meant. Judged by the rules for the use of ordinary language, the Zen doctrine is meaningless; but, if I were to have a satori (a mystical experience), I would both understand what it meant and know that it is true. Leaving aside the issue of the cognitivity or truth of such a mystical experience, which will be the topic of Chapter 8, the following reply could be made to his claim that only the mystic will be able to understand the doctrine. I, along with a host of other nonmystics, understand this doctrine along with other mystical claims, such as those concerning timeless duration and an illimitable life that is had all at once. If nonmystics did not understand the writings of mystics, there wouldn't be such a hefty sale of mystical literature within the "straight" community.

This belies the claim of mystics that their experience is uniquely ineffable, being beyond any conceptualization or description. No doubt, it cannot be described while one is having it, but that is also true of nonmystical experiences, such as wrestling with an alligator, that admit of subsequent description. Nor is the description of a mystical experience a substitute for it in that it is qualitatively isomorphic with it, but, again, this is true of nonmystical experiences, such as a sense experience of a red patch. In both cases, the description, though not a phenomenological replica of the experience it describes, is such that it enables us to identify this experience were we to have it.

I believe that the real reason for the mystic's claiming some sort of unique ineffability for their experience is to be found in the inestimable significance and value it has for them. It seems that the more highly we prize some experience, the more we shun applying concepts to it. Like the composer who shuns writing program notes for her symphony because she fears, and rightly so, that eventually the reading of the program notes will take the place of actually listening to the music, the mystic is afraid that the concepts by which the experience is described will become surrogates for this experience itself. Both persons are telling us by their refusal to conceptualize their experience that it is the direct experience itself that counts and that language is a very poor substitute.

But how is it that we can understand these claims without having had mystical experiences? I don't know, nor do I know of any satisfactory account, but I do know that we understand what the mystics are saying, in spite of their language appearing, on purely syntactical grounds, to violate the ordinary canons for informative discourse. If a sportscaster were to say, "Joe Montana is dropping back to pass while remaining in place," my reaction would be, "What a schmuck, he is contradicting himself," but when it is said in the *Isa Upanishad,* in reporting the phenomenological content of the mystical experience, that it stirs without moving, I understand. I apply a different logic to the mystical claim than to the empirical one; for instance, I do not ask, as I would in the Joe Montana case, whether it stirs and remains at rest *at one and the same time,* for unitive mystical experiences are phenomenologically timeless, containing no distinctions between different times within their content.

Similar considerations hold for sayings like "It's full and it's empty" and "The stone and the tree are one." If the former is said by someone peering into the fridg, he's a candidate for Bellevue; but if it is said by someone who has just finished doing *zazen,* we might consider booking him on a lecture tour of college campuses. If the gardener says that the stone and tree are one, we consider replacing him; but if it is said by Meister Eckhardt in a sermon describing a "nature" type of mystical state, we say, "How profound!" Obviously, the contexts in which these things are said is crucial in supplying the key for their interpretations, including the sort of logical standards we appeal to in understanding and evaluating them. I don't know what the "logic" of mystical discourse is, but I do know that it is radically different from that of "straight" discourse.

I venture to speculate that the reason nonmystics can understand these "contradictory" notions is that they have had experiences that are steps along the way to fully developed unitive mystical experiences: altered states of consciousness, such as drunkenness and drug-induced highs, the empathetic identification with another in a love relationship, especially when it involves the joining of the flesh ("I've got you under my skin"), aesthetic experiences of reconciliation between opposites, for instance, the union of joy and tragedy in the allegretto movement of Beethoveen's Seventh Symphony (and don't ask if the joy and tragedy occur at one and the same time, since they permeate the entire experience of the movement), and last, but not least, the poorman's "oceanic experience" upon sinking into a hot tub.

Too often the rationalistic theist muddies the waters by trying to show that the notions of a timeless present and timeless duration make sense according to the canons of ordinary discourse. This is clearly evident in the Kretzmann–Stump exposition. At the heart of their account is the claim that the timeless and temporal present, along with timeless and temporal duration, are species of the same generic notions of present and duration respectively. (As we shall see in the next chapter, they also claim, with equal implausibility, that there is a generic notion of simultaneity that has both a temporal and nontemporal species.) What is basically wrong with this account is that it runs together incommensurable languages. If the mystical notions of a timeless present and a timeless duration were species of the same genus as are the temporal present and temporal duration respectively, there should be considerable overlap in their logics. They should at least obey the same laws of logic, such as the law of noncontradiction. But, as seen above, they don't. There isn't any ordinary sense of duration other than the temporal one. By cutting the notion of the eternal present loose from its mystical roots, they block the only way in which sense can be made of it and thereby do a great disservice to the doctrine that they attempt to defend against the charge of meaning-lessness.

Their attempt to make rational sense of the notion of a timeless mind also commits the sin of cutting a mystical doctrine loose from its mystical roots. God has an illimitable *life* and thus must be alive and possessed of a mind; but he has this "life" all at once. Thus, he must enjoy a mental life of some sort that does not involve any kind of temporal succession or duration. The proper thing to say about this is that it is a mystically rooted notion that makes no sense in terms of what these expressions mean in ordinary language. Maybe the quickest and most direct way of showing the absurdity of a timeless mind is as follows: A mind is conscious, and consciousness is a temporally elongated process.

Obviously, not everyone agrees with this. Stump and Kretzmann attempt to make good ordinary sense of a time-less mind by claiming that there are many psychological or mental states that do not require temporal duration. Inductive support can be given for my claim that consciousness is essentially temporal by meeting any alleged counterexamples, such as those given by them. They give knowing as a counterexample:

> Knowing seems to be the paradigm case; learning, reasoning, inferring take time, as knowing does not. In reply to the question 'What have you been doing for the past two hours?' it makes sense to say 'Studying logic' . . . but not 'Knowing logic'.[6]

Willing and awareness are other examples they give of mental states that one can have atemporally.

While they are right that it makes no sense to ask "How long have you been knowing logic?" since knowing logic is a state, not a process, they fail to see that it does make sense to ask "How long have you known logic?" and "When did you begin (cease) to know logic?" Furthermore, one could not be in the state of knowing that *p* without having dispositions to engage in various sorts of episodes, such as having occurrent beliefs that p, employing that p in one's reasoning, and so on, just as one could not be in love without having dispositions to perform various actions, such as caring for, protecting, cherishing, and so on, the loved one. While these states fill time in a homogeneous manner, they require having dispositions to engage in temporal episodes, occurrences, or processes. This raises an especially acute problem for the timelessly eternal Deity of the great medieval theists, who is supposed to have pure actuality and therefore no unrealized dispositions. Thus, God's being in one of these states, such as loving or knowing, would require that he not have any unrealized dispositions but instead be engaging in all of the actions that one in such a state is disposed to do. But these actions take time to perform.

The same points hold with respect to the extrinsic aspects of God's timeless eternality. Our ordinary concept of causation involves some sort of temporal relation, which can be that of simultaneity, between cause and effect. This holds even for the notion of agent causation in which the cause is not an event but a person. God's timeless causation is a species of such agent causation but one that has no temporal relation to its temporal effect. Our ordinary concept of causation does not make room for timeless causation; but it might make sense within the mystical tradition, with its idea of the eternal intersecting time at every moment. Mystics claim to directly experience this intersection between time and eternity – that all times are one, namely, the present. And we might be able to make sense of the idea of timeless causation on such an experiential basis. Again, we seem forced to give a mystical interpretation of God's timeless eternity.

So far it has been argued that the intrinsic and extrinsic features of God's timeless eternity can be understood only in mystical terms. But the theist must pay a significant price for going this mystical route, namely, he winds up with a God who is a nonperson. A person has a mind and thus endures in time. It has purposes, intentions, and goals and interacts with other persons, which, again, require it to have a temporal mode of existence. The personal God of the Scriptures qualifies as a person in this sense: He has purposes and interacts with his creatures. The Deity to whom the authors of the Bible prayed was taken to be someone with whom they had communion, someone who comforted, counseled, and warned them, and on occasion, answered their prayers. They conceived of themselves as having a two-way interaction with God. Their words and actions brought about certain reactions from God; for instance, their prayers moved God to respond, their actions caused God to intercede, and so on. Such two-way interaction makes no sense on the theory of a timelessly eternal God, for all of his states and actions occur within a single timeless present and cannot be the effect of anything that happens in time. God's absolute aseity requires this. Our words and deeds, rather than being causes of God's will, merely fit into a pattern that God timelessly wills and knows. Thus, in making God an absolutely perfect being, the medieval theists cut God off from his creatures.[7]

There were, of course, deep motives for this depersonalizing of God. It was assumed by the medieval theists, as it was by the Greeks before them, that there is something inherently inferior about the temporal compared with the timeless. Being temporal was an infliction, a sort of body odor from which everything of this world reeked. For a complex set of reasons, some psychological having to do with the fear of death and decay, others socioeconomic concerning their disdain for the inferior class of people who were forced to manipulate changing objects, they assumed that true being must be found in what is immutable and independent of anything that might limit or destroy it, an absolutely simple being, thus the doctrine of the divine simplicity. Such a reality is the sort that mystics take themselves to be in touch with via their experiences – an eternal one, an undifferentiated unity, that is, an absolutely simple being that admits of no distinctions. But such a timeless reality is not a person. Furthermore, as we shall see when we consider various ontological arguments in Chapter 6, the necessity of God's existence seemed to require that he be timeless, for only such a being's existence can be deduced from its essence.

The underlying problem of theism is that it wants its God to play contradictory roles – to be both a person and a mystical reality that is beyond being, time, and distinctions. The doctrine of the Trinity is an attempt to resolve this contradiction by giving God, through the different members of the Trinity, both of these aspects, Jesus the Son being the personal God to whom we can relate in a personal way and God the Father being the mystical reality – the absolutely simple being who is beyond being and distinctions – to whom we have access through unitive mystical experiences. This doctrine is not all that different from Eastern forms of mysticism in which an eternal one or undifferentiated unity somehow undergoes emanation into lesser deities of a personal sort, which emanations eventually flow back into its oneness. I am convinced that the doctrine of the Trinity makes sense only on mystical grounds, for, on the surface, it appears contradictory by its identifying the three members of the Trinity with each other but refusing to allow them to have all their properties in common, thereby violating Leibniz's law.

Not surprisingly, Stump and Kretzmann also try to make good rational sense of this doctrine. Their way out of the problem of how we can identify the persons of the Trinity without having to apply Leibniz's law to them is to hold that each of them has its properties qua that member of the Trinity. Thus, the proposition that Christ died is to be understood as "Christ with respect to his human nature (or qua man) died."[8] If ever a predicate were referentially transparent, it is "dies" or "gets crucified," pace what they claim. Being crucified or dying, unlike being loved, does not occur under a concept or description. It would have been a bad joke for the Roman executioners to have said to Jesus, "Don't feel bad. We're crucifying you only qua Son, not qua Father."

Concerning the extrinsic features of God's eternality, only that of timeless causation has been considered. An even more serious problem concerns the epistemological relations that such a being has to the temporal universe. It appears that his timeless immutability precludes his knowing certain facts about the temporal world, such as what is happening right now. This is one of the reasons that it seems impossible to have personal interactions with such a God. The next chapter will consider the omniscience–immutability argument against such a God, and it will be argued that it succeeds. And, as a result, we will have to make due with a temporal God, the nature of which will partially emerge as a result of this argument, to which we now turn.

Chapter 3

The omniscience–immutability argument

This argument's initial set is composed of these three propositions:

1. God essentially knows all and believes only true propositions;

2. God essentially does not change from one time to another in respect to any nonrelational property; and

3. There are true temporal indexical propositions (to be called "A-propositions") to the effect that certain events and/ or times are now past, present, or future.

Theism's commitment to 1 and 2 results from its conceiving God to be essentially both omniscient and immutable; and it is committed to 3 because, as pointed out in the previous chapter, theism (at least as represented by Judaism and Christianity) is a historically rooted creed that accords not only reality but significance to the sort of A-facts over which 3 quantifies, such as that the world came into being in the *past*, has reached a certain stage in its spiritual development at *present*, and awaits a *future* day of judgment.

The qualification on God's omniscience, that he believes only true propositions, which will be dropped in the future for the sake of brevity, is due to our not wanting to allow an omniscient being to go around having any false beliefs, even if he does know every true proposition. Notice that an omniscient being must not only know of every true proposition that it is true but must also know every true proposition. As we shall see later in this chapter, these are not the same, since one could know that some proposition is true without knowing it.

The reason for the restriction of God's immutability to non-relational properties, in which a nonrelational property is one that an individual could possess even if there were not to exist any other nonuniversal particulars, save for spaces and times, is to escape such "Cambridge" changes in God as being thought about by Jones at one time but not at another, herein the change being in Jones rather than in God. How the argument proceeds from here depends on whether it has as its target the timelessly eternal God of St. Augustine or the omni-temporally eternal God of the Bible, that is, a God that endures throughout a beginningless and endless time and logically could not begin or cease to exist. If it is the former, it argues that a timeless being cannot know an A-proposition, and therefore God isn't omniscient; and, if the latter, that in order literally to keep up to date, God would have to change in his temporal indexical beliefs from one time to another, and thereby is not strictly immutable. A contradiction results in either case. Since we are intent on following up the preceding chapter's concern with the viability of the conception of a timelessly eternal God, we shall first consider the version of the argument that is directed against this sort of Deity and then go on to see how it fares when it is deployed against the omnitemporal God. It will turn out that only the latter escapes the argument, and only if we give up his strict immutability.

No contradiction can be deduced from the initial set 1–3. It is necessary to add the following supposedly necessary additional premise:

4. It is conceptually impossible for a timeless being to know an A-proposition,

from which it follows, in conjunction with 3, that

5. God (conceived of as timelessly eternal) does not know every true proposition,

which contradicts 1. Thus, God both is and is not omniscient.

Faced with this contradiction, our theist must deny at least one of the premises of the above argument, either 1, 2, 3, or 4. Premise 2 cannot consistently be denied, since God's immutability is a logical consequence of his being timelessly eternal: A being that is not in time at all cannot change in the non-Cambridge properties it has from one time to another. Denial of 3 is not an attractive option, for the reasons already given, nor is the denial of 1, since omniscience is usually taken by theists to be at least a soft- if not hard-core property of God. It is the added premise 4 that the theist will want to dispute, many of the great medieval theists, for example, arguing that God could timelessly know A-propositions. Obviously, the defender of the omniscience–immutability argument owes us an explanation and defense of 4, since it is not clear, much less acceptable, without further ado.

The first thing that must be done toward this end is to clarify the very troublesome notion of an A-proposition. We will restrict our treatment to contingent propositions. An A-proposition is expressible by (but not necessarily only by) the use or intentional tokening of an A-sentence, that is, a sentence that is such that successive tokenings of it by the same person, at the same place, and with the same meaning logically could express propositions that differ in truth-value.[1] It must also be stipulated that the sentence is used with the same meaning on each of these occasions. The grammatical device that is used in Indo-European languages to render sentences nonfreely repeatable in time is the tense of a verb, while in Chinese and Eskimo it results from the inflection of a noun. The meaning of an A-sentence is given by its "tokening rule," which specifies the conditions under which an intentional tokening or use of it expresses a true proposition or, as some would put it today, a rule that takes us from a context of tokening, of which the relevant feature is the time of tokening, to a truth-value. (Throughout this book I am adopting the convention that a tokening of "now" or other temporal indexical term refers to the time of tokening rather than the time of its being perceived, which is our usual, but not universal convention.) For instance, the tokening rule for

59

the English sentence "Event E is now present (past, future)" requires of a true tokening of it that it be simultaneous with (later than, earlier than) event E.

A B-proposition, however, is one that is expressible through the use of a freely repeatable sentence and describes a temporal relation between two events and/or times, for instance, "Event E is (timelessly) earlier than event E'." It is freely repeatable in that it is logically impossible that successive tokenings of it, with the same meaning, can express propositions that differ in truth-value. A freely repeatable sentence will be called a "B-sentence."

Care has been taken to give only a sufficient condition for being an A-proposition, namely, being expressible by the use of an A-sentence, thereby leaving it open whether an A-proposition also is expressible by the use of a B-sentence. If the latter were to be the case, it could be shown that every A-proposition is identical with some B-proposition, that is, a proposition expressible by the use of a B-sentence. This would afford the theist a way out of the omniscience–immutable argument, since God could timelessly know an A-proposition via timelessly knowing the B-proposition with which it is identical, which certainly is possible, if timeless knowledge itself is possible. The previous chapter cast doubt on the possibility of the latter, and this chapter will argue against the possibility of a B-reduction, that is, the doctrine that every A-proposition is identical with some B-proposition, thereby presenting a two-pronged attack against this strategy for escaping the argument. Appeal to a B-reduction, however, is only one of many ways of rebutting it, as we shall see.

Given this account of an A-proposition, why should we accept 4's contention that only a being in time can know an A-proposition? A. N. Prior has given both a negative and positive defense of 4.[2] The former consists in an argument against the chief ground for denying 4 – the B-reduction. Since, as we shall see when we consider Castaneda's rebuttal based on a timeless way of knowing an A-proposition in *oratio obliqua,* there are other grounds for denying 4 than that supplied by the B-reduction, Prior's negative defense suffers from incompleteness. We will consider it anyway and then go on to criticize his positive argument for 4.

Against the B-reduction's claim that every A-proposition is identical with some B-proposition, Prior repeats his earlier objection from his article "Thank Goodness That's Over."[3] When we say of some particularly unpleasant experience – the final examinations – "Thank Goodness that the final examinations are over (past)," we are not expressing the same proposition as we would were we to say "Thank goodness that the final examinations occur (timelessly) at t_7 (or are (timelessly) 2000 years later than the birth of Christ)"; for why should we be glad about the latter? In brief, Prior's argument is that the A- and B-propositions in question are not identical, since one could be glad about the former but not the latter. Prior's point can be generalized to all propositional attitudes, since one could believe, know, and the like that the final examinations are now past without having the same propositional attitude to the B-proposition that these exams occur (timelessly) at t_7.

Herein Prior is implicitly appealing to (at least the only-if part of) the following propositional-attitude-based criterion for propositional identity:

PA. Proposition p is identical with proposition q if and only if it is not possible that someone who understands both p and q have a propositional attitude at some time T toward one of them that she does not have toward the other.

A similar type of propositional-attitude-based criterion can be given for determining when two sentences express the same proposition:

PA'. The sentences "s" and "s'" express the same proposition at some time T if and only if it is not possible that someone who understands the meaning of both "s" and "s'" have a different propositional attitude at T toward what "s" expresses than toward what "s'" expresses.

"At some time *T*" was inserted in both PA and PA' so as to make them applicable to A-propositions and A-sentences, respectively. Similar qualifications would have to be added to make them applicable to other types of indexical propositions and sentences.

These criteria could aptly be called the "Fregean criteria," since it was Frege who stressed the crucial role that propositions play as objects of propositional attitudes. These criteria are the most demanding ones and will play a key role when we examine versions of the B-reduction that have appeared subsequently to Prior's criticism of the B-reduction. But even if Prior's negative defense of 4 is not completely convincing because it fails to consider new versions of the B-reduction, as well as Castaneda's *oratio obliqua* way of denying 4, his positive defense of 4 could be completely satisfactory, and we now turn to it.

In support of 4, Prior claimed that an A-proposition "isn't something that God or anyone else could know timelessly, because it just isn't true timelessly."[4] Herein Prior employs the Aristotelian-scholastic-Lukasiewicz terminology according to which an A-sentence expresses the same proposition whenever it is tokened, albeit one that changes in truth-value. When this argument is reformulated in my stated alternative terminology for A-sentences, it comes to this:

4a. For every A-sentence there are at least two times such that this sentence expresses propositions that differ in truth-value when tokened at these times.[5]

Therefore,

4. It is conceptually impossible for a timeless being to know an A-proposition.

Prior is attempting to deduce 4 from the mere definition of an "A-sentence," and I am unable to see how 4 follows from this definition.[6]

That more must be said in defense of 4 than that supplied by 4a is also evident by the fact that no less a philosopher than Peter Geach flatly denied 4, no doubt with Prior in mind, and moreover did so without accepting either the B-reduction (which he rejects) or the possibility of timelessly knowing an A-proposition in *oratio obliqua*. In other words, Geach claims that God can timelessly know an A-proposition in *oratio recta*, even though no A-proposition is identical with any B-proposition. Geach begins by giving the following simple rule for God's omniscience: " 'God knows that p' is true if and only if the plain 'p' is true." He goes on to say:

> We need not lose our heads in dealing with tensed propositions; we need only stick to the simple rule I have just given. In 1939 it was true to say 'Hitler is alive'; it was therefore true to say in 1939 'God knows that Hitler is alive'. In 1970 it was true to say 'Hitler is dead'; it was therefore true to say in 1970 'God knows that Hitler is dead'.[7]

Notice that no temporal qualification is made on when God knows. Whatever he knows, he knows timelessly. What is temporally qualified is the proposition he knows and when we time-bound creatures can truly say that God timelessly knows this proposition.

There is an ambiguity in Geach's presentation that must be clarified before we can evaluate his position. When I now say "God knows that Hitler is now dead," am I ascribing to God knowledge of the very same A-proposition as the one I express by my present use of "Hitler is now dead" in the *oratio obliqua* clause? This question gets down to whether the occurrence of "now" in the *oratio obliqua* clause expresses God's present-tense indexical mode of reference to the present as well as my own. As Hector-Neri Castaneda has so ably shown, an indexical word, such as *"now,"* always has the widest scope in a sentence, even if it occurs in an *oratio obliqua* clause, because it expresses the speaker's own indexical reference.[8] The question is whether in cases in which an indexical word occurs in an *oratio obliqua* construction attributing a belief, desire, and the like to someone it also expresses this person's own indexical reference. Castaneda denies that it does. In many cases it does not, especially those involving personal indexicals. If I say "Jones knows that I am tired," the occurrence of "I" expresses my own first-personal indexical reference, not also Jones's; for were Jones to have employed this mode of indexical reference, he would have referred to himself rather than me. In this case, the *oratio obliqua* clause abstracts from how Jones refers to me and thereby underdetermines the proposition known by Jones. But the issue is not so clear cut with "now." Ordinary usage, in my opinion, is not sufficiently precise to determine whether an occurrence of "now" in an *oratio obliqua* clause attributing a belief, and the like to a person does or does not indicate this person's indexical reference as well as the speaker's.

If we take such an occurrence of "now" as expressing only the speaker's indexical reference, we abstract from how the person in question refers to the present moment and thereby underdetermine the proposition he believes, and so on. On this construal, Geach would have failed to show that God can know an A-proposition; for it could be true that God knows that Hitler is now dead without God making a present-tense indexical reference to the present moment and thus without God knowing any A-proposition. In this case we underdetermine the proposition known by God.

We can, of course, simply decide to construe an *oratio obliqua* occurrence of "now" or any indexical word as expressing both the speaker's and the believer's indexical reference; and we could adopt the convention that when and only when an *oratio obliqua* construction is represented in the explicit paratactic manner are we so to construe it. If I say "God knows that (this). Hitler is now dead," the *oratio obliqua* occurrence of "now" expresses both my and God's indexical reference, and, thereby, I do attribute to God knowledge of the very same A-proposition as I express by my use of "Hitler is now dead" in the *oratio obliqua* clause. Thus, Geach winds up with the seemingly bizarre position that God is able to make a present-tense indexical reference to the present moment *without doing so at any time!*[9] But many a bizarre claim is true, and thus it behooves us to find some cogent argument against Geach.

Such an argument is to be found in Robert Coburn's version of the omniscience–immutability argument, directed against the timelessly eternal Deity:

> If a being is omniscient, then presumably it follows that this being knows everything which (logically) can be known. But it is easy to see that an eternal being could not know everything which (logically) can be known, and this is because some of the facts which (logically) can be known, are knowable only by temporal beings, by beings who occupy some position (or some positions) in time. . . . assume that the idea of a non-temporal knower makes sense. Then ask, could such a knower know, e.g., that today is May 12, 1962? The obvious answer, I submit, is that it could only if it could use temporal indicator words. For otherwise, it could not express and *a fortiori* could not entertain a truth such as the above. But a necessary condition of being able to use temporal indicator words is being an occupant of time. Hence, God's alleged eternity is logically incompatible with his alleged omniscience.[10]

Before we can properly understand and criticize this argument, it must be given an explicit mounting. In the following, Coburn's use of an indicator word will be replaced by that of the tokening of an A-sentence in which the tokening is intentional. Further, each of its premises is a necessary conceptual truth, as is required, since the conclusion, 4, has to be a necessary truth if it is to be permissible to add it to the initial set of an atheological argument:

4b. A person can know a proposition only if she can truly express it [premise];

4c. A person can truly express a proposition only if she can truly token a sentence that expresses this proposition [premise];

4d. A person can truly express an A-proposition only if she can truly token a sentence that expresses this proposition [from 4c];

4e. An A-proposition is expressible only by the tokening of an A-sentence [premise];

4f. A person can truly express an A-proposition only if she can truly token an A-sentence [from 4d and 4e];

4g. A person can truly token an A-sentence only at a time [premise];

4h. A person who can truly token an A-sentence exists in time [from 4g]; and

4. It is conceptually impossible for a timeless being to know an A-proposition [from 4b, 4f, and 4h].

This argument is valid, but its premises stand in need of further elucidation and justification.

Premise 4b must not be taken as requiring of someone who knows a proposition that she can give overt expression to it in some public language. (Let us not forget Gunga Din and James's deaf mute.) For the sake of argument we can assume the possibility of an in-principle private language and thereby permit our Deity to express his thoughts in his own private Deitese language.

To establish 4c we must begin with the fact that knowing entails believing, which in turn entails having either a certain occurrent thought or the disposition to have this thought. Since God is pure actuality, he has no unfulfilled dispositions, although he does have counterfactual possibilities in that he varies across possible worlds in which he exists. As a result, all of his thoughts are occurrent. Now, to think something occurrently is to say something to oneself, to express a proposition even if only in one's mind or heart. Here we must appeal to an important thesis championed by Peter Geach and Wilfrid Sellars that such internal sayings are to be understood as an analogical extension of the overt use of language. This means that we are to construe a person's saying some proposition to herself as involving a mental tokening of a sentence that has the same meaning or plays the same role as does a sentence by which her thought could be publicly expressed. To summarize: Premise 4c requires of a knower of a proposition that she can either publicly express it by tokening a suitable sentence or mentally token (or be disposed to token) a sentence that has the same meaning as some sentence by which this proposition can be publicly expressed.

Premise 4d is just a substitution instance of the universal proposition 4c and needs no further comment. Premise 4e, which is a denial of the B-reduction, is not explicitly asserted by Coburn, but plainly it is required for the derivation of 4f. More will be said about 4e when we consider rebuttals based upon the B-reduction. Premise 4g is necessary in virtue of the tokening rules for A-sentences that specify the sort of temporal relation that must hold between the tokening event and the event reported for a true proposition to be expressed. Because the tokening must stand in a temporal relation to the event reported, the tokening must occur at a time. And this seems to entail 4g, since a person cannot do something at a time without existing at that time.

I will defend this reconstructed version of the Coburn argument against a number of possible objections. Hopefully, this will enable us to gain a greater understanding of and justification for its various premises.

God's timeless tokening of A-sentences. The Augustinian doctrine of God's timeless causation of effects in time, which was expounded in the preceding chapter, can be marshaled against premise 4g. Doubt has already been cast on whether this doctrine makes any (nonmystical) sense, but, for the sake of argument, we will grant the intelligibility of timeless causation. Given the doctrine of timeless causation, it might be claimed that God can truly express A-propositions by timelessly bringing it about that tokens of A-sentences occur at different times in a way that satisfies the tokening rules.[11] He might accomplish this by bringing it about that a rainbow has for a brief time the sign design of "Mary is now baking pies."

The need for God to bring about all these A-sentence tokens opens the door for the following sort of inductive argument against God's existence: God, being essentially omniscient, must know every true proposition in every world in which he exists. Therefore, in every world in which both God and A-facts exist, he brings about the occurrence of an A-sentence token for every A-proposition that is true in that world. The empirical evidence available to us in this world indicates that this is not the case! The theist, of course, can have faith that these tokens occur on some remote galaxy or the like, but this is a pretty bizarre thing to have to accept on faith – a blabber-mouth Deity who must publicly remark on everything. There should be a new hymn, "We Believe In Our Heavenly Bringer About of A-sentence Tokens." Or he might offer as an apologia that we wouldn't be able to recognize these tokens were we to come upon them, since they would be in Deitese.

A far more serious objection to the timeless causation rebuttal of 4g is that it abuses the tokening rules for A-sentences. These rules specify what temporal relations must hold between an *intentional* tokening and the reported event, for only an intentional tokening of an A-sentence *expresses* an A-proposition. Thus, an intentional tokening of an A- sentence involves the thinking of the thought or proposition expressed by the tokening. This requires that the thinking of the proposition expressed by the tokening of the A-sentence is simultaneous with the tokening. As a consequence, the thinking of the proposition must have the same temporal relation to the reported event as does the tokening, if the relevant tokening rule is to be satisfied. But this is exactly what a timeless God cannot do. God's occurrent believing and thinking of an A-proposition (remember that he has no dispositional potentialities), unlike the occurrence of the A-sentence token he causes, has no temporal relation to any event, and this results in a failure to satisfy the relevant tokening rule. Furthermore, God believes all at once, in a single timeless present, every A-proposition (e.g., that E is now past, present, and future), which hardly satisfies the tokening rules.

There is another path that leads to 4g. It begins with the conceptual truth that a person cannot express a proposition unless she can understand the expression of this proposition by someone, in which the "someone" can be herself. God cannot understand the expression of an A-proposition by anyone, including himself, since to do so he would have to determine the temporal relation between the tokening of the A-sentence and his perceiving it; but his perceiving it stands in no temporal relations.

At this point, our proponent of the timeless causation rebuttal might take the desperation tack of charging us with being unduly anthropomorphic in requiring the Deity to jump through the same conceptual hoops as we mortals do, in particular, of having to satisfy our tokening rules if he is to have knowledge of, and thereby be able to express, A-propositions. It is sufficient if his occurrent believings of A-propositions stand in timeless relations to the reported events that are counterparts to the temporal relations of precedence and simultaneity that are required by the tokening rules. Let us first consider a nontemporal counterpart relation to simultaneity and then consider what such a counterpart would be for precedence.

Stump and Kretzmann supply us with a nontemporal counterpart to temporal simultaneity that relates a timelessly eternal Deity to every event and moment of time, and it will be instructive to determine whether it can help us to make sense of this Deity's knowing A-propositions. They begin by claiming, as is their wont, that our ordinary notion of temporal simultaneity, that is, existence or occurrence at one and the same time, is a species of a generic notion of simultaneity that means "existence or occurrence at once (i.e., together)."[12] Another species of this genus is what they call "ET-simultaneity." This relation holds between the timelessly eternal God and every moment of time and event because each of the latter is "observed as temporally present" by God, and God, in turn, is observable by an observer at each of these times as eternally present, supposedly through a mystical experience, though they do not commit themselves to this interpretation.[13] Their account assumes that successive mystical experiences apprehend one and the same eternal present, an assumption that will be challenged in Chapter 8.

Why couldn't God timelessly know an A-proposition, at least a present-tense one, by standing in this relation of ET-simultaneity to the event reported by this proposition?

In the first place, there isn't any nontemporal generic notion of simultaneity. The *O.E.D.* has this entry under "simultaneity": "from the Latin *simul*, at the same time." If they were right that there is a generic sense of "simultaneity" meaning "existence together," it would be correct to say that two fictional characters that exist together in the same novel are simultaneous and that two numbers that exist together in the same number system are simultaneous!

This departure from ordinary language is not decisive, since Stump and Kretzmann could maintain that their ET-simultaneity relation, by whatever name we decide to call it, is sufficiently analogous to ordinary simultaneity that it should allow God to have knowledge of present-tense A-propositions by standing in this relation to the event reported by such a proposition. Just how *relevantly* analogous is ET-simultaneity to ordinary simultaneity? The relevant features of the analogy concern the respective roles these relations play as relations, that is, the manner in which they order things. Ordinary simultaneity is reflexive, symmetrical, and transitive, but ET-simultaneity is only symmetrical. It cannot be transitive; for, if it were, any two times would have to stand in the ET-simultaneity relation to each other since each has this relation to God, which would violate the requirement that the relata in an ET-simultaneity relation are a timelessly eternal being and a temporal entity. And for the same reason, the relation cannot be reflexive. Thus, it has only one out of the three logical features of ordinary simultaneity. This makes it look quite disanalogous to simultaneity, and thereby gives us no reason for thinking that God's standing in it to the event reported by a present-tense A-proposition satisfies the tokening rule that requires of a true tokening of a present-tense A-sentence that it be simultaneous with the reported event.

Even if the Stump–Kretzmann strategy were to work for God's knowledge of present-tense A-propositions, and it doesn't, it would fail to show how he can know past- and future-tense A-propositions. To accomplish this they would have to concoct a nontemporal counterpart relation to ordinary precedence, call it "ET-precedence," that again would have an eternally present and temporal entity as its relata. Given the ontological disparity between its relata, it must be irreflexive and nontransitive, for the reasons already given. And, also like ET-simultaneity, it will be symmetrical. By giving the relation these logical properties, it avoids introducing any succession within God's timeless eternity or requiring him to bear any temporal relations to temporal entities. And it could be claimed by Stump and Kretzmann that God, in virtue of standing in ET-precedence to the event reported by a future-tense A-proposition, can know it, since this relation is sufficiently analogous to the ordinary-precedence relation between tokening and reported event that is required by the tokening rule.

As with ET-simultaneity, the analogy with its temporal counterpart is very thin. Again, only one out of the three logical properties of the latter is fulfilled. Ordinary precedence is irreflexive, asymmetric, and transitive while ET-precedence is irreflexive, symmetric, and nontransitive. And one out of three just isn't good enough for it to count as a *relevant* analogue to the ordinary relation. To allow God to know A-propositions in virtue of standing in ET-simultaneity and ET-precedence relations to worldly events is on a par with a radically multivocalist theory that permits God to count as benevolent even though he does not satisfy our ordinary criteria for being benevolent. In both cases it is a dishonest piece of equivocation.

The B-reduction. This family of rebuttals argues that every A-proposition is identical with some B-proposition, and thus by knowing the latter God also knows the former. The first version of this rebuttal to be considered was developed by Nelson Pike for the expressed purpose of refuting Coburn's argument.[14] Pike begins by correctly pointing out that a timeless God, in virtue of his knowledge of B-propositions that report a temporal relation between an A-tokening and the event it reports, can know when time-bound persons express true A-propositions. For instance, God can know the B-proposition that Smith's tokening of "*E* occurs now" is (time-lessly) simultaneous with *E* and thereby know that the A-proposition expressed by Smith is (timelessly) true in virtue of satisfying the relevant tokening rule. If Smith should be called upon to justify his A-assertion, he would do so by pointing out that it satisfied the relevant tokening rule, that is, he would assert this very B-proposition. And, fur-thermore, God also would offer this B-proposition to justify his knowledge of the B-proposition that the A-proposition expressed by Smith is (timelessly) true. And, Pike controver-sially adds, this identity in justification shows that the latter B-proposition that the A-proposition expressed by Smith is (timelessly) true is identical with the A-proposition expressed by Smith. And, in virtue of this identity, God timelessly knows the A-proposition expressed by Smith.

There are several flaws in this. In general, it is not true that a person cannot know that the proposition expressed by another is true without knowing this very proposition. There are at least two cases in which this does not hold. In one case a suitable justification cannot be given; for instance, I can know that the mathematical proposition expressed by some noted mathematician is true but fail to know this proposition because I cannot derive or prove it. A more relevant case is one in which I cannot express the proposition known by another, thereby failing to satisfy requirement 4b for knowl-edge; for instance, I can know on the basis of reliable eyewit-ness reports that the first proposition expressed by Smith yesterday is true and yet not know this proposition because I cannot express or specify it. And this is exactly the predica-ment God seems to be in regarding the A-proposition expressed by Smith: He cannot express it since he cannot truly token an A-sentence. That God can identify but not express this A-proposition is not paradoxical once we realize that there are two different ways of identifying a proposition. In one we use a noun "that"-clause that expresses the proposition, that is, has a sense that is the proposition; for instance, one says "that snow is white." In the other we use a non-specifying singular identifying expression, for instance, "Smith's favorite proposition." Pike fails to show that God can identify an A-proposition in the specifying manner. And if God cannot specify it, he cannot know it.

Another flaw in the argument from sameness of justificatory responses for two assertions to identity of propositions asserted is the assumption that what is asserted is identical with how it is justified. Pike is right that we justify an assertion of an A-sentence by stating a B-proposition indicating that the relevant tokening rule is satisfied, that is, that the tokening bears the proper temporal relation to the event reported. But obviously, the A-proposition asserted is not identical with the justificatory B-proposition, since the latter alone entails that a token bears some temporal relation to the reported event. The A-proposition that it is now raining could be true even if no tokens were to occur now. The sentence, "It is now raining even though no tokens occur now," is pragmatically self-refuting in that every tokening of it expresses a *contingently* false proposition.

An interesting new version of a B-reduction can be developed from Kripke's views on rigid designators and a criterion for propositional identity based on the semantics of possible worlds, namely:

PS. The proposition p is identical with the proposition q if and only if they have the same truth-value in every possible world.

Consider any A-proposition, say the one expressed by now tokening "E occurs now." The temporal indexical word "now" means the same as "this time" and, in some contexts, "at this time," and thereby denotes a moment of time (whatever that might turn out to be). Therefore, there is a true identity proposition, say that t_7 is now. Both the indexical word "now" and the proper name "t_7" are rigid designators in that they denote in every counterfactual proposition in which they occur the same individual as they do when used in a categorical proposition about the actual world. Therefore, if "*d*" is rigid, the proposition expressed by "*d* might not have been *d*" is false. Both "now" and "t_7" are rigid designators by this test. As a consequence, the proposition expressed by the identity sentence "t_7 is now" is necessarily true if true at all. Given that it does express a true proposition, it follows that there is no possible world in which now – this very moment of time, namely, t_7 – is not identical with t_7. And, since *E* occurs now, there is no possible world in which *E* occurs now but does not occur at t_7. Therefore, that *E* occurs now and that E occurs (timelessly) at t_7 have the same truth-value in every possible world and, thus, by PS, are identical.

The only thing suspect in this B-reduction is its criterion for propositional identity. PS is a far weaker criterion than PA, and the question is which one should be operative in our discussion of God's omniscience. It seems that PS not only is inadequate in general, since it yields the counterintuitive result that there is only one necessary (impossible) proposition, but demands too little of an omniscient being. God would not be disqualified from being omniscient according to PS were he to believe that $2 + 2 = 4$ but fail to believe that $2 + 3 = 5$. Thus, PS permits God to have a second-class sort of omniscience, which is definitely not the sort we expect of the being than which none greater can be conceived.

The co-reporting thesis. That we cannot permit God to have a second-class sort of omniscience also undermines this way out of the Coburn argument. It is based on a far more modest claim than that made by the B-reduction – that for every A-proposition there is some B-proposition that reports one and the same event, in which the event reported by a proposition is the event referred to by its participial nominalization. That *S* is Fing reports the event of *S*'s Fing. Thus, the co-reporting thesis claims that for every A-proposition there is a B-proposition such that their participial nominalizations are co-referring. This seems correct, given that temporal indexical terms like "now" denote a moment of time.

Consider the A-proposition expressed by now tokening "*S is F*ing now." As already seen, "now" denotes a moment of time, and thereby there is a true proposition identifying now with a moment of time, say that t_7 is now. As a result, the B-proposition that *S* is (timelessly) F*ing at t_7 is co-reporting with that *S* is F*ing now, since *S*'s F*ing now is one and the same event or state of affairs as *S*'s F*ing at t_7, the reason being that these events involve the same subject instantiating the same property at the same time. While our timeless Deity, for the reasons given by Coburn, cannot know the A-proposition that *S* is F*ing now, he can timelessly know the B-proposition that *S* is (timelessly) F*ing at t_7. Thus, a timeless God can know of every event, including events such as *S*'s F*ing now.

But this way out attributes a second-class omniscience to God. God, on this account, does know of every event but not under every true description. He knows what is going on now, but he doesn't know of these events that they are occurring now. The co-reporting way out receives a spurious plausibility from an ambiguity in "God knows of *S*'s F*ing now" that exactly parallels the aforementioned ambiguity in "God knows that *S* is F*ing now" in regard to whether the *oratio obliqua* occurrence of "now" indicates both the speaker's and God's indexical reference or only the speaker's. Since the co-reporting thesis agrees that it indicates only the speaker's, it must say the same about the occurrence of "now" in "God knows of *S*'s F*ing now." And this gives the game away.[15]

The elimination thesis. Yet another possible escape from Coburn's argument is supplied by a radical theory of indexicals that has been developed by John Perry in two articles of unsurpassed clarity and brilliance.[16] It is radical because it denies the very existence of the sort of A-propositions whose existence is asserted by the claim of premise 3 that there are true A-propositions. These propositions are supposed to resemble nonindexical ones in that both are a complete, unified Fregean sense compounded of the senses of the subject and predicate of a sentence that expresses this unified sense. Such a Fregean proposition or "thought," in addition to serving as the sense of this sentence, also serves as its indirect reference (i.e., its direct reference when the sentence occurs in *oratio obliqua*) and most importantly the object of propositional attitudes. Let us follow Perry and call such propositions "traditional" or "de dicto" propositions. Perry has an argument for the elimination of de dicto A-propositions, as well as other de dicto indexical propositions, in favor of what he calls "de re" propositions; and it will turn out that a timeless God can know these de re propositions.

Perry begins by clearly demonstrating that the traditional Fregean theory does not fit indexical propositions. The A-sentence "Now is when *E* occurs" obviously has the same sense or meaning from one time to another, since the sense or meaning of "now" is invariant over time, although its referent is not. And yet one could believe what this sentence expresses at one time but not believe what it expresses when tokened at another time. This shows that the sense of this A-sentence cannot be identified with what it is that someone believes who believes the proposition or thought it expresses when tokened at some time. The source of the difficulty is that the predicate of a subject–predicate sentence supplies an incomplete sense (e.g., the sense of "_____ is when *E* occurs") that requires a sense completer supplied by the subject expression so as to form a complete, unified sense, that is, a de dicto proposition. But the subject of an indexical sentence (and for the sake of simplicity indexical sentences whose subject alone is indexical are to be considered) is not fitted to serve as a sense completer, for the reason just given. Plainly, if we are to go on believing in the existence of de dicto indexical propositions, we must modify this traditional theory.

The most likely way to do this, and one that Frege himself seemed to pursue, is to continue to hold that indexical words are sense completers but impute to them a sense of limited access that varies with the context, as opposed to the context-invariant senses that other words have. Every time "now" is tokened, it has a different sense that is apprehendable only at that time, and similarly for other indexical words. As a result, the proposition or complete, unified sense expressed by a tokening at t_7 of "Now is when E occurs" can be apprehended or thought only at t_7; and only Jones can grasp or apprehend the proposition he expresses by tokening "I am F." The sense that "now" has at t_7 cannot be conveyed by any nonindexical or fully general description, since the replacement of "now" by such a description results, according to PA, in a different proposition being expressed at t_7.

The notion of a sense that is private or of limited access is anathema to Perry, as it is to a host of contemporary defenders of de re propositions, and thereby he cannot accept the existence of de dicto indexical propositions that involve such a sense:

> Such a theory of propositions of limited accessibility seems acceptable, even attractive, to some philosophers. Its acceptability or attractiveness will depend on other parts of one's metaphysics; if one finds plausible reasons elsewhere for believing in a universe that has, in addition to our common world, myriads of private perspectives, the idea of propositions of limited accessibility will fit right in. I have no knockdown argument against such propositions, or the metaphysical schemes that find room for them. But I believe only in a common actual world.[17]

Perry develops his de re theory of indexical propositions so as to avoid countenancing these mysterious private senses and perspectives. Instead of thinking of the sense of an indexical sentence as the proposition or thought it expresses in some context, he proposes that we think of it as the "role" of the sentence, a role being specified by what we have called a tokening rule. And instead of thinking of the proposition expressed by an indexical sentence in some context (i.e., as tokened by some person, at some time, and place, etc.) as a complete, unified sense – an abstract entity composed of abstracta – we are to think of it as an ontological mixed bag –

a pair comprised of the value or referent of the indexical subject expression in that context and the incomplete sense of its predicate. For relational sentences with more than one indexical subject expression, for instance, "This hit that," the de re proposition expressed in some context will be an ordered n-tuple comprised of a sequence of the different values of its indexical words in that context and the incomplete sense of its relational predicate. This ontological mixed bag is called a "de re" proposition. It is true just in case the value or referent of its indexical subject expression in that context falls under or is an instance of the concept denoted by the incomplete sense of its predicate. For instance, my tokening of "I swim every day" expresses this de re proposition: the pair made up of Richard Gale the man (which is the referent of my use of "I") and the incomplete sense of "____ swims every day." And it is true because Richard Gale – the value of "I" in that context – falls under the concept being-someone-who-swims-every-day, which is denoted by the incomplete sense of "____ swims every day."

The next step is to identify a de re proposition with the *information* conveyed by the tokening of an indexical sentence in a certain context. Perry says of the tokening on August 1, 1976, of "Russia and Canada quarrelled today" that it

> seems to yield just this information:
> (i) an incomplete sense, that of 'Russia and Canada quarrelled';
> (ii) an object, the day August 1st, 1976.
> (i) and (ii) do not uniquely determine a thought, but only an equivalence class of thoughts. Belonging to this equivalence class will be just those thoughts obtainable by completing the sense of 'Russia and Canada quarrelled' with a sense completer which determines, as reference, August 1st, 1976. I shall call thoughts related in this manner *informationally equivalent*. [18]

Herein we have the key to escaping Coburn's argument. God can timelessly know a B-proposition, for instance, that Russia and Canada quarrel (timelessly) on August 1, 1976, that is informationally equivalent to the de re A-proposition that is expressed by tokening on August 1, 1976, "Russia and Canada quarrelled today." And thereby God knows this de re proposition, that is, its informational content. If it should be objected that God still does not know the de dicto A-proposition that is expressed by the tokening of this A-sentence on that date, the reply would be that there aren't any such propositions and not even an omniscient being can be required to know what isn't there to be known.

While I sympathize with Perry's worry about indexical sense completers of limited access, I believe that he has exaggerated the problems they give rise to and, more seriously, that his own de re theory faces far greater problems. Perry's eliminative claim that de dicto indexical propositions are nothing but de re propositions, unlike the eliminative claim that demons are nothing but hallucinatory experiences, is based on purely conceptual considerations consisting in arguments to the effect that such de dicto propositions give rise to puzzlements and perplexities. While he admits that his argument for their elimination is not "knockdown," a better description of it would be a light jab that misses. His "argument" amounts to little more than an expression of his intuitive bias against "private perspectives." But since many, in fact a majority, of philosophers have accepted such perspectives, the onus would seem to be on Perry to make us unhappy with them by showing the conceptual problems to which they give rise. But this he has not done. I now hope to show that we should not run in horror from de dicto indexical propositions of limited access because they are not private in any objectionable way.

The first thing to note is that these propositions stand in relations of logical entailment to each other; for instance, that S is now F at t_7 logically entails, on the assumption that there is a later time t_9, that it will be the case at t_9 that S would have been F two time units prior to then. Let us call sentences that differ only in their personal, spatial, or temporal indexical expressions "differently indexed counterparts"; for instance, the pairs "S was F" and "S is now F," and "I am F" and "He is F." The appropriate tokening of differently indexed counterparts can express differently indexed counterpart de dicto propositions that are at least logically equivalent if not identical. The propositions expressed respectively by tokening at t_7 "S is now F at t_7," and at a later time t_9 "S was F at t_7," mutually entail each other, on the previous assumption that these times exist, just as do the propositions expressed, respectively, by my tokening of "I am F" and your tokening of "He (pointing to me) is F." Thus, even if it were true that each de dicto indexical proposition is apprehendable or expressible only in a single context, we can still apprehend or express in other contexts a differently indexed counterpart proposition that entails this proposition. And this should go a long way to allaying our worries about the "limited accessibility" of de dicto indexical propositions.

Furthermore, by appeal to the intuitively plausible principle that if X knows both p and that p entails q then X knows q, it can be shown that any indexical proposition can be known in a different context than that in which alone it is expressible; for, in general, people know that differently indexed counterpart propositions entail each other. This indirect way of knowing an A-proposition is of no help to a timeless God, since he is unable to express, and a fortiori unable to know, a differently indexed counterpart proposition to any A-proposition.

Perry's worries about indexical words as sense completers also applies to proper names if Kripke is right that they aren't replaceable by a description. Just as we had to settle with something like being-now as the current sense of "now," we must accept being-Socrates as the sense of "Socrates," the only difference being that the latter has a contextindependent sense; but the problem posed by senses of limited accessibility, supposedly, has already been solved. Of course, Perry might find being-Socrates just as objectionable as being-now and extend the scope of his de re theory to cover propositions expressed by sentences containing such proper names, which is commonly done by defenders of de re propositions.

Not only is the de re elimination theory not properly motivated, it faces serious conceptual problems of its own. It will be argued that the de re theory fails to offer a suitable object for an indexical belief as well as a suitable bearer of a truth-value.

According to Perry, when someone believes an indexical proposition, the object of belief is not a de dicto proposition but one of his ontological mixed-bag de re propositions consisting of an incomplete sense and the object that is the value or referent of the indexical expression in that context. This is a variant on Russell's multiple relation theory of judgment, according to which belief is an ordered $n + 1$-tuple relation whose relata are the believer and the n number of objects referred to by the subject(s) and predicate of the sentence expressing her belief: And it faces the same serious problems.[19]

There has been a standard objection to the multiple relation theory that applies with equal force against the de re theory, namely, that it fails to account for the unity of what is believed, said, and the like, since it gives us a mere heap, reported by a laundry list, as the accusative. To say or believe something is not to refer successively to different items. A tip-off that something is amiss surfaces with Perry's misuse of "information" when he tells us that the tokening of "Russia and Canada quarrelled today" on August 1, 1976, "seems to yield just this *information* (i) an incomplete sense, that of 'Russia and Canada quarrelled'; (ii) an object, the day August 1st, 1976"; for, if I were without further ado to present you with Jones the man as I say "the incomplete sense of '____ is a fireman'," I would not be said to have informed you of anything nor to have expressed a belief. Of course, were I to have done this in response to the request "Present me with a man and tell me of an incomplete sense that refers to a concept under which this man falls," I would be informing you of something, because, in effect, I would be saying "Jones (this man here) falls under the concept referred to by the incomplete sense of '____ is a fireman'." But this blown-up Platonic proposition, like the proposition that Jones instantiates firemanness, is a de dicto proposition, not one of Perry's de re propositions.

Because a de re proposition lacks an internal articulation and unity, it is categorically unsuited to be the bearer of a truth-value, and thereby also unfit to serve as a relatum in an entailment relation. Were I, without any special stage setting, to present you with the man Jones as I say "is the incomplete sense of '____ is a fireman'," it would be conceptually absurd for you to reply "That's true," for I have not presented you with a suitable subject of a truth-value. And since a de re proposition categorically cannot have a truth-value, it is unable to entail or be entailed by anything. But as seen in the discussion of differently indexed counterpart propositions, indexical propositions do enter into entailment relations. They also have such relations to nonindexical propositions. The A-proposition that S is now Fing at t_7 entails the B-proposition that S is (timelessly) Fing at t_7. All of this is rendered anomalous on the de re theory.

In defense of Perry's de re theory against the charge that there are conceptual absurdities in taking a de re proposition to be an intentional accusative and the bearer of a truth-value, it could be said that his theory is not supplying us with a paraphrase type of analysis, such that the *analysans* is categorically substitutible for the *analysandum* in every context, but rather with a semantic or truth-condition type of analysis. It is not claiming that instead of saying "Jones believes that here is 42nd Street and Broadway," we could have said "Jones believes that" followed by an act of pointing to 42nd Street and Broadway as we say "the incomplete sense of '____ is 42nd Street and Broadway'." It is giving us the truth-conditions for Jones's indexical belief. If this is all it is doing, the de re theory is a very unperspicuous philosophical theory, since it fails to account for the object of an indexical belief and the like. And since the de dicto theory attempts to explain these things, it is, to that extent, a better theory.

The quasi-indicator theory. Castaneda has developed a theory of "quasi-indicators" or quasi-indexicals in a series of articles that represent the finest treatment of indexicals by any philosopher, and he has put this theory to use in refuting Kretzmann's temporal version of the omniscience-immutability argument – the one directed against the omnitemporal God.[20] But since his refutation can easily be extended so as to apply to a timeless version of the argument, it will be considered in this section; for, if it succeeds against the latter, it also succeeds against the former, since anything that can be known timelessly can be known at a time (but possibly not vice versa). Basically, this rebuttal is directed against premise 4e of Coburn's argument, because it attempts to show that an A-proposition can be expressed by the use of a non-A-sentence in *oratio obliqua* containing a quasi-indicator, thereby refuting the claim that an A-proposition is expressible only by the tokening of an A-sentence. This refutation is extremely subtle and requires that we first get control over the notion of a quasi-indicator.

Briefly, a quasi-indicator makes an anaphoric reference within an *oratio obliqua* construction attributing a propositional attitude to someone and indicates what sort of indexical reference this person made. In the sentence "Jones believes that he himself is rich," "he himself," in the first place, makes an anaphoric reference within the scope of a referring expression ("Jones") outside of the clause. But it is more than your ordinary bound variable or relative pronoun, for it also indicates that Jones's belief is expressed or thought by him through the use of a first-person indexical reference, such as "I." Had we simply said "Jones believes that he is rich," we would not attribute any such first-personal indexical belief to Jones, since the use of "he" in the *oratio obliqua* clause, if indexical, would express the point of view of the speaker. And this would result in our underdetermining the proposition Jones believes, since we would be leaving undetermined how he referred to the subject of his belief.

Now for the controversial part of his theory. Through the use of a quasi-indicator, we can express in *oratio obliqua* the *very same* proposition as is expressed by someone else through the use of an indexical sentence. If I say "Yesterday Jones said that it is then t_7," the occurrence of "then" within the *oratio obliqua* clause, in addition to making an anaphoric reference to yesterday in virtue of falling within the scope of "yesterday," also indicates that Jones made a present-tense indexical reference to that time by tokening a sentence synonymous with "It is now t_7" in my language. Through the use of the quasi-indicator "then," I succeed in expressing in *oratio obliqua* the very same A-proposition that Jones expressed in *oratio recta* through the tokening of an A-sentence.

This doctrine is pressed into service in refuting Kretzmann's contention that an omnitemporal God cannot know at any time the very same A-propositions that he or someone else could express in *oratio recta* at other times by the tokening of A-sentences. First, Castaneda shows how God could express all of these propositions at a single time; for if he can't express them he can't know them. Next, he shows how he can know them at a single time.

Kretzmann's somewhat confused claim that

> First such a being (God) knows that it is now t_1 (and that it is not now t_2) and then it knows that it is now t_2 (and that it is not now t_1)[21]

is perspicuously rendered by the use of quasi-indicators as

6. At t_1, X knows (tenselessly) that it is (tenselessly) *then* t_1, but not t_2, and at t_2, later than t_1, knows that it is *then* t_2, but not t_1.[22]

This, in turn, is recast so as to show how at a single time, t_1, X can know that someone knows at t_2 an A-proposition that is expressed by X at t_1 via the use of a quasi-indictor:

7. Time t_2 is later than t_1, and at t_1 X knows both (1) that it is then$_{t_1}$ t_1, but not t_2, and (2) that somebody knows (or would know) at t_2 that it is (would be) then$_{t_2}$ t_2, but not t_1[23]

in which the quasi-indicators "then$_{t_1}$" and "then$_{t_2}$" carry subscripts that indicate which date-name outside of the *oratio obliqua* clause binds them. It will be important later to realize that a subscript does not turn the quasi-indicator "then" into a constant but only serves as an aid in locating the constant that binds the subscripted word.

Proposition 7 does not by itself show that at t_1 X knows the very same A-proposition that he or someone else knows at t_2 in *oratio recta*. An additional premise is needed, and Castaneda finds it in the principle of the transitivity of knowledge:

> T. If a sentence of the form 'X knows that a person Y knows that . . . ' formulates a true statement then the person X knows the statement formulated by the clause filling the blank.[24]

He goes on to point out that

> this principle must be carefully understood: it establishes a sort of transitivity of knowledge, but it does *not* say anything about detaching expressions of the form 'Y knows that . . . '.[25]

All that remains to be done is to plug into formula T the relevant parts of 7. This results in

7a. At t_1 X knows . . . that somebody knows at t_2 that it is then$_{t_2}$ t_2

and has the consequence that at t_1 X knows the very same A-proposition that someone knows at t_2 – the one that he would express at t_2 by tokening "It is now t_2."

Before we evaluate this beautifully ingenious refutation, it will be shown that it can and ought to be reformulated so as to apply to a timeless Deity. To see why this ought to be done, let us begin with the following objection:

> Even if your Deity X at every time can know in *oratio obliqua* the very same A-propositions that are expressible in *oratio recta* by the tokening of A-sentences at other times, it still is the case that he must change the way in which he expresses these A-propositions from one time to another; for instance, at t_1 he expresses in *oratio recta* that it is then$_{t_1}$ t_1 but does not do so for the A-proposition that at t_2 it is then$_{t_2}$ t_2, but he

changes at t_2 in that he no longer expresses the former A-proposition in *oratio recta* but must do so in *oratio obliqua*. And this change in the way God formulates his beliefs compromises his immutability.

An easy way out of this problem is supplied by the realization that there is no need to place X (God) at a moment of time in order for X to know an A-proposition in *oratio obliqua*. To see this we only need to rewrite 6 by substituting "and X timelessly knows" for "and at t_1 X knows" and make our time-bound knower someone other than X.

7′. Time t_2 is later than t_1, and X timelessly knows both (1) that at t_1 someone knows (or would know) that it is then$_{t_1}$ t_1, but not t_2 and (2) that somebody knows (or would know) at t_2 that it is (would be) then$_{t_2}$ t_2, but not t_1.[26]

The reason why we can place our *oratio obliqua* knower X "outside" of time is that the sentences that express his beliefs (e.g., "at t_1 someone knows that it is then$_{t_1}$ t_1"), because they contain quasi-indicators, are freely repeatable B-sentences. And this is the vital nerve in the refutation – that, pace 4e, an A-proposition can be expressed by a B-sentence that contains quasi-indicators.

Unfortunately, although 7′ helps to avoid the mutability problem, it creates a problem of its own in that it clashes with religious orthodoxy. According to theism God is essentially omniscient, that is,

8. God is omniscient in every possible world in which he exists.

It also is the case for theism that God is free to create finite, time-bound knowers or not to. Therefore,

9. There are possible worlds in which both God and time exist but no time-bound knowers.

But the Castaneda-style solution using 7′ saves God's omniscience in a temporal world by making him into an epistemic Count Dracula who must live off the blood of his time-bound *oratio recta* knowers of A-propositions, which has the consequence that

10. There are no possible worlds in which both God is omniscient and time exists but no time-bound knowers do.

From 8 and 10 it follows that

11. It is not the case that there are possible worlds in which both God and time exist but no time-bound knowers do.

And this flatly contradicts theism's belief in 9.

Thus, the choice between employing 7 or 7' in a refutation poses a dilemma, for we wind up either compromising God's immutability or departing from theistic beliefs. But it will turn out that there is an escape from this dilemma, because a 7'-style refutation really does not require that there be finite, time-bound knowers. But first it will be shown that both of these refutations suffer from an additional flaw: The principle of the transitivity of knowledge T not only is false but also is misused in these refutations.

This principle is subject to the same sort of counterexamples and restrictions as is the previous principle that a person cannot know that the proposition expressed by another is true without knowing this very proposition. Just as I could know that the proposition expressed by another is true but not know it because I lack a suitable justification for this proposition, I can know that another knows this proposition and lack this needed justification for it. Both principles, furthermore, must be restricted to cases in which the proposition expressed or known by the other person is completely specified, and this means that both the subject and predicate sense components be specified or expressed. If propositional underdetermination is allowed within the blank space of T, the following sort of counterexample can be constructed: In the case in which "X knows that Y knows that concerning (or of) the F that it is G," the proposition that Y knows is underdetermined because we are not told how Y refers to the F; he could have been ignorant that this individual is the F and instead referred to it by a proper name. And, therefore, it does not follow that X knows the very same proposition that Y does.

The relevant part of 7' (and 7) says "X knows timelessly (knows at t_1) that somebody, Y, knows at t_2 that it is then$_{t_2}$ t_2." The crucial question is whether this also is a case of propositional underdetermination in the final "that"-clause – the one that is inserted in the blank space of T. It could be argued with some plausibility that it is not, because the quasi-indicator "then$_{t_2}$" tells us how Y refers, namely, through the use of a present-tense indexical word such as "now." Unfortunately, its final that-clause – "that it is then$_{t_2}$ t_2" – does not alone specify a complete proposition since "then$_{t_2}$" occurs within it as a free variable, no longer being bound by the occurrence of "at t_2" outside of the that-clause. Thus, the relevant part of 7' (7) is not fit to be plugged into the blank space of T once T is restricted, as it must be, to completely specified propositions.

It might be thought that this problem of failing to specify a complete proposition in the final that-clause is easily solved by moving the "at t_2" from outside to inside the final that-clause, resulting in "X knows timelessly (at t_1) that somebody, Y, knows that at t_2 it is then$_{t_2}$ t_2." But now it becomes clear that neither Y nor X know any A-proposition at all. The proposition that at t_2 it is then$_{t_2}$ t_2 is identical with the tautology that t_2 is t_2, which is a B-proposition since it is expressed by a freely repeatable sentence. Assuming, pace Perry, that there are de dicto A-propositions, that it is now t_2, by Leibniz's law, is not identical with that t_2 is t_2 (or that at t_2 it is then$_{t_2}$ t_2) because only the latter has the property of being knowable a priori. God, of course, can timelessly know that t_2 is t_2, but this gives no reason to think that he can timelessly know the A-proposition that it is now t_2. That he can know these tautologies in *oratio recta* shows that nothing is gained by making God into an epistemic Dracula who must live off the *oratio recta* blood of time-bound knowers.

The response to this might be that the proposition that at t_2 it is then$_{t_2}$ t_2 cannot be identified with the proposition that t_2 is t_2, since only the former identifies an A-proposition, namely, the one that is expressible by tokening at t_2 the

A-sentence "It is now t_2." This response has a spurious plausibility because it fails to distinguish between the specifying and nonspecifying mode of identifying a proposition. While "that at t_2 it is then$_{t_2}$ t_2" does identify an A-proposition, it does not do so in a specifying manner, as does the tokening now of "that it is now t_2." As seen, *T* requires that a complete specification of a proposition be inserted in its blank space. While "that at t_2 it is then$_{t_2}$ t_2" does completely specify a proposition, it is the B-proposition that t_2 is t_2. What is tricky is that it also identifies in a nonspecifying manner an A-proposition. Thus, the phrase "the proposition that at t_2 it is then$_{t_2}$ t_2" identifies both an A- and B-proposition but does so in a specifying manner only for the latter.

The limitations on a perfect being's omniscience. This refutation accepts Coburn's argument for 4 but escapes the contradictory conclusion of the omniscience–immutability argument by rejecting the account of God's omniscience given in premise 1 in favor of a weaker one that not only permits but conceptually requires that God not know A-propositions. It will be recalled from Chapter 4 that it proved necessary to give the following restricted definition of God's omnipotence:

O_3. For any proposition p, if it is logically possible that God bring it about that p, then God can bring it about that p.

The strategy is to restrict God's omniscience in an analogous manner to what it is logically consistent for God to know:

O_5. For any proposition p, if it is true that p and it is logically possible that God know that p, then God knows that p.

What must be done is to demonstrate that from O_5, in conjunction with other necessarily true propositions, it can be deduced that it is conceptually impossible that God know an A-proposition, thereby showing that his failure to do so does not impugn his omniscience, assuming that O_5 is true.

This demonstration goes as follows: It begins with the conceptual truth that

12. God is an absolutely perfect being.

Then it argues that necessarily

13. An absolutely perfect being is timeless,

by appeal to the alleged conceptual truth that

14. Any temporal being has the possibility of ceasing to exist.

Since having even the mere logical possibility of ceasing to exist is an imperfection, it follows that necessarily

15. God (i.e., an absolutely perfect being) is timeless.

And by appeal to

4. It is conceptually impossible that a timeless being know an A-proposition,

it deduces the desired conclusion that

16. It is conceptually impossible that God know an A-proposition.

And since God's omniscience, as defined by O_5, excuses him from having to know any proposition that it is logically or conceptually impossible that God know, his failure to know A-facts does not constitute a counterexample to his omniscience.

This refutation of the omniscience–immutability argument faces two insuperable difficulties. First, it creates a very virulent version of the paradox of perfection, by comparison with which the Chapter 1 paradox of perfection created by the O_3 and O_4 definitions of God's omnipotence is quite mild. Whereas many are content to live with the latter, few, including myself, will be able to stomach the former. While we are not crushed by the thought that God, in virtue of his absolute perfection, is barred from playing football, committing suicide, or performing a morally wrong act, we are by the thought that it precludes his knowing any A-proposition. His O_5-type omniscience appears far inferior to that possessed by some possible nonperfect being who, in virtue of not having to be timeless, can know everything that God knows plus all the true A-propositions. (The conceptual possibility of such a nonperfect omniscient being assumes that a being can have some but not all of the divine perfections, and thus that the doctrine of the divine simplicity is false, which has already been argued for in Chapter 1.)

God's inability to know A-propositions in virtue of his timeless eternality, not only is a blight on his omniscience, but also is another factor that contributes to his being religiously unavailable. A religiously available God is one with whom we can commune. But we can commune only with beings who share our tensed perspectives, who know how it goes with us right now, and not just how it goes timelessly with us at t_7, even if now is t_7. In other words, they must be beings of whom the song title "My Time Is Your Time" is true. It matters very much to us when we seek solace, guidance, and encouragement from a person that they are aware of our present situation and, in turn, can be a living presence to us when they offer such solace, guidance, and encouragement. Only a being possessed of knowledge of A-facts could be a suitable object of such intentions of ours. The God who is the apparent object of direct experiences of God's presence interacts with us as a living presence, and thus possesses knowledge of A-facts concerning us. He carries on an A-type discourse with us. Thus, if we are to be true to the phenomenology of religious experiences of God's presence, we must conceive of the God who is the object of such experiences as a being in time who is possessed of knowledge of A-facts concerning us.

A second major difficulty with the restricted-omniscience way out of the omniscience–immutability argument is that its claim that 14 is a conceptual truth is quite dubious, since there is a long-standing tradition within Western theism, deriving from the Bible, that accepts as meaningful the concept of an omnitemporally eternal God. That the language game involving the concept of an omnitemporal Deity has been played by so many for so long counts against the claim that 14 is a necessary conceptual truth. I know of no good argument for it being necessary that any being in time has the logical possibility of ceasing to be. Nor, as will be argued in Chapter 6, does an ontological argument have any more chance of succeeding for a timelessly eternal God than it has for an omnitemporally eternal one.

Not only does there appear to be no good argument for why a highest being, a being than which none greater can be conceived, must be timeless, there is a good argument for why it must be temporal. Such a being must be a person, but only a temporal being can qualify as a person. Part of the justification for this was given in Chapter 1, when it was argued that a person must have a mind and that a mind must have temporal endurance, the reason being that consciousness is a temporally elongated process. A conscious being is a Sartrian for-itself that is always running ahead of itself into the future. The concept of a strictly immutable, completely actualized personal God is an impossible one, an attempt, as Sartre brilliantly portrayed in his *Being and Nothingness*, to have a God that is both a for-itself and at the same time an in-itself, that is, a being whose existence is wholly contained within a single moment, which could well be a timeless present that has no past or future, and yet transcends this moment into its future. The penetrating phenomenological analyses of the temporally "ekstatic" mode of existence of persons given by Heidegger and, before him, by James, Bergson, Dewey, and Husserl, bring out the necessity for such a self-conscious being to have retentions of its past that inform its present experience in the formation of future projects.

The results of a *conceptual analysis* of a person agree with those of the previous *phenomenological analyses*. A person, within forensic and moral contexts, must be an agent that performs intentional actions so as to bring about some goal or end. But to have a goal or end, the agent must have desires and values. But only a temporally incomplete being can have a desire or intention or will something, since one cannot desire, intend, or will what one already has. The rich man does desire and intend to be rich, but what he desires is the continuation of his richness into the future. And he does not yet have these future wealthy states.

An agent, furthermore, is a morally responsible being. But someone can be morally responsible only in a community of other morally responsible agents with whom he interacts, as will be argued at some length in Chapter 9. A timeless God cannot interact with other agents, since he cannot be causally affected by what they do, nor, as just argued, can he affect them in personal ways that matter. It is not an accident that those theists who conceived of God as timeless, although they thought he could timelessly bring about effects in the world, were careful to deny that anything in the world could in turn affect him. (The petitionary prayer of working theists makes no sense on this view.) This doctrine of one-way inter-actionism makes God a nonagent, since he is rendered unable to be a member of a community of agents who interact with each other and mutually hold each other morally responsible. And without community there can be no communion, thereby rendering the timeless God religiously unavailable. The latter requires two-way interactionism between Deity and creatures. God, or should I say we, pay too great a price for his aseity. If this is absolute perfection, my vote is for something less exalted.

If we are right that a timeless God, in virtue of being a person, must be temporal, his inability to know A-facts is the least of his worries. *If* the argument for the former is sound, there is no need for the omniscience–immutability argument, since the former alone establishes the conceptual absurdity of the concept of a timelessly eternal God. But this is a big *if*, since philosophical arguments never are conclusive, and thus it is wise to make use of as many weapons as are available to us in our attempt to undermine the concept of a timelessly eternal God. Even if our multipronged attack on this concept is not decisive, it can still be shown that the concept of an omnitemporal Deity is a more attractive and serviceable one. Not only does it render God religiously available but also gives us an easy way out of the omniscience–immutability argument, as will now be shown, something that was not possible for the timeless Deity.

The version of the omniscience–immutability argument that is directed against the omnitemporal God begins with the same initial set as does the timeless version:

1. God essentially knows all and believes only true propositions,

2. God essentially does not change from one time to another in respect to any nonrelational property; and

3. There are true A-propositions.

It then goes on to argue that it is necessary that

17. Any being who knows every true A-proposition will have to change the way in which he expresses or is disposed to express his indexical beliefs from one time to another,

from which it follows, in conjunction with 1 and 3, that

18. God (conceived of as omnitemporally eternal) changes in the way he expresses or is disposed to express his indexical beliefs from one time to another.

And this contradicts 2. Thus, God both is and is not immutable.

The atheologian's argument for 17 draws upon the points made in the above discussion of Castaneda. Assuming there to be moments of time t_1 and t_2, at t_1, but not t_2, a being who knows every A-fact tokens or is disposed to token a sentence synonymous with our "It is now t_1" and at t_2, but not t_1, a sentence synonymous with "It is now t_2." Such a being, therefore, changes from t_1 to t_2 in either the manner in which she formulates her A-beliefs in *oratio recta* or its dispositions so to formulate her A-beliefs.

The theist who conceives of God as being omnitemporally eternal will rightly reject the premise 2 demand for God to be strictly immutable. This can be supported by showing, first, that the traditional arguments for strict immutability are unacceptable, and, second, that there are ways of restricting

God's immutability that do not endanger his exalted status as that than which none greater can be conceived. And this is what will now be attempted.

There are two traditional arguments for strict immutability: the Platonic argument that any change in an absolutely perfect being would represent a deterioration in it and thereby disqualify it as being absolutely perfect; and the Aristotelian argument, which is the one that weighed most heavily with the great medieval theists, that an absolutely perfect being must enjoy complete actuality.

Of the two arguments, the Platonic is the most vulnerable, since it is implausible to assume that any change in God is for the worse; it might have a neutral outcome.[27] The response to the Aristotelian argument, which also applies to the Platonic one, is that any being that has strict immutability is a nonperson for all of the reasons previously given: He cannot, for example, be conscious, perform intentional actions, have any goals or ends, will anything, interact with other persons, and so on. Aristotle's god of pure actuality might be an object of intellectual love, as might be Euclidian geometry, and serve as an explanation of the final causes of worldly changes, but he is conceptually unfit to be a relatum in a two-way love relationship or one of communion, this being due to his status as a nonperson.

What is to be rejected is the Greek assumption that underlies both the Platonic and Aristotelian arguments – that true being, a highest form of being, must be timeless. Such an assumption, no doubt fathered by a fear of death and the vicissitudes of time, as well as a disdain for the changeable world that was the object of concern for the "lower" class of people in their society, as John Dewey so insightfully pointed out, must be rejected by any theism that postulates a personal God. It is a totally perverse assumption, and it is amazing that the great medieval theists should have accepted it. Philosophy makes for strange bedfellows indeed.

We know that God, in virtue of being a person, cannot be strictly immutable. The only question is how mutable he is, and this must be answered in a way that does not

95

compromise his status as an absolutely perfect being. That an omnitemporal God must undergo some change is an immediate consequence of his enduring in time. If Don Rickles should be fortunate enough to meet God at the pearly gates, he could say to God what he has been saying for years to Henny Youngman – "You're old!" While in one sense this is obviously true – God is not only old but infinitely old – it is false in the sense intended; for, unlike Youngman (and who says names have descriptive sense), God has not become decrepit and feeble, has not aged in this pejorative sense. If aging or growing older in the chronological sense is a purely relational change, involving having different external relations to different events or moments at different moments of time, God's aging presents no problem. But, if, as I suspect is the case, this change involves a change in his monadic properties, the omnitemporal version of God's immutability must be restricted to properties for which it is not a logical consequence of his omnitemporality that he change in respect to them.

Furthermore, God's immutability must not be so strict as to preclude his knowing A-facts. This requires that he continually change in the manner in which he expresses or is disposed to express his A-beliefs in *oratio recta* discourse. Such changes do not compromise his absolute perfection by lessening in any way his omniscience, for his change of mind from one time to another does not result in his holding incompatible beliefs – his believing at one time what he had disbelieved at an earlier one. Furthermore, he knows at every time everything that it is logically possible to know at that time; since at every time he knows both every A-proposition truly expressible in *oratio recta* at that time and for every A-proposition truly expressible in *oratio recta* only at another time a differently indexed counterpart A-proposition that entails it. As argued, there is ground for contending that he even knows the latter and not just entailers of it.

What is required of an absolutely perfect being is not that he not change in any of his nonrelational properties but that he not change in respect to any one of his perfections, such as omnipotence, omniscience, omnibenevolence, sovereignty, and so on. And the omnitemporal Deity, having all these perfections essentially, is assured of not changing over time in respect to them, only in the way in which he manifests them from one time to another. Many of these manifestations or displays are accidental, such as his manner of being conscious and his cognitive relation to the changing universe, and thus the need to readjust his *oratio recta* A-beliefs over time. Certainly, these sorts of accidental change do not disqualify him as being an absolutely perfect being. Quite to the contrary.

This, in conjunction with Chapter 2, completes my polemic against the viability of the concept of a timelessly eternal God and support for that of an omnitemporally eternal God. Atheological arguments, especially the creation–immutability and omniscience–immutability arguments, proved valuable tools in developing a more adequate conception of the nature of God in respect to his temporality and mutability, illustrating the underlying thesis of this book concerning the positive value of atheological arguments. In the next chapter we shall consider an atheological argument that is initially directed against God being both omnipotent and omnibenevolent, this being the famed argument from evil. It will turn out that it is not just these two divine perfections that are brought into prominence but also those of omniscience and sovereignty, since some of the escapes from this argument are based upon attempts to restrict one or more of them.

Chapter 4

The deductive argument from evil

The existence of evil poses both a logical and empirical problem for theism, forming the basis of both a deductive argument that attempts to deduce a contradiction from the
existence of both God and evil and an inductive argument
that contends that it is improbable that God is the creator of
a world that contains the amount and kinds of evils found in
this one. Since the deductive argument tries to prove that
there is no possible world that contains both God and evil, all
the theist need do to rebut it is to show that it is logically
possible that God and evil coexist, and this can best, maybe
only, be done by actually describing a possible world in
which both exist. In such a world God will have a good
reason or morally exonerating excuse for permitting evil.
Such a response constitutes a *defense*. To rebut the inductive
argument, the theist must construct a *theodicy*, which is a
defense plus an empirical argument for the actual existence
of the possible world articulated in the defense.

Often a defense is confounded with a theodicy, resulting
in the bogus demand that the theist produce a theodicy as a
rebuttal of the deductive argument. H. J. McCloskey, as an
example, first espouses the deductive argument. "Evil is a
problem for the theist," he says, "in that a contradiction is
involved in the fact of evil on the one hand, and the belief in
the omnipotence and perfection of God on the other."[1] He
shows a surprisingly short memory span because later in his
essay he says of a certain defense that "it does not in itself
provide a justification for the evil in the universe. It shows

simply that the evil which occurs *might* have a justification."[2] And when he discusses the free will defense (hereafter FWD), he says that it "can at best show that moral evil *may have* a justification, and not that it has a justification."[3] These admissions are inconsistent with his earlier claim that theism is inconsistent in holding that both God and evil exist. He seems to be requiring of an adequate defense that it also succeed as a theodicy, which belies a serious conceptual confusion on his part. It is desirable, of course, that a successful defense have the makings of a plausible theodicy, but this is not logically required. Our concern is exclusively with the logical problem of evil and the various defenses it elicits, especially the FWD.

THE DEDUCTIVE ARGUMENT

The deductive argument has been around at least since the time of Epicurus, but until recently it has been stated only in the following sort of loose, intuitive manner:

> Whence evil? Is God able but unwilling to prevent it? Then he is not benevolent. Or is God willing but unable to prevent it? Then he is not all powerful. God, therefore, is either not all powerful or not benevolent.

And since the God of traditional theism has both of these properties essentially, it follows that this Deity does not exist. Supposedly, the proposition that such a Deity exists, coupled with the admission that evil exists, leads to the contradiction that God both is and is not benevolent (omnipotent). But it is not apparent how it does. Obviously, some suppressed premises are being implicitly appealed to in this deduction.

It is to the great credit of J. L. Mackie that he was the first to try to make an honest argument out of it by explicitly spelling out these needed additional premises. He begins with the informal statement of the argument:

In its simplest form the problem is this: God is omnipotent; God is wholly good; and yet evil exists. There seems to be some contradiction between these three propositions, so that if any two of them were true the third would be false.[4]

Let us explicitly mount these three propositions that together form the initial set of propositions accepted by theism:

1. God is omnipotent;
2. God is wholly good (omnibenevolent); and
3. Evil exists.

Mackie is going to attempt to deduce the negation of 3 from 1 and 2, but he is going to require some additional premises to do this.

Before we deal with what these additional premises are, it must be noted that propositions 1 and 2 admit of both an existential and attributive reading, according to which they mean respectively "There exists a being, God, who is omnipotent (omnibenevolent)" and "God is conceived of or described in the 'God'-story as a being who is omnipotent (omnibenevolent)." They must be given the existential reading, for otherwise the argument would face refutation by the following fallacious parallel argument, in which its premise about Santa Claus is to be read attributively:

In its simplest form the problem of deserving children not receiving a Christmas present is this: *Santa Claus brings a present to every deserving child at Christmas.* Tom is a deserving child, and yet Tom did not receive a Christmas present. There seems to be some contradiction between these three propositions, so that if any two of them were true the third would be false.

From this set of three propositions no one would think that it followed that Tom did receive a Christmas present, assuming that the italicized premise about Santa Claus is interpreted attributively as a description of the "Santa Claus"-story. For this reason, if we read 1 and 2 attributively, we must add that God exists to the initial set.

Now for the needed necessary additional premises:

> However, the contradiction does not arise immediately; to show it we need some additional premises, or perhaps some quasi-logical rules connecting the terms "good," "evil," and "omnipotence." These additional principles are that good is opposed to evil, in such a way that a good thing always eliminates evil as far as it can, and that there are no limits to what an omnipotent thing can do. From these it follows that a good omnipotent thing eliminates evil completely, and then the propositions that a good omnipotent thing exists, and that evil exists, are incompatible.

Thus, we are to add these two additional premises:

4. A wholly good (omnibenevolent) being eliminates and prevents every evil he can; and
5. There are no limits to what an omnipotent being can do

in which I have taken the liberty of adding "and prevents" in 4, since a being would not qualify as omnibenevolent if he allowed some preventable evil to occur, even if he thereafter eliminated it. (Think of all the volunteer firemen who torch buildings so that they can have the fun of putting out the fires.) With these extra premises it is easy to deduce a contradiction in the following way:

6. It is not the case that evil exists [from 1, 2, 4, and 5]; and
7. Evil exists and it is not the case that evil exists [from 3 and 6].

Faced with this contradiction, the theist must give up at least one of the propositions in the initial set, since the additional premises must be necessary. But are they?

Mackie is well aware that they must be. That is why he calls them "quasi-logical rules." Why did he not call them "definitions"? That would fit nicely with his implied linguistic theory of necessity. The reason, no doubt, is that such definitions are not to be found in any ordinary dictionary. Nevertheless, they are supposed to be true in virtue of normative rules or conventions that are implicit in our use of language, such that speakers are willing to offer and accept correction when there is a deviation from them.

The trouble with calling 4 and 5 quasi-logical rules is that our, and certainly the theist's, use of language does not square with them. They misdescribe the language games in which the concerned terms are used. Pace 4, we often feel justified in bringing about or not preventing some evil so that a greater evil can be avoided (e.g., the surgeon causing a patient to feel pain in the course of amputating a limb or a parent disciplining a child) or an outweighing good realized (e.g., suffering the agony of writing a paper refuting the FWD). And one will find very few theists, if any, who accept the premise 5 account of omnipotence. Mackie is well aware of this, for when he considers various defenses he is willing to allow the theist to use "omnipotence" and "benevolence" in ways that deviate from these rules. While he lodges objections to these defenses, he does not object to them on the grounds that their use of these terms is at variance with 4 and 5. (One wonders what perversity lead Mackie initially to formulate his deductive argument in a way that he knew was unacceptable.) There are numerous places where he shows a willingness to replace 4 and/or 5 with some more restricted proposition.

One such place is his consideration of the defense that holds that God could not create a world containing good without permitting some evil, because there logically cannot be one without the other, this being based upon some significant contrast principle. (Surprisingly, it turns out that if the Pink Panther were the Deity, he couldn't make everything pink.) This defense obviously employs a weaker version of 5, namely,

5_1. An omnipotent being can bring about any logically possible state of affairs.

Mackie is willing to give his theistic opponent this weaker account when he writes:

> It may be replied that these limits are always presupposed, and the omnipotence has never meant the power to do what

is logically impossible, and on the present view the existence of good without evil would be a logical impossibility. This interpretation of omnipotence may, indeed, be accepted as a modification of our original account which does not reject anything that is essential to theism, and I shall in general assume it in the subsequent discussion.[5]

Mackie's discussion of the good-requires-evil defense also makes clear that it rejects 4. That God cannot logically bring about good without allowing some evil is supposed to morally exonerate him for permitting some preventable evil, pace 4; for this was the price that had to be paid to have any good at all, and the good supposedly far outweighs the evil.
    Mackie has a response to this, but it is not based upon this defense's departure from 4.

> It will provide a solution for the problem of evil only if one is prepared to say 'Evil exists, but only just enough evil to serve as the counterpart of good'. I doubt whether any theist will accept this.[6]

Herein Mackie shows himself willing to accept this defense's replacement of his original 4 with something more qualified, such as

4_1. An omnibenevolent being attempts to bring about the best overall situation he can; or
4_2. An omnibenevolent being tries to eliminate and prevent every morally unjustified evil,

in which a morally unjustified evil is one that is not necessary for either the realization of an outweighing good or the prevention of a greater evil. To block this defense Mackie is implicitly replacing his original premise 3 with the stronger

3_1. There are evils in excess of what is required for there to be a significant contrast with evil.

It is not clear that the proponent of this defense is willing to grant 3_1.

Another example of Mackie's willingness to permit the replacement of his 4 and 5, respectively, by 4_1 or 4_2 and 5_1 is his discussion of the defense that holds that the universe is better off as a whole with some evil in it than if there were none. Sometimes this is given an aesthetic twist, but more often it is cashed in in terms of the soul-building defense: It is a better overall state of affairs for there to be a gradual overcoming of evil in the course of the spiritual and moral development of free creatures than a statically good world. His account of the latter defense makes clear that it accepts neither 4 nor 5. It rejects 5 because it holds that it is logically impossible for God to bring about this overall better situation without permitting some preventable evil, which plainly does not impute totally unlimited power to God. As for 4, the following shows that Mackie replaces it with 4_2:

> But does it still hold that good and evil are opposed? Not, clearly, in the sense that we set out originally: good does not tend to eliminate evil in general. Instead, we have a modified, a more complex pattern. First order good (e.g. happiness) *contrasts with* first order evil (e.g. misery): these two are opposed in a fairly mechanical way; some second order goods (e.g. benevolence) try to maximize first order good and minimize first order evil; but God's goodness is not this, it is rather the will to maximize *second* order good. We might, therefore, call God's goodness an example of a third order good.[7]

The relevant point is that the existence of first-order evil is a logically necessary condition for the existence of second-order good consisting in the good character traits of courage, fortitude, sympathy, and benevolence in the face of suffering. Not even an omnipotent God could bring about the latter without the former, and, moreover, it is better overall to have a world that contains the two than one containing first-order good alone.

Again we find Mackie objecting to a defense that eschews his original 4 and 5 in favor of their weaker cousins on grounds other than this, for he counters this defense on the ground that it leads to a vicious infinite regress. We begin with the problem of finding a morally exonerating excuse for God's permitting first-order evils, such as physical and mental suffering. This defense holds that such evils are logically necessary conditions for the emergence of second-order goods of benevolence, courage, and the like and that these goods far outweigh the first-order evils, thereby exonerating God for allowing them. But there is still the problem of second-order evil – badness of character, such as malevolence, cowardice, cruelty. And this type of evil is far more serious than first-order evil.

> We should, therefore, state the problem of evil in terms of second order evil, and against this form of the problem the present solution is useless. An attempt might be made to use this solution again at a higher level, to explain the occurrence of evil (2), i.e. second order evil. . . . But even if evil (2) could be explained in this way, it is fairly clear that there *would be* third order evils contrasting with this third order good: and we should be well on the way to an infinite regress, where the solution of a problem of evil, stated in terms of evil (n), *indicated* the existence of an evil ($n + 1$), and a further problem to be solved.[8]

This infinite regress, supposedly, is vicious, because the very problem that is addressed by the account on the first level recurs on each level in the regress. The bogey man never stops chasing us, always being just one level away from catching us.

There is a fatal flaw in this vicious infinite regress argument. It fails to satisfy a necessary condition for such an argument to succeed, namely, that every proposition reporting the existence of the problem on level n *logically entail* a proposition reporting the existence of the same type of problem on level $n + 1$. Mackie's claim that the existence of evil on any level n "indicates" the existence of evil on level $n + 1$ doesn't satisfy this entailment requirement, because he does not show that if there is a good on any level n there also is evil on level $n + 1$. His claim that "there would be" is at best an empirical generalization. As a result, it is open to the theist to stop the regress by claiming that there is good on some level without any accompanying evil on that level; for instance, it could be said that there is good (3) – intentions to produce goodness of character – without any evil (3) – intentions to produce badness of character. It could be an empirical fact that benevolent beings are capable of forming higher-order intentions than malevolent beings. After all, they're more highly intentioned!

Yet another place where Mackie operates with weaker versions of 4 and 5 is in his discussion of the FWD, in which he sees it as a special version of the preceding n-order-evils-are-justified-because-they-are-necessary-for-outweighing-$n + 1$-order-goods. Herein the free will of created persons is a third-order good that far outweighs the second- and first-order evils it occasions. According to Mackie's account of the FWD, moral responsibility for these evils stops with these created middle-men; it does not reach through to God. As we shall see when we discuss versions of the FWD published subsequently to Mackie's essay, responsibility, but not blame, is allowed to reach through to God. Mackie presents us with a highly implausible, strawman version of the FWD.[9] He makes the wild claim that according to the FWD, "second order evils, such as cruelty, are logically necessary accompaniments of freedom, just as pain is a logically necessary pre-condition of sympathy."[10] He demolishes this fantastic claim by pointing out the logical possibility of all free persons always freely doing what is right. The point here is not that he presents a strawman version of the FWD but that he is willing to allow a defense to operate with weaker versions of 4 and 5.

The crucial question is what happens to Mackie's deductive argument when his quasi-logical rules are replaced by something more acceptable, for instance, 5 by 5_1 and 4 by 4_1 or 4_2? No contradiction can now be deduced; for, from

1. God is omnipotent;
2. God is omnibenevolent;

3. Evil exists;

4_1. An omnibenevolent being attempts to bring about the best overall situation it can; and

5_1. An omnipotent being can bring about any logically possible state of affairs

it follows only that

6_1. The actual world is the best overall situation, that is, the best of all possible worlds.

And 6_1, unlike

6. It is not the case that evil exists,

is not obviously inconsistent with 3. And when 4_1 is replaced with

4_2. An omnibenevolent being tries to eliminate and prevent every morally unjustified evil,

it follows only that

6_2. It is not the case that morally unjustified evil exists.

And again there does not appear to be any logical clash with 3. Mackie might try to salvage his argument by replacing 3 with

3_1. Morally unjustified evil exists,

but the theist is not going to grant this. The fate of Mackie's argument is that either it must use additional premises that are unacceptably strong or it must require the theist to grant too much in regard to what kinds of evils exist.

THE INDUCTIVE ARGUMENT FROM COMPLETE ENUMERATION

We should not be surprised that the deductive argument does not work. Philosophy just isn't that easy. A battle between two long-lived philosophical traditions, such as theism and atheism, is not going to end like a Mike Tyson fight with just one haymaker. But the logical problem of evil can survive the demise of the deductive argument. With a little imagination one can screw out of the essays by Mackie and McCloskey an inductive argument from complete enumeration, laced with a good deal of conceptual analysis, for the proposition that it is logically impossible that both God and evil exist. Attempts to show that some proposition is necessary or impossible through an inductive argument are not uncommon. The use of a computer to establish some proposition as a theorem appeals to various empirical facts concerning the working of a computer. In philosophy, arguments for something being a necessary conceptual truth often proceed piecemeal by an empirical inquiry into the way language is used.

The inductive argument from complete enumeration, unlike the previous inductive argument that posed the empirical problem of evil, makes no mention of the amount and kinds of evils that exist. It begins with some conceptual analysis. If it is not true that it is logically impossible that both God and evil exist, then there must be some possible world in which both God and evil exist. In any such world, God must have a morally exonerating excuse for permitting evil. Therefore, it must be logically possible that God have such an excuse. It is at this point that the inductive argument from complete enumeration is brought to bear to show that all of the different types of excuses that we can think of are conceptually inapplicable to God in virtue of his essentially being omniman. Unlike men, God cannot plead any limitation in power, opportunity, or knowledge. This inductive enumeration, of course, might be incomplete; but it is up to the theist to show that it overlooks a kind of excuse that is available to God in the face of evil.[11]

The theist cannot sit back and say that this enumerative inductive argument fails to establish conclusively that it is logically impossible that God have a morally exonerating excuse for permitting evil, since our power of imagination is limited and therefore it is logically possible that there is some such excuse that we failed to take into consideration. Nor can the theist claim that the onus rests with the atheologian to prove conclusively that it is logically impossible for God to have such an excuse, and not on the theist to argue that it is possible.[12] This response won't do for at least two reasons. First, while it is true that the atheologian is required to support his claim of impossibility, the theist in turn is required to support its possibility, since it is an essential tenet of theism that such an excuse should be available to God; otherwise no defense of God in the face of evil is possible. Each has the burden of supporting their respective modal claims. Neither has the option of sitting out this dance. Second, as Terence Penelhum has shown, the theist attributes a certain sort of moral character to God, namely, one that agrees with the moral code that the theist accepts, though she may fail to live up to it in practice, and this greatly limits the kind of justification that could be given for God's permitting evil; and, for this reason, the induction by complete enumeration argument has considerable plausibility.[13] It is not being claimed that Mackie and McCloskey intended to structure their argument in this way, only that they do in fact try to show why all the types of excuses we can think of could not apply to God, and that this could serve as the basis of an induction by complete enumeration argument.

Theists certainly have not sat out this dance. Their tradition is rich in attempts to construct a defense in which God's morally exonerating excuse is articulated in great detail. We have already come upon a smattering of them in our critique of Mackie's essay. And we now turn to our main task – the critical assessment of these defenses. We can forget about the aesthetic defense that justifies evil by the contribution it makes to the overall beauty and interest of the totality; for to impute such a purpose to God does not square with the moral code of traditional theism, as represented in Judaism and Christianity. That God would have, for example, the overriding Leibnizian aim of creating a world that achieves a maximum of diversity with a minimum of explanatory principles is a distinctively Greek ideal that might apply to the Demiurge of the *Timaeus* or his modern-day counterpart, the

God of Sir James Jeans, or even the god of Oscar Wilde, were he to have one, but it could not apply to the Deity of biblically based theism.

Of more pertinence is the soul-building theodicy of St. Irenaeus and John Hick. According to this theodicy, which also can double as a defense, God has created a moral proving ground in which imperfect men, in an environment frought with evils, have the opportunity to develop, *according to their own free will,* in their moral, spiritual, and intellectual perfection, ultimately to come to know and love God. That God should have such a distinctively unutilitarian goal is a reflection of the theist's own antiutilitarian moral intuitions. The theist's moral code places great stress on intrinsically valuable states for a person to be in and gives equal importance to the manner in which they are brought about, namely, by the subject's own free endeavorings. This is a type of causal theory of value.

The FWD shares the same causal theory of value and also accords great importance to the existence of free will, so much so that it uses it to exonerate God for permitting the evils that result from the misuse of free will by created persons. The two defenses complement each other, the soul-building one justifying certain natural evils, such as disease and famine, as necessary for the significant employment of free will by creatures, the FWD justifying the evils that result from this employment. Though they complement each other, they face different sorts of challenge, such that one of them might fail and the other succeed. The ensuing discussion will focus exclusively on the FWD, but it will turn out that the very reason why it fails, namely, that God has a freedom-canceling control over created beings, also undermines the soul-building defense, since it too requires that God create free persons in the manner described by the FWD.

THE FREE WILL DEFENSE

This defense concerns itself only with so-called moral evil – evil that is in some way attributable to the free will of finite persons, not necessarily members of our biological species. Initially it has nothing to say about nonmoral evils, often misleadingly called natural or physical evils, misleadingly because it implies that the self and its faculty of free will are unnatural or nonphysical, which begs some pretty big questions. The usual examples of such evils are floods, earthquakes, famines, and the like. If we take a broad enough view of "attributable to," so that not only positive use of free will but also failure to use it or use it effectively can count, it might turn out that these examples of natural evils really are moral evils.

But even if this is granted, the FWD is still powerless to rebut the atheological argument based on natural evil. It will not do to say, as does Alvin Plantinga, that all the natural evils appealed to in this argument might be species of moral evil, for instance, caused by very powerful free nonhuman agents, such as the devil. While this is true, it fails to realize that the atheological argument based on natural evil is an impure atheological one, due to the proposition that there is natural evil being taken to be only contingent by the theist. In denying that there is in fact any natural evil, it is not shown that the initial set of this argument does not entail a contradiction. And, if it does, so does the proposition that the conjunction of the propositions in its initial set is possibly true. Thus, to neutralize the deductive argument based on natural evil, Plantinga must show not just that every alleged natural evil really is or could be a moral evil but that *it is logically impossible that there be a natural evil.* And that he has not done. Nor do I think it can be done. And if so, we must recognize that the FWD can work as a defense of God only for moral evil.

Before we get embroiled in the different versions of the FWD, it will be helpful to have an overview of what they share in common. All of them employ weaker versions of God's omnipotence and benevolence than that given by 5 and 4. They begin with the "intention premise":

8. It is God's intention to create the best overall situation or the best world that he can.[14]

This is followed by the "normative premise" that rank orders possible worlds in terms of goodness:

9. A world containing free persons who freely perform both right and wrong actions, but for the most part go right, is better than any possible world devoid of free persons.

The next two premises, which are respectively the "incompatibilist premise" and the "God-could-be-unlucky premise," have the job of blocking the objection that any free persons created by God will always freely go right, resulting in moral good sans moral evil:

10. God cannot cause or determine in any way what a created person freely does; and

11. It is logically possible that God is contingently unable to create free persons who always go right.

In the possible world in which God is unlucky in the manner described in 11, he is morally exonerated for creating Mr. Rogers-type people, you know, "the very same people who are bad some time are good some time."

The intention premise, 8, faces the objection from Chapter 1 that there is no world that is the best of all possible worlds. To avoid this difficulty, it could be reconstrued as holding that it is God's intention to create a "very good world," that is, a world in which there is moral good sans moral evil. His benevolence would not be impugned by his creating a world containing 1,000 free persons who are paragons of moral virtue, when he could have created a world containing 1,001 such beings, and so on. In the ensuing discussion we will understand 8 in this watered-down manner.

Even atheologians, with one minor exception, are willing to grant 9.[15] Considerable fire has been directed at 10, but the most vulnerable premise by far is 11. The trick is to restrict one of God's omniproperties so as to account for how he could be unlucky and not be able to realize his first choice and thereby have to settle for second best – the world with a favorable balance of moral good over moral evil – without compromising this omniproperty so that it renders God less than that than which none greater can be conceived. By varying the story we tell about the circumstances under which God is unlucky, we get different versions of the FWD that make different types of morally exonerating excuse available to God.

The story told in the Plantinga version tinkers with God's omnipotence. His being able to create moral do-gooders depends upon contingent facts beyond his control concerning what possible free persons would do if God actualized them. Herein God's excuse is that of a lack of opportunity, similar to I can't play the piano now because no piano is present or I couldn't save the patient because I lacked the necessary surgical instruments or medicine. The story in the Robert M. Adams version finds God's exoneration in an excusable lack of knowledge, since there is supposed to be no way he could have known in advance the moral evils that would result from his creation of free persons. (How could I have known that the apple I gave to the trick-or-treater contained deadly poison, since I bought it at my friendly neighborhood supermarket.) Herein it is God's omniscience that is being played with. Both versions will face the problem of whether they have watered down the concerned omniproperty too much. Our exposition of these two versions will begin with Plantinga's and then bring in Adams's version as a way of escaping a formidable objection, but it will turn out that the Adams version faces even more formidable objections, thereby leaving us with no clearly viable version of a FWD. And the cause of the failure of the FWD – the impossibility for the God of traditional theism to create free persons – also undermines the soul-building defense.

The Plantinga version

Plantinga's version of the FWD is a thing of beauty that, it is safe to say, will serve as one of the cornerstones in theism's response to evil not just for many years to come but for many centuries. Because of its importance, it will be subject to the sort of careful, detailed critical exposition that would be an exercise in misplaced pettiness for a lesser work. His first published formulation, titled "The Free Will Defence," appeared in *Philosophy in America* (hereafter PA).[16] This article was reprinted verbatim as chapter 6 in his *God and Other Minds* with the addition of a final section that briefly attempts to neutralize the inductive argument from evil and the mysterious deletion of a paragraph on page 195 of PA that explains why God cannot control the free acts of persons. A new version, employing the ontology of possible worlds, appeared as chapter 9 of his *The Nature of Necessity* (hereafter NN). A more popular presentation of this version was given in his *God, Freedom, and Evil* (hereafter GFE). In the course of my exposition it will be shown that the PA and possible-worlds versions differ only in their terminology, not their ontology. (His argument does gain in formal rigor, however, by the use of the possible-worlds terminology.) My exposition will jump around between these different published presentations of his FWD. In his "Self-Profile" in the 1985 *Alvin Plantinga* Profiles Volume, (hereafter SP),[17] he attempts to meet objections to the incompatibilist premise and suggests a way in which the FWD can be formulated so that it does not require that God foreknows what will result from his creation of free persons, thereby moving quite close to the Adams version, whose defense is built on just this limitation in God's knowledge. For this reason we will hold off discussion of the new version of the FWD in SP until we discuss the Adams version.

As indicated, the heart of the FWD is the story that is told of the possible circumstances under which God is unable to realize his first choice and thereby is morally exonerated for creating the morally mixed-bag world. For Plantinga the story will involve some contingent factor beyond God's control that renders him unable, through a lack of opportunity, to realize the goody-goody world. Mackie and his cohorts are going to argue that God's omniproperties logically preclude there being any such factor. Herein we find an instance of what has become the standard objection to any FWD – the

God-can-do-more objection. No one has yet pressed the opposite objection that God cannot do as much as Plantinga requires without negating the freedom of the persons he creates. It will turn out that this is the telling objection.

The most prominent of the God-can-do-more objections are based on either causal or theological compatibilism, the former arguing that since an act can be both free and causally determined, God could have assured the realization of his first choice by a suitable selection of deterministic causal laws and the initial state of the universe, the latter that since an act can be both free and determined supernaturally by God, he could have realized this simply by willing that it be so. These supernaturally determined events need not be causally determined by anything within the universe. Plantinga develops his FWD in a highly dialectical manner in the course of responding to these two compatibilist-based objections, beginning with that of the causal compatibilist. We will follow the dialectic of his exposition.

The causal compatibilist objection

This objection holds that since an action or choice can be both free and causally determined in the sense of admitting of a Hempelian deductive-nomological explanation (i.e., a proposition reporting the action or choice is deducible from the conjunction of causal laws and propositions reporting conditions prior to it, without being entailed by the latter alone), God can make certain that all of the free persons he creates always freely go right by (A) ordaining that certain strict deterministic laws hold, and (B) creating persons in circumstances such that they would be determined by these laws always freely to go right.[18] It takes considerable intelligence to find just the right combination of laws and initial conditions, but this should be no problem for an omniscient being. Once God has done (A) and (B), he can sit back like the God of Deism and just watch the inevitable beneficient unfolding of what their conjunction entails.

The deductive argument from evil

Plantinga does not consider the case in which events admit of only a Hempelian inductive-statistical-type explanation, no doubt because such a case could not serve as the basis for an objection to the FWD. The reason is that if God were to determine that probabilistic laws hold, regardless of how high the probabilities, and determine the initial state of the universe, it would not logically ensure that persons always freely go right. Were God to try to determine this morally desirable situation in this fashion, he could be faulted by the causal compatibilist objector for not availing himself of the better option of laying down strict deterministic laws so as to logically ensure this outcome.

Plantinga's initial response to the causal compatibilist objection is to deny that it is consistent to say that some act is both free and causally determined:

> When we say that Jones acts freely on a given occasion, what we say entails . . . that either his action on that occasion is not causally determined, or else he has previously performed an undetermined action which is a causal ancestor of the one in question. (PA 189)

He expands on this purely negative account of freedom on pages 165–6 of NN:

> If a person S is free with respect to a given action, then he is free to perform that action and free to refrain; no causal laws and antecedent conditions determine either that he will perform the action, or that he will not. (see also GFE 29)

The dispute between Plantinga and the causal compatibilist is the modern-day continuation of the medieval dispute between Molina and Scotus over whether freedom is to be understood in terms of the "freedom of indifference" or only the "freedom of spontaneity." Whereas the modern-day defender of the freedom of spontaneity – the causal compatibilist – basically follows the Hobbes–Hume account of freedom as absence of external compulsion (with the added

116

requirement of an absence of internal or psychological compulsion), Plantinga, the Libertarian, requires that the agent has both the power to do the act and the power to refrain, with this requiring an absence of causal determination but not agent determination.

Plantinga, however, does not try to refute the causal compatibilist.[19] Instead he makes a present of the word "freedom" to Flew, compatibilist objector, and reformulates his FWD using a different locution:

> The Free Will Defender can simply make Flew a present of the word 'freedom' and state his case using other locutions. He might hold, for example, not that God made men free and that a world in which men freely do both good and evil is more valuable than a world in which they unfreely do only what is good; but rather that God made men such that some of their actions are *unfettered* (both free in Flew's sense and also causally undetermined) and that a world in which men perform both good and evil unfettered actions is superior to one in which they perform only good, but fettered, actions. By substituting 'unfettered' for 'free' throughout this account, the Free Will Defender can elude Flew's objection altogether. (PA 189)

This strategy for eluding the causal compatibilist's objection is endorsed, although not stated, in NN and GFE. On pages 170–1 of NN he writes:

> And a person is free with respect to an action A at a time t only if no causal laws and antecedent conditions determine either that he performs A at t or that he refrains from so doing. This is not a comment upon the ordinary use of the word 'free'; that use may or may not coincide with the Free Will Defender's.

And when he considers Flew's objection in footnote 14 on page 32 of GFE, he refers the reader back to his earlier discussion in PA in which he develops the make-Flew-a-gift-of-the-word response.

This strategy for meeting the causal compatibilist's objection is, in my opinion, a disaster.[20] First, if Plantinga really intends to make a present of the word "freedom" to the compatibilists, and thereby let them decide its meaning, his account turns out to be inconsistent because almost all of them have insisted that a necessary condition for an action's being free is that it is causally determined. They have claimed that a causally undetermined action is a chance, fortuitous occurrence that cannot be attributed to the doer of the action in such a way that he is morally responsible for it.[21] When it is realized that the compatibilist requires that an action is free only if it is causally determined, as well as physically and psychologically uncoerced, Plantinga's account is seen to be inconsistent; for it may then be stated as follows:

> God made men such that some of their actions are unfettered (both free in Flew's sense of being both causally determined and neither physically nor psychologically coerced and also causally undetermined).

The consistency problem is easily solved by redefining "unfettered" as "neither physically or psychologically coerced nor causally determined," only now to face the objection that there is nothing particularly valuable about such "unfettered" actions; and, as a consequence, the objector is no longer willing to grant the normative premise when it is reformulated in terms of such actions. The reason for this, as stated, is that they equate a causally undetermined action with a random or chance occurrence for which the agent cannot be held responsible. Mackie, the causal compatibilist, writes:

> If freedom is randomness, how can it be a characteristic of will? And, still more, how can it be the most important good? What value or merit would there be in free choices if these were random actions which were not determined by the nature of the agent.[22]

Thus, Plantinga's attempt to reformulate his FWD in terms of "unfettered" actions, even when formulated consistently, fails to achieve the desideratum of avoiding an ultimate clash of intuitions between himself and the causal compatibilist critic. All he achieves by this maneuver is to shift the clash of intuitions from the incompatibilist premise to the normative one.

By the time Plantinga came to write his "Self-Profile," he realized that his former strategy of making a present of the word "freedom" does not work for the reasons just given, and he disowned it with the rather understated remark, "I now think this way with the difficulty too short" (SP 45). He realizes that there is no way he can avoid a clash of intuitions with the compatibilists, but now he is willing to tough it out and assert his incompatibilist intuition in opposition to theirs. As he sees it, the nub of the dispute is whether his Libertarian conception of a free act is viable in that the agent can be held responsible for it. A free act, for the Libertarian, is not a mere chance, random, or accidental occurrence, since it is "agent determined" by a nonempirical self in a way that defies scientific description and explanation.[23] Plantinga does not fill in his Libertarian theory, but from what little he says it appears that he is in the same camp as Aristotle, James (in his great account of the will in *The Principles of Psychology*), Campbell, Chisholm, Taylor, and Sartre. In support of the viability of his theory, he gives God as an example – the ultimate uncaused-causer whom we emulate every time we serve as the unmoved-mover of one of our own limbs. Plantinga thinks that it is unreasonable for his critic not to grant the viability of this conception of God.[24]

By challenging the compatibilist objector, Plantinga does not achieve his original desideratum of avoiding a clash of intuitions, but at least he is confident that his Libertarian concept of a free act is a viable one. He fails to see that his clash with his compatibilist opponent is not confined solely to the viability issue but also breaks out on the normative level; for it is conceivable that his opponent would (begrudgingly) grant him the viability of his concept of a free act but then go on to deny that such acts have the sort of value that is required for the normative premise to be acceptable. And were the dispute to shift to this normative level, there is no doubt that Plantinga again would be willing to get into the "Tis-Tisn't" sort of shouting match with his opponent.

What are we to make of these clashes of intuitions over the viability and, assuming viability, the value of a Libertarian free act? It would be naive in the extreme to think that these disputes are to be resolved by appeal to "ordinary language"; for while "ordinary usage" at Calvin College and Notre Dame University might favor Plantinga's intuitions, what counts as ordinary usage at the establishments frequented by Flew and Mackie might well support theirs. Just how shaky our intuitions are in this matter is apparent to anyone who has taught the free will–determinism issue to a group of introductory students. It takes no more than thirty seconds to turn them into a wild-eyed lynch mob of incompatibilists and about sixty seconds to turn them back into compatibilists. In my opinion, nothing short of an extensive metaphysical theory of the self conjoined with a normative theory about the forensic and ethical dimensions of personal responsibility will "settle" this dispute, meaning that this is not the sort of issue that gets settled. It certainly is too quick to dismiss Plantinga's FWD because one's intuitions do not support its normative premise. And since the FWD is countering the charge of logical inconsistency against theism, maybe all that should be required of it is that it be valid and not employ any plainly implausible premise. Judged by this weak standard, Plantinga earns at least a draw with his compatibilist critic. The FWD is still alive.

I believe that there is available to Plantinga a workable strategy for achieving his original desideratum of avoiding any clash of intuitions with the causal compatibilist: find some freedom-canceling condition accepted by the latter that is present in the case in which God predetermines the behavior of persons in the nomic manner mentioned. While causal compatibilists do not recognize the mere fact that an action is causally determined as freedom canceling, they do accept certain ways in which an action is causally determined as freedom canceling. Even the crudest of them recognize physical compulsion as freedom canceling, and this is extended by more recent compatibilists to actions that result from psychological compulsions. Most of them, with one minor exception, recognize ways in which one person can usurp another person's free will by gaining a habitual ascendancy over their will, such that all or most of their behavior is caused by, or under the causal control of, the former.[25] They accept, for example, cases of extensive brainwashing, posthypnotic suggestion, or intentional control over the inputs to a brain-in-a-vat as freedom canceling. There are recognized limits to how far one person can go in causally controlling the behavior of another person without negating the latter's freedom. Now God is a person, but his control over created persons is even more extreme than in these man–man cases; not only does he sufficiently cause all of their behavior by bringing about certain instantial conditions and have the counterfactual power to produce alternative behavior, he also creates the causal structure of the universe, whereas finite controllers merely take advantage of a given causal structure. The causal-compatibilist-based objection, therefore, winds up being inconsistent, for it imputes to God this agreed upon freedom-canceling control over created persons and yet holds that they are free.[26]

The causal compatibilist might search for some disanalogy between the man–man cases and the God–man case that precludes applying to the latter the same freedom-canceling principles that hold for the former. The actions of the finite controllers are events in the universe that event-cause in some nomic manner the behavior of the victims. But God's act of willing is not an event in the universe, and it does not event-cause in some nomic manner the instantial conditions in the universe that in turn event-cause the behavior of the created persons, but instead agent-causes these conditions. Thus the causal chain linking God's initial act of will with the subsequent behavior of created persons is a mixed bag of agent and event causes. It could then be contended that whereas causation is transitive for causal chains that involve only event causation, it is not for mixed causal chains. And, as a consequence, God's act of will is not the cause of the behavior of created persons; and thus God does not have a freedom-canceling control over created persons. I see little plausibility in this response. Suppose I agent-cause my arm to rise, which in turn event-causes molecules of air to be displaced. Certainly I, the person who agent-causes my arm to rise, cause this displacement. And if it be asked whether I event-cause or agent-cause the displacement, the answer is that I do neither, since my act of will is connected with the displacement by a mixed causal chain. To demand that it is one or the other is implicitly to rule out such mixed causal chains.

I conclude that my strategy enables Plantinga to win a decisive victory over his causal compatibilist objector. My "gift," however, will turn out to be a Trojan horse, since it will be seen that the account given in Plantinga's own FWD of the relation between God and created persons runs afoul of the very same freedom-canceling principle as is appealed to in my refutation of the causal-compatibilist-based objection. Watch out for philosophers bearing gifts.

The theological compatibilist objection

Plantinga views this as the more serious of the two God-can-do-more challenges to his FWD. God does not have to utilize any mixed causal chains to predetermine the behavior of persons. He can agent-determine it directly by his supernatural will. The theological compatibilist sees no incompatibility between an action's being free and yet determined by God in this manner. For this reason it is within God's power to create free persons who always freely go right; and, thus, he cannot be excused for failing to do so on grounds of inability or lack of opportunity or even lack of knowledge since whatever God can predetermine by his will he can infallibly foreknow. This objection is not confined to the atheologian, since many of the great theists have been theological compatibilists. Such theists must find a defense that is independent of the FWD.

Plantinga's way with this objection is, first, to ferret out its crucial presupposition, then argue against it, and finally utilize this argument for the purpose of describing a possible world in which God has a morally exonerating excuse for allowing moral evil. He begins by considering Mackie's following presentation of the theological-compatibilist-based objection:

> First I should query the assumption that second order evils are logically necessary accompaniments of freedom. I should ask this: if God has made men such that in their free choices they sometimes prefer what is good and sometimes what is evil, why could he not have made men such that they always freely choose the good? If there is no logical impossibility in a man's freely choosing the good on one, or on several, occasions, there cannot be a logical impossibility in his freely choosing the good on every occasion. God was not, then, faced with a choice between making innocent automata and making beings who, in acting freely, would sometimes go wrong: there was open to him the obviously better possibility of making beings who would act freely but always go right. Clearly, his failure to avail himself of this possibility is inconsistent with his being omnipotent and wholly good.[27]

It would seem that Mackie is appealing to the Leibnizian doctrine, called "Leibniz's lapse" by Plantinga for reasons that will soon emerge, that

LL. God can actualize any possible world.

This is a consequence of the stated logically restricted account of omnipotence:

5_1. An omnipotent being can bring about any logically possible state of affairs.

No party to the dispute wants to doubt that among the logically possible worlds are ones that contain moral good sans moral evil, so the only issue is the acceptability of LL.

Plantinga is quick to present counterexamples to it. If God is not a necessary being, LL and 5_1 must be restricted to possible worlds or states of affairs in which God exists. But this might not be enough; for, if there are necessary beings such as numbers and properties that do not admit of creation or destruction, they must undergo yet further restriction. And, also, let us not forget about the absurdity of God's having to play *causa sui* by actualizing himself. To meet these counterexamples, they can be recast as:

LL_1. God can actualize any possible world w such that it is logically consistent that God actualizes w; and

5_2. An omnipotent being can bring about any state of affairs s such that it is logically consistent that an omnipotent being bring it about that s. [28]

Mackie's objection can be reformulated so as to accommodate these more restricted accounts of what God, an omnipotent being, can do. It has been agreed that among the possible worlds are morally perfect ones. And since it is not logically inconsistent that God actualize one of them, it follows that God can do so; and, given his benevolence, it follows that any possible world containing free persons that God actualizes contains moral good sans moral evil. But plainly this is not the case.

The crucial presupposition in Mackie's reformulated objection is

M. It is necessary that God can actualize a possible world in which all free persons always freely go right.

This is necessary because what it is logically consistent for God to actualize cannot vary across possible worlds. Plantinga is going to argue for the negation of M:

−M. It is possible that God cannot actualize a possible world in which all free persons always freely go right.

This will be called the "depravity proposition" because it claims that every possible free person could be depraved in that were God to attempt to actualize any one of them, the resulting concrete person would freely go wrong at least once. As a step along the way to proving −M, Plantinga will prove that

CL. It is necessary that there is some possible free person that God cannot actualize,

which will be referred to as the "counter-Leibniz proposition." Once −M is established, Plantinga can complete his FWD by adding that in the possible world in which what −M claims to be possible is realized, God is morally exonerated for settling for his second choice – the creation of the Mr. Rogers-type persons.

Before we can understand Plantinga's arguments for −M and CL, we must see what he means by "possible person" and "possible world," as well as their instantiation and actualization respectively. The PA version works with possible persons, the NN and GFE version with possible worlds, but, it will be seen, the ontology is exactly the same, only the terminology being different. A possible person is a higher-order Platonic entity, being a set of abstract properties that may or may not be instantiated, while a possible world is a set of abstract states of affairs (or propositions) that may or may not obtain (or be true). More precisely, a possible person is a maximal compossible set of properties each of which could be possessed by a single person (PA 193).[29] The set is compossible in that it admits of the logical possibility of coinstantiation by a single concrete individual, and it is maximal because for every property that could be possessed by a person, either this property or its complement is included in the set. A possible person is the same as a Leibnizian complete concept of a person. A possible world, however, is a maximal compossible set of states of affairs or properties. I will use "universe" to refer to a maximal spatiotemporal aggregate – the totality of what exists and happens in space and/or time – and "cosmos" to refer to the maximal aggregate of actually existent entities. Whatever exists in the universe also exists in the cosmos but not necessarily vice versa, since abstract entities such as numbers exist in the cosmos alone.

For Plantinga there must be one and only one cosmos, as well as universe, and a given cosmos must actualize one and only one possible world.

Another way in which Plantinga conceives of a possible world is as a maximal compossible set of abstract propositions, that is, all the propositions that would be true were that world to be actualized. Such a set is called a "world book," and corresponding to every possible world is such a world book. A given cosmos makes true one and only one world book. It is important to emphasize that possible persons, possible worlds, and world books are abstract possibilia. Each is a way things might be, and that is not something locatable in space and/or time. Moreover, these possibilia are necessary entities and thus exist in every possible world.

It should be apparent that the same Platonic ontology informs both the possible person and possible world formulations of the FWD. What is more, given Plantinga's definitions, it follows that every possible person is identical with some possible world, though not conversely, since some possible worlds are devoid of persons. This is a consequence of the fact that the only restriction Plantinga places on a property that is a member of the set that is a possible person is that it is possible for a person to have it. This allows us to include relational properties and by using sufficiently rich spatial and temporal relational properties, for instance, being born so many years after the last dinosaur died, being a person who dies while there is a full eclipse of the sun, and so on, we can come out with a complete description of an entire cosmos, including all of the other personal inhabitants of it.

Of special interest for our purpose is a possible significantly free person, that is, a possible person containing the property of being free in respect to some action having moral significance. For such a person there is at least one morally significant action A and set of circumstances C such that this person includes the disjunctive property of either-freely-doing-A-or-freely-refraining-from-doing-A-in-C. Since a possible person is maximal, it also includes the property of doing

A or the property of not doing A. For every possible free person containing the property of freely-doing-A-in-C there is a numerically distinct possible person that includes all of the same properties except for including freely-refraining-from-doing-A-in-C instead. Let us call such a pair of possible free persons an "incompatible pair." Whenever you freely perform an action, you instantiate one member of such a pair to the exclusion of the other. In what follows we shall consider only significantly free possible persons and, for short, will call them "possible persons."

With these terminological and ontological points out of the way, we can begin to approach Plantinga's argument for CL, the counter-Leibniz proposition. The argument attempts to show that for any incompatible pair, God will be contingently unable to actualize one person in the pair. Let our specimen incompatible pair be P and P_1, who include all of the same properties save for P's including freely-doing-A-in-C and P_1's instead including freely-refraining-from-doing-A-in-C. Our revised Leibnizian of the LL_1 type will hold that each is such that God can actualize or instantiate it, though he cannot, of course, coinstantiate them. Plantinga, the Libertarian, disagrees, because he thinks it is logically inconsistent that God actualizes or instantiates either of them. The reason is that God's actualizing or instantiating P, for example, consists in his causing there to exist a person having all of the properties included in P, and thereby God causes or determines this person freely to do A in C; but this is logically inconsistent according to the incompatibilist premise. For the Libertarian it must be the agent herself that is the (agent-) cause of a free act, not some condition external to the agent, though such conditions might limit the range of possibilities from which the agent can choose and "incline" it in a certain direction, requiring greater effort of will for it to pursue an opposite course of action.

If God cannot actualize a possible person simply by supernaturally willing that it be actualized, how does he do it? It is here that Plantinga has an incredibly ingenious and controversial story to tell. Again we must begin with some terminology.

What God does is to actualize what I will call a "diminished possible person" and then leave it up to the created person what it will freely do. Each possible person contains a diminished possible person that is its largest proper subset of properties that is such that for any action A, it neither includes or entails freely doing A nor includes or entails freely refraining from doing A, in which a property F includes or entails another property G just in case it is logically impossible that F be instantiated and G not be. (What I call a "diminished possible person" corresponds with Plantinga's second definition of a "possible person" on page 196 of PA. His dual use of "possible person" in PA creates difficulties for the reader, which, I hope, my terminology helps to avoid.) We will also refer to such a subset as a "freedom neutral" set of properties. Each property included in a set of properties could be freedom-neutral and yet the set as a whole not be, for the set could contain either - freely - doing - A - or - freely - refraining - from - doing-A and doing A. Any incompatible pair will contain as proper subsets the same diminished person or set of freedom-neutral properties. Thus, P's diminished person, DP, is numerically one and the same as DP_1 – the diminished person corresponding to P_1. God performs the same creative act when he endeavors to actualize P as he does when he endeavors to actualize P_1, namely, he supernaturally wills that the diminished person DP be instantiated or actualized. Intuitively, we can think of this as God's creatively determining every feature of the universe up until the time at which the created person, the instantiator of DP, freely does A or freely refrains from doing A. Since P and P_1 are each identical with some possible world, it follows that this is the same creative act God performs in actualizing either of these two worlds.

The question is what would result if God were to instantiate DP. Would the instantiator of this diminished person or set of freedom-neutral properties freely do A or freely refrain? Plainly, the instantiator must do one or the other, since he has the disjunctive property of either-freely-doing-A-or-freely-refraining-from-doing-A. Thus, it is either true that

F. If *DP* were instantiated, the instantiator would freely do
A; or

F'. If *DP* were instantiated, the instantiator would freely
refrain from doing *A*.

Let us call a subjunctive conditional whose antecedent
reports the instantiation of a diminished possible person and
consequent the performance of a free action by the instantiator a "free will subjunctive conditional," for short, an "F-
conditional."[30] If F is true, then were God to instantiate *DP*, it
would result in *P*'s being actualized; whereas, if F' is true,
were God to actualize *DP*, it would result in P_1's being actualized. Since F and F' are logically incompatible, it follows that
if F is true God is unable to actualize P_1, and if F' is true God
is unable to actualize *P*. But necessarily, one of them is true
and therefore necessarily true that God cannot actualize *P* or
cannot actualize P_1, which proves CL.

This proof assumed that the law of conditional excluded
middle holds for F-conditionals. Herein the necessarily true
disjunction is formed not from the disjunction of an F-
conditional with its negation, as is the case when the weaker
law of excluded middle is applied, but from the disjunction of
an F-conditional with an F-conditional containing the same
antecedent and the denial of the former's consequent, as is
the previous case with the disjunction of F and F'. In SP,
Plantinga gives a proof for CL that applies only the law of
excluded middle to F-conditionals. It begins with what Plantinga calls "Lewis's lemma," which, when translated into my
terminology, says that God can actualize a possible person *P*
containing the property of freely doing *A* only if it is true that
if God were to actualize its diminished person *DP*, the instantiator would freely do *A*. It next is claimed by appeal to the
law of excluded middle that it is either true or false that F. If
it is false, then, given Lewis's lemma, God cannot actualize *P*;
and, if it is true, then he cannot actualize P_1. As we shall see
when we consider Adams's version of the FWD, it is controversial whether an F-conditional could be true. Even if they
all were necessarily false, the law of excluded middle version

of the proof of CL would work; for if both F and F′ are false, then God can actualize neither P nor P_1.

From Plantinga's argument for CL, it is only a few short steps to the establishment of the depravity proposition, $-M$. At the outset let us confine ourselves to possible persons that include the property of being free with respect to only one action, such as our forementioned persons P and P_1. What we establish then can be generalized to more complex possible persons. Any incompatible pair of such simplified persons is a Dr. Jeckyl and Mr. Hyde pair, the former being the one that contains the property of freely doing A (which is the morally right thing to do), the latter the property of freely refraining from doing A (which is the morally wrong thing to do). It has already been shown in the argument for CL that God might not be able to actualize P, the Dr. Jeckyl member of the pair, since F could be false. But what could be true for this particular Dr. Jeckyl and Mr. Hyde pair could be true for all of them. Every incompatible pair of this sort could be such that it is true that if God were to instantiate the diminished possible person common to both, the instantiator would freely do the morally wrong alternative. Under such unfortunate circumstances, God can actualize only Mr. Hydes, and therefore will not attempt to instantiate any of these simple possible persons, assuming that his brand of benevolence requires that there be a favorable balance of moral good over moral evil.

The result can be generalized so as to apply to more rich possible persons that contain the property of being free in respect to more than one action. It could still be the case for every such person that it is true that if God were to actualize its diminished person, the instantiator would freely go wrong with respect to at least one of these actions. And this suffices to establish $-M$ – that it is possible that God cannot actualize a possible world in which all free persons always freely go right.

At this point Plantinga can complete his FWD by claiming that in the possible world in which the truth-values of the F-conditionals preclude God from actualizing any Dr. Jeckyls or, more generally, possible persons containing the property of always freely doing what is right, he is excused for creating the Mr. Rogers sort of persons, provided for the most part they freely go right, which I am sure is true for the Mr. Rogers types. In such a world God can plead that he did the best he could but was screwed by those damned F-conditionals.[31] This compares with Scotty saying to Captain Kirk, "Sorry about that, Skipper, but I gave it all the phaser power I had." This completes our rough sketch of Plantinga's FWD account of the possible world in which God is unlucky and thereby morally exonerated for allowing moral evil.

Those damned F-conditionals

The account given so far of Plantinga's story of creation fails to deal with some key issues concerning F-conditionals: their modal status; God's knowledge of them; and from whence they derive their truth-values, assuming that they have them at all. Different ways of handling these issues produce different versions of the FWD. It will now be shown that Plantinga's FWD is committed to the following theses about F-conditionals:

I. Every F-conditional has a contingent truth-value, that is, is contingently true or contingently false,

II. God knows the truth-value of all F-conditionals prior to his creative decision, and

III. God does not determine the truth-values of F-conditionals.

Theses I and II together make up the doctrine of God's "middle knowledge," which doctrine is rejected by the Adams's version. Each of these theses will now be examined in some detail.

Another way of formulating the doctrine of God's middle knowledge is that God foreknows for every diminished possible person what free actions would be performed were that person to be instantiated. This is an important consideration, since in assessing one's responsibility and blame for some event, questions of what was known and when it was known are relevant. We can imagine a belligerent newscaster asking "Just what did God know? and When did he know it?" For Plantinga, God cannot get away with the Ronald Reagan-type response:

> In the first place, there wasn't anything to be known (since F-conditionals lack a truth-value). In the second place, no one told me what their truth-values were. And, moreover, if they had, I wouldn't have understood what they were talking about. And, furthermore, I don't remember what happened, but if I did remember anything it would be that I was told about their truth-values too late – after I had made my creative decision.

(That Reagan can get away with this type of answer and God cannot shows that Reagan is more powerful than God, since he can do something that God cannot.) Many of the things that Plantinga says in the PA and NN-GFE formulations preclude God's taking this know-nothing tack:

> Now God is said to be omniscient and hence knows, with respect to any person he proposes to create, whether that person would or would not commit morally evil acts. (PA 192)

> The atheologian's proper retort, I think, is as follows. Suppose we conclude that not even God can cause it to be the case that I freely refrain from *A*. Even so, he *can* cause me to be free with respect to *A*, and to be in some set *S* of circumstances including appropriate laws and antecedent conditions. He may also know, furthermore, that *if* he creates me and causes me to be free in these circumstances, I will refrain from *A*. (NN 172)

These two quotations are not decisive, because Plantinga is attributing a belief in God's middle knowledge to his theological compatibilist objector. But he does not challenge this belief. The following quotations are decisive, because Plantinga speaks in the first person:

Our question is really whether there is something Curley would have done had this state of affairs been actual. Would an omniscient being know what Curley would have done – would he know, that is, either that Curley would have taken the bribe or that he would have rejected it? The answer, I should think, is obvious and affirmative. There is something Curley would have done, had that state of affairs obtained. (NN 180)

The following makes clear that God possesses his middle knowledge prior to his creative decision:

Further, God knows in advance what Curley would do if created and placed in these states of affairs. (NN 185–6)

Similar remarks are made in GFE, Curley, the crooked politician, being replaced by Maurice, the oatmeal eater:

Now God no doubt knows what Maurice will do at time t, if S' obtains. He knows which action Maurice would freely perform if S' were to be actual. (GFE 42–3)

The following is of special importance, since it clearly attributes a contingent truth-value to an F-conditional:

Now we merely supposed that DP is such that if it is instantiated, its instantiator will perform A. And this supposition, if true at all, is merely contingently true. (PA 195; I have altered Plantinga's names so as to match my above example of an F-conditional.)

Together these quotations make clear that Plantinga attributes middle knowledge to God and thereby prevents him from taking the Reagan "excusable" ignorance or lack of knowledge way out; for when God creates free persons, he already knows what they will do and thus doesn't watch the unfolding of their personal histories in the way in which "hockey parents," for example, watch their son play in a game, holding their breath, hoping that he will come through and being disappointed when he does not – Oh! He just gave up the puck in his own zone! Oh! He just took a dumb penalty! This shows that the Holiday Inn slogan "The best surprise is no surprise" isn't always true, judging by the amount of moral evil there is.

While it is clear that Plantinga accepts theses I and II in the version of the FWD given in the PA and NN-GFE formulations, our question is whether this version requires that he accept them. From what little he says about omniscience, it appears that he thinks that II is entailed by I: If F-conditionals have contingent truth-values, then God knows what they are at the time of his creative decision. This entailment holds if we accept, as he seems to, the tough account of omniscience given by traditional theism – that God essentially knows every true proposition.[32] For this reason, the only issue is whether his FWD requires thesis I, and we can confine ourselves to this issue alone.

Given Plantinga's Libertarian account of F-conditionals, it is not obvious that thesis I is true; for, according to this Libertarian theory, the consequent of an F-conditional is not determined by any antecedent condition(s). Such conditions, at best, can render it probable that the consequent will be realized once the antecedent is actualized by inclining the free person in the direction of what it reports. We shall find that it is on this basis that Adams argues that it is conceptually or logically impossible that F-conditionals be true and that they thereby could not have a contingent truth-value; they are necessarily not true, which is the case if they are either necessarily false or necessarily neither-true-nor-false, that is, truth-valueless.

Adams's argument for the denial of thesis I was published after Plantinga's three published formulations of his FWD.[33] When Plantinga subsequently reconsidered his FWD in SP, he was again ready to take the ecumenical route to avoid a clash with his critic, in this case Adams, by reformulating his FWD in terms of mutually acceptable propositions. (We recall the disastrous result of his earlier ecumenical effort when he made a gift of the word "freedom" to his causal compatibilist objector and reformulated his FWD in terms of the technical notion of "unfettered.") His hope now is to find a formulation that will not require either thesis I or II, thereby avoiding a clash with Adams:

> An interesting project would be to develop in detail a version of the FWD that does not involve either middle knowledge or F-conditionals (counterfactuals of freedom). (SP 50)

That there are F-conditionals means "that F-conditionals have a determinate truth value" (SP 49). I assume that by "determinate truth value" he means "contingent truth value" and not that fatalistic notion of now being unpreventably true or unpreventably false, which, according to the Arabic commentators on Chapter 9 of *de Interpretatione* is probably what Aristotle meant when he said of propositions about future contingents that they are not yet either determinately true or determinately false. That there are F-conditionals, thereby, is just another way of expressing thesis I.

What follows is supposed to be a "simplified" (!) version of the argument from NN for CL and $-M$, which has already been sketched. It makes explicit what is only implicit in the NN formulation, namely, Lewis's lemma, which says, in my terminology, that God can actualize a possible person containing the properties of freely doing $A_1 \ldots A_n$ only if it is true that if he were to instantiate its diminished person, the instantiator would freely do $A_1 \ldots A_n$. This argument, like the NN one, applies only the law of excluded middle to F-conditionals, not the stronger law of conditional excluded middle, and thereby works even if every F-conditional is false. Under this condition, given Lewis's lemma, God cannot actualize any possible person and thereby cannot actualize one containing the property of always freely going right. For this reason he concludes:

> Indeed, strictly speaking the present argument doesn't depend upon the assumption that any F-conditionals are true; it could be, for all the argument presupposes, that all such F-conditionals are false. (SP 52)

But that the arguments for CL and −M go through, and must go through, if all F-conditionals are false hardly shows that his FWD works even if there are no F-conditionals, which is what he thinks he accomplishes by formulating his argument without appealing to the law of conditional excluded middle. It is one thing for all F-conditionals to be false and quite another for them to lack a contingent truth-value because they are necessarily not true.

Plantinga seems to forget that his FWD does not consist only in the proofs of CL and −M but also must go on to describe, utilizing −M, the possible world in which God is morally exonerated for permitting moral evil. In such a world God succeeds in actualizing a possible person, from which it follows in accordance with Lewis's lemma that some F-conditional is true in that world; and, therefore, it is false that every F-conditional is necessarily not true, pace Adams. Thus we see that the FWD has both a negative and a positive component. The negative one concerns the conditions under which God is unable to create certain kinds of possible persons: The arguments for CL and −M perform this negative task. The positive component concerns the conditions under which God is able to create certain free persons: This is contained in the description of the "unlucky" world in which God is excused for allowing moral evil. Plantinga's ecumenical effort fails, because the positive component requires thesis I.

It does not work even for the negative component. This will be shown by deducing an explicit contradiction from the conjunction of the premises of his argument for CL in NN (which is the same as that in SP) with the denial of thesis I – that F-conditionals necessarily are not true. This argument attempts to prove that given any two possible worlds in which God exists, W and W^*, such that there is a person who freely does action A in W but freely refrains from doing A in W^*, either it is contingently impossible that God actualize W or contingently impossible that God actualize W^*.

For let W be a world where God exists, where Curley is free with respect to the action of taking a $20,000 bribe, and where

he accepts it; and as before, let T be the largest state of affairs God strongly actualizes in W. God's actualizing T (GT) includes neither Curley's accepting the bribe (A) nor his rejecting it ($-A$); so there is a world W^* where God strongly actualizes T and in which Curley rejects the bribe. Now
(24) $GT \rightarrow A$
is either true or false. If (24) is true then by the previous argument God could not have actualized W^*. On the other hand, if (24) is false, then God could not have actualized W (NN 182–3),

in which "$\rightarrow$" means "subjunctive conditionally implies" and "God's strongly actualizing T" means that God's supernatural will is the sole free cause of T,[34] in which T, according to my terminology, is the diminished Curley possible person or Curley's freedom-neutral properties.

My indirect proof of thesis I, relative to the premises of this argument, will utilize these abbreviations: "L_l" and "M_l" mean, respectively, "it is logically necessary that" and "it is logically possible that" and "M_c" means "it is contingently possible that." It begins with the denial of thesis I:

−I. L_l every F-conditional is not true,

to which are then added the premises of the former argument. It is apparent that the law of excluded middle is applied to F-conditionals, giving us

12. Every F-conditional is true or false.

Other obvious premises are

13. W is a possible world in which God exists; and
14. W^* is a possible world in which God exists.

The next two premises are based on Lewis's lemma:

15. L_l [(it is true ($GT \rightarrow A$) $\supset$ ($-M_c$ God actualizes W^*)]; and
16. L_l [(It is false ($GT \rightarrow A$) $\supset$ ($-M_c$ God actualizes W)].

Plantinga assumes, furthermore, that it is logically, although maybe not contingently, possible that God actualize any possible world in which he exists:

17. L_1 $(w)(w$ is a possible world in which God exists $\supset M_1$ God actualizes w).

From $-I$ it follows that

18. $(p)(p$ is an F-conditional $\supset L_1 p$ is not true).

It is the case that

19. $(GT \rightarrow A)$ is an F-conditional.

And from 18 and 19 it follows that

20. $L_1(GT \rightarrow A)$ is not true.

From 16 it follows that

21. L_1 $[M_c$ God actualizes $W \supset$ It is true $(GT \rightarrow A)]$.

And by an uncontested theorem of modal logic it follows from 20 and 21 that

22. $L_1 - M_c$ God actualizes w.

And this entails that

23. $-M_1$ God actualizes w.

Given that w is a possible world in which God exists, it follows from 17 that

24. M_1 God actualizes w.

And by conjoining 23 with 24, we have our explicit contradiction.

It must be reiterated that this is not intended to be an indirect proof of thesis I, only a demonstration of the logical commitment to it by the premises of Plantinga's argument for CL. Its success as an indirect proof of thesis I hinges on the acceptability of Lewis's lemma, of which 15 and 16 are special instances; but we must postpone discussion of this until we have completed our expositions of both the Plantinga and Adams versions of the FWD. Right now our only concern is with how F-conditionals enter into Plantinga's FWD. It has already been shown that his FWD is committed to theses I and II – the doctrine of God's middle knowledge – that F-conditionals have contingent truth-values that are known to God. But whence do they derive their truth-values?

One possible answer, which Plantinga rules out by appeal to his incompatibilist premise 10, is that God determines their truth-values. God's sovereignty must be restricted, in accordance with the 5_2 account of omnipotence, to what it is logically consistent for God to bring about or determine. Plantinga claims that if God were both to determine an F-conditional's truth-value and actualize its antecedent, he would in effect be determining what the created person freely does, which is inconsistent with it being done freely (PA 195). Such dual determination is freedom canceling in the same way that God's determining both what deterministic laws hold and the initial state of the universe negates the freedom of the actions that inevitably result from their conjunction.

Even if Plantinga's incompatibilism is acceptable, it shows only that God cannot *both* determine an F-conditional's truth-value and actualize or instantiate its antecedent, not that he couldn't do either of these alone. Supposedly, given God's free will, there are some possible worlds in which God does not elect to create free persons. Why couldn't he determine the truth-values of F-conditionals in such worlds? Might there not be possible worlds in which God comes upon pre-existent persons who instantiate some diminished possible person and then determines the truth-values of the relevant F-conditionals concerning them? In both kinds of possible world, God does only half the job, determining the truth-values of the F-conditionals, rather than determining only which F-conditionals, if any, get their antecedent instantiated, as is the case in the Plantinga story of creation. Plainly, neither Plantinga nor the theistic tradition in general is willing to countenance such possible worlds, but no one, to my knowledge, has devised any explicit argument against them. Three arguments will now be advanced for the conclusion that God does not determine the truth-values of F-conditionals in any possible world.

The first argument was given by William Wainwright in a letter to me. The following is a modified version of this argument. It attempts to deduce a contradiction from the assumption that God makes any F-conditional true. Let our randomly chosen F-conditional be our old favorite:

F. If *DP* were instantiated, its instantiator would freely do *A*.

Assume for the purpose of indirect proof that

26. God makes it true that if *DP* were to be instantiated, its instantiator would freely do *A*.

This entails the following two propositions:

27. If *DP* were instantiated by God, its instantiator would freely do *A*; and
28. If *DP* were instantiated by God, God would make it true that its instantiator freely does *A*.

Next comes the incompatibilist premise of the FWD:

10. God cannot cause or determine in any way what a created person freely does.

And from the conjunction of 10 and 28, it follows that

29. If *DP* were instantiated by God, its instantiator would not freely do *A*.
30. Propositions 27 and 29 are logically inconsistent; and
31. It is not true that God makes it true that if *DP* were instantiated, its instantiator would freely do *A*.

This argument is vulnerable on two counts. The inference of 28 from 26 is dubious; and 30 rests on the controversial law of conditional excluded middle. Still the argument is not without some interest and merit.

The next two arguments, which also appeal to some theological incompatibilist premise, are based upon the following principle concerning God's sovereignty, which I will call the "principle of sovereign type-invariance":

P. If in one world God determines whether or not a certain type of entity exists, happens, or is the case in that world or part thereof then God determines in every world in which he exists whether or not this type of entity exists, and so on, in that world and every part thereof; and, if God determines in any world the truth-value of a proposition, then he determines the truth-value of every proposition of that type in every world in which he exists.

This principle is consistent with 52. It allows there to be types of states of affairs that fall outside the domain of God's sovereignty, such as the existence of abstract entities and the truth of necessary propositions. Although the principle of sovereign type-invariance has never been explicitly stated, I believe that it is implicitly assumed by the traditional accounts of God's sovereignty. The denial of P leads to anomalies. If we permitted God to exercise sovereignty over the existence, say, of rocks in world w but not in another world w' in which he also exists or in one region of w but not another, it would raise anomalous questions: "Why does God's sovereignty extend just that far and no further?" "Why does he have the rock concession in w but not w'?" "Is there someone else who also must get a piece of the action?" Okay Big Al, you control the southside of Chicago and I got the northside.

This is the first argument based upon P:

32. Whether or not there exist free persons, that is, whether or not any F-conditionals have their antecedents instantiated, is the type of thing that falls within God's sovereignty [premise];

33. In some possible world God determines whether any F-conditionals get their antecedent instantiated [from 32];

34. In every world in which God exists, he determines whether any F-conditionals get their antecedent instantiated [from P and 33];

35. In some world God determines that some F-conditional's antecedent is instantiated [premise];

36. It is logically inconsistent for God to determine both that some F-conditional's antecedent is instantiated and its truth-value [one version of theological incompatibilism];

37. In some possible world God does not determine the truth-value of F-conditionals [from 35, 36, and *P*]; and

38. In no possible world does God determine the truth-value of an F-conditional [from *P* and 37].

I believe that this argument does the trick. Its one controversial point is the theological incompatibilist premise 36. It will be argued for when I raise my God-cannot-do-as-much objection to Plantinga's FWD.

The second argument based upon *P*, which also appeals to 36, is based on the nature of God's decision whether or not to create free persons. It first attempts to prove that God must have middle knowledge when he makes this decision, and thereby that F-conditionals have truth-values prior to his decision. Next it gives an indirect proof for it being impossible that God be the determiner of these prior truth-values. The argument, formally mounted, goes this way:

34. In every world in which God exists, he determines whether any F-conditionals get their antecedent instantiated [from *P* and 33];

39. It would be reckless to decide whether or not to instantiate an F-conditional's antecedent without first knowing its truth-value [premise];

40. An omnibenevolent being would never make a reckless decision [premise];

41. God is essentially omnibenevolent [premise];

42. God would never make a reckless decision [from 40 and 41];

43. In every possible world in which God exists, he knows the truth-values of the F-conditionals prior to his deciding whether or not to instantiate any of their antecedents[35] [from 39 and 42];

44. In every possible world in which God exists, F-conditionals have truth-values prior to God's deciding whether or not to instantiate any of their antecedents [from 43];

45. In some possible world God determines the truth-values of the F-conditionals prior to his decision whether or not

to instantiate any F-conditional's antecedent [assumption for indirect proof];

46. God's determining the truth-values of the F-conditionals is in effect a decision not to actualize any of their antecedents [from 36];

47. God decides not to instantiate the antecedent of any F-conditional prior to his decision whether or not to instantiate any F-conditional's antecedent [from 45 and 46];

48. There is no possible world in which God determines the truth-values of the F-conditionals prior to his decision whether or not to instantiate any F-conditional's antecedent [from 45 to 48 by indirect proof]; and

49. There is no possible world in which God determines the truth-values of the F-conditionals [from 44 and 48].

This third argument for thesis III is far less compelling than the second one. The premise 40 claim that an omnibenevolent being would never make a reckless decision – a decision whose outcome is unknown – will be seen to be the basis for an objection to any version of a FWD sans middle knowledge; and it will be found to be without plausibility. In spite of misgivings about the first and third arguments, I believe that together these three arguments make out a pretty good case for thesis III.

If God does not determine the truth-values of the F-conditionals, who or what does? There is an answer to this that is implicit in the Platonic ontology employed in Plantinga's FWD. Since possible persons, including diminished possible persons, are sets of abstract properties, they exist in every possible world, as do all abstracta. Abstract entities have both essential and accidental properties. The number 2 has the property of being even in every possible world but has the property of being Igor's favorite object in only some. Our old friend, diminished possible person *DP*, being a set of properties, has the property of containing the same properties in every possible world, such as the property of being free with respect to *A*. However, it also has some accidental properties, among which is the following: being-such-that-if-it-were-instantiated-its-instantiator-would-freely-do-A. In some worlds it has it and in others not. In virtue of this, the F-conditional, that if *DP* were instantiated, its instantiator would freely do *A*, is true in some worlds but not others. It is all right to call this funny property of *DP* a "dispositional property" provided we are clear that it is not a disposition of *DP* to freely perform *A* if instantiated (abstract entities, with the possible exception of God, cannot perform actions) but a disposition to have its instantiator freely do *A*.

But what, it will be asked, determines whether a diminished person has one of these funny dispositions? As they used to say in the Bronx, "Don't ask!" Here's where the regress of explanations hits the brick wall of brute, unexplainable contingency. There are no further elephants or tortoises upon whose back this contingency rests. This brings to a close our account of how those "damned F-conditionals" enter into Plantinga's FWD, and we are now in a position to consider objections to this defense.

Objections to Plantinga's FWD

The omnipotence objection. In Plantinga's story of creation, the F-conditionals are God's kryptonite, limiting his power in a similar way to that in which fate limits the powers of the Greek gods. In both cases there is a force or power above and beyond the control of individuals that limits their powers to do what they want. The idea that God must be lucky, that he must be dealt a favorable poker hand of F-conditional facts, if he is to be able to realize his first choice – the creation of a universe containing moral good sans moral evil – strikes some as blasphemous, as a radical distortion of the orthodox concept of God's omnipotence.

Has Plantinga gone too far in watering down God's omnipotence? There is some cause for alarm. It isn't that the limitations placed upon God clearly violate the 5_2 (and O_3 and O_4) account of omnipotence, for there is a way in which the theological incompatibilist can read "God brings it about that all persons always freely do right" that renders it logically inconsistent. It is rather that the limitations placed on God's power do not adhere to Plantinga's own claim that "roughly, there are no non-logical limits to God's power" (NN 167 and GFE 17). One would think that a logical limitation to God's power is one that he is subject to in every possible world in which he exists. For example, in no possible world is God able to bring it about that there exists a squared circle or that $2 + 2 = 5$. But whether God is able to instantiate a possible person containing the property of always freely doing what is right varies across possible worlds in which he exists. God's being subject to such a contingent limitation is quite different from and more worrisome than his being subject to "logical," that is, world-invariant, limitations. It looks like we are getting close to violating the spirit if not the letter of the principle of sovereign type-invariance.

Because of this contingent limitation in God's power, it no longer can be deduced that

6₁. The actual world is the best of all (logically) possible worlds

from the fact that God is omnipotent and omnibenevolent, and an omnibenevolent being attempts to bring about the best overall situation he can. Rather, it follows only that

6₃. The actual world is the best of all contingently possible worlds.

In thus avoiding Leibniz's lapse, we might be falling prey to Plantinga's lapse.

While Plantinga might be guilty of not fully facing up to the extent of the limitations he places on God's omnipotence, there still is a case to be made out for his contingent-limitation account. William Wainwright, in a very sharp paper, tries to make out this case.[36] He correctly points out that historically, the concept of omnipotence has been imprecise and took some note of the need to limit God's power so as to accommodate creaturely freedom. This provides a precisification of the concept of omnipotence some room within which to maneuver. Finally, he says of worlds in which God is screwed by the contingent truth-values of the F-conditionals that he is less lucky in those worlds but not less perfect than in those worlds in which their truth-values allow him to realize his first choice. In the latter-type world, "he would perhaps be *better off* but it is not clear that he would be *better.*"[37] The problem with this is that it understands God's perfection solely in terms of his benevolence. If meaning well is all that is required of a perfect being, we wind up with a lot of bungling, incompetent "perfect" beings.

Maybe the best response to the omnipotence objection is that while Plantinga's account of omnipotence is not every theist's cup of tea, it might be the one that will prove most digestible and healthy for theism in its effort to construct an adequate defense. As pointed out in Chapter 1, there is a tremendous conceptual gap between the notion of "God almighty" in the Old Testament and its highly theoretic reconstruction by the great traditional theists. For this reason, the contemporary theologian must not be frozen by fear of offending against "orthodoxy," that is, the theories of these traditional theists, any more than present-day physicists should fear disagreeing with past physicists. In every area of human endeavor that allows for some form of measurement or evaluation of performance, we find progress. Why should philosophy be any different?

God-can-do-more objections. So far we have not challenged Plantinga's various theological incompatibilist claims, most notably premise

10. God cannot cause or determine in any way what a created person freely does; and
36. It is logically inconsistent for God to determine both that some F-conditional's antecedent is instantiated and its truth-value.

We shall critically evaluate three objections by the theological compatibilist to such incompatibilism: the Gabby Hayes objection; the God's-grace objection; and the just-in-the-nick-of-time objection.

The Gabby Hayes objection. One strategy available to the theological compatibilist, which has been vigorously pushed in recent times by Nelson Pike, is to object that Plantinga gives a misleading description of what God must do in order to assure that created persons always freely do right. Pace Plantinga, he does not create free persons and then cause them freely to do various actions, which would be inconsistent. Instead he creates people that he foreknows will freely do these actions. According to Pike he is like the employer who hires those whom he knows will do a good job on their own rather than one who hires them and then makes them do a good job. This presents us with the "enabling" view of God's creation of free persons and assures us that it is necessarily within God's power to instantiate the do-gooder-type possible persons, given that there are possible persons containing the property of always freely going right.

Pike supports this enabling view of creation by an analogy between God's instantiating a possible person containing the property of always freely doing right and the opening of the door of a cage that releases persons whom one foreknows will always freely go right.[38] This analogy relegates God to a minor Gabby Hayes-type role – a roustabout in a rodeo who merely opens the chute of a stall (as he delivers one of his immortal lines, "Okay, men, let's cut her loose!") enabling John Wayne to gain entrance onto the floor of the arena so that he can flawlessly ride his bucking bronco, as Gabby knew he would.[39]

Unfortunately, this analogy limps on all four hoofs. To make God out to be a Gabby Hayes-type enabler hides from us the extent of his control over the behavior of created persons. When Gabby cuts John Wayne loose so that he can gain entrance into the arena, his action is only a necessary cause of Wayne's subsequent brilliant performance. Gabby did not create or determine the additional causal factors that also were necessary for this performance, especially the ones internal to Wayne, such as his strength, skill, and courage: The 20th Century Fox studio created those. But when God creates free persons, he does determine all of their physical and psychological powers and dispositions, which play such an important role in determining their behavior, be it on a Libertarian or causal compatibilist theory. Even worse, God's willing that a certain possible people be instantiated is alone a sufficient cause not only of the existence of concrete people but also of their instantiating each and every property included in these possible people, including properties like freely-doing-*A*. Whereas Gabby's opening of the chute was only one among many necessary causes of Wayne's brilliant ride, God's will alone is a sufficient cause of all actions performed by created persons. God is a predeterminer, not just a foreknowing enabler. That God does not create the *abstract* persons he instantiates is irrelevant to whether he assumes a freedom-canceling control via his predetermining will over the *concrete* persons he creates.[40]

Another misleading aspect of the analogy is the assimilation of God's instantiating possible persons to the opening of a cage's door. Since there necessarily exist possible persons containing the property of always freely going right, we are assured that there is a cage in which are contained a bunch of do-gooder intentioned creatures just dying to get out so that they can help old ladies across the street and mow their neighbor's lawn gratis. All that remains is for Gabby to "cut 'em loose." But whereas we can understand what might prevent Gabby from being able to open the door – he had uttered his famous line "Make mine a whiskey, and make it quick!" once too often and was immobilized with the DTs – we cannot imagine what could prevent God from being able to open the door. And Pike thinks this destroys the FWD. What Pike conveniently leaves out of his charming rodeo analogy is the role played by those damned F-conditionals – the very heart of the FWD. While Plantinga readily concedes that it is necessary that there are possible persons containing the property of always freely doing right, he denies that it is necessary that any one of them have a diminished possible person that has the funny dispositional property of being-such-that-if-it-were-instantiated-its-instantiator-would-always-freely-do-right. It is a contingent matter, necessarily beyond God's control according to thesis III, whether any of them have such a diminished possible person. If by some unfortunate luck none of them do, then God is unable to "open the door" of the goody-goody cage. In possible worlds in which the F-conditionals have unfavorable truth-values, God is no better off than a DT-immobilized Gabby Hayes, suffering from Delirium Theologicum in those worlds.

The God's-grace objection. Adams points out that certain eminent past theists, most notably Molina and Suarez, who, like Plantinga, also imputed middle knowledge to God, nevertheless went on to claim that in the case of every created person, God has the power through the knowing use of his grace to get this person freely to do what is right. He quotes Suarez:

> It is alien to the common doctrine . . . and to the divine perfection and omnipotence, and is therefore of itself incredible enough, to say that God cannot predetermine an honorable free act, in particular and with all its circumstances, by His absolute and effective will, the freedom of the created will still being preserved.[41]

Adams endorses this:

> There is an infinite variety of natural and supernatural ways in which God can work on us inwardly, assisting our reasoning, affecting our feelings and perhaps our beliefs and desires, without causally determining our responses.[42]

Since Adams rejects causal compatibilism, I assume that the qualification "without causally determining our responses" means that although God's supernatural grace determines our responses, it does not do so by bringing about conditions that are sufficient event-causes of them. Plantinga could grant that God's behind-the-scenes machinations could render it more likely that a creature will freely do right, but it must stop short of determining such a free act, pace both Suarez and Adams.

Why are Suarez and Adams so sure that God can use his grace to get these persons freely to go right? Is it that they believe that there is no inconsistency in God predetermining this? This is theological compatibilism, and reasons have just been given for rejecting its enabling version of God's creation of free persons. Or are they assuming that the truth-values of the F-conditionals, although not God determined, are always such that there is something God can do that will bring about that these people always freely do right? For example, when God sees W. C. Fields about to freely drink the fatal glass of beer, he remembers that it is true that if W. C. Fields at that moment were to have an image of his sweet wife and children, he would freely refrain from taking it. But this just begs the question against Plantinga's claim that W. C. Fields, along with everybody else, could be the instantiation of a Mr. Hyde or a depraved diminished possible person.

Another way of playing Adams's grace objection is as a variant on the forementioned omnipotence objection, herein the point being that Plantinga's denial that it is logically necessary that God, by the use of his foreknowing grace, can make everyone always freely do right is "alien to the common doctrine" concerning omnipotence, to use Suarez's expression. And to this the answer must be the one already given. Treat the accounts of omnipotence given by Suarez, Aquinas, Plantinga, and so on as so many theories, and then subject them to critical analysis to determine which of them offers the best systematic account of God's nature and relation to the universe, especially its free creatures. We must not prejudge this issue by assuming that the final word was said about this hundreds of years ago, any more than we should assume that the best physicists or high hurdlers existed in the Middle Ages. It is reported that St. Thomas's extreme obesity hurt his times in the high hurdles, though not as much in the low hurdles.

The just-in-the-nick-of-time objection. The theist grants the existence of both morally wrong free choices (and actions) and the suffering of innocent persons that results from them. A defense, accordingly, must be given for both types of evils. The answer of the FWD is that there are possible worlds in which God is contingently unable to create free persons without there being both types of evils. The objection counters that God can use his middle knowledge, which he is conceded to have by the FWD, to prevent both types of evils by stepping in just in the nick of time.

The first type of evil is preventable by God's interceding just before individuals freely make or perform some morally wrong choice or action that God foresees will occur if he does not interfere. When God foresees that they will freely do right, he leaves them alone. By adopting this policy of selective interference, God prevents all moral evil but does not negate the free will of created persons. Thus, he can have his cake and eat it too, pace the FWD. The second type of evil is preventable by God's interceding just after the morally wrong free choice or action occurs so as to causally quarantine the culprits from the surrounding world, rendering them causally impotent like the derelicts I used to pass on my way to school whom I knew were forming the most evil intentions but fortunately were too wasted to carry them out – if only they could have gotten their fingers on that red button, or me for that matter. Again, God succeeds in preventing the type of evil in question without negating the free will of created persons.[43]

The Free Will Defender has a ready response to both types of preventive strategies. The objection to the first strategy is that it is logically inconsistent for God to both create free persons and have the intention of preventing them from choosing or performing the morally wrong alternative that their freedom makes available to them. Given that God has this intention and that his will is necessarily effective, they cannot avoid doing what is morally right. But a choice or action is free only if avoidable. Therefore, these created persons aren't free after all.[44] The principle that freedom entails avoidability has not been without doubters, both past and present. There is Locke's famous counterexample of the man locked in a room who gladly and willingly remains because of the delightful company. The moral is that even though his remaining in the room is unavoidable, he still remains there of his own free will.[45] I think that Locke and his supporters are confounding his remaining in the room *gladly* with his remaining there *freely*. It is a fact, a very distressing one, that some people gladly accept being in bondage; just look at the prevalence of "bondage"! Another wrinkle in the Locke example is that the man might be glad to remain in part because he is ignorant of the fact that he cannot leave. Were he to believe that he freely remains, he would be mistaken. That he might be the sort of person who does not mind acting under false beliefs, provided he is conscious in a pleasant manner, is irrelevant to whether he really is free.

Richard Swinburne, in his treatment of evil in *The Existence of God*, gives a rather convincing objection to the causal-quarantining strategy. What is of value according to the moral intuitions of the theist is not having just free will but *significant* free will in virtue of which created persons have control not only over their own life but over other parts of the universe as well, including the well-being and future of their species. Furthermore, if God were always to intervene just in the nick of time, created persons no longer would attach any importance to their possession of free will. They could indulge themselves, knowing that no harm will result: "I have a great idea, dear, let's kill the children." And if it should be suggested that God could take a page out of the book of the Evil Demon and systematically deceive these persons so that they are not aware that "superman" always appears just in the nick of time, the reply is that this is inconsistent with his not being a deceiver.

The God-cannot-do-as-much objection. This objection stands in sharp contrast to the preceding God-can-do-more objections, for it claims that God cannot consistently do as much as he is required to do by the FWD in his creation of free persons. It will be argued at some length that God, in virtue of having middle knowledge, has a freedom-canceling control over created persons. And because these created middlemen aren't free, the buck of moral blame for seeming moral evils cannot stop with them but must reach through to God, which destroys the FWD's attempt to show how God can escape blame, although not responsibility, for these evils. I will begin by making the distinction between blame and responsibility.

In general, a person is responsible for an occurrence that she was *fully able* to prevent, that is, had the power, opportunity, and requisite knowledge to prevent. God, for example, is responsible for moral evil, since he could have prevented it by electing not to create any free persons. An especially pertinent case is that in which a person delegates some of her power to another but retains the power to revoke the delegated power.[46] In a dual-control student-driver car, the instructor can throw a switch that gives the student control over the car but still retain the power to regain control over the car by flipping the switch the other way. If the car should be involved in some foreseeable untoward incident while the student is in control, the instructor, along with the student, is responsible, but it could be that only the student is blameworthy. Whether the instructor shares blame will depend on whether she has a good reason for not having retaken control of the car, for instance, the resulting harm was minor and the student can best learn by being left free to make mistakes.

The relation of God to created free persons is similar. By creating free persons God delegates some of his power to them, but he still retains the power, called "overpower" by Pike, to rescind their power, either in part or wholly. The first version of the just-in-the-nick-of-time objection was based on God having overpower plus middle knowledge. Because God can withdraw his gift of free will – flip the big switch – he is responsible along with created free persons for the moral evil they cause. But, like the driving instructor, he might have a good excuse that frees him from sharing the blame with those to whom he has delegated some of his power. The FWD supplies such an excuse. God can be responsible but not blameworthy for the evils caused by created beings only if they are free. But, I will now argue, they are not according to the Plantinga story of creation. He never succeeded in flipping the switch that gave them the power to freely control their own lives.

The first stage of my argument establishes that God causes the actions of created free persons according to the FWD. I'll begin with a fallacious argument for this that can then be fixed up to work. According to the FWD, when God instantiates a diminished possible person, say *DP*, there is a true F-conditional known to God to the effect that if *DP* were instantiated, its instantiator would freely do *A*. This shows that *DP*'s being instantiated is *sufficient for* the instantiator's freely doing *A*. But God's willing that *DP* be instantiated is *causally sufficient for DP*'s being instantiated. Since causation is transitive, it follows that God's willing that *DP* be instantiated is *causally sufficient for* the instantiator's freely doing *A*.

The fallacy in this argument for God being the cause of a creaturely free action jumps right out at us. *DP*'s being instantiated is only *subjunctive-conditionally sufficient for* the instantiator's freely doing *A*, not *causally sufficient for* it, at least according to the Libertarian account given by the FWD. Since one of the links in the sequence going from God to *A* is noncausal, the principle of the transitivity of causation cannot be applied. By interposing the indeterministic process reported by the F-conditional between God's initial act of will and the eventual doing of *A*, the FWD supposedly cuts the link of causal sufficiency between them. God's act of will is only causally necessary at best for *A*, since if he were not to have willed as he did, *A* would not have occurred.

The first thing that must be done in fixing up this fallacious argument is to show that under certain circumstances, a sufficient cause can reach through the interposition of a relation of subjunctive-conditional sufficiency of an indeterministic sort. Then it will be shown that this very circumstance obtains in the FWD. Consider this stochastic machine: When its button is pressed, a stochastic process, such as the decay of a radioactive element or the spinning of a wheel of fortune, is triggered, the outcome of which determines whether a poisonous gas will be released into a crowded stadium that will result in the deaths of fifty thousand innocent people. It might be necessary to add for you sports fans that they would die before seeing the end of the game, this qualification being necessary so that you are convinced that this is a truly evil outcome. When the button is pressed, either this outcome will ensue or it won't. Therefore, either it is true that if the button were to be pressed, this horrendous outcome would ensue or it is true that if the button were pressed, this outcome would not ensue. Let us assume, furthermore, that we mortals cannot discover by any discursive methods which of these subjunctive conditionals is true, any more than we can for similarly matched F-conditionals.

Imagine the case in which I chance on the scene and inadvertently press the button, resulting in the horrendous outcome. Given that I did not have "middle knowledge" of what would result from pressing the button and did not intend to bring about or even risk bringing about this outcome, I am blameless for the resulting evils. Furthermore, I do not even cause these evils. Were we to infer by appeal to the transitivity of causation that I cause them, we would be guilty of the above fallacy.

Let us change the circumstances so that I now have middle knowledge via some ESP faculty and press the button so as to bring about the deaths. In this case my action is a sufficient cause of the deaths, and is so in spite of the interposition of a stochastic process. Furthermore, I am blameworthy for the deaths, unless I have got a mighty good excuse, for instance, they were British soccer fans.

While there is no doubt that this is what people on the street would say, it might be objected that their concept of causation is confused; for the only difference between the two cases is my psychological state, what I know and intend, and how can this determine whether or not I cause the deaths? If what was at issue was the physicist's concept of causation, this would be a powerful objection. But this is not the concept of causation in question. Rather, it is the forensic one that concerns moral and legal responsibility and blame, which is the very concept that figures in the FWD, since it is concerned with the assignment of responsibility and blame to God and man.

Plantinga could grant that I do cause the deaths in the second case but claim that there is a crucial disanalogy between my relation to the deaths and God's relation to moral evil on his account that shows God not to be the cause of such evil. It is in the nature of the intervening stochastic process. In my case it involves a nonintentional physical process, for instance, the spinning of a wheel of fortune or the like, whereas in the God case it involves the free actions and choices of created persons. This makes all the difference in regard to whether the initial agent is the cause of and blameworthy for the resulting evils. A sufficient cause can reach through an intervening stochastic process only if the initial agent is morally blameworthy for the outcome. In my case there weren't any later free interveners who could be blamed for the deaths, but in God's case there are later free interveners, the created free persons, who can take the "fall" for there being moral evil. And, as a result, I am blameworthy for and thereby the cause of the evil outcome, but God, in virtue of having later free middlemen to take the rap, is neither blameworthy for nor the cause of moral evil.

But it is not clear why causation and blame cannot reach through even a "free choice" stochastic process. Why couldn't both God and the free middlemen be causes of and blameworthy for moral evil? Against this possibility appeal might be made to the Hart–Honore thesis from their *Causation and the Law* that the occurrence of a voluntary or free act between the initial and outcome events "negatives" the former as a cause of the latter, and thereby relieves the initial perpetrator of any blame for the outcome.

This is one of the very few philosophical theses I know of that is plainly false. (In some rare cases philosophy is easy.) The clearest counterinstance is that of the contract murder. In spite of the subsequent free action of the hired killer, the contractor does not escape sharing both causal responsibility and blame for the resulting death.

But Plantinga need not resort to the implausible Hart–Honore thesis to render God blameless for moral evil. While both God and created free persons were fully able to have prevented moral evil, only the latter are to blame for it, since only God could have a morally exonerating excuse for not doing so. God, not they, is the creator of the universe, and thus he alone could say that his allowing such evil was the price that had to be paid for there existing any free persons at all, which is something like my "They were British soccer fans!" excuse for intentionally pushing the button. In both cases, the evil in question was necessary for the realization of an outweighing good.

Notice that the response that has been made on Plantinga's behalf does not claim that God does not cause moral evil, only that he is not blameworthy for it since he has an excuse that cannot be available to created free middlemen. This excuse collapses if these middlemen are not free, since then the buck of blame could not stop with them. And this is just what I will now argue.

Since God creates free persons with middle knowledge of what will ensue, he sufficiently causes the free choices and actions of these persons. This alone does not negate the freedom with which these acts are done, for one person can cause another to act without thereby rendering the act unfree. As a rule, the more that the external event only triggers a deep-seated character trait or natural disposition of the agent, the less difficulty there is in treating it as not abrogating the free will of the affected agent.[47] When I induce a person of amorous nature to call Alice for a date by telling him that she is desirous of going out with him, I cause him to act but do not usurp his free will since prominent among the causes of his action are his own deep-seated character traits, which were not imposed on him by me. I didn't have to "work on him" – drug, hypnotize, brainwash him – to call Alice. Unfortunately, God's way of causing created persons to act is not of this innocent sort. It is freedom canceling.

My argument for this is anthropomorphic in that it applies the same freedom-canceling principles that apply to man–man cases to the God–man case. Whether it is permissible to reason in this anthropomorphic manner will be considered subsequently. Obviously, any analogy between man and God will be an imperfect one, since there are such striking disanalogies between the two. For this reason I do not see my argument as in any way conclusive. At best, it might take the smirk off the face of a Free Will Defender and replace it with a worried grin. I will try to derive these freedom-canceling principles by examining paradigm cases in which one human or finite person has a freedom-canceling control over another.

The case of the sinister cyberneticist. Imagine a *Stepford Wives*-type situation in which a cyberneticist operates on his wife's brain or replaces it with a preprogrammed computer analogue, so that he can inculcate in his wife the desired psychological makeup comprising various desires, wants, dispositions, and so on. As a consequence, she is always amorous, anxious to cook, clean, and so on. To an uninformed observer her actions will appear free and voluntary, since they emanate from and are explainable by her own psychological makeup. But her cyberneticist husband has imposed this makeup on her. Her lack of freedom of the will is not due to the fact that this makeup has been determined by factors external to herself (no man being either an island or a *causa sui*), but rather to the manner in which it has been determined, namely, through the machinations of another person for the purpose of controlling her responses to stimuli. The cases of the Insidious Hypnotist- and *Manchurian Candidate*-type Barbaric Brainwasher who have gained a habitual ascendancy over the will of another by inculcating in them a certain psychological makeup are similar.

Our intuitions about these cases suggest the following freedom-canceling sufficient condition for man–man cases:

C_1. If M_1's actions and choices result from psychological conditions that are intentionally determined by another man M_2, then these actions and choices are not free.

Under these circumstances, M_2 has a freedom-canceling control over M_1, not in virtue of determining M_1's actions and choices, but rather causing M_1 not to have a mind or will of his own. It isn't so much M_1's actions and choices that are not free but M_1 himself; and in virtue of M_1's lack of global freedom, his specific actions and choices are not free.

The case of the evil puppeteer. Stromboli has poor Pinnochio wired up in such a way that he controls his every movement. An observer who fails to notice the wires might falsely believe that Pinnochio's behavior was fully free and voluntary. Stromboli controls Pinnochio, not via having imposed on him an inner network of dispositions, motivations, intentions, and the like, but by exerting a compulsive force over him that renders such inner factors irrelevant. There need not be actual wires connecting the controller with the "puppet." It could be a wireless radio hookup such as exists between a controller and a remote-control toy airplane or between the Horrible Dr. Input and a brain in a vat that in turn has a radio-control hookup with a shell body in the manner described in Daniel Dennett's "Where Am I?"

By a coincidence that rivals that of the preestablished harmony case, it could be the case that every time the external controller causes the puppet to perform some movement, the puppet endeavors on its own to perform this movement. This is a case of causal overdetermination in which there is more than one sufficient cause of a given occurrence. While the puppet's action is unavoidable in that it would have made this movement even if it had not endeavored to, there are those, like Locke, who would still call it free. Reasons have already been given for rejecting their claim.

What is it about these cases that makes us say the controller, be it the Evil Stromboli or the Horrible Dr. Input, has a freedom-canceling control? It is that most of the "victim's" behavior is caused by and subject to the whim of the controller. This suggests that

C_2. M_2 has a freedom-canceling control over M_1 if M_2 causes most of M_1's behavior.

Is God's relation to created persons in the FWD such that it satisfies C_1 and/or C_2? If it satisfies either, no less both, the FWD is in trouble, as would be the soul-building defense as well. I submit that it satisfies both, and thus it is time for the nervous smile to replace the smirk.

It is clear that it satisfies C_1, since according to the FWD, God intentionally causes a created free person to have all of her freedom-neutral properties, which include her psychological makeup. The Free Will Defender will make the Libertarian claim that these inner traits only "incline," but do not causally determine, the person to perform various actions or act in a certain regular manner, but this does not make the God–man case significantly disanalogous to the type-1 man–man cases; for even if we imagine that our intentional psychological-trait inducers could render it only probable according to various statistical laws that their victims would behave in certain characteristic ways, they still would exercise a global freedom-canceling control in which the person is rendered nonfree due to her not having a mind of her own.

The God–man relation in the FWD also satisfies C_2; for, when God instantiates diminished possible persons or sets of freedom-neutral properties, he does have middle knowledge of what choices and actions will result, and thereby sufficiently causes them. And he does so quite independently of whether or not he is blameless for the untoward ones among them.

Because God sufficiently causes the actions of created persons, Plantinga's attempt to distinguish between "determinate" (i.e., freedom-neutral) and "indeterminate" properties at page 195 of PA in terms of what God can and cannot cause a person to have, as well as his distinction between God's "strongly" and "weakly" actualizing a state of affairs at page 173 of NN in terms of what God does and does not cause to be actual, do not work; for whatever God weakly actualizes he sufficiently causes to be actual. At page 49 of SP, he draws the distinction between strong and weak actualization in a way that does not rest on the cause–not cause distinction:

Let us say that God *strongly* actualizes a state of affairs S if and only if he causes S to be actual and causes to be actual every contingent state of affairs S^* such that S includes S^*; and let's say that God *weakly* actualizes a state of affairs S if and only if he strongly actualizes a state of affairs S^* that subjunctive-conditionally implies S.

These new definitions allow for God's willing that some diminished possible person be instantiated being *a* sufficient cause of the instantiator freely doing A. The basis of the distinction between strong and weak actualization now is between God's act of will being *the* (sole) sufficient cause of an event and its being only *a* sufficient cause due to there being a free middleman whose will is also a sufficient cause of it.

Plantinga would agree that *if* God's relation to created persons satisfies C_2, he has a freedom-canceling control, for he has said that "If God *causes* them always to do only what is right, then they don't do what is right freely" (SP 45). But Plantinga might be conceding too much in accepting C_2.

There are at least two objections to C_2. David Blumenthal has offered an interesting objection to C_2. He begins by asking us to imagine that M_1 is "massively ignorant" in that for every action M_1 performs, there is an unknown fact such that if M_1 were to have known it, M_1 would have refrained from doing it. There is another person M_2 who knows all of these facts that are unknown to M_1. So far there is no problem about M_2 having a freedom-canceling control over M_1. Although M_2 has the power to cause all of M_1's actions by feeding M_1 the relevant facts at the right time, M_2 does not actually exercise this power. We are now to imagine that M_2 exercises this power by informing M_1 on every occasion of the relevant unknown fact, thereby causing all of M_1's actions. We have already seen that I can cause someone to call Alice for a date by informing him of some relevant unknown fact without usurping his free will in doing so. Why can't I similarly cause all of his actions without thereby negating his free will in doing them?

This slide from some to all is suspect. People have different intuitions about the all case. Michael Slote suggested that M_1 would feel dependent upon M_2's ubiquitous timely advice, so much so as to feel bereft of the sort of independence that is necessary for being free. Just think of the cold sweat that would engulf M_1 if he were called on to act before M_2 called him. He could say to M_2 what many a mother has said to her offspring, "What's the matter, you never call." M_1 would have the same sort of radical doubts about his own agency as he would if M_2 were correctly to predict his every action, in spite of his best efforts to falsify them.

Be this as it may, God's way of causing our actions in Plantinga's FWD is less benign than is M_2's, for God's instantiating a diminished person alone *sufficiently* causes all of the instantiator's actions. (The truth of the relevant F-conditional is not among the causes of these acts, since a proposition cannot cause anything.) To be on the safe side, C_2 might be narrowed so that it is required that M_2 sufficiently cause most of M_1's behavior.

Another objection to C_2, even in its narrow version, is that for M_2 to have freedom-canceling control over M_1, it is not enough that M_2 sufficiently cause most of M_1's behavior: M_2 also must have *counterfactual control* over M_1 in virtue of which M_2 can cause M_1 to behave in ways other than those in which M_1 in fact behaves. Whereas Stromboli and Dr. Input have this additional counterfactual control over their victims, God does not have it over created persons; for while God causes the instantiator of *DP* to do *A*, he does not have the power to cause this instantiator to do other than *A*, given that it is true that if *DP* were instantiated, its instantiator would freely do *A*. God could have prevented the instantiator from doing *A* by not instantiating *DP*, but this is not causing the instantiator to do other than *A* – nonexistent persons do not act.

Granted that there is this disanalogy between God and our finite controllers in that only the latter have this sort of counterfactual control, what follows? Not that God does not have freedom-canceling control over created persons in virtue of satisfying C_2 (as well as C_1), but that there is a stronger sufficient condition for having freedom-canceling control that he does not satisfy, namely,

C_3. M_2 has a freedom-canceling control over M_1 if M_2 causes most of M_1's behavior and also has the counterfactual power to cause M_1 to act differently from the way in which M_1 in fact acts.

But that there is this *additional* sufficient condition for one man to have a freedom-canceling control over another does not show that C_2 and C_1 are not also each sufficient conditions; for, in general, to satisfy one sufficient condition for being X does not require satisfying every sufficient condition for being X.

The objector might retort that having counterfactual control is necessary for having freedom-canceling control: The "if" in C_3, accordingly, is to be replaced by "only if." This is not particularly plausible for two reasons. First, if C_3 is turned into a necessary condition, it follows that C_1 is unacceptable and that, therefore, the Sinister Cyberneticist and the like do not have freedom-canceling control, which is not what we want to say. Second, God, although lacking counterfactual control, has an additional power over created persons that Stromboli and Dr. Input do not have – God both creates and determines the psychological makeup of his "victims." This additional power of God should at least counterbalance his lack of counterfactual power and thereby make him at least as good a candidate as our finite controllers for having freedom-canceling control.

Furthermore, it should be obvious by now that the FWD's gambit of having something other than God determine the truth-values of the F-conditionals does not succeed in showing that God does not cause the free acts of created persons. Stromboli and Dr. Input were not excused from being the cause of their victim's behavior because they did only half the job – determined the causally relevant instantial conditions but not which causal laws hold. Analogously, God is not excused from being the cause of the free acts of created persons because he did only half the job – determined which diminished possible persons get instantiated but not the truth-values of the relevant F-conditionals. If this does not convince you, try these counterfactual thought experiments. Our finite controllers do only half the job by determining which causal laws hold after they come upon their victim in some instantial state, and God does only half the job by determining the truth-values of the F-conditionals after he comes upon concrete instantiations of various diminished possible persons. Certainly, we want to say of both God and the finite controllers in these thought experiments that they cause their victim's behavior and have a freedom-canceling control in virtue of C_2 alone.

So far, it appears that God's relation to created persons satisfies both C_1 and C_2 (but not C_3) and that he thereby has a freedom-canceling control over them. But there still remain some disanalogies between the God–man and man–man cases that have not been explored. One of them concerns the fact that the finite controllers in our type 1 and 2 cases were a sinister bunch who meant no good for their victims, whereas God is benevolent and intends the best for his created beings. This makes no difference in regard to having freedom-canceling control but only in how the movie is titled. One is titled "The Horrible (Sinister, Insidious, Barbaric) Dr. Input (Cyberneticist, Hypnotist, Brainwasher)" while the other is titled "The Incredible (Fabulous, etc.) Supernatural Predeterminer." One is a horror movie, and the other is not; but neither involves free persons.

Another tack is to argue that God's relation to man is so disanalogous to man's relation to man as to render the freedom-canceling principles, such as C_1 and C_2, that hold for the latter inapplicable to the former. It is not just that God is quite different from men – in the lingo of the streets, "He is something else!" – but that he is different in just those respects that make these principles inapplicable to his relation to created persons. He is literally out of it, not a part of the universe. No insult intended, but he is as unnatural as you can get; in fact, he is supernatural. He does not cramp our elbow room in the way in which finite men do. Unlike these universe mates who block our path and physically compel and coerce us, God is not pushing, elbowing, or kneeing anyone in the subway, or putting a gun to anyone's head ("Your money or your salvation!"). In these respects he is crucially unlike our bevy of sinister finite controllers. These people ride herd on their fellowman. God does not do so (shades of Gabby Hayes and John Wayne again). This is not an epistemological point concerning our being unaware of God's causal efficacy in bringing about things in the world, but an ontological one having to do with the radical difference in the way his causal efficacy works from that in which a finite controller's works.

It is just such antianthropomorphic considerations that are at the foundation of theological compatibilism. And I am very sympathetic to them. Were I to be a theologian in my next reincarnation as a result of my sinful life in this one, this is the line I would run. Unfortunately, Plantinga cannot avail himself of this strategy for averting the objection that God assumes a freedom-canceling control over created persons in his FWD. The reason is that his FWD must take the anthropomorphic route in its rejection of theological compatibilism, for it claims that God cannot determine the free acts of persons without negating their freedom. And the only basis for this claim is that if one man were to do this to another, it would be freedom canceling. In other words, God cannot get away with determining the free actions of men, because this would violate C_1 and/or C_2 – the very principles that operate in man–man cases.

We cannot allow Plantinga to be a good-time anthropomorphist: to reason anthropomorphically when warding off the objection of the theological compatibilist, and then refuse to do so for the purpose of rebutting the charge that God has assumed a freedom-canceling control over created persons. Thus, Plantinga is caught on the horns of a dilemma. If he reasons anthropomorphically, his FWD collapses because it imputes to God a freedom-canceling control over created persons. And if he does not reason anthropomorphically, again his FWD collapses, this time because it has no reply to the objection of the theological compatibilist. But either he reasons anthropomorphically or he does not. Therefore, his FWD collapses.

But it would be quite premature for me to write "Q.E.D." after my above argument for the God-cannot-do-as-much objection that Plantinga's FWD is logically inconsistent; for Plantinga, or one of his followers, could mount a counter-argument for why God does not cause the free actions of created persons in his story of creation. One such counter-argument, which I owe to the fertile minds of Jonathan Dancy and Donald Turner, goes as follows: They begin by taking seriously Plantinga's claim that when God creates free persons, he leaves it up to them what they shall freely do. This has the consequence that it is they who determine the truth-values of F-conditionals through their own free actions. A consequence of this view is that F-conditionals that do not get their antecedent instantiated are truth-valueless. Since an F-conditional has its antecedent instantiated in some but not all possible worlds, an F-conditional is not necessarily either true or false: In the actual world there are F-conditionals that are neither true nor false. This is not such a bizarre result as to totally discredit their argument, since F-conditionals are such queer birds. My argument for God being the sufficient cause of all the actions of created persons was based on Plantinga's thesis II that God has middle knowledge when he created them. But, Dancy and Turner urge, the actions of these persons is the cause of their middle knowledge – their knowing the F-conditionals in question. God's decision to instantiate an F-conditional's antecedent is determined or explained by his middle knowledge of what will result from his doing so. Therefore, God's decision to instantiate an F-conditional's antecedent is caused or explained by the instantiator's action, rather than vice versa as I would have it; and, thereby, God is not the cause of this action, since we are not going to allow a circle of causes or explanations.

The following is an explicit mounting of their argument:

50. An F-conditional is made true or false by the instantiator's action [premise];
51. God's decision to instantiate the antecedent of an F-conditional is determined or explained by his middle knowledge [premise];
52. God's middle knowledge is determined or explained by the action of the instantiator [from 50];
53. God's decision to instantiate the antecedent of an F-conditional is determined or explained by the instantiator's action [from 51 and 52]; and
54. God's decision to instantiate the antecedent of an F-conditional does not determine or explain the instantiator's action, that is, is not the cause of this action [from 53 in virtue of causation being asymmetric].

The Dancy–Turner argument is clearly in the spirit of Plantinga's FWD, especially in its imputation of middle knowledge to God at the time or stage at which he deliberates about instantiating the antecedents of different F-conditionals. At that time or stage, he is fully apprised of the truth-values of every F-conditional that has a truth-value, which, according to premise 50 of the Dancy–Turner argument, means every F-conditional whose antecedent he will instantiate, since only they have a truth-value.

This can be shown to lead to a contradiction. My reductio argument will avail itself of an omnitemporal God that engages in deliberation prior to his creative decision, but everything I say can be recast in terms of a timelessly eternal God and the order of explanation or determination in his nontemporal deliberation and decision (see note 35 on this point). My argument is as follows:

55. It is impossible that an agent deliberate while knowing what decision she will make or knowing of an event for which her decision is a causally necessary condition [premise];

56. God's instantiation of an F-conditional's antecedent is a causally necessary condition for the existence of its instantiator, as well as its subsequent action [premise];

57. It is impossible that while God deliberates about instantiating an F-conditional's antecedent, he know either that its instantiator exists or that it performs some action [from 55 and 56];

58. God has middle knowledge while he deliberates about instantiating an F-conditional's antecedent [Plantinga's thesis II and granted by premise 51 of the Dancy–Turner argument];

59. God has middle knowledge of an F-conditional only if he instantiates its antecedent [from premise 50 of the Dancy–Turner argument];

60. It is possible that there is some F-conditional such that while God deliberates about instantiating its antecedent, he already knows whether or not he decides to instantiate it [from 58 and 59]; and

61. It is impossible that there is some F-conditional such that while God deliberates about instantiating its antecedent, he already knows whether or not he decides to instantiate it [from 57].

I conclude that my God-cannot-do-as-much objection has considerable force against the Plantinga version of the FWD, since it imputes middle knowledge to God. Without it, God's instantiating the antecedent of a true F-conditional would no longer count as a case of his causing the instantiator to do what the consequent reports. Created persons, then, could serve as the sole suitable scapegoats for moral evil. This naturally gives rise to the question whether a viable version of a FWD can be constructed that denies middle knowledge to God.

Versions of the FWD sans middle knowledge

Since God's middle knowledge is comprised of the conjunction of

I. Every F-conditional has a contingent truth-value; and

II. God knows the truth-value of all F-conditionals prior to his creative decision,

there will be two ways of constructing a FWD sans middle knowledge. The first version, which is ably championed by Adams, denies thesis I and thereby II, since not even an omniscient being can know what isn't true. This renders God blameless for permitting moral evil, since he could not have known in advance the moral evils that would result from his creation of free persons. The second version, which is hinted at by Plantinga on page 52 of SP, accepts thesis I but denies II, again rendering God blameless in virtue of an excusable lack of knowledge. Herein there was something to be known, unlike the first version, but there was no way in which God could have divinely known it. God winds up as a hockey parent after all.

Because both versions have God instantiate the antecedent of F-conditionals without foreknowledge of what the created persons will freely do, they face the objection that God is acting in a recklessly immoral way by shooting craps at our expense.[48] The reckless objection has already been adumbrated by these two premises in the third argument for thesis III:

39. It would be reckless to decide whether or not to instantiate an F-conditional's antecedent without first knowing its truth-value; and

40. An omnibenevolent being would never make a reckless decision.

An omnibenevolent being would not create free persons without middle knowledge because it would be immoral to take such a risk.

No red-blooded theist would accept the wimpy moral intuition underlying the reckless objection and would give God's creation of free persons in both versions as a counterexample. The objection also faces an ad hominem-type rebuttal in that no existent person, except for a few gripers, are apt to make it; for, if God hadn't elected to roll the dice, they wouldn't even exist, and, supposedly, they are glad that they do.[49]

Although both versions make the same excusable lack of knowledge excuse available to God, they differ significantly in their epistemological and metaphysical underpinnings, and thus require separate consideration. The outcome of our discussion will be that both versions face formidable objections: The first version, because of its denial of thesis I, renders it anomalous how God is able to create any free persons; and the second version waters down God's omniscience in an unacceptably anthropomorphic manner.

First version. Adams develops this version in the course of defending the attack on middle knowledge by certain late-sixteenth-century Dominicans against their Jesuit opponents, Molina and Suarez. Adams's denial of thesis I is built upon the Libertarian account of F-conditionals, according to which the act reported by the consequent is neither causally determined nor determined by anything other than the instantiator of the antecedent. Given this account, he does not see how an F-conditional could possibly be true. Thus, it appears to be logically or conceptually impossible for it to be true and therefore it necessarily lacks a truth-value. Unlike the "neuter" or "indeterminate" propositions of Lukasiewicz, it does not become true or false with the passage of time. Adams says that he doubts if they "ever were, or ever will be, true."[50] This means that even if the antecedent should be instantiated and the instantiator subsequently perform the action reported by its consequent, the F-conditional does not become true. And a fortiori this sequence of events does not show that the F-conditional was true all along, for there is no present truth to cast a backward shadow. Adams gives us a choice between F-conditionals being necessarily false and being necessarily neither-true-nor-false. The common denominator of these options is that F-conditionals necessarily are not true.

Adams's argument for the denial of thesis I is not made fully explicit. One who denies thesis I is typically a warranted-assertibility theorist who holds a proposition to be true only if it is in principle epistemically supportable. But this isn't Adams's line, for he says that a proposition reporting a future contingent (e.g., the sea fight tomorrow, which we finally know didn't happen since Khrushchev decided not to challenge Kennedy's blockade of Cuba), although in principle not warrantedly assertible, "can be true by correspondence to the actual occurrence of the event they predict."[51] This suggests that for Adams a necessary condition for a proposition being true is that it have an external correspondent. The "external" qualification precludes the correspondent of the proposition that p being the fact that p; for, given that a fact is a true proposition, this would make that p the correspondent of that p.

In the previous discussion of III, it was suggested that for Plantinga the external correspondent of the true F-conditional, that if DP were instantiated, its instantiator would freely do A, is the abstract diminished possible person DP having the funny dispositional property of being-such-that-if-it-were-instantiated-its-instantiator-would-freely-do-A. According to Adams's commentary, Suarez also held this view. While not objecting to this account's Platonism, Adams objects that he does not

> have any conception, primitive or otherwise, of the sort of *habitudo* or property that Suarez ascribes to possible agents with respect to their acts under possible considerations.[52]

This autobiographical fact hardly constitutes a refutation of the Suarez–Plantinga position. The rejection of a position by saying "I do not quite understand this" has mercifully gone the way of rejection by appeal to desert landscapes. Not being able to understand is not always an achievement. I suspect that the reason Adams does not understand what it is for a diminished possible person to have one of the "dispositional" properties is that he does not see how an F-conditional can be true, and his reason for this will emerge in our discussion of whether thesis I is true, to which we now turn.

In our previous defense of thesis I, which was relativized to the premises of Plantinga's FWD, it was shown that for Plantinga, I is a consequence of the law of excluded middle:

> Our question is really whether there is something Curley would have done (had he been offered the bribe). . . . The answer . . . is obvious and affirmative. There is something Curley would have done, had that state of affairs obtained (NN 181).

If *DP* were instantiated, given that its instantiator has the disjunctive property of either-freely-doing-*A*-or-freely-refraining-from-doing-*A*, its instantiator either freely does *A* or freely refrains. Thus, it is either true that

F. If *DP* were instantiated, its instantiator would freely do *A*; or true that

F′. If *DP* were instantiated, its instantiator would freely refrain from doing *A*.

So far I cannot find anything to object to. According to Lewis's lemma, if neither F nor F′ is true, it follows that God is unable to instantiate either P or P_1, in which P and P' form an incompatible pair having *DP* in common and differing only in that P contains freely-doing-*A* while P' contains freely-refraining-from-doing-*A*; for if it is not true that if God were to instantiate *DP*, its instantiator would freely do *A*, God is unable to instantiate P, and likewise mutatis mutandis for P_1. And this can be generalized, so that if no F-conditional is true, God cannot instantiate any possible person, which would be the shipwreck of the FWD, since any possible world in which God is morally exonerated for allowing moral evil is one in which he succeeds in creating free persons and thus is able to do so.

Adams, surprisingly for a Free Will Defender, says something that seems to imply that God is unable to instantiate any possible person: "In other words, I deny that God could have made free creatures who *would* always have freely done right."[53] This seems to say that God couldn't have instantiated any possible person containing the property of always freely doing right by instantiating its diminished possible person, because the relevant F-conditionals are not true. I assume that this is why Adams put *"would"* in italics. But this reason for God's being unable to instantiate any goody-goody possible person can be generalized to all possible persons, since no F-conditional is true. Thus, God is unable to instantiate even a Mr. Rogers-type possible person. Adams is not rejecting Lewis's lemma – quite to the contrary. It is exactly because he accepts it and denies thesis I that he reaches the anomalous conclusion that God cannot instantiate any possible person.

Maybe my interpretation of Adams is unduly uncharitable, for certainly as a Free Will Defender he does not want to wind up with this anomalous conclusion. Another way of understanding him is as denying both thesis I and Lewis's lemma, rather than denying thesis I and accepting Lewis's lemma, which resulted in anomaly. On this new interpretation, that God instantiates *DP* and this is followed by the instantiator freely doing *A* entails that God was able to instantiate *P* but not that F was true. But this new position is not without the appearance of anomaly, for it seems obvious that F would be rendered true by this sequence of events. Adams better have a very good argument for why our intuitions deceive us in this matter; however, I can't find any such argument in his essay. I get the feeling that he is making impossible demands on an F-conditional: First, neither its antecedent nor anything else can nomically necessitate its consequent; and, second, for it to be true, there must be this very relation of nomic necessitation between them. That the antecedent probabilize the consequent in virtue of various dispositions and inclinations of the instantiator of *DP* isn't enough.

At this point, Adams, no doubt, will throw the ball back into Plantinga's court and ask him to supply an explanation of how F could possibly be true. Plantinga's previously stated claim that there is something Curley would have done if offered the bribe suggests a "minimalist" account of F-

conditionals. While F-conditionals usually involve a probabi-
lizing relation between their antecedent and consequent due
to a set of freedom-neutral properties often containing dispositional properties, they need not. For an F-conditional to be
true, it suffices (though isn't necessary) that the instantiation
of its antecedent both precede and be necessary for the event
reported by its consequent. This minimalist view could aptly
be called the "stage-setting" account. F is true if the instantiation of *DP* is in fact followed by the instantiator's freely
doing *A*, since the former is necessary for the ensual of the
latter. While the law of conditional excluded middle holds for
stage-setting subjunctive conditionals, it does not apply to all
subjunctives, such as "If I were now to snap my fingers,
Caesar would have freely crossed the Rubicon," in which
there isn't the right sort of conditional–ensual relation, in this
case because there is neither the right sort of temporal order
between what is reported by antecedent and consequent nor
the required stage-setting relation. Because a stage-setting
F-conditional need not involve anything more than the
instantiation of its antecedent both preceding and being necessary for the event reported by its consequent, it will resist
a possible worlds analysis in terms of the closeness relation
between different worlds;[54] for a world in which the instantiator of *DP* freely does *A* and one in which it freely refrains
from doing *A* need not involve any other difference between
them, such as a difference in their deterministic or statistical
laws.

I think that this stage-setting analysis of F-conditionals in
terms of their truth conditions captures the ordinary way
in which they are used and explains why we are perplexed by
the claim that *DP*'s instantiation could be followed by its
instantiator freely doing *A* without it being true that if *DP*
were instantiated, its instantiator would freely do *A*. This is
just as anomalous as saying that God's instantiation of *DP*
could be followed by the instantiator freely doing *A* without
God having been able to instantiate *P*.

Would it help if this first version of a FWD sans middle knowledge were to be changed so as to allow an F-conditional, ini-

174

tially truth-valueless as Adams contends, to become true or false when its instantiator performs her free action? Dancy and Turner, after being confronted with my reductio counterargument to their above argument, developed a variant that is based on this Lukasiewicz manner of viewing F-conditionals. According to their variant on the Adams FWD, an F-conditional lacks a truth-value at the time or stage of God's deliberation, thereby denying thesis II, and acquires a truth-value only after God has instantiated its antecedent and the instantiator does the deed reported by the consequent. (Those that go uninstantiated remain forever truth-valueless – poor devils.) It is still the case that the instantiator makes the F-conditional true; and, moreover, since God lacks middle knowledge, it destroys my God-cannot-do-as-much objection. God is in very much the same situation as the person who touched the button of the stochastic machine in ignorance of what the outcome would be, the only difference being that the former, unlike God, did not know that his action created a certain risk of there being an evil outcome, thereby rendering God, unlike this person, responsible for what ensues. But, supposedly, since it was worth taking the risk, God is rendered blameless for any evil outcome of his "pressing the button." This argument, if successful, establishes that God is not the cause of the actions of created persons, thereby neutralizing my God-cannot-do-as-much objection.

This Dancy–Turner variant on the Adams FWD is subject to the same basic objections. By denying that F-conditionals have any truth-value, and thereby are not true, at the time or stage at which God deliberates and makes his creative decision, it winds up denying Lewis's lemma, just as the Adams FWD did. And this renders it anomalous how God is able to instantiate any possible person, say P, who includes diminished possible person DP and freely doing A; for if it is not true that if DP were to be instantiated its instantiator would freely do A, it seems impossible for God to instantiate P, and similarly for any other possible person you choose. Furthermore, if God instantiates DP and the instantiator freely does

A, the concerned F-conditional thereby "becomes true," as Dancy and Turner maintain. But does this not cast a shadow backward, rendering it true all along that if *DP* were instantiated, its instantiator would freely do *A*, pace their claim? I believe that the only response that can be made to these objections must invoke a warranted assertibility theory of truth; but this runs into the "True" and "Fact" cigarette problem (see footnote 51).

Second version. This version accepts both thesis I and Lewis's lemma, understood in terms of minimalist stage-setting F-conditionals, and thereby escapes both types of anomalies. Its special gimmick is to deny II, thereby enabling God to reply to the newscaster's question by saying that although there was a truth of the matter at the time he deliberated about creating free persons, there was no way he could have known then that these moral evils would result from his decision to instantiate certain diminished possible persons. This second version, because it accepts theses I and III, also makes available to God, in addition to the excuse of ignorance, the I-was-screwed-by-those-damned-F-conditionals excuse of Plantinga's FWD. The latter excuse, of course, could be offered by God only after the fact, not at the time of his creative decision, as it can be in the Plantinga version.

It is plain that in accepting thesis I and rejecting II, the second version rejects the traditional definition of God's omniscience according to which God knows every true proposition and is replacing it with the weaker definition that

O_5. For any proposition p, if it is true that p and it is logically possible that God know that p, then God knows that p.

It was shown in Chapter 3 that O_5 creates a very virulent version of the paradox of perfection in that it winds up imputing to God a lesser degree of omniscience than that possessed by some possible nonperfect being. But there is no reason for the second version to use such a watered-down account of God's omniscience. It can, instead, employ

O_6. For any proposition p, if it is true that p and it is logically possible for anyone to know that p, then God knows that p

in which God's omniscience is not relativized to what it is logically possible for God, a perfect being, to know but to what it is logically possible for anyone to know, thereby eluding the paradox of perfection.

The problem is why is it logically impossible for anyone to know an F-conditional in advance? The answer is that knowledge requires a justificatory explanation and none could be given in advance for an F-conditional, since neither its antecedent nor anything else determines its consequent. This certainly holds true for finite persons, since their knowledge is discursive and thus in need of a justificatory explanation. But God is supposed to know things in his own inimitable supernatural way that is denied to us finite beings, just as he is supposed to be able to do or bring about things that we cannot, such as create things ex nihilo. Moreover, we cannot even conceive of how God knows and does these things, though we can, pace Berkeley, conceive of there being things that we cannot conceive of. Maybe God's justification for believing an F-conditional that has not yet had its antecedent instantiated is that he knows that he is God and thereby omniscient and thus whatever he believes is true. To restrict God's omnipowers to what we can conceive of is a radical anthropomorphizing of God. For this reason a traditional theist cannot adopt this second version.

But this is not the end of the matter, since the "traditional" account of God's omniscience is a theoretical reconstruction of the biblical notion of an all-knowing personal Deity that in spite of his essential omniscience, is through and through temporalistic. Because God is time bound, he does not know everything about the future, such as what future decisions he himself will make[55] and what responses will be made by created persons to his overtures. He periodically turns into Charles Bronson because of his disappointment at these responses. Contemporary process theologians give a theoretical reconstruction of God's omniscience that is closer to the temporalistic God of the Bible. Such a view dovetails nicely with the overall thrust of Chapters 2 and 3 – that a strictly immutable timeless God is a nonperson that is not religiously available.

If the price that must be paid to have an adequate defense of God in the face of moral evil is to go with this biblical-style notion of God's omniscience, then it is worth it. One might worry whether such a sharp divergence from the traditional account does not change the referent of the word "God" from what it had when used by the great medieval theists. If the account in Chapter 1 of how "God" refers is basically correct, the answer is no; for contemporary process theologians are not rejecting any one of God's hard-core properties, such as being that than which none greater can be conceived and being eminently worshipable. They are only giving a different analysis from that given by the medievals of what constitutes the lower-level, soft-core determiners of these hard-core emergent properties. Furthermore, and of greatest importance, they are members of the same ongoing religious community, the role of the God-idea in their religious language game being the same as it was for the medievals.

Chapter 5

The argument from world-relative actuality

This atheological argument differs sharply from the ones considered in the preceding three chapters in two important respects. First, it has never been given before. Second, it fails to undermine in any way the traditional conception of God and therefore is not an occasion for theists to go back to the drawing board and redesign this conception.

Why, then, consider it? The reason is that it brings into clear relief an overlooked feature of this conception concerning God's "absolute actuality." God, as creator, has a standpoint that is "outside" of or independent of possible worlds – the infinitely many different ways that things could be. God's existence or actuality is absolute, not being in any way relative to one of these worlds: He exists or is actual simpliciter. In his role as creator, God contemplates them and makes a unique creative decision as to which one alone shall be actual simpliciter. His choice is unique because, of all the creative choices he might have made, this choice alone is actual simpliciter, not just actual relative to some world. As a result of the absolute nature of God's creative choice, one world has a special sort of ontological honor bestowed upon it consisting in it alone having absolute actuality, that is, being the actual world simpliciter. Thus, the absoluteness of God's perspective as creator is propagated down the line via his unique creative choice to a particular world. And what is more, the universe – the largest spatiotemporal aggregate of objects and events – that is created by his unique actualization

179

of one possible world itself has an absolute, unqualified existence. It exists simpliciter.

This theistic view of actuality and existence as absolute or non-world relative is challenged by David Lewis's extreme version of modal realism according to which *"every way* that a world could possibly be is a way that some world *is."*[1] Logical space is a plenitude of isolated physical worlds, each being the actualization of some way in which a world could be, that bear neither spatiotemporal nor causal relations to each other.[2] This means that no world is *"absolutely* actual" or *"actual simpliciter."*[3] The formal mode version of this thesis is that the predicate "is the actual world (or is actual)" really is a disguised two-place predicate of the form "____ is actual at ____." There is an ontological parity between worlds because for every world w, it is the case that w is actual at w and only at w.[4] No world qualifies, therefore, for the coveted title of being *the* actual world. There is no such title to be won since there is no such thing as being actual simpliciter, "is actual" being a two-place predicate. This is the thesis of ontological parity. Not even God qualifies as being actual simpliciter. His actuality, along with the actuality of his creative choice, also is world relative. He exists in many different worlds; and, for each world w in which he exists, he chooses in w that w be actualized. No one of these creative choices is special or unique, which, if true, completely undermines traditional theism.

The ontological parity thesis helps to clarify and support Lewis's shocking claim that worlds other than the one that we take to be alone actual do not differ in "kind" or their "manner of existing" but only in their contents from this world.[5] Since our world is a maximal aggregate of spatiotemporally related objects and events, so are these other worlds. This results in the plenitude of isolated concrete worlds.

Lewis has another account of what a possible world is in terms of a "way things could have been."[6] The ontological parity thesis not only does not support but undermines this account. From the following four propositions,

1. Other worlds do not differ in kind from the world we take to be actual;
2. Our world is a maximal spatiotemporal aggregate;
3. A spatiotemporal aggregate has a spatiotemporal location determined by the spatiotemporal regions occupied by its parts, that is, it occupies the same spatiotemporal regions as do the objects and events that form its parts; and
4. A way things could have been (or are) has no spatiotemporal location;

it follows that

5. A world is not a way things could have been.[7]

Lewis has an argument for the thesis that actuality is world relative that is based upon the premise that "actual" is an indexical term.[8] This argument, although not intended as such, constitutes the basis of an atheological argument. It is in no way based upon the claim that a possible world is a way things could have been. Peter van Inwagen makes the baffling claim that "Lewis's only argument for the existence of more than one possible world depends upon his identifying worlds with ways things could have been."[9] To be sure, this definition does occur as the key premise in Lewis's preliminary Quinean-style argument for our prima facie ontological commitment to possible worlds in virtue of our quantifying over them when we say that *there are* many ways things could have been.[10] The indexical argument, however, is quite distinct from this argument, although both support the conclusion that there is a plurality of worlds. Van Inwagen errs, therefore, when he speaks of "Lewis's only argument for the existence of more than one possible world."

The indexical argument receives its first and fullest presentation in "Anselm and Actuality."[11] In his later *Counterfactuals* and *On the Plurality of Worlds*, Lewis gives a brief summary of the argument, along with some minor refinements, and refers his reader back to the fuller presentation in "Anselm and Actuality."[12] Accordingly, we will focus on this presentation and bring in the later refinements when relevant.

The key premise of the indexical argument for world-relative actuality is that "actual" and cognate expressions are indexical expressions that are analogous to "now," "here," and "I":

> I *suggest* that "actual" and its cognates should be analyzed as indexical terms: terms whose reference varies, depending on relevant features of the context of utterance. The relevant feature of context, for the term "actual," is the world at which a given utterance occurs. According to the indexical analysis I *propose*, "actual" (in its primary sense) refers at any world w to the world w. "Actual" is analogous to "present," an indexical term whose reference varies depending on a different feature of context: "present" refers at any time t to the time t. "Actual" is analogous also to "here," "I," "you," "this," and "aforementioned" – indexical terms depending for their reference respectively on the place, the speaker, the intended audience, the speaker's acts of pointing, and the aforementioned discourse.[13]

Lewis's use of "I suggest" and "I propose" permits two interpretations. They can be understood as having assertional illocutionary force that is somewhat weaker than that of "I assert (state)." Herein Lewis would be purporting to describe the actual way in which "actual" is used, it being claimed that "actual" functions in the way that indexical terms do in ordinary discourse. Or they can be understood as having the illocutionary force of "I hereby stipulate that." Herein there would be no claim that "actual" is used indexically, only that the author stipulates that he will so use it. If Lewis is only stipulating that we use "actual" in the way in which indexical terms are used, he would be unable to support his ontological parity thesis by this move, since this thesis is about our ordinary concept of actuality – not some made-up one that renders his ontological parity thesis true by definition. Thus, we will interpret Lewis as purporting to describe our ordinary use of "actual." There is, of course, plenty of middle ground between purely descriptive and stipulative definitions, such as revisionary definitions that are justified by various arguments. If Lewis's account were revisionary in this sense, he would have to justify his revision of ordinary usage (e.g., by appeal to his cost–benefit argument adumbrated in footnote 8), and thus the indexical argument would not stand on its own two feet, which supposedly it does.

That "actual" refers at any world w to w is further refined so as to deal with its cognates and their different semantic relations:

> To speak more precisely: at any world w, the name "the actual world" *denotes* or *names* w; the predicate "is actual" *designates* or *is true of* w and whatever exists in w; the operator "actually" is *true of* propositions true at w, and so on for cognate terms of other categories.[14]

Thus, it isn't only "is actual" that is a disguised two-place predicate but also "is true" and "exists": the latter require expansion respectively into "is true in world ____" and "exists in world ____." Ordinarily, when it is said that p is true, it means that p is true in the actual world. Thus, if "is actual" is indexical, so is "is true" and "exists." When what is said to be true or existent is necessary, it will not be important to expand the grammatical one-place predicate, but it is when the item is contingent. It will be futile, therefore, to argue for the monadic nature of actuality by appeal to a monadic concept of truth or existence. An example of such futility is Robert M. Adams's argument that there is only one world that is actual simpliciter because there is only one world that has a *book* containing propositions all of which are true simpliciter, in which a book for a given world is the set of all propositions true in that world, that is, that would be true were that world to be actualized.[15]

Alongside of the world-relative use of "exists," Lewis recognizes an absolute, non-world relative use, though this is not clearly marked out in ordinary language. There is for him an existential quantifier that is totally unrestricted in its domain, ranging over all the possible worlds and their contents. Thus, Lewis can say without contradiction that *there are* (unrestricted) things that do not (actually) exist (restricted).[16] This is analogous to there being a temporal quantifier that is unrestricted among times so that it can be said without contradiction that there are (timelessly) times that are not now present.

If "the actual world" and "is actual" are indexical, there should be some explicitly indexical phrase that can replace them without change of sense. Based on what Lewis says, there appear to be two different indexical expressions that can do this job, one employing "I" and the other the demonstrative "this." According to the first-person parsing, "the actual world" and "is actual" mean, respectively, "the world in which I exist" and "is in the world in which I exist." The following quotations speak in favor of this construal:

> If we take an a priori point of view and ignore our own location among the worlds the big difference between the actual world and other worlds should vanish.[17]

> I said that when I use it, 'actual' applies to my world and my worldmates; that is, to the world I am part of and to other parts of that world.[18]

When discussing the above distinction between the restricted and unrestricted quantifiers, he says that

> they may be restricted to our own world and things in it. Taking them as thus restricted, we can truly say that there exist[s] nothing but our own world and its inhabitants.[19]

Furthermore, Lewis's reply to Adams's indifference argument rests on such a first-person analysis. Adams's objection to the ontological parity thesis is that it is unable to account for our strong want or preference that the actual world be without evil, to which Lewis responded that this involves the irreducibly indexical want that the world in which I exist be without evil.[20]

The demonstrative rendering of "the actual world" and "is actual" takes the form "this world" (or "the maximal spatio-

temporal aggregate containing this") and "is spatiotemporally related to this" (or "is part of the maximal spatiotemporal aggregate containing this"). This rendering is supported
by the repeated use of "this world" and "this-worldly"
throughout *On the Plurality of Worlds* as paraphrases of "the
actual world." Later it will be shown that neither the first-
person nor demonstrative paraphrases hold *salva veritate*.

On either of these two indexical paraphrases it is required
that individuals do not exist in more than one world; otherwise "the world in which I exist" or "the maximal spatiotemporal aggregate containing this" would fail to have a unique
referent. Given that Lewis holds to the indexical analysis of
actuality, it is no accident that he also holds to a theory of
world-bound individuals, of which counterpart theory is one
example. Thus, any objection to the theory that no individual
(save some abstracta) exists in more than one world also is an
objection to the indexical theory of actuality. In my opinion,
this is most unfortunate for Lewis, since it seems obvious to
me, as well as to a host of his critics, that when I say of some
person that he could have done other than he in fact did, I am
speaking about how that very person acts in some counterfactual situation and not about some counterpart to his in
another world. Since I am not prepared to discuss counterpart theory in this book, I will not press this objection.

There will be much to say later about whether "actual" is
indexical, but right now our concern is in figuring out how
the ontological parity thesis is supposed to follow from the
premise that "actual" is indexical.[21] Supposedly, there is
some argument that shows that no time, place, or person is
respectively now, here, or I absolutely or simpliciter in virtue
of "now," "here," and "I" being indexical that works in an
analogous way for "actual." Lewis gives us some hint how to
fill in this do-it-yourself argument when he writes:

If we take a timeless point of view and ignore our own location in time, the big difference between the present time and
other times vanishes. That is not because we regard all times
as equally present, but rather because if we ignore our own

location in time we cannot use temporally indexical terms like "present" at all. And similarly, I claim, if we take an a priori point of view and ignore our own location among the worlds the big difference between the actual world and other worlds should vanish.[22]

Before we try to develop this into an argument, it will be necessary to give a brief account of indexicality, similar to that which was given in Chapter 3.

As Lewis puts it, what is peculiar to indexical terms is that their "reference varies, depending on relevant features of the context of utterance."[23] An indexical term could be said to have as its meaning a rule that takes us from a context of tokening to a value or referent. The relevant contextual feature differs from one indexical term to another. A token of "now" denotes the time of the tokening, "here" (when used without an act of ostension) the place of the tokening, "I" the person doing the tokening, and so on. "The actual world" is supposed to behave analogously to these indexical terms. "The relevant feature of context, for the term 'actual,' is the world at which a given utterance occurs."[24] A token of "the actual world" denotes the world in which the token occurs.

On the basis of this analogy, the following argument could be constructed, in which an analogy is drawn between "the actual world" and "now" or "the present":[25]

THE INDEXICAL ARGUMENT

6. The tokening at any time t of "Now (or the present) is t" expresses a true proposition [based on the tokening rule for "now"];

7. No time is now simpliciter [from 6];

8. "The actual world" is an indexical term that is analogous to "now" [Lewis's premise];

9. The tokening at any world w of "The actual world is w" expresses a true proposition [from 8 by changing the relevant contextual feature of utterance from a time to a world]; and

10. No world is the actual world simpliciter [from 9].

It will be shown that this argument fails on both material and formal grounds. Two of its premises, namely, 8 and 9, are false; and it contains two serious nonsequiturs – the inferences from 6 to 7 and from 9 to 10. "The actual world" is not indexical, and, even if it were, nothing would follow about actuality being world relative.

To begin, it will be shown why "the actual world" is not indexical. Four significant disanalogies between it and "now" (or the indexical terms of your choice – it doesn't matter) will be unearthed, namely, that unlike "now," "the actual world" (i) does not always take the widest scope, (ii) is not a rigid designator, (iii) is not replaceable *salva veritate* by any recognized indexical expression, and (iv) does not contribute to different propositions being expressed when a sentence containing it is tokened at different relevant contexts.

(i) In our discussion of Hector Castaneda's account of quasi-indicators in Chapter 3, it was shown that an indexical word always has the widest scope, even if it occurs in an *oratio obliqua* clause, because it expresses the speaker's own indexical reference. As a rule, when I assert the sentence "Jones believes that Mary is baking pies now," the *oratio obliqua* occurrence of "now" expresses only my own indexical reference, and thereby I underdetermine the content of Jones's propositional belief, since I do not specify the manner in which Jones referred to the time at which Mary is baking pies – whether by an indexical expression, proper name, or definite description. I could just as well have made the explicitly de re assertion "In regard to now, Jones believes that Mary is baking pies at this time," in which "this time" is a bound variable. By contrast, when I assert the sentence "Jones believes that the actual world is a place of evil," I do not underdetermine the proposition believed by Jones, since the embedded occurrence of "the actual world" expresses not my but Jones's reference. The explicit de re formulation "In regard to the actual world, Jones believes that it is a place of evil" is not synonymous in this case. That an *oratio obliqua* occurrence of an indexical term, unlike "the actual world," takes the wide scope should become even more apparent by considering the case in which I assert that Jones believes that this world is not the actual world. While I am attributing to Jones a radically false belief concerning what is actual, I am not attributing to him the even more radical confusion of believing what is expressed by the pragmatically self-falsifying sentence "This world is not the actual world," in which a pragmatically self-falsifying sentence is one every tokening of which expresses a contingently false proposition. He may be a bit crazy, but he is not that crazy.

(ii) Whereas indexical terms are rigid designators according to the account given in Chapter 3, namely, "d" is a rigid designator just in case the proposition expressed by a tokening of "d might not have been d" is false, "the actual world" is not. Any tokening of

11. Now (I, here) might not have been now (I, here)

expresses a false proposition but not so for every tokening of

12. The actual world might not have been the actual world.

A tokening of 12 expresses a true proposition when the narrow scope is given to its modal operator – there is a world that is the actual world and it is possible that it not be the actual world – rather than the wide scope – it is possible that there is a world that both is the actual world and is not the actual world. Numerous counterfactual stories can be told in which the world that in fact is the actual world fails to be. If any feature of the actual world were to have been different, for instance, someone were to have chosen other than he actually did, some other world would have been the actual world. But no counterfactual story can be told in which now – this very time – is a different time than it in fact is. Certain ordinary ways of talking might suggest that this can be done. When the impatient bridegroom says to his bride during the wedding ceremony, "If it were now 9 P.M. rather than 3 P.M., we would be making love," he is not imagining a counterfactual situation in which now is not identical with the time it is in fact identical with, namely, 3 P.M., but is saying only that whereas they are (regretfully) not making love now at 3 P.M., they will be at 9 P.M. Similarly, when I say to you that if I were you I would buy treasury bonds, I am not imagining a situation in which I am identical with someone else, but am saying only that anyone in your situation prudentially ought to buy treasury bonds.

Lewis has a ready response to the charge that "actual" is not indexical because it is not always used rigidly. His strategy is not to deny the latter but instead to save the analogy by denying that every indexical term is always used rigidly. He distinguishes between a *primary* sense of "actual" in which it refers to the world of utterance, even in a context where another world is under consideration, and a *secondary* sense in which it shifts its reference in such a context.[26] A primary use is rigid, referring to the world in which it is used or uttered even when another world is envisaged, but a secondary use is nonrigid because the reference shifts to the envisioned world. But something similar happens to some but not all indexicals, thereby salvaging the analogy:

> Compare 'now,' which is normally rigidified, with 'present,' which may or may not be. So you say 'Yesterday it was colder than it is now,' and even in the scope of the time-shifting adverb, 'now' still refers to the time of utterance. Likewise you say 'Yesterday it was colder than it is at present,' and the reference of 'present' is unshifted. But if you say 'Every past event was once present,' then the time-shifting tensed verb shifts the reference of 'present.' I suggest that 'actual' and its cognates are like 'present': sometimes rigidified, sometimes not.[27]

In this passage Lewis fails to show that "at present" has both a rigid and nonrigid use, for his example of its nonrigid use is "Every past event was once present." Herein "at present" does not even occur, only the nondesignator "present," which in this use means the same as "happening." "Every past event was once at present" is either illformed or contradictory. One might think that a more favorable example for Lewis's purpose is "he," which has both an indexical use in which it means "this man" and an anaphoric use as a relative pronoun. But this is an uninteresting case of an equivocation in which the latter has no connection with the former. The occurrence of "present" in "Mary is baking pies at present" and "Mary's baking pies once was present" are a similar sort of uninteresting equivocation. By showing that "the actual world" can shift its reference in some counterfactual assertions, Lewis is unwittingly undermining his indexical theory of actuality, since it makes it appear as if "the actual world" is a nonrigid definite description, similar to "the first person to write out a jazz orchestration," which shifts in its reference when used in the counterfactual sentence "If the first person to write out a jazz orchestration were to have been W. C. Handy instead of Jelly Roll Morton, then Jelly Roll Morton would still claim to have been the first." (He had a big ego.)

(iii) Another reason for believing that "the actual world" is not indexical is that it is not replaceable *salva veritate* by an explicit indexical phrase and, in particular, not by Lewis's two candidates – "the world in which I exist" and "this world" or their variants.[28] We will begin with the first-person analysis.

Whereas it is true that

13. It is possible that I do not exist in the actual world,

it is false that

14. It is possible that I do not exist in the world in which I exist.

This counterexample to the first-person analysis does not beg the question against counterpart theory, since it does not require that I inhabit more than one world.

Things go no better for the analysis in terms of "this world" or "the maximal spatiotemporal aggregate containing this." Because "this world" is rigid and "the actual world" is not, it is true that

12. The actual world might not have been the actual world

but false that

15. This world might not have been this world.

"The maximal spatiotemporal aggregate containing this" also flunks the substitutible *salva veritate* test, for while it could be true that

16. Jones disbelieves that the actual world is the maximum spatiotemporal aggregate containing this,

it almost certainly is false, unless he is in pretty bad shape, that

17. Jones disbelieves that the actual world is the actual world.

While it is relatively easy to criticize the first-person and demonstrative analyses, it is more difficult to explain how very able philosophers could have accepted them. My speculative explanation is that their acceptance is based on a failure to distinguish between the meaning of a designator and the way in which we fix its reference, to make use of Kripke's distinction. It probably is the case that many of us are prepared to fix the reference of "the actual world" by employing the indexical phrase "this world" or "the world in which I exist." Were our madman Jones to ask me which world is the actual one, I might reply "This world," as I point to some object around me. That I fix the reference of "the actual world" by using "this world" does not show that they have the same sense, and thereby will be intersubstitutible *salva veritate.*

(iv) Because "the actual world," unlike "now," is a non-rigid definite description, we should expect there to be this further disanalogy: A sentence containing "the actual world" expresses the same proposition when tokened at different worlds whereas one containing "now" expresses different propositions when tokened at different times. It is apparent that tokenings of "t_1 is now" at different times involve a shift in the time referred to by "now" and express different propositions; but, disanalogously, due to the fact that "the actual world" is a nonrigid definite description, tokenings of "w_1 is the actual world" at different worlds, although involving a shift in the world referred to by "the actual world," express the same proposition. This disanalogy, in turn, gives rise to this further disanalogy: While it is true that

6. The tokening at any time t of "Now is t" expresses a true propositions,

it is false that

9. The tokening at any world w of "The actual world is w" expresses a true proposition.

That there is this disanalogy, no doubt, is not obvious. Some might quibble that 6 is true only if it is explicitly relativized to the English language, since another language might contain a sign design similar to "Now is t" that has a different meaning. Furthermore, it is true that successive tokenings of "t_1 is now" express different propositions only if the successive tokenings are in English.[29] I gladly accept these amendments. But even when similar amendments are made in 9, it is false. It is a universal proposition, but it doesn't hold for every case. Imagine that the actual world is not w but w_1. In that case it would not be true that the proposition expressed by the tokening at w of "w is the actual world" is true. We can protect 9 from this kind of counterexample by restricting its truth-ascription to the world of the tokening. This gives us

9'. The tokening at any world w of "The actual world is w" expresses a true proposition at w.[30]

But this gives the game away, for there was no need to relativize the truth-ascription of 6 analogously to the time of the tokening, as is done by

6'. The tokening at any time t of "Now is t" expresses a true proposition at t.

It is interesting to note that when "this world" is substituted for "the actual world" in 9, it results in the true proposition that

9″. The tokening at any world w of "This world is w" expresses a true proposition.

Herein, as in 6, there is no need to relativize the truth ascription, thereby bringing out yet another disanalogy between "the actual world" and "this world."

Another strategy for salvaging 9 is to say that "the actual world" designates each world rigidly at that world.[31] But this move is revisionary; by now it should be clear that "the actual world" is not used rigidly but instead as a nonrigid definite description. As already stressed, when Lewis "proposes" and "suggests" what is the use of "the actual world," he must be taken as describing our ordinary use of this phrase. Were he merely stipulating that we use it rigidly because he prefers this way of talking, it would have no more philosophical interest than that he prefers Jockey shorts to Fruit-of-the-Loom briefs.

The myth underlying the indexical theory of actuality is that the *transmundane* contexts of worlds for the use of "the actual world" is analogous to the *intramundane* contexts of times, places, and persons for the use, respectively, of "now," "here," and "I." The myth, in short, is that in addition to these intramundane indexicals, there is also a special transmundane indexical – "the actual world." But whereas the times, places, and persons that are the referents, respectively, of tokenings of "now," "here," and "I" are interrelated parts of a single universe or Lewis-world, the worlds that are the referents of tokenings across worlds of "the actual world" bear no such systematic interrelations to each other. The only relation between worlds that I can think of that might yield a system is that of the proximity relation between worlds, but this relation, in addition to being highly problematic, seems a very thin analogue to the spatiotemporal relations between different times, places, and persons within a single universe. Not only do the referents of these intramundane indexicals bear systematic relations to each other, so do the indexical propositions expressed by tokening differently indexed counterpart sentences containing these indexicals at these different contexts, which is a familiar story from Chapter 3. The proposition expressed by tokening today "Today is when event *E* occurs" is at least logically equivalent to, if not identical with, the proposition expressed by tokening tomorrow the differently indexed counterpart to this sentence, "Yesterday is when event *E* occurred." But I cannot imagine anything analogous for worlds, since I have no idea of what would be a differently "indexed" counterpart to a sentence containing "the actual world."

The indexical argument, in addition to containing the radically false premises 8 and 9, also commits two serious non sequiturs. It is totally mysterious how

7. No time is now simpliciter

is supposed to follow from

6. The tokening at any time *t* of "Now is *t*" expresses a true proposition.

And likewise for how

10. No world is the actual world simpliciter

follows from

9. The tokening at any world *w* of "The actual world is *w*" expresses a true proposition.

We know in the case of 7 and 6 that the entailment doesn't hold, because 6 is true and 7 false and entailment is truth preserving. But is 7 really false? Lewis does not think so, for he writes:

> If I am right, the ontological arguer who says that his world is special because his world alone is the actual world is as foolish as a man who boasts that he has the special fortune to be alive at a unique moment in history: the present.[32]

Pace Lewis, the boaster obviously is right. Would Lewis also contend that when I say that I am Richard Gale (though this is nothing to boast about) this is not true if it means that I am

Richard Gale simpliciter or absolutely? Certainly my statement is true without any relativization to persons – that I am
Richard Gale at Richard Gale. Similarly, when I assert at the
time I am writing this sentence that time t_1 is now, what I say
is true and not in need of any relativization to a time – that t_1
is now at t_1. Another way of putting this is that the proposition I express by tokening at t_1 "t_1 is now" is true simpliciter
and, moreover, true without relativization to any time, as we
saw in the case of 6. Again, we find that Lewis's account does
not square with actual usage, and he cannot take the revisionary route since this winds up in the wonderful world of
haberdashery. Similar points hold concerning the connection
between 10 and 9, with the difference that 9, unlike 6, is false.
The predicate "is the actual world" is no more a disguised
two-place predicate than is "is now (the present)."

The problem, again, is to give some therapeutic account of
how a bright person could be misled into accepting such a
false thesis. The explanation, again, might be in terms of the
failure to distinguish between the way in which the reference
of a token of a referring term is fixed and the sense this token
has. The following describes the tokening rule for fixing the
reference of a token of "the present" in English:

18. The tokening of "the present" at any time t refers to t.

From 18 it might wrongly be inferred that

19. The tokening of "the present" at any time t means the
same as "the time that is present at t."

And from 19 it does follow that

20. The predicate "is the present" is a two-place predicate.

A similar argument can be given for "is the actual world"
being a two-place predicate. From the following description
of the rule for fixing the referent of a token of "the actual
world,"

21. The tokening of "the actual world" at any world w
refers to w,

it is wrongly inferred that

22. The tokening of "the actual world" at any world w means the same as "the world that is actual at w."

This would establish the ontological parity thesis, namely,

23. The predicate "is the actual world" is a two-place predicate.

Unfortunately for this thesis, the inferences of 19 from 18 and 22 from 21 fail because 18 and 21 are each true and 19 and 22 each false. Theses 18 and 21 each truly describes the referring rule in English for the use of "the present" and "the actual world" respectively. That 19 and 22 are each false can be established by showing that the tokens they claim to have the same sense are not substitutible *salva veritate*.

It is true that at any time t that

24. It is knowable a priori that t is the time that is present at t,

but it is not true that at any time t that

25. It is knowable a priori that t is the present.

Similarly, it is true that in any world w

26. It is knowable a priori that w is the world that is actual in w,

but it is not true that in any world w

27. It is knowable a priori that w is the actual world.

Given these differences in sense between tokenings of the expressions in question in the very same relevant contexts (time or world), it follows that the expressions will not be substitutable *salva veritate* in propositional-attitude contexts. I could believe that w is the world that is actual in w but not believe that w is the actual world, or know that time t is the time that is present at t but not know that t is the present.

This completes my critique of the indexical argument. It is misleading to speak of it as *the* indexical argument, since there are other arguments that begin with Lewis's premises that "actual" is indexical and terminate in his conclusion that being actual is world relative. Maybe a more interesting and viable indexical argument can be constructed on Lewis's behalf; but I must leave this task to my superiors, since I have done the best I can.

CONCLUSION

One and only one theory of actuality – the indexical theory – has been considered, and it has been found wanting, thereby saving theism from an atheological argument based upon this theory. The results of my discussion, however, are not wholly negative. It has been shown that "the actual world" is a nonrigid definite description and "is actual" is a monadic predicate. While these theses do not constitute a full-blown theory of actuality, any such theory must square with them. It is not my purpose in this book to construct such a theory, since it would take me too far afield. Nor am I up to the task. But I want to caution those who attempt it. Because "is actual" is monadic, it must not be inferred that being actual is a simple property that one and only one world possesses. This is not so much wrong as unhelpful, for there are properties and there are "properties."[33] Ordinary, paradigmatic properties, such as being red, are the sort of thing that an individual can possess in different modal manners, for instance, actually as opposed to merely possibly being red. If being actual is supposed to jump through the same conceptual hoops as do these ordinary properties, a vicious infinite regress is generated by the simple property theory of actuality. It analyzes "X is actual" into "X has the property of actuality," but the latter means "X actually (as opposed to only possibly) has the property of actuality," which, in accord with this theory, must be analyzed into "X has the property of actually having the property of actuality," and so on ad infinitum.[34] The regress is vicious because it is one of meanings or analyses rather than one of only entailments. It would appear to be fundamentally wrong to try to reduce a modality to a property. The modal manner in which an individual has a property is not itself a property. The actual world does not differ from other worlds in that it alone possesses the property of actuality but in that it alone actually has existence. Maybe it is existence that is the sought after simple property.

This completes my discussion of atheological arguments. I trust that you have found your excursion through them to have positive value in helping find a more adequate and defensible conception of God. It is now time to turn to the theological arguments for it being rational to believe that God exists. We shall begin with the epistemological or truth-directed arguments and then go on in the final chapter to consider some pragmatic arguments for faith.

Theological arguments

Chapter 6

Ontological arguments

An ontological argument attempts to deduce the existence of God from an analysis of the conception of God, thereby showing that it is necessary that God exists. From the mere logical possibility that this conception of God is instantiated, it is supposed to follow that it is necessarily instantiated. It has been dogmatically pronounced by a long line of philosophers from Hume up through the logical positivists that an ontological argument cannot work, since existence can never be a logical consequence of an entity's essence. This dogma is called into question by what appear to be perfectly legitimate ontological arguments for certain types of *abstract entities*, that is, entities that could not logically be located in either space and/or time, such as numbers, properties, and propositions. God, as conceived of by the great medieval theists, is such an abstract entity, though differing from these abstracta in having a life (an illimitable one at that, which is supposed to be had all at once!) and also having a causally efficacious will that can timelessly bring about effects in the universe.[1] Given God's status as an abstract entity, the question naturally arises whether the same style of deductive reasoning from premises knowable a priori to an existential conclusion, such as figures so prominently in mathematics in which existential questions are internal to the system, being decidable by deductions from axioms and definitions, might not also apply to the existence of God. It certainly would be a blatant begging of the question to deny that it can. It is no accident that the ontological argument is the darling of the mathematically inclined theistic philosophers in the Platonic tradition, those who think that the mathematical method of reasoning is the pathway to true knowledge.

This chapter will consider many different types of ontological arguments. The first is based on a weak version of the principle of sufficient reason according to which everything has a possible explanation and argues that a contradiction follows from the assumption that God does not exist consisting in there both being and not being a possible explanation for this negative state of affairs. The second version, of which there are several variants, is based on some premise that is supposed to formulate a necessary truth about abstract entities in general, from which, in conjunction with other necessary premises, God's existence is supposed to follow. The third is the famous argument in chapter 2 of *St. Anselm's Proslogion,* and attempts to deduce a contradiction from the assumption that a being than which none greater can be conceived does not actually exist, namely, that the being than which none greater can be conceived could be greater (or could be conceived to be greater). The fourth, and final version to be considered, is based on a tougher set of requirements than those supposedly laid down by Anselm for qualifying as a being than which none greater can be conceived and employs necessary existence, rather than plain old existence, as one of the great-making properties. It will turn out that none of them works. The moral that will emerge from our discussion is that the philosopher who gives an ontological argument is playing with fire. To make it work she must up the ante, soup up her conception of God so much that it opens the door for an ontological disproof based on deductions from this very conception, which is just what will be seen to befall the fourth version in particular. More generally, it will be shown to be a fundamental mistake either to argue for the necessary existence of God or to conceive of God as having necessary existence. God should not be the sort of entity that necessarily exists; for, if he is so conceived, it follows that he does not and cannot exist.

THE WEAK SUFFICIENT REASON VERSION

This argument is a simplified version of one given by James F. Ross, which he in turn owes to Scotus, but I believe that it is a worthy popularization of their argument.[2] We must begin with the conception of God as an unsurpassably great being – a being than which none greater can be conceived. Such a being must be totally unlimited and thereby invulnerable to any outside force that could prevent it from existing or even cause it to exist. This is a conceptual truth about God. The other premise in this argument is a weak version of the principle of sufficient reason, according to which for every individual that exists or does not exist, there is a *possible* explanation for the fact that it exists or the fact that it does not exist. The strong version of this principle requires that there actually be such an explanation, rather than that there just possibly be one. According to the strong version, nothing can have a brute, inexplicable existence or nonexistence. Obviously this is not something that the opponent of the ontological argument is going to grant. Furthermore, there appears to be no good argument for it. But the weak version should not be the occasion for any wrangling; for, certainly, it should be at least possible that there is an explanation for the existence or nonexistence of any entity.

From these two premises the argument proceeds via an indirect proof. Assume that God, so conceived, does not exist. From this it follows that there is a possible explanation for this negative existential fact. Yet in virtue of God's conceptually based unpreventability, it is not possible that anything could explain it. Thus, there both is and is not a possible explanation for the fact that God does not exist.

The following is an explicit mounting of this argument:

1. It is impossible that anything prevent the existence of God [conceptual truth];

2. For every individual *x*, if it is a fact that *x* exists or a fact that *x* does not exist, it is possible that there is an explanation

for the fact that *x* exists or the fact that *x* does not exist [weak version of the principle of sufficient reason];

3. God does not exist [assumption for indirect proof];

4. It is possible that there is an explanation for the fact that God does not exist [from 2 and 3];

5. It is not possible that there is an explanation for the fact that God does not exist [from 1];

6. It is and it is not possible that there is an explanation for the fact that God does not exist [from 4 and 5]; and

7. It is false that God does not exist [from 3 thru 6 by indirect proof].

And, since a contradiction was deduced from the proposition that God does not exist, it shows that this proposition is not only false but necessarily false. It is necessary that God exists!

While there is little to question with either premise 1 or 2, the inference of 5 from 1 is most dubious. It implicitly assumes that the only possible explanation for the fact that some individual does not exist is a causal one in terms of something that (causally) prevents the existence of this individual. But this is plainly not the case. One possible explanation for why some individual does not exist is an argument that shows a logical absurdity, such as a contradiction, in the claim that it exists. For instance, we can give a noncausal explanation for why the largest integer does not exist consisting in a reductio argument against its existence. Another type of a noncausal explanation of a negative proposition is in terms of some positive reality that logically precludes the denied state of affairs. For instance, the reason that I am not now in San Francisco is that I am now in Pittsburgh. My being in Pittsburgh now does not causally prevent but logically precludes my being in San Francisco now. Similarly, the reason the rug is not blue is that it is red, and so on.[3]

It is exactly such an explanation for a negative proposition in terms of a positive reality that logically excludes the denied state of affairs that is possible for the nonexistence of God. For instance, the reason that God does not exist is that there exists some positive state of affairs that logically precludes his existence, such as a *morally unjustified evil*, that is, an evil that is such that it is logically necessary that God would not allow it to occur, such as an evil that serves no good purpose. Such evils will serve as the linchpin on which will hinge my argument later in this chapter against it being necessarily true that God exists.

What is more, the proponent of the above argument is inconsistent in inferring 5 from 1. Just as it is not logically possible that anything causally prevents God's existence, it is not logically possible that anything causes his existence either; yet according to this argument, there is an explanation for his existence consisting in this very ontological argument. Herein the ontological arguer does recognize an explanation for an individual's existence or nonexistence that is not causal. If all explanations of existence and nonexistence must be causal, there cannot be a successful ontological proof or disproof. And this undercuts the very purpose of the above argument, since it is intended to be an ontological proof of, and thereby explanation for, God's existence.

Ontological arguments from God's abstractness

This is a neglected, but nevertheless interesting type of a priori argument for it being necessary that God exists that is based upon the conception of God as an abstract entity. What is distinctive about this kind of argument is that it employs some premise that is such that the argument works only if it represents a necessary truth about abstract entities. Four different specimens of it will be critically evaluated – St. Anselm's argument in Part I of his *Reply to Gaunilo*, along with Norman Malcolm's two variations on it in his "Anselm's Ontological Argument," plus a simplified version of my own that clearly brings out the essence of these arguments. It will be shown that all four arguments face the objection that their alleged necessary truth about abstract entities is question begging. Furthermore, each argument will be shown to be uncompelling by construction of a parallel argument that contains its alleged necessary truth about abstract entities and other premises that are no less plausible than those of the original but whose conclusion is logically incompatible with that of the original. And, in a later section of this chapter, it will be shown that there are independent reasons for thinking it false that it is necessary that God exists and thus for holding suspect any argument that has this proposition as its conclusion.

Anselm writes:

> I insist, however, that simply if it can be thought it is necessary that it exists. For 'that-than-which-a-greater-cannot-be-thought' cannot be thought save as being without a beginning. But whatever can be thought as existing and does not actually exist can be thought as having a beginning of its existence. Consequently, 'that-than-which-a-greater-cannot-be-thought' cannot be thought as existing and yet not actually exist. If, therefore, it can be thought as existing, it exists of necessity.[4]

This is a subtle and beautiful argument; but it cannot be fully appreciated, no less shown to be valid, until it is translated into the logistical form of contemporary modal logic.

The argument attempts to prove that if "that-than-which-a-greater-cannot-be-thought" (to be abbreviated as "God") can be thought, then God exists of necessity. It takes the form of a conditional proof in which we begin with the assumption of the antecedent proposition, which will be understood as

8. It is possible that God exists,

based on the assumption that for Anselm, whatever "can be thought" is logically possible.

Two premises are then added. Both are intended as necessary truths, as they must be if Anselm is to be allowed to use them in his attempt to deduce from 8 that God "exists of necessity," which is to be rendered as

C. It is necessary that God exists.

The first says that God "cannot be thought save as being without a beginning," which will be represented as

9. It is not possible that God begins.

That God cannot have a beginning in time is a logical consequence of Anselm's conception of God as an abstract entity. Following the Boethian–Augustinian conception of God's eternality as involving timelessness rather than everlastingness or omnitemporality, Anselm rightly deduces that it is not possible that God begins to exist; for, were God to do so, he would begin in time and thus be in time. The second added premise, also assumed to be necessary, is supposed to hold, or at any rate must hold if the argument is to succeed, for every abstract entity. It says that "whatever can be thought as existing and does not actually exist can be thought as having a beginning." In accordance with the previous way of understanding "can be thought," this will be paraphrased as

10. It is necessary that, for any x, if it is possible that x exists and x does not exist, then it is possible that x begins.

From 8–10 we are supposed to deduce C, at which point we can close the scope of our initial assumption 8 and deduce that if 8 then C. And since Anselm's opponent is supposed to grant him the truth of 8, C can be deduced by modus ponens.

To demonstrate that C is entailed by 8–10 it is helpful to translate 8–10 into a C. I. Lewis-style modal logical form and make use of the axioms of both S4 and S5. The following is the Lewis-style translation and argument.

Anselm's argument from God's abstractness

8. M God exists[5] [assumption for conditional proof];
9. $-M$ God begins [necessary truth];
10. $L(x)[Mx$ exists and $-x$ exists) $\supset Mx$ begins] [necessary truth];

11. $L[(M$ God exists and $-$ God exists) $\supset$ M God begins] [from 10 by universal instantiation];

12. L $-$ God begins [from 9 by definition of L];

13. LL $-$ God begins [from 12 by axiom of S4];

14. $L[$ $-M$ God begins $\supset$ $-(M$ God exists and $-$ God exists)] [from 11 by transposition];

15. $L[L$ $-$ God begins $\supset$ $(M$ God exists and $-$ God exists)] [from 14 by definition of L];

16. L $-(M$ God exists and $-$ God exists) [from 13 and 15 by axiom of modal logic $L(p \supset q) \supset (Lp \supset Lq)$)];

17. $L($ $-M$ God exists or God exists) [from 16 by DeMorgan axiom];

18. $L(M$ God exists $\supset$ God exists) [from 17 by definition of $\supset$];

19. LM God exists [from 8 by axiom of S5];

20. L God exists [from 18 and 19 by axiom of modal logic in step 16]; and

21. M God exists $\supset$ L God exists [from 8–20 by conditional proof].

Notice that if the material implication in 10 is not itself necessary, it can only be deduced that if it is possible that God exists, then God exists. And this isn't a bad day's work. The need to appeal to the axioms of S4 and S5 will not be questioned now. What they collectively say is that a proposition's modality is invariant among possible worlds.

Norman Malcolm's two variations on this argument are directed against an opponent who says that although nothing could prevent God from existing, it nevertheless is the case that God's existence is contingent in that it is both possible that God exists and possible that he does not. In the first argument, Malcolm replies that "from the supposition that it could happen that God did not exist it would follow that, if He existed, He would have mere duration and not eternity,"[6] which, I assume, is meant to be a substitution instance of a necessary universal truth. This consequence, however, is absurd, since we conceive of God's eternality as excluding "as senseless all sentences that imply that He has duration."[7]

This argument can be explicitly formulated as an indirect proof that attempts to deduce a contradiction from the supposition that it is possible that God does not exist.

Malcolm's first argument

22. M −God exists [assumption for indirect proof];

23. M God exists [granted by Malcolm's opponent];

24. $L(x)[M$ −x exists $\supset$ (x exists $\supset$ x has duration)] [necessary truth];

25. $L[M$ −God exists $\supset$ (God exists $\supset$ God has duration)] [from 24 by universal instantiation];

26. LM −God exists [from 22 by axiom of S5];

27. L(God exists $\supset$ God has duration) [from 25 and 26 by axiom $L(p \supset q) \supset (Lp \supset Lq)$];

28. $L($ −God has duration $\supset$ −God exists) [from 27 by transposition];

29. L −God has duration [necessary truth];

30. L −God exists [from 28 and 29 by axiom in step 27];

31. −M God exists [from 30 by definition of L];

32. M God exists and −M God exists [from 23 and 31 by conjunction]; and

33. −M −God exists [from 22−32 by indirect proof].

In this argument we again find the two essential ingredients of the special type of a priori argument under consideration. It contains a premise – 29 – that is a logical consequence of the conception of God as an abstract entity, and another premise – 24 – that must hold necessarily for abstract entities if the argument is to be sound. Both of these ingredients are also found in Malcolm's second argument:

> If God . . . does not exist then He cannot *come* into existence. For if He did He would either have been *caused* to come into existence or have *happened* to come into existence, and in either case He would be a limited being, which by our conception of Him He is not. Since He cannot come into existence, if He does not exist His existence is impossible. If He does exist

He cannot have come into existence (for the reasons given), nor can He cease to exist, for nothing could cause Him to cease to exist nor could it just happen that He ceased to exist. So if God exists His existence is necessary. Thus God's existence is either impossible or necessary. It can be the former only if the concept of such a being is self-contradictory or in some way logically absurd. Assuming that this is not so, it follows that He necessarily exists.[8]

This very complex argument can be shown to be valid without the use of either S4 or S5. The following is an explicit formulation of the argument.

Malcolm's second argument

34. $-M$ God is limited [necessary truth];

35. L [God came into existence $\supset$ (God is caused to do so or God happened to do so)] [necessary truth];

36. L (God is caused to do so $\supset$ God is limited) [necessary truth];

37. L ($-$God is limited $\supset$ $-$God is caused to do so) [from 36 by transposition];

38. L $-$God is limited [from 34 by definition of L];

39. $-M$ God is caused to come into existence [from 37 and 38 by axiom $L(p \supset q) \supset (Lp \supset Lq)$];

40. $-M$ God happened to come into existence [by same kind of argument as given for 39];

41. L [$-$(God is caused to come into existence or God happened to come into existence) $\supset$ $-$God came into existence] [from 35 by transposition];

42. $-M$ God is caused to come into existence and $-M$ God happened to come into existence [from 39 and 40 by conjunction];

43. $-M$ (God is caused to come into existence or God happened to come into existence) [from 42 by axiom of modal logic $-M(p$ or $q) \equiv (-Mp$ and $-Mq)$];

44. L $-$(God is caused to come into existence or God happened to come into existence) [from 43 by definition of L];

The weak sufficient reason version

45. L −God came into existence [from 41 and 44 by axiom in step 39];
46. God does not exist [assumption for conditional proof];
47. $L(x)[(x$ does not exist and Mx exists) ⊃ Mx comes into existence] [necessary truth];
48. $L[($God does not exist and MGod exists) ⊃ MGod comes into existence] [from 47 by universal instantiation];
49. −MGod came into existence [from 45 by definition of L];
50. −(God does not exist and MGod exists) [from 48, and 49 by modus tollens];
51. God exists or −MGod exists [from 50 by DeMorgan axiom];
52. −MGod exists [from 46 and 51 by Disjunctive Syllogism];
53. God does not exist ⊃ −MGod exists [from 46–52 by conditional proof];
54. God exists [assumption for conditional proof];
55. L(God exists ⊃ −MGod begins or ceases to exist) [necessary truth];
56. −MGod begins or ceases to exist [from 54 and 55 by modus ponens];
57. $L(x)[(x$ exists and Mx does not exist) ⊃ Mx begins or ceases to exist] [necessary truth];
58. $L[($God exists and MGod does not exist) ⊃ MGod begins or ceases to exist] [from 57 by universal instantiation];
59. −(God exists and MGod does not exist) [from 56 and 58 by modus tollens];
60. −God exists or −MGod does not exist [from 59 by DeMorgan axiom];
61. −MGod does not exist [from 54 and 60 by disjunctive syllogism];
62. God exists ⊃ −MGod does not exist [from 54–61 by conditional proof];
63. (God does not exist ⊃ −MGod exists) and (God exists ⊃ −MGod does not exist) [from 53 and 62 by conjunction];
64. God exists or God does not exist [tautology];
65. −MGod exists or −MGod does not exist [from 63 and 64 by constructive dilemma];

211

66. M God exists [granted by Malcolm's opponent];

67. $-M$ God does not exist [from 65 and 66 by disjunctive syllogism]; and

68. L God exists [from 67 by definition of L].

While this argument is far more complex than its two predecessors, it is of a piece with them. Each of these argument contains a premise that is either identical with or a close cousin of one of its premises. This argument's premise

47. $L(x)[(x$ does not exist and Mx exists) $\supset Mx$ comes into existence]

appears to be identical with Anselm's premise

10. $L(x)[(Mx$ exists and $-x$ does not exist) $\supset Mx$ begins],

assuming that "come into existence" means the same as "begin." Also, its premise

57. $L(x)[(x$ exists and Mx does not exist) $\supset Mx$ begins or ceases to exist]

is a close cousin of Malcolm's first argument's premise,

24. $L(x)[M -x$ does not exist $\supset (x$ exists $\supset x$ has duration)]

agreeing in their antecedents when exportation is applied to 24 and differing only slightly in their consequents. What is common to all four propositions, which will become evident as we proceed, is that they are true only if no abstract entity can have a contingent existence.

Before showing why this requirement is question-begging, it will be helpful to construct a simplified version of these three arguments that makes this requirement explicit.

The simplified argument

69. $L(x)[x$ is an abstract entity $\supset (Lx$ exists or Lx does not exist)] [necessary truth];

70. L [God is an abstract entity $\supset (L$ God exists or L God does not exist)] [from 69 by universal instantiation];

71. God is an abstract entity [necessary truth];
72. L God exists or L God does not exist [from 70 and 71 by modus ponens];
73. −L God does not exist [granted by opponent of argument]; and
74. L God exists [from 72 and 73 by disjunctive syllogism].

OBJECTIONS TO ARGUMENTS
FROM GOD'S ABSTRACTNESS

The first objection to be lodged against all four arguments is that each contains as a premise an alleged necessary truth that is question-begging. The conception of a question-begging argument is a dialectical one, since it concerns what propositions the opponent of the argument is willing to concede *prior to* the presentation of the argument. Not every valid deductive argument will be question begging. The valid argument that Socrates is mortal because all men are mortal and Socrates is a man will beg the question only if the person to whom it is directed initially rejects either of its premises. It will not be fair for the opponent of the argument, *after* it has been given and discovered to be valid, to charge that it *begged* the question, for at that time he was willing to grant its premises.

What is the dialectical context of our four arguments? This gets down to what are the *prior* beliefs of the opponent of these arguments. The opponent is characterized by Malcolm as having the prior belief that God is a contingent being – that "it might just happen that He did not exist."[9] When this belief is combined with the opponent's prior acceptance of the Anselm–Malcolm conception of God as an abstract entity, it becomes clear that the opponent will not grant premises 69, 10, 24, and 57; for he could offer God himself as a counterexample to each of them.

He can offer this abstract, but contingent God as a counterexample to the premise 69 claim that necessarily every abstract entity is either a necessary or impossible being. And exactly the same counterexample can be offered to 10, 24, and 57. Given his prior belief in the contingency and abstractness of God's existence, the opponent would say that there is a possible set of circumstances under which their antecedents are true and consequents false. For 10 it involves a possible world, w_1, in which God might exist but does not, and for 24 and 57 a possible world, w_2, in which God exists but might not. But in neither w_1 nor w_2 is it possible for God to begin (cease) or have duration. Thus, 10 is false in w_1 and 24 and 57 false in w_2. And since these propositions are supposed to be necessary – true in every possible world – all three are false.

Against such an opponent, an Anselm or Malcolm must mount an argument to show that there is a logical inconsistency in the conception of an abstract contingent God. But they cannot, without begging the question, use their arguments to accomplish this. As was said, their arguments have largely been neglected. I think we now can see why. It is because they are blatantly question-begging.

There is yet another way to discredit these arguments: Show that for each of them there is a parallel argument that contains its alleged necessary truth about abstract entities – 69, 10, 24, or 57 – and other premises that are no less plausible than those of the original but whose conclusion is logically incompatible with that of the original. To do this we only need form the conception of a greatest conceivable abstract demon or devil, which will be abbreviated as GCAD, also short for greatest conceivable cad. In addition to being nonspatial and nontemporal, the GCAD will be omnipotent, omniscient, and, most important, sovereign. Of course, it will be omnimalevolent, which is the only property that distinguishes it from God. When each of our four arguments is reformulated in terms of the GCAD in place of God, an argument results whose premises are no less plausible than those of the original (since it seems just as possible that our GCAD exists as that God does) but whose conclusion is logically incompatible with that of the original. Since all these arguments are valid, these parallel arguments render the premises of the original arguments dubious, in particular premises 69, 10, 24, and 57.

It might be questioned why it is logically impossible for both God and the GCAD to exist. It is not because there would exist two omnipotent beings, but rather because there would exist two sovereign beings. A sovereign being completely and uniquely determines every feature of any world in which it exists, which is such that it is logically consistent that this being completely and uniquely determines it. Thus, if two providential beings existed in a given world, each would completely and uniquely determine everything in that world that it is consistent for either one of them alone completely and uniquely to determine, thereby resulting in the contradiction that some things in this world both are and are not completely and uniquely determined by one of the two sovereign beings.

The only way to block this refutation is to argue that it is not possible for a being to have one of the divine perfections without having all of them. In Chapter 1 it was argued that there is no good argument for this and, more strongly, that the doctrine of the divine simplicity is a most implausible doctrine.

It is important to note that even if it could be proven that a being could not have one of the divine perfections without having all of them, it would not save Anselm's argument and Malcolm's second argument from refutation by a parallel argument that uses the concept of an omnitemporally eternal God in place of that of a timelessly eternal God. The theistic tradition is pretty much split down the middle with respect to these two different ways of understanding God's eternality. All of the great medieval theists, as well as Berkeley and Schleiermacher, have defended the timelessly eternal view, while the omnitemporally eternal view is that of the Bible, along with the Nicene Creed and most Protestant theologians, not to mention present-day process theologians. It has already been argued at some length in Chapters 2 and 3 that the religiously available God of the everyday working theist cannot be timelessly eternal. Malcolm could not consistently attack the intelligibility or viability of this omnitemporal conception of God, for he defends the viability of his own timeless conception of God on the grounds that this conception enters into language games that are actually played. But exactly the same can be said, only more so, on behalf of the omnitemporal conception of God.[10] What Malcolm must do is to argue that it is necessary that any temporal being has the possibility of ceasing to exist; but, as argued in Chapter 3, it is unlikely that any such argument can succeed. There seems to be nothing contradictory or absurd about the conception of an omnitemporally eternal God, that is, a God that exists throughout a beginningless and endless time and logically could not begin or cease to exist. Plainly, the onus is on Malcolm to show that this conception of God, which has entered into the language games of working theists throughout the ages, is not viable. This he has not done.

Anselm's argument and Malcolm's second argument work equally well for the greatest conceivable omnitemporally eternal being.[11] But then we again wind up with incompatible conclusions, this time between a sovereign timeless God and a sovereign omnitemporal God. One does not escape this problem by appeal to the doctrine of the Trinity, in which one of its members is the timelessly eternal and another the omnitemporally eternal God. The reason is that, if taken in a literal, nonmystical manner, it violates Leibniz's law, since these Gods are supposed to be identical and yet differ in some of their properties, one being temporal and the other not. It was suggested in Chapter 2 that this doctrine must be interpreted as a mystical doctrine, but then it cannot be appealed to in order to save a piece of rational theology, such as the arguments of Anselm and Malcolm.

Again, the moral to be drawn is that the premises, in particular 10 and 57, of the original arguments are suspect. And since 10 and 57 are of a piece with premise 24 in Malcolm's first argument in that the same sort of metaphysical intuitions that lead one to accept or reject one of the former do likewise for the latter, it also renders this argument uncompelling. There is another way to discredit our four arguments, based on an argument for it being impossible that God necessarily exists, that will be explored later.

ANSELM'S VERSION

Our concern now is with the version of the ontological argument that Saint Anselm presents in Chapter 2 of *Proslogion*. Many silly arguments have been attributed to Anselm by people who obviously have never read the text. Sometimes it is said that he engaged in the sleight of hand maneuver of defining the word "God" in such a way that it included, among other divine perfections, the property of having existence. From this it follows only that no nonexistent individual could be God. Whereas a nonexistent being, for instance, Merlan, could be a magician, no such merely fictional or mythical being could qualify as God. But this is perfectly consistent with the proposition that there exists no individual that is God. To conceive of God as being essentially existent leads to the same dead end, for it entails only the tautology that God is existent in every possible world in which God exists, which, again, is quite consistent with there existing no individual that is God. It does not help to add the additional premise that God, so defined or conceived, is a possible being or could exist, since it would follow only that the individual that is God in some possible world is existent in that world, not that this world is the actual world or that this individual actually exists.

Fortunately, this is not St. Anselm's argument, for he does not argue from, but to, God having existence. He begins with the conception of God as a being than which none greater can be conceived, leaving it open whether any individual that qualifies as such must be existent. To be sure, there is an additional premise having to do with existence being a great-making property, but there is no attempt to include being existent in the conception or definition of God or a being than which none greater can be conceived. There is no doubt that in Chapter 2 he is employing the concept of plain old existence, not necessary existence. Whether he had other versions of an ontological argument in Chapter 3 and his *Reply to Gaunilo* that employed such modalized existence is a controversial issue that will be left alone. (I believe that the text is not decisive and that if he had such a version, it was not clearly worked out in his own mind.)

Let us begin by quoting Anselm's formulation of the argument in Chapter 2.

> Now we believe that You are something than which nothing greater can be thought. . . . Even the Fool . . . is forced to agree that something-than-which-nothing-greater-can-be-thought exists in the mind, since he understands this when he hears it, and whatever is understood is in the mind. And surely that-than-which-a-greater-cannot-be-thought cannot exist in the mind alone. For if it exists solely in the mind even, it can be thought to exist in reality also, which is greater. If then that-than-which-a-greater-cannot-be-thought exists in the mind alone, this same that-than-which-a-greater-*cannot*-be-thought is that-than-which-a-greater-*can*-be-thought. But this is obviously impossible. Therefore there is absolutely no doubt that something-than-which-a-greater-cannot-be-thought exists both in the mind and in reality.[12]

This is a turgid piece of reasoning that cries out for clarification. My strategy will be to give at the outset my own interpretation of it in the form of an explicit indirect proof, bearing in mind that it is only one among several ways of drawing an argument out of the text, and then go on to clarify its premises and indicate their textual basis.

Anselm's Chapter 2 argument

75. God is that than which a greater cannot be thought [true by definition];

76. It is possible that that than which a greater cannot be thought exists [granted by fool opponent];

77. That than which a greater cannot be thought does not exist [assumption for indirect proof];

78. For any individual x, if it is possible that x exists and x does not exist, then x could be greater [necessary truth];

79. If it is possible that that than which a greater cannot be thought exists and that than which a greater cannot be thought does not exist, then that than which a greater cannot be thought could be greater [from 78 by universal instantiation];

80. That than which a greater cannot be thought could be greater than it is [from 76, 77, and 79 by modus ponens];

81. It is not the case that that than which a greater cannot be thought does not exist [from 77–80 by indirect proof].

And since a contradiction, namely, proposition 80, has been deduced from the assumption that God, conceived of as a being than which a greater cannot be thought, does not exist, in which use was made of only necessarily true propositions, it follows that it is necessary that God exists.

Premise 75, the "definitional premise," should not occasion much difficulty, but often students who read Anselm for the first time object that it does not accurately describe the way in which they conceive of or define God. If it was a lexical definition, its failure to agree with ordinary usage would be a serious flaw. But for the purposes of Anselm's argument, it can function as a purely stipulative definition, the point being that when God is so conceived or defined, it can be demonstrated that he exists.

Another difficulty they have with the definitional premise is that they do not understand what is meant by a being than which a greater cannot be thought. To make sense of this conception, it must be placed in a religious context. God, understood as that than which a greater cannot be thought, plays a special role in the religious language game as an eminently worshipable and obeyable being. It will be recalled from the discussion in Chapter 1 that this constituted one of God's hard-core properties, but a higher-level, emergent one.

There will be lower-level determiners of it, such as being essentially omnipotent, omnibenevolent, omniscient, and the like. This supplies some positive content to the conception, but there is also a negative component to it, since this being is conceived of having each of these lower-level perfections in an *un*limited manner. Herein Anselm goes a long way with the negative approach to the divine; but, unlike a Pascal, who thinks that our inability qua finite creatures to form a fully positive conception of God's true nature or essence bars us from being able to argue either for or against the existence of God, Anselm sees it as no barrier, his earlier argument being proof that it isn't.

Premise 76, the "possibility premise," is far more controversial. The opponent of the argument – the Fool of the Scriptures who denied that God exists – supposedly understood that whose existence he was denying. Anselm uses "understand," "understandable," and "in the mind" in a somewhat technical way so that from the fact that any individual satisfies either of them, it follows that it has the logical possibility of existing.[13] If the Fool were to deny that the being than which a greater cannot be thought is not understandable in the sense of being logically possible, the onus would be on him to show that this concept is in some way absurd or contradictory. Supposedly, the Fool is not able to do this, and thereby is committed to accepting 76.

Nor will it do for the fool to charge that 76 begs the question, since if it is not granted, Anselm cannot deduce his desired conclusion 81; for this is an after-the-argument refusal to grant a premise, whereas what is in question in determining whether an argument begs the question is the before-the-argument beliefs of the argument's opponent. And supposedly the Fool is willing to grant 76 before he knows what is coming.

Step 77 is the assumption for indirect proof, and it is a shortened version of Anselm's claim that "it exists solely in the mind." What is at issue is not whether God has intentional existence as an object of thought but whether he has first-class, mind-independent existence. From the assumption that he does not, a contradiction – 8o – is supposed to follow.

To show this it must be assumed that existence is a great-making property. Premise 8o, the "great-making premise," presents one way of formulating this doctrine based on Anselm's claim that "if it exists solely in the mind even, it can be thought to exist in reality also, which is greater." Following the principle of minimal ordinance – that an argument should not have stronger premises than are absolutely required for it to be valid – 8o is the weakest interpretation of the text that will do the trick. There are stronger versions of the existence-is-a-great-making-property doctrine, for instance, that any individual that exists is greater than any individual that does not. But why use them and run the risk of refutation if they are not essential to the argument's validity?

In 8o a comparison is drawn not between a nonexistent entity and some *other* existent entity in respect to their relative degrees of greatness but between the greatness possessed by a *single* entity in two different circumstances, in one of which it exists and the other in which it does not. If there are no other relevant differences between these circumstances, the individual is greater in the circumstance in which it is existent. Some, such as C. D. Broad, find such a comparison to be suspect, because they believe that we cannot talk about the greatness of a nonexistent being. But it is not obvious that this is so, for we do talk about the greatness of purely fictional and mythical beings.

Another ground for attacking 8o is based on the denial that existence is a great-making property in anything. In support of this, Norman Malcolm points out that if President Bush were to ask his advisors to make up a list of the properties that it is desirable for a secretary of defense to have, they might put on their list such properties as being chaste, being a teetotaler, having no previous business relationships with defense companies, but they would not list having existence.[14] The response to this is that we do not do so because the context makes clear that we are restricting ourselves to existent beings. It is strange to find Malcolm going on to defend the doctrine that necessary existence, that is, the impossibility of failing to exist, is a great-making property, for it would seem that in general the only reason why being necessarily or essentially F is great-making or desirable is that being plain old F is great-making or desirable. We would not prefer that an individual be essentially benevolent rather than just benevolent unless we deemed benevolence itself desirable. But if what was in question was malevolence, we would prefer the malevolent to the essentially malevolent being. Malcolm, therefore, seems to be inconsistent in upholding necessary existence as a great-making property but denying that existence is.

The crucial step in the deduction is 80, the "reductio step." It is based on Anselm's claim "For if it exists solely in the mind even, it can be thought to exist in reality also, which is greater." My interpretation is based upon the earlier assumption that for Anselm "what can be thought" is what is possible or could exist. Thus, if that than which a greater cannot be thought can be thought to be greater than it is, it follows that that than which a greater can be thought could be greater than it is. This is taken to be contradictory by Anselm, so that he can close the scope of the assumption made in 77 and deduce its falsity.

But is the reductio step really contradictory? At first glance it appears to be so. How could that than which a greater cannot be thought be greater than it is? A good case can be made out that it is not.[15] The first step in the refutation is to realize that an individual has existence or status in more than one possible world and its greatness can vary across these worlds. The Brando character in Chapter 1 who said that he could have been a contender is implicitly saying that he exists in other possible worlds than the actual one and that in some of these he is a contender and thereby greater in that world than he is in the actual one. All of us believe that we could have done better than we in fact did and that thereby we are greater in some possible world than we are in the actual world. But we should take solace in the thought that there are possible worlds in which we do a lot worse. Ah, the glory and the misery of possible-worlds fantasizing.

Given that an individual exists in more than one world, there is a crucial ambiguity in

80. That than which a greater cannot be thought could be greater than it is.

The phrase "than it is" is incomplete, failing to specify a world. Is it the actual world that is in question or the world in which it realizes its greatest perfection, that is, the one in which it is essentially (omnipotent, omniscient, omnibenevolent, and so on), which shall be called maximal excellence? If this being were not to exist in the actual world, for instance, to have a merely mythical or fictional status in this world, then it would be true that it could be greater than it is in the actual world, though not in the world in which it realizes maximal excellence. Superman, for example, in virtue of failing to exist in the actual world, could be greater than he is in the actual world. Maybe he could even be greater than he is in the world depicted by Marvel Comics, for he could be free of his vulnerability to kryptonite.

This way of giving a noncontradictory rendering of 80 becomes quite compelling once a possible-worlds rendering is given of the possibility premise

76. It is possible that that than which a greater cannot be thought exists.

Given that what is possible is what is realized in at least one possible world and that an individual's greatness must be relativized to a world since its greatness varies across worlds, 76 is to be translated into

76_1. There is a possible world w and an individual x, such that x exists in w and the greatness of x in w is not exceeded by that of any individual in any possible world.

While it is not possible that this individual x be greater than it is in w, wherein it realizes maximal excellence, it is possible that x could be greater than it is in the actual world, for it might fail to exist in the actual world. Anselm cannot employ his argument to show that it is not possible that x fails to exist in the actual world, since from 76_1, in conjunction with the other premises of the argument, it cannot be deduced that w is the actual world and thereby that x exists in the actual world. If 76_1 is strengthened so that it is claimed that w is the actual world, it would rightly be charged by the Fool with begging the question. I believe that the 76_1 rendering of the possibility premise, along with the realization that an individual's greatness is world relative, destroys Anselm's argument by showing that the reductio step fails to present us with a contradiction. The next version, the one based on necessary existence, gives us a way of avoiding this objection.

THE NECESSARY EXISTENCE VERSION

The clearest and most viable formulation of this version is given by Alvin Plantinga in *The Nature of Necessity*, pp. 213–21. (Again, we find Plantinga taking the lead among his contemporaries: Were it not for his brilliance and creativity, I never would have been moved to write this book.) It departs from the Anselm Chapter 2 version in the analysis it gives of a being than which a greater cannot be thought. The latter analyzes this in terms of having maximal excellence – being essentially omnipotent, omniscient, omnibenevolent, sovereign, and so on. Supposedly, any being that instantiates maximal excellence in any possible world w has a greatness in w that is not exceeded by that of any being in any possible world. Thus, 76_1 can be rephrased as

76_2. There is a possible world w in which the property of having maximal excellence is instantiated.

While we can be assured by the modal nature of maximal excellence that the being who instantiates maximal excellence in w does not have any lesser degree of greatness in any possible world in which it exists, we still have no reason to think that it exists in the actual world.

According to the basic intuition underlying the necessary existence version, the determination of the greatness of a being in some world depends not only upon how it goes with this being in that world but also upon how it goes with this being in other possible worlds – the logical space that surrounds this being and determines its possibilities. This intuition is shared by the Anselm version, since it required that the being who instantiates a greatest greatness have in every possible world in which it exists all of the great-making omniproperties. It did not go far enough, however, and see that necessary existence – the impossibility of failing to exist – was also required of a being than which a greater cannot be thought. Thus, the new version replaces 76_2 with the stronger possibility premise that

76_3. There is a possible world w in which the property of having *unsurpassable greatness,* that is, maximal excellence plus necessary existence, is instantiated.

With this premise it can be deduced that the being, call it Fred, who instantiates having unsurpassable greatness in w does exist and has maximal excellence in the actual world. Since Fred has essentially all the properties that comprise maximal excellence, it has these properties in every possible world in which it exists. And, given that the actual world is a possible world and that Fred exists in every possible world in virtue of having necessary existence, it follows that Fred exists and has maximal excellence in the actual world.[16]

We would be imposing on the Fool opponent of the ontological argument if we were to demand that he grant the new possibility premise 76_3 on the grounds that he accepted the former possibility premises $76–76_2$. He might be a fool but he is not a complete schmuck. He can point out that this new possibility premise involving unsurpassable greatness is considerably stronger than the previous ones involving only maximal excellence. Furthermore, he could charge 76_3 with begging the question. That it is blatantly question-begging becomes manifest when the earlier argument is reformulated in logistical terms employing S5 as follows:

82. God is an unsurpassably great being [by definition];

83. An unsurpassably great being is maximally excellent, that is, essentially omnipotent, omniscient, and so on, and necessarily existent [by definition];

76_3. There is a possible world w in which the property of unsurpassable greatness is instantiated [granted by fool (??)];

84. $M(\exists x)(x$ is maximally excellent and necessarily existent) [from 76_3 by the principle that x exists in some possible world $\equiv$ It is possible that x exists];

85. $ML(\exists x)(x$ is maximally excellent) [from 84 by definition of "necessarily existent" – X is necessarily existent $\equiv$ It is necessary that X exists]; and

86. $L(\exists x)(x$ is maximally excellent) [from 85 by theorem of S5 that $MLp \supset Lp$].

And since it is necessary that there exists a maximally excellent being , there actually exists a maximally excellent being, who, by definition, is God. Such a being, in other words, exists in the actual world.

Before considering the crucial question of whether the Fool will grant 76_3, something ought to be said about the S5 theorem, that $MLp \supset Lp$, which is appealed to in the deduction of 86 from 85. It is not clear what this theorem means, no less that it is true. This theorem requires that the accessibility relation between worlds is reflexive, transitive, and symmetrical. One world is accessible to another if a being (or possible being) in the latter can know the former's world book, that is, all of the propositions true in that world. A proposition is possible if it is true in some world, and necessary if true in every world. Thus, if it is possible that it is necessary that p, it follows that that p is necessarily true in some world w, but it qualifies as necessarily true in this world because in this world a being could discover that it is included in every other world book. There are problems with the S5 doctrine that every world is accessible to every other one, especially in regard to indexical propositions and the epistemological grounds on which a person can determine the truth-values of propositions in other worlds, but we will let them pass since they don't directly concern the issue under consideration.

The explicit S5 formulation of Plantinga's argument brings out just what is involved in the Fool's acceptance of the possibility premise 76_2. It would be unreasonable to ask him to assent to a proposition until he fully understands what it means. Once the Fool understands what unsurpassable greatness involves – in particular that it involves necessary existence – and that for an entity to have necessary existence is for it to be necessary that it exists, and, moreover, accept the S5 theorem that what is possibly necessary is necessary, he would have to be quite a schmuck to grant 76_3. In granting 76_3, he is in effect granting that it is possible that it is necessary that God, conceived of as an unsurpassably great being, exists. And that is something the opponent of the ontological argument would not want to do once he knows what is entailed by the combination of these modal operators within S5. The principle of informed consent applies to disputation and not just within the area of biomedical ethics.

While it seems clear that 76_3 begs the question, there remains the larger question of whether it is true. If people were simply to deny it, they would be pitting their modal intuition against Plantinga's. This would result in a philosophical stalemate that would satisfy Plantinga's larger purpose of showing that it is not irrational or epistemically impermissible to believe that God exists; for his argument is valid and has premises that are just as probable or likely to be true as any or all propositions that are incompatible with them.

A more promising strategy for rebutting 76_3, as well as Plantinga's claim that even if his argument does not succeed as a piece of rational theology, at least it shows that religious belief is epistemically permissible, is to find some property that (i) intuitively seems more likely to admit of the possibility of instantiation than does having unsurpassable greatness and (ii) is *strongly incompatible* with it in that if either property is instantiated in any possible world, the other is instantiated in none. It is not difficult to produce properties that satisfy (ii), for instance, Plantinga's own example of the property of having *near maximality*, which is possessed by a being just in case "it does not exist in every possible world but has a degree of greatness not exceeded by that of any being in any world."[17] But such properties are intuitively on a par with having unsurpassable greatness, neither possessing greater intuitive possibility of instantiation than the other; and thereby they do not satisfy condition (i).

Just slightly, but only slightly, less artificial is that of being a maximally great omnimalevolent being – our GCAD who essentially has all of the properties that make up maximal excellence, save for malevolence in place of benevolence.[18] That this property is strongly incompatible with unsurpassable greatness is due to the logical impossibility of there existing in the same world two beings that are both sovereign for the reason already given. The ontological arguer might challenge the possibility of this property being instantiated by appeal to Plantinga's ontological argument. While this would be question-begging, it still is not clear which of the two strongly incompatible properties (if not both) is to be relegated to the junk heap of the logically impossible.

But we need not resort to such artificial examples, since we have ready at hand properties that do satisfy both (i) and (ii). One example is the property of being a morally unjustified evil, that is, an evil that is such that the God of traditional theism could not be morally excused for permitting it. Such an evil, which is familiar to us from Chapter 4, is one that can neither be attributed to the use of (or failure to use) free will by finite persons nor be shown to be necessary for the realization of some outweighing good or the prevention of a greater evil. An example of such an evil is a supernova that destroys a planet containing sentient beings without this resulting from any finite person's use of or failure to use free will nor this being necessary for the prevention of an even greater evil or the realization of an outweighing good; for instance, we never would have known how much Jones meant to us if we hadn't lost him in that supernova. There is no possible world in which both God, an unsurpassably great being, and morally unjustified evil exist, since it is a conceptual truth that God is both willing and able to prevent such an evil. But if the property of having unsurpassable greatness is instantiated in any world, it is instantiated in every one. Therefore, the possibility premise 76_3 is logically incompatible with

87. There is a possible world in which the property of being a morally unjustified evil is instantiated.

A theist who does not impute a necessary existence to God can accept 87 and then go on to construct a defense or theodicy for different types of moral and natural evil, depending on whether it is the deductive or inductive argument from evil that is being rebutted. But the problem of evil for the theist who either accepts an ontological argument or imputes necessary existence to God takes a far more acute form. It is the modal problem of evil, concerning the very *possibility* of there being a morally unjustified evil, the theistic response to which must take the form of an argument for the impossibility of there being an evil for which God does not have a morally exonerating excuse. It is not enough to give a FWD, since this still leaves open the possibility of a morally unjustified natural evil, such as the example of the supernova. What these theists must establish is that it is more likely that it is possible that having unsurpassable greatness is instantiated than that being a morally unjustified evil is. At a minimum, they can challenge the intuitions underlying 87 with their own counterintuitions favoring 76_3.

There is an even more plausible property that satisfies (i) and (ii), namely, being a world in which every free person always freely does what is morally wrong or, in other words, being a world that contains moral evil sans moral good. This will prove to be an especially troublesome objection for Plantinga, since it will be shown that the very intuitions that establish that this property satisfies (i) and (ii) are those that enter into his own FWD. But this will have more than a mere ad hominem interest, since these intuitions are both widely shared among professional theologians and working theists and plausible on their own. First, it will be shown why it is reasonable to think that this property has the possibility of being instantiated, then, why it is strongly incompatible with having unsurpassable greatness.

It is both a basic tenet of any FWD and granted by every right-thinking person that

88. There is a possible world containing free persons.

The FWD is committed to this by its account of how it is possible for God to create free persons, namely, by actualizing their diminished possible persons. Whatever is possible is the case in some possible world. Now a free person cannot only make a morally wrong choice on *any* occasion but on *every* one as well. Thus,

89. There is a possible world in which some free person always freely does what is morally wrong.

What holds true for *any* free person in this respect also holds for *all* free persons. Therefore,

90. There is a possible world in which every free person always freely does what is morally wrong.

While neither 89 nor 90 is entailed by Plantinga's FWD, they rest on the same sort of intuitions as do some of its key premises. It would be most odd, although not contradictory, for someone to accept the FWD's depravity premise.

–M. It is possible that God cannot actualize a possible world in which all free persons always freely go right.

but deny 89 or 90. The reason is that the depravity premise rests on the possibility that the F-conditionals would have contingent truth-values such that if any of their antecedents were to be instantiated, it would result in the occurrence of at least some moral evil. According to the FWD, and rightly in my opinion, their contingent truth-values could be even more unfavorable, so that it would result in moral evil sans moral good, that is, every free person always freely going wrong. This still does not entail 90. What must be added is that in some possible world in which the F-conditionals have such unfavorable truth-values, some of them have their antecedents instantiated, be it by God or mere chance. (It will turn out that it is only by the latter, since it would be inconsistent for Plantinga's God to do so.) This certainly seems possible. More needs to be said in defense of 90, but first it will be shown why it is logically incompatible with 76_3.

Plantinga's above ontological argument shows that from

76_3. There is a possible world w in which the property of having unsurpassable greatness, that is, maximal excellence plus necessary existence, is instantiated,

it can be deduced that

86. $L(\quad x)(x$ is maximally excellent$)$.

And 86 in turn entails that

91. There is an individual, who, by definition, is God, and both exists and has maximal excellence in every possible world.

Since 76_3 entails 91, if 91 is incompatible with 90, so is 76_3. The following is a demonstration, based upon the premises of the FWD, of the incompatibility of 91, and thereby 76_3, with 90.

A logical consequence of 91 is that

92. God both exists and has omnibenevolence, omniscience, and sovereignty in every possible world,

since, by definition, a maximally excellent being is essentially (omnibenevolent, omniscient, and sovereign). Since God exercises his sovereignty in every possible world, he completely and solely determines every feature of every world that it is consistent for him completely and solely to determine. According to the FWD, given that it is consistent for God to create free persons (though not also to determine what they freely do – that is why the F-conditionals do not have their truth-values determined by God), it follows that

93. In every possible world in which there exist free persons, God creates them.

Plantinga's FWD accepts theses I and II – the doctrine of God's middle knowledge – that requires God to know in every world in which he exists the contingent truth-value of every F-conditional. From this and 92 it follows that

94. God both exists and has middle knowledge in every possible world.

The next link in the demonstration is that

95. An omnibenevolent being who knows that he can prevent a situation in which every free person always freely does what is morally wrong will do so.

In addition to being plausible on its own, 95 is supported by the normative premise of the FWD that

96. A world containing free persons who freely perform both right and wrong actions, *but for the most part go right*, is better than any possible world devoid of free persons

because the very same moral intuition that requires the *"but for the most part go right"* qualification in 96 also supports 95. (The reader is referred back to the discussion of this premise in Chapter 4, where it is called "9.") From 93, 94, and 95, it follows that

97. In every possible world God will prevent it from being the case that every free person always freely does what is morally wrong.

In every possible world in which the contingent truth-values of the F-conditionals are such that if any one(s) of them were to have its antecedent instantiated, it would result in moral evil sans moral good, God has middle knowledge of this and will prevent any F-conditional getting its antecedent instantiated by electing not to create any free person. (Remember that God is sovereign in this matter and that the principle of sovereign type-invariance holds, so that no F-conditional could get its antecedent instantiated by chance.) And in conjunction with 93, this entails that

98. There is no possible world in which every free person always freely does what is morally wrong.

And from this it can be concluded that the property of being a world in which every free person always freely does what is morally wrong is strongly incompatible with having unsurpassable greatness, that is, that 90 is incompatible with 76_3. Furthermore, since 90 rests on far stronger intuitions than does 76_3, it is 76_3, and thereby Plantinga's ontological argument, that is to be rejected.

Theists who believe that God has necessary existence and thereby accept 76_3 are not going to accept this demonstration of the falsity of 76_3. The sort of rebuttals that are available to them will depend upon what tenets they hold in addition to 76_3. First we shall consider the possible responses of the Plantinga-type theist – the one who accepts 76_3 as well as the premises and intuitions that underlie Plantinga's FWD. Such theists have very few options for rebutting the above demonstration of 90. For instance, they can't explain how God could permit the possibility envisioned by 90 to come to pass in terms of his lacking middle knowledge, thereby morally exonerating him for creating free persons all of whom always freely go wrong on the basis of an excusable lack of knowledge. An Adams-type theist can say this but not a Plantinga-type, since the former, unlike the latter, denies that God has middle knowledge.

One possible move is for the Plantinga-type theist to deny that God is essentially benevolent. This will require a redefinition of "maximal excellence" so that to qualify as such, a being must be only plain old benevolent, though it still must essentially have all of the other omniproperties. In any possible world in which all free persons always do what is morally wrong, God will exist and have middle knowledge. He just won't be morally at his best. In fact, he will qualify as a real cad in such worlds. This downgrading of what is required of a maximally excellent being, however, clashes with the first premise of the necessary existence version of the ontological argument:

82. God is an unsurpassably great being.

A being that has this sort of watered-down maximal excellence intuitively does not seem to qualify as an unsurpassably great being or a being than which a greater cannot be thought. It presents us with an insuperable case of the paradox of perfection.

The Plantinga-type theists might just outright reject 90 by appeal to their intuitions that it is more likely that having unsurpassable greatness admits of the possibility of instantiation than does being a world in which all free persons freely do what is morally wrong. The problem with this is that, as argued above, the very premises and intuitions that enter into their FWD support the possibility of the latter, that is, 90. Another problem for them is that even if they could establish on some ground that 90 is false, they could still be challenged by a weaker and thereby more intuitively powerful version of 90, say

90'. There is a possible world in which the majority of acts freely performed by persons are morally wrong.

This weakened version of 90 is incompatible with the normative premise of their FWD

96. A world containing free persons who freely perform both right and wrong actions, *but for the most part go right*, is better than any possible world devoid of free persons,

since it requires a favorable balance of moral good over moral evil, something not realized in the 90'-type possible world.

Plainly, theists who accept 76_3 but do not buy in on all the premises of Plantinga's FWD, especially the doctrine of middle knowledge, have a better chance of refuting 90. They can appeal to one of the versions of a FWD sans middle knowledge from Chapter 4 to show how 90 is consistent with 76_3. It has already been argued in that chapter that such versions do not work. But even if one of them did, they would still face two problems. Their FWD at best meets the challenge posed by 90 but not that based upon the seeming possibility of there being a *morally unjustified evil*. Furthermore, by denying middle knowledge to God, they significantly limit his omniscience, and this seems hard to square with their identification of God with an unsurpassably great being in premise 82 of their ontological argument.

The most reasonable move for this type of theist to make is to challenge my claim that intuitively it seems that being a morally unjustified evil or a world in which all free persons always freely do wrong more likely admits of the possibility of instantiation than does having unsurpassable greatness. Both Phil Quinn and Peter van Inwagen wrote to me that their modal intuitions are the reverse of mine. My response to them is that our prima facie modal intuitions speak in favor of my intuitions, and thus the onus is on them to show that they are not to be trusted. This might be done by showing, in regard to 90 for example, that upon a deeper analysis, it turns out to be impossible that all free persons would always freely go wrong. It might be argued that a free person must be rational and that on at least some occasions, rational beings will realize that it is in their own best interest to do the morally right thing, since thereby they keep afloat the practice or institution of following moral rules, which furthers their own prudential interests. This Kantian-style argument against 90 is weak, since we can conceive of a possible world, such as one in which the Evil Demon is in charge, in which on every occasion that a free choice is to be made, the agent has good reason to believe that the prudential thing to choose is the morally wrong alternative.

I conveyed these considerations in a letter to Phil Quinn, and he wrote back that he rejected my placing the onus on him. His justification was that immediately upon opening and reading my letter in the office of the philosophy department at Notre Dame, he asked the first seven people he met whether they thought it was possible that being a morally unjustified evil or a world in which everyone always freely goes wrong be instantiated, and to a person they denied its possibility. I, in turn, conducted my own modal intuition poll at the office of the philosophy department at the University of Pittsburgh after I opened his letter, and, not surprisingly, everyone I consulted thought it possible that these properties be instantiated. This clash of modal intuitions between the persons at these two departments raises an intriguing possibility. Might it not be a good idea to complement the long-standing rivalry between the football teams representing these two great institutions with a Modal Intuition Bowl involving these two rival departments?

If the participants in this bowl are restricted to the members of the two philosophy departments, it might seem that the result will be a tie (unless someone is throwing the game), the reason being that the participants are sufficiently tutored in philosophy to know what will result from their assenting to or denying the possibility of these properties being instantiated. But there are ways of finding a winner. One way we might try to resolve the deadlock is to widen the scope of our poll and ask some "ordinary" people who have not been perverted by the study of philosophy to give their modal intuitions. I actually left the philosophy department office and put the question to such people – a janitor, maintenance man, barmaid, and the like – and each had modal intuitions that matched mine.

Furthermore, I question the consistency of the Notre Dame-types who refuse to countenance the possibility of these properties being instantiated because they know the problem such an admission would pose for their brand of theism. If their modal intuitions really did favor 76_3 over the possibility of these properties being instantiated, why do so many of them feel it necessary to construct a defense, as well as a theodicy, for what *seem* to be morally unjustified evils? Premise 76_3 *alone* constitutes a perfectly adequate defense of God against any type of evil. It would appear that the reason they feel a need to construct a defense other than that based on an acceptance of 76_3 is that they are not all that sure of 76_3. Thereby they violate one of the basic rules of the Modal Intuition Bowl – be consistent in your modal intuitions! Furthermore, their modal intuition in favor of 76_3 over its rivals seems to be motivated by their desire to use it for the purpose of giving the stated ontological argument in which it occurs as the key premise. But this argument makes use of some very hairy and dubious assumptions, such as each world being accessible to every other one.

Maybe the strongest reason for not accepting at face value their professed modal intuition in 76_3 is that the concept of an unsurpassably great being is very complex and problematic, giving rise to all of the atheological arguments that were discussed in Chapters 1–4 concerning omnipotence, omniscience, benevolence, and sovereignty, especially when these properties are had essentially. Compared with the idea of an unsurpassably great being, that of a morally unjustified evil or a world in which everyone always freely goes wrong is a relatively simple and unproblematic one. This should tilt the balance in favor of the latter being instantiatable, regardless of what our *initial* intuitions might be. After all, they are only prima facie intuitions and thereby defeatable by subsequent conceptual analyses of the sort that have been given in the earlier parts of this book.

Chapter 7

Cosmological arguments

One of the fondest memories of most of us is the time we nailed our parents with the regress of why-questions, the crowning point of which was when we triumphantly asked, "Yeah, so who made God?" At this point we were told to go play marbles in traffic. Little did our parents realize that the cosmological argument could have served as Jim Dandy to the rescue; for it demonstrates that our initial explanatory demand must ultimately terminate with a self-explaining explainer, in which a self-explaining being is one whose existence is entailed by its nature or essence, that is, one for whom there is a successful ontological argument.

But if there is a successful ontological argument, as the cosmological argument supposedly proves, why screw around with the cosmological argument? Why not go right for the jugular and give this ontological argument, thereby having an end to the matter of whether God exists? This was one of Kant's objections to the cosmological argument. This charge of redundancy misses the mark, since there could be a successful ontological argument even if we were unable to give it. Thus, we could know on the basis of the cosmological argument that there is a successful ontological argument and thereby that God exists, but not be smart enough to give it.

The most telling objection that can be lodged against the cosmological argument is that it is impossible for such a being to exist, thereby showing that this argument's conclusion is necessarily false. Any argument for an impossible conclusion, to say the least, leaves something to be desired, whether in the way of validity or soundness. This will be the ground on which every version of the cosmological argument will be attacked. The points made in the Chapter 6 criticisms of ontological arguments will form the basis of my polemic.

Before getting down to a detailed analysis of different versions of the cosmological argument, it will be helpful to describe their generic nature. A cosmological argument is made up of three components: (a) a contingent existential fact, (b) an explanatory argument, and (c) a version of the principle of sufficient reason (hereafter PSR). It begins by demanding an explanation for the existential fact in (a) or some fact that it entails in conjunction with certain other premises or assumptions. This is followed by an argument in (b) that purports to demonstrate that this fact or the fact generated by it can be explained only in terms of the causal efficacy of a self-explaining God, or something very like God, which will be called a "theistic explanation." And, finally, there is in (c) a version of PSR, suitably tailored so as to require that there be an explanation for the sort of fact of which the initial fact or the one entailed by it is an instance. The conjunction of (a)–(c) entails that there is a theistic explanation of the fact in question and thereby that there exists a self-explaining God.

Different versions of the cosmological argument result from different explanatory demands. St. Thomas, in his First Way, begins with the fact that one object is moved by another, in the Second Way that one object's existence is simultaneously dependent upon another. Sometimes the existential fact is quite humble, such as that there exists something rather than nothing or that there exists at least one being whose existence is dependent upon the causal efficacy of another. Often it is a more rich fact, for instance, that there exists this universe, comprised of all the specific objects and events it contains. Herein what requires explanation is a maximal spatiotemporal object.

This existential fact component, as well as the PSR one, is not knowable a priori. It is desirable that the existential fact be either undisputable or, even better, of a sort one of whose species or determiners is bound to obtain, thereby assuring that no matter what the actual world is like, there will be such a fact to be explained; for instance, no matter what possible world gets actualized, there will be some one world book that is true simpliciter and for which an explanation can be demanded. Few versions realize the latter, though some come close. For instance, if the explanatory demand concerns why there exists a certain concrete aggregate of individuals that comprise the universe, it can be repeated no matter what individuals the universe contains, provided there is at least a spatiotemporal aggregate of some kind. A cosmological argument that begins with the existential fact that there exists something also comes very close to realizing this desideratum, if not fully realizing it.

It is also desirable that the existential fact be of a sort that cannot in principle either be scientifically explained or require no explanation relative to some possible scientific theory; for instance, that there exists something. History amply demonstrates that it is unwise to make a theistic explanation a competitor to a scientific explanation. This desideratum is often violated by the cosmological arguments given by scientists, especially cosmologists, who, if they are steady-state theorists, ask what causes hydrogen atoms continually to come into existence or, if big-bang theorists, what precipitated the primordial cosmic explosion. They might even hark back to Descartes and ask why material objects persist in being or why matter is conserved.[1] They indict science with being necessarily incomplete because it cannot in principle explain the cosmological fact in question.

What they fail to realize is that their explanatory demand concerns a kind of fact that is either in principle scientifically explainable or not in need of any explanation relative to some possible scientific theory. Certainly, it is conceivable that someday science would be able to explain what brought about the initial cosmic explosion that presently serves as a unique point singularity. Furthermore, whether it is incumbent on us to explain why certain objects persist in being or, contrariwise, why hydrogen atoms come into being will depend on the scientific theory we accept, in particular what sort of conservation laws it incorporates. Relative to Aristotelian science, the fact of motion required explanation but not so relative to Newtonian science with its first law of motion. And if what requires an explanation is why some law or theory holds, it is possible that it would be explainable by some more inclusive law or theory, such as was the case with the explanation of the Galilean law of free fall in terms of Newton's law of gravity. The strategy of the cosmological arguer should not be to ask why some specific law or theory holds but rather why there is any lawlike regularity at all. All of the versions of the cosmological argument that will be considered in this chapter have explanatory demands that necessarily fall outside the purview of science.

It is the explanatory argument component that distinguishes a cosmological argument from inductive theological arguments, such as the teleological argument or the argument from the widespread lawlike regularity and simplicity of the world. The latter are inferences to the best explanation, the claim being that the theistic explanation of these existential facts is superior to its competitors or that these facts make it likely or probable that there exists a being very much like God whose causal efficacy explains these facts. The explanatory argument of a cosmological argument, in contradistinction to these inductive arguments, tries to *demonstrate* that the only *possible* explanation of these facts is the theistic one in terms of God's will. Sometimes it is not clear whether an argument based upon facts of natural design, order, beauty, and the like is a cosmological or inductive argument due to it not being made manifest whether the theistic explanation of these facts is supposed to be the only possible one or only the most probable one.

There are numerous versions of the PSR that vary in strength, from the strongest version requiring that every true proposition have an explanation to a relatively weak one requiring only that there is an explanation for the coming into existence of any individual. The Ross–Scotus version of the ontological argument in Chapter 6 employed an even weaker version requiring only that every fact have a possible explanation. The principle of minimal ordinance, that an argument should not have stronger premises than is required, will apply. Thus, if the explanatory demand in (a) requires that a certain fact of type F have an explanation, the version of the PSR that occurs in (c) will require only that every F-type fact has an explanation. It is generally conceded that there is no way to establish the PSR, even in its weaker form, and, as a result, any cosmological argument can be stopped dead in its tracks by calling into question the version of the PSR that enters into its (c) component. We will hold off discussing until the very end of the chapter what happens to the cosmological argument when its PSR is not granted. Surprisingly, it will turn out that denial of the PSR does not have as deleterious consequences for the cosmological argument as has usually been supposed.

Three versions of the cosmological argument will be considered, each being based on a different explanatory demand. The first, the "concrete-aggregate" version, demands an explanation for the existence of some concrete, that is, spatiotemporal, aggregate, this sometimes being the universe as a whole, the maximal spatiotemporal aggregate, or the succession of events and/or objects that comprise history as a whole or at least up until the present. The second demands an explanation for a special sort of general existential fact – that there exists at least one dependent being, that is, a being whose existence is explained in terms of the causal efficacy of another being. The third version, which no one has yet given, has as its initial existential fact that a certain world book is true simpliciter, in which a world book is comprised of all the propositions that would be true were a certain possible world to be actualized. This version will prove to be superior to the others but still subject to the same fatal problem that afflicts every cosmological argument – that its conclusion is impossible.

CONCRETE-AGGREGATE VERSIONS

Scientific explanations are by nature piecemeal, explaining one *part* of the universe in terms of some other *part*, with appeal being made to some sort of nomic connection of a deterministic or statistical sort that connects them together. But what, asks the proponent of one version of the concrete-aggregate version of the cosmological argument, explains the existence of the universe as a whole? We find Leibniz, in "On the Ultimate Origin of Things," writing:

> And even if you imagine the world eternal, nevertheless since you posit nothing but a succession of states and as you find a sufficient reason for them in none of them whatsoever, and as any number of them whatever does not aid you in giving a reason for them, it is evident that the reason must be sought elsewhere.

And, in more recent times, Richard Taylor has made the same demand that there be an explanation of the existence of the universe-as-a-whole:

> But it is at least very odd and arbitrary to deny of this existing world the need for any sufficient reason, whether independent of itself or not, while presupposing that there is a reason for every other thing that ever exists.[2]

Both authors assume some version of the PSR requiring that every individual has an explanation of its existence and then go on to treat the universe as a whole as an individual, and thereby subject to this version of the PSR. Leibniz gives a brief sketch of the explanatory argument that demonstrates the impossibility of explaining the existence of the universe as a whole in a nontheistic way, for instance, by appeal to some individual within the universe. To do so in the latter manner, supposedly, would violate the principle that no individual can be a self-cause, since the intrauniverse individual that is invoked to explain the existence of the universe as a whole would have to explain, among other things, its own existence.

The concrete-aggregate version finds its fullest and most forceful presentation in Part II of Samuel Clarke's 1705 *Demonstration of the Being and Attributes of God*. The argument is presented in two stages. The first attempts to prove that there is a being who necessarily exists and is the causal explainer of the world of dependent beings, the second that this being is the God of traditional theism. The argument of the first stage, which will be our primary concern, employs a fairly strong version of the PSR that holds that whatever exists (and not just whatever comes into existence), even if it be omnitemporally eternal, has an explanation of its existence. The explanation for a being's existence will be either an externalistic one in terms of the causal efficacy of some other being, in which case it is a "dependent being," or an internalistic one in terms of its own nature, it then being an "independent being." Given this distinction between the two ways in which a being's existence can be explained, Clarke's version of the PSR can be expressed as:

PSR$_1$. Every existing thing has a reason for its existence either in the necessity of its own nature or in the causal efficacy of some other being.

Armed with PSR$_1$, Clarke gives the following argument for the existence of a necessary being:

1. Every being is either a dependent being or an independent being [PSR$_1$];
2. Either there exists an independent being or every being is dependent [from 1 by logical equivalence];
3. It is false that every being is dependent [premise];
4. There exists an independent being [from 2 and 3 by disjunctive syllogism]; and
5. There exists a necessary being [from 4 by definition of an *independent being* as one for which there is a successful ontological argument].

This is to be called the "main argument." It contains two premises, 1 and 3, both of which are controversial. There is little that Clarke can say in defense of 1, but we will not worry about this until the end of the chapter. It would be wrong to say that this premise begs the question, since it does not entail 5, no less that God exists. Because PSR_1 and that God exists occupy the same upper echelon in many philosophers' wish book does not show any logical connection between these propositions, only at best a psychological one.

However, Clarke does have something to say in defense of 3. He presents the following "subsidiary argument" for it:

3a. If every being is dependent, then the whole of existing things consists of an infinite succession of dependent beings;

3b. If the whole of existing things consists of an infinite succession of dependent beings, the infinite succession itself must have an explanation of its existence;

3c. If the existence of the infinite succession of dependent beings has an explanation, then the explanation must lie either in the causal efficacy of some being outside the succession or it must lie within the infinite succession itself;

3d. The explanation of the existence of the infinite succession of dependent beings cannot lie in the causal efficacy of some being outside of the collection;

3e. The explanation of the existence of the infinite succession of dependent beings cannot lie within the succession itself; therefore,

3. It is false that every being is dependent[3] [from 3a to 3e].

The reason why there is an infinite succession of dependent beings if all beings are dependent is that each such being owes its existence to the causal efficacy of its immediate dependent predecessor and there cannot be a "circle of causes," such as A causing the existence of B, B of C, and C in turn of A. There could be such a circle of causes if time is either topologically closed in the manner envisioned by Reichenbach, Grunbaum, and Goedel (given any three non-simultaneous events each is temporally between the other two) or open with local closed causal loops, such as portrayed by Robert Heinlein in his stories "All You Zombies" and "By His Bootstraps," in which a person literally is his own mother and father due to a sex-change operation followed by a backward time journey to enable this person to copulate with his earlier self. Clarke, being a good Newtonian, did not countenance the possibility of such closed causal loops, no less a topologically closed time, but their possibility does not undermine his argument; for if time were to form one big closed causal loop comprised of a *finite* number of dependent beings, he could still demand an explanation, in the name of PSR_1, of the entire causal loop, just as he had demanded an explanation of the entire *infinite* linear succession of dependent beings.[4]

There is an existential assumption underlying Clarke's argument that has not yet been made explicit, and, without which, the subsidiary argument fails. Before presenting the main argument, Clarke assumes that at every moment of time in an infinite past, there has existed some being or other. Actually, he can get by with the weaker existential assumption that there exists at least one being, be it dependent or independent. Unless he makes an assumption that is at least as strong as the latter, it is not true that

3b. If the whole of existing things consists of an infinite succession of dependent beings, the infinite succession itself must have an explanation;

for if there were to exist nothing, it would be true that the whole of existing things consists of dependent beings, since $(x)Fx \equiv -(\exists x)-Fx$, but there would not be an infinite succession of dependent beings to be explained.[5]

Thus, it turns out that when Clarke's argument is completely fleshed out, the initial existential fact that comprises component (a), that there exists at least one being, is not the fact about which the explanatory demand is made and which is shown in component (b) to admit of no explanation other than a theistic one. Rather, this initial existential fact, in conjunction with PSR_1 and the indirect proof assumption that every being is dependent, generates that which requires explanation – the infinite succession of dependent beings. The following is an explicit mounting of Clarke's argument that has the virtue of combining the main and subsidiary arguments as well as making explicit how his explanatory demand grows out of this assumption in conjunction with certain premises and assumptions.

The combined concrete-aggregate formulation

6. There exists at least one being [existential-fact premise];

1. Every being is either a dependent being or an independent being [PSR_1];

2. Either there exists an independent being or every being is dependent [from 1 by logical equivalence];

7. Every being is a dependent being [assumption for indirect proof];

8. There is an infinite succession of dependent beings [from 6 and 7 by principle that there cannot be a circle of causes];

9. This infinite succession of dependent beings is itself an individual [premise];

10. There is an explanation for the existence of this infinite succession of dependent beings [from 1 and 9 by universal instantiation];

11. The explanation for the existence of this infinite succession of dependent beings is in terms of the causal efficacy of either a dependent or an independent being [from 1 and 10];

12. The explanation for the existence of this infinite succession of dependent beings is not in terms of the causal efficacy of an independent being [from 7];

13. The explanation for the existence of this infinite succession of dependent beings cannot be in terms of the causal efficacy of a dependent being [premise];

14. There is no explanation for the existence of this infinite succession of dependent beings [from 11 to 13 by modus tollens and DeMorgan theorem];

15. There both is and is not an explanation for the existence of this infinite succession of dependent beings [from 10 and 14 by conjunction];

16. It is false that every being is a dependent being [from 7 to 15 by indirect proof];

4. There exists an independent being [from 2 and 16 by disjunctive syllogism]; and

5. There exists a necessary being [from 4 by definition of an independent being].

The problematic premises in this argument are 9 and 13, which correspond, respectively, to 3b and 3e in the subsidiary argument, and we shall now consider some objections to them. Since PSR$_1$ quantifies over individuals, the infinite succession of dependent beings is not covered by PSR$_1$ unless it qualifies as an individual. For different reasons it has been doubted that it so qualifies. These sceptical doubts would also apply to the maximal spatiotemporal aggregate, and thus undermine every concrete-aggregate version of the cosmological argument. The fact that we have names for these entities – "the history of the world" for the infinite succession of dependent beings and "the universe" for the maximal spatiotemporal aggregate – is not decisive in allaying such doubts. But what are the grounds for doubt?

In opposition to Clarke's PSR$_1$-based demand that there be an explanation for the infinite succession of temporal beings since it qualifies as an individual in its own right, Rowe writes:

> But such a view of the infinite collection is implausible, if not plainly incorrect. Many collections of physical things cannot possibly be themselves *concrete* entities. Think, for example, of the collection whose members are the largest prehistoric beast, Socrates, and the Empire State Building. By any stretch of the imagination can we view this collection as itself a concrete thing? Clearly we cannot. . . . At best our knowledge of

the things (both past and present) comprising the universe and our knowledge of their interrelations would have to be much greater before we would be entitled to view the *sum* of concrete things, past and present, as itself something *concrete*. (p. 135; see also p. 145)

Rowe's argument against premise 9 of my combined formulation and 3b of the subsidiary argument needs some filling out, especially in regard to what a "concrete entity" is. Furthermore, it is not clear what sorts of knowledge we would have to possess before we would be entitled to take the whole of dependent beings as a single concrete entity.

Rowe gives us no reason why the largest prehistoric beast, Socrates, and the Empire State Building (which sounds like the beginning of a Johnny Carson "What do . . . have in common?") are not parts of a single concrete entity, and we must supply some account on his behalf. It would seem that a concrete entity must have a nature or essence – the what-it-is – that specifies the manner in which its spatial parts are concatenated and function in relation to each other. Think of the song "Dry Bones" as a case in point. For this reason a concrete entity can be identified as being of a certain sort or type in virtue of its size and shape and, most important, by the way its spatial parts are interrelated so as to achieve certain distinctive functions. Often such objects move as a whole. A barker at an auction who wanted me to move down front said "Move the feet and the body follows." Finally, and most important, an object's nature will present us with a way of conceiving of it that is either pragmatically useful in helping us to get around effectively in the world or intellectually satisfying by employing scientific notions that help us to understand why the object behaves as it does. The manner in which the periodic table defines the nature of the different elements is a good example of the latter. Let us call an object that has a nature that satisfies the preceding conditions a "sortal object" and its nature a "sortal nature." Obviously, the concrete aggregate composed of Rowe's three disjointed objects is not a sortal object or, as he would say, a "concrete entity."

The underlying assumption in Rowe's objection is that *if there is a causal explanation of X then X is a sortal object.* The reason why it is illegitimate to ask for the causal explanation of the infinite succession of dependent beings or the maximal spatiotemporal aggregate is that it does not qualify as a sortal object. But Rowe's assumption is false, facing numerous clear-cut counterexamples. A heap of twenty rocks is not a sortal object, not moving as a whole or having a sortal nature, yet it makes sense to ask for the cause of its existence, which could be the person who assembled the rocks into a heap.

The distinction between sortal and nonsortal *objects* has only a rough *event* analogue, since there seems to be no temporal analogue to the essentially spatial notion of an Aristotelian *natural kind* that has just been articulated. And do not confuse the issue by bringing up the concept of *unnatural acts.* A sortal event would be one whose concept prescribes the manner in which its temporal parts are concatenated, for instance, a baseball game. The cause of a sortal event, such as a war, can be something above and beyond the several causes of the battles that make up the war, such as the king whose decree brought about the war. Similar considerations hold for a nonsortal event, such as the "event" comprised of the succession of Jones running in place, Smith falling down, and Brown singing "Dixie." There could be a common cause of this conjunctive event consisting in some person hiring these three people to perform their respective acts, just as Nero is the cause of a strange succession of events by his issuing the order "Let the games begin." Much more will be said shortly about common causes of concrete aggregates, both sortal and nonsortal, but for now we can conclude that Rowe's objection to 9 and 3b fails because its assumption is not true in general.

Instead of denying that the infinite succession of dependent beings or the maximum spatiotemporal aggregate qualifies as an "individual," it might be said that an adequate formulation of the PSR should not count them as individuals and thereby require that they have an explanation. The reason they should not be subject to the PSR is that they are unique in virtue of involving the totality. Bertrand Russell, in his BBC debate with Father Copleston, seemed to make this point when he said in opposition to Copleston's demand that there be an explanation for the universe as a whole that "you're looking for something which can't be got" and "you have to grasp this sorry scheme of things entire to do what you want, and that we can't do."[6] Russell is making a stronger claim than that we have no right to assume that there is an explanation for the existence of the maximum spatiotemporal aggregate; for this would just be to call into question the PSR – a perfectly legitimate thing to do. Rather, he is making the stronger claim that there (conceptually) could not be such an explanation. But why not?

There are two reasons that he might give. When asked why it is illegitimate to explain the existence of the universe as a whole, he responded that such a request rested on the fallacy of composition in which it is assumed that a whole must have the same properties as its parts:

> I can illustrate what seems to me your fallacy. Every man who exists has a mother, and it seems to me your argument is that therefore the human race must have a mother, but obviously the human race hasn't a mother – that's a different logical sphere.[7]

In saying that the human race is in "a different logical sphere" than are individual men, Russell seems to be taking the human race to be an *abstract* set. To be sure, abstract entities do not have causes, but this example is crucially disanalogous to the case of the universe versus parts of the universe in which both members are concrete entities, the universe occupying the same space-time region as does its parts. Thus, there does not seem to be any obvious category mistake in asking for the cause of the universe. As Rowe has pointed out, the cosmological arguer who requires a causal explanation for the existence of the universe does not do so on the basis of each of its parts having such an explanation, which would be subject to the charge of a fallacy of composition, but rather on the basis of the PSR and the universe being an individual in its own right.

But there is another way in which Russell might support his claim that there cannot be an explanation for the totality. It would be based on his scientism – his deep-seated belief that all knowledge is scientific knowledge. Knowledge requires an explanation, and, in the case of scientific knowledge, such an explanation will be a piecemeal, intraworld affair in which one state or event within the universe is nomically hooked up with another. Since all knowledge is scientific and all scientific explanations are intraworld, there cannot be any explanation for the existence of the totality, the world itself, at least none that could qualify as knowledge constituting. I have heard many philosophers of science echo a similar sentiment. But that's all it is – a sentiment. The cosmological arguer will rightly charge Russell with begging the question by assuming at the outset that all knowledge is scientific because only scientific explanations qualify as *real* explanations.

Now for what is generally conceded to be the most powerful objection – that premises 13 and 3e wrongly assume that there can be an explanation of a whole or aggregate above and beyond the several explanations for the parts or members that make it up. This objection is raised by Hume in the ninth paragraph of Part 9 of his *Dialogues Concerning Natural Religion:*

> Did I show you the particular causes of each individual in a collection of twenty particles of matter, I should think it very unreasonable should you afterwards ask me what was the cause of the whole twenty. This is sufficiently explained in explaining the parts.

This implies that since each one of the infinitely many dependent beings in Clarke's succession has an explanation, the infinite succession is thereby explained, pace premises 13 and 3e. This objection has been forcefully reiterated in recent times by Paul Edwards, who imagines a group of five Eskimos standing together in New York City:

> Let us assume that we have now explained in the case of each of the five Eskimos why he or she is in New York. Somebody then asks: "All right, but what about the group as a whole; why is it in New York?" This would plainly be an absurd question. There is no group over and above the five members, and if we have explained why each of the five members is in New York we have *ipso facto* explained why the group is there. It is just as absurd to ask for the cause of the series as a whole as distinct from asking for the causes of individual members.[8]

The principle underlying the Hume–Edwards objection is:

HE. If the existence of every member of a collection (group, succession, and the like) is explained, the existence of the collection, and the like, is thereby explained.

There are two things to note about this principle. First, it applies to concrete collections or aggregates, since a group of five Eskimos and a collection (heap) of twenty particles of matter have spatiotemporal location. Second, it is intended as a necessary conceptual truth. This is especially clear in the case of Edwards, who says that it would "plainly be absurd" to ask why a group exists after the existence of each of its members has been explained. The modal status of HE is less clear in Hume's case, for he says only that it would be "very unreasonable" to raise this question about the collection. He usually is understood as holding HE to be necessary (and my colleague Annette Baier, a *real* Hume expert, assures me that this is what he intended, which is enough for me). And this is how he will be understood.

The HE principle is just plain false. Numerous counterexamples have already been given to it, involving both sortal and nonsortal objects. The existence of each and every rock in a heap of rocks could be causally explained, each one owing its existence to some prisoner swinging a sledgehammer, and yet there could be a causal explanation for the existence of the heap, for instance, in terms of the assembling activity of some other prisoner, above and beyond the several explanations for the rocks in the heap. Of course, there might not be, but that there might be suffices to refute HE, understood as being a necessary conceptual truth. A sortal object, such as an automobile, could have an explanation for its existence in terms of the activities in a Detroit assembly plant that is above and beyond the several explanations for each part of the automobile, for instance, the carburetor was made by Delco-Remy in Chicago, the starter motor by United Motors in Kansas City, and so on.

The exact cause of HE's failure is that explanation is not closed with respect to conjunctive introduction, that is, is not "agglomerative," to use Michael Slote's helpful terminology.[9] What this means is that the following is an invalid argument form:

There is an explanation for X (or the fact that p);

There is an explanation for Y (or the fact that q); therefore,

There is an explanation for X and Y (or the fact that p and q).

It could be noncoincidental that A is in the Sludge Falls Bank at T – there is an explanation for why he is there at T, for instance, his boss, B, sent him there to make a deposit. And it also could be noncoincidental that C is in this bank at T, for instance, his boss, D, sent him to make a withdrawal. And yet it could be coincidental that A and C are both in the bank at T. There might be no explanation of this conjunctive fact. And, again, there could be an explanation of this fact above and beyond the several explanations of its conjuncts, for instance, B and D have the same boss, E, who ordered them to order their subordinates, A and C, respectively, to be in the bank at T so he could win a wager.

Not only could there be an explanation of a concrete aggregate or conjunctive fact above and beyond the several explanations of its parts or conjuncts, in some cases it is reasonable to assume that there is such an explanation. As Wesley Salmon has convincingly argued, when "confronted with what appears to be an improbable coincidence, we seek a common cause of this improbability."[10] Edwards's example of the group of five Eskimos standing together in New York, unfortunately for its intended purpose, is just such a case. It is reasonable to seek an explanation for the entire group's being there even after we have for each of the Eskimos an explanation for why he or she is there: for instance, Eskimo 1 won a trip to New York in a lottery; Eskimo 2 is on assignment from the Sludge Falls Courier, and so on. There could be a Mister Big operating behind the scenes to bring about the several causes of these Eskimos being there; he rigged the lottery, bribed the editor of the paper to send the reporter there, and the like.

It would be a serious mistake, however, for the cosmological arguer to appeal to the common-cause principle in support of her demand that there be an explanation for the totality above and beyond the several explanations of its parts, to defend, à la Mark Lane and Cyril Wecht, the conspiracy theory of the universe – "Don't try to tell me that there isn't some capo de tutti de capi, a celestial Carlos Marcello, behind all these electrons, stars, and galaxies." The common-cause principle can be applied only to an *improbable* coincidence, but the universe or totality, being a unique, one-shot affair, could not be said to be such since there could be no prior evidence concerning the frequency with which such totalities came about. But the cosmological arguer need not make the strong claim that it is *probable* that there is a common cause of the universe as a whole, only that it is *possible*. And this, in conjunction with the PSR, entails that there is such an explanation.

Another mistake that underlies the HE-based objection to 3e and 13, in addition to the assumption that explanation is agglomerative, is the belief that it is extensional, that is, that the principle of substitutivity *salva veritate* of coreferential expressions and coreporting sentences holds within the blank spaces of "____ explains ____." Plainly, Edwards is assuming this when he says that "there is no group over and above the five members, and if we have explained why each of the five members is in New York we have *ipso facto* explained why the group is there." Supposedly, because the group is nothing "over and above the five members," that is, is identical with these members, any explanation of the latter *ipso facto* is an explanation of the former.

Unfortunately for Edwards, "explains" is a nonextensional context. That the president of the Sludge Falls Bank was publicly convicted of embezzlement, in conjunction with certain generalizations of folk psychology, explains why there was a run on the Sludge Falls Bank, but not why the event that led to the downfall of Sludge Falls occurred at that time, even though the run on the Sludge Falls Bank is the event that led to the downfall of Sludge Falls. And that the only man in Sludge Falls with 712 hairs on his head was publicly convicted of embezzlement, along with the same generalizations of folk psychology, does not explain why there was the run on the bank, even though the president of the Sludge Falls Bank is the only man in Sludge Falls who has 712 hairs on his head.

To make sense of the nonextensionality of explanation, as well as for the fact that its explanans entails (in some cases) its explanandum, we must view explanation as a relation between abstract propositions, that is, we explain one fact, that is a true *proposition*, by reference to other facts. This point is often unperspicuously formulated in terms of the explanandum and explanans containing events or objects "under a description."

In order to square with the nonextensionality of explanation, the concrete-aggregate versions of the cosmological argument must be recast so that what requires explanation is not some concrete aggregate, such as the infinite succession of dependent beings or the universe as a whole, but instead the true proposition that reports the existence of these concreta.

But exactly what is the proposition that requires explanation in a concrete-aggregate version of the cosmological argument? There are three different ways of construing the explanandum, yielding three different variants of each of the different versions of the cosmological argument: (1) that A and B and so on are concatenated in the way they are; (2) that there exists A and B and so on together; and (3) that there exists A and B and so on together and that they are concatenated in the way they are.[11] Whether or not the infinite succession of dependent beings or maximal spatiotemporal aggregate admits of the possibility of explanation by some dependent being or member of this spatiotemporal aggregate respectively might depend upon which of these three interpretations we adopt.

If we adopt the "assemblying" interpretation (1), we are assimilating the demand to explain the infinite succession or the universe to the earlier demand to explain what caused the various parts of an automobile to become concatenated in the way they are, which was explained in terms of what went on in a Detroit assembly plant. Herein there is no demand to explain the very existence of the different parts, only their being concatenated as they are. Supposedly, the explainer of the manner in which the infinitely many dependent beings get successively concatenated cannot itself be a member of this succession, since then it would have to operate on itself.

But it is not obvious that this is impossible. I can be the assembler of an orchestra of which I am a member and even conduct from the piano. There might, however, be a special problem with a member of the infinite succession of dependent beings that terminates in the present serving as the assembler of it, since this would require that this being causally operate on, for instance, manipulate or control, dependent objects that precede it in the temporal succession. But causation cannot go backward from a later to an earlier time.[12] This response presupposes that time is open, that is, that its generating relation is *later than,* and thus fails to address the possibility of a closed causal loop. The cosmological arguer, in my opinion, should grant this limitation to her argument and add as an a posteriori premise that there is good empirical evidence that the time of the actual world is open. Herein she makes it manifest that her argument does not hold in every possible world, which is hardly news, since it was obvious all along that the PSR does not hold in every possible world. That the argument works in the *actual* world should be enough to satisfy the interests of theism.

Interpretation (2) of the explanatory demand escapes the need to make these messy qualifications, for it requires an explanation for the fact that *A* and *B* and so on all exist together. Herein it is apparent that the causal explainer of the existence of each and every dependent being cannot itself be a dependent being, for then it would have to be the *proximate* cause of its own existence; and this is impossible even if it is possible that an object be a *remote* cause of its own existence in a closed time or Heinlein-type closed causal loop.

Interpretation (3) is a conjunction of (1) and (2), and thereby inherits both of their strengths, making a stronger explanatory demand than does either alone, but escapes the problem that confronted the assemblying interpretation. An adequate explanation of the totality must explain both the existence of each and every part of it as well as their coming to be concatenated as they are. Even if an internalistic account could be given for the concatenation, it could not be given for the existence of the parts. Thus, even if the cosmological fails on interpretation (1), it could still work on interpretation (3), as well as (2). Plainly, the cosmological argument, whatever version it takes, should go with interpretation (2) or, even better, (3).

THE GENERAL FACT VERSION

This version is ably defended by William Rowe in his important book, *The Cosmological Argument*. It has the same main argument as Clarke's and also attempts an indirect proof of its premise

3. It is false that every being is dependent,

based upon the assumption that 3 is false. But, whereas Clarke generated from this assumption, in conjunction with

6. There exists at least one being,

the demand to explain the existence of the infinite succession of dependent beings, understood as a concrete aggregate, Rowe derives from them the quite different demand to explain why there exists at least one dependent being. And, furthermore, both argue that on the assumption that every being is dependent, their explanatory demand cannot be met without some sort of vicious circularity, be it in the order of causation or explanation. Given that their explanatory demands are so different, it could be that one of their vicious circularity arguments works while the other does not.[13] I have given a somewhat idealized reconstruction of Rowe's actual argument; and, before I explicitly formulate it in the same combined manner as I did Clarke's, I will show how it naturally evolves out of a critical analysis of the text.

The point at which Rowe departs from Clarke's version is in his interpretation of the infinite succession of dependent beings for which the subsidiary argument demands an explanation. Whereas Clarke took it to be a *concrete* aggregate, having the same spatiotemporal location as its parts, Rowe conceives of it as an *abstract* set.[14] Rowe is well aware that it is conceptually impossible for there to be a causal explanation for the existence of an abstract set. To avoid this absurdity he interprets the question "Why does set X exist?" as "Why does set X have the members it does rather than none at all?" Notice that it is possible to explain the existence of every member of X without thereby explaining why X has at least one member rather than none at all. This would refute an HE principle that applies to abstract sets, which, not surprisingly, is how Rowe understands this principle.

There is an ambiguity in Rowe's account of what is involved in explaining the existence of a set. When we are asked to explain why some individual a is a member of set X are we required to explain why a exists or instead why a has the set-defining property? If we are to explain, for example, why a is a member of the set of contingent beings, are we required to explain why a exists or why a is a contingent being, for which the explanation might be that a is a horse and horses are essentially contingent beings? Rowe does not explicitly resolve this ambiguity, but his discussion for the most part favors the former interpretation, and this is how he will be understood. Thus, to explain the existence of set X is to explain why there exist the various members of X rather than none at all.

Whereas, for the most part, Rowe construes the demand to explain the existence of X in this manner (see pp. 138, 139, 144, 145, 154, 159), there are places where he demands more of an explanation of a set. At two places he requires that an explanation of the existence of the set of dependent beings, A, tell us why "A has the members it has rather than some other members or none at all." The addition of "rather than some other members" will raise the hackles of those philosophers who recoil from negative events in horror because they think we lack adequate criteria of identity for unrealized possibilities. That sinister character, Smokey the Bear, the very one who ate a Boy Scout alive just to get his hat, was fond of snorting, "Only you can prevent forest fires!" I guess one accomplishes this feat by not dropping matches in a dry forest and the like. But how many times did you not do these sorts of things yesterday? How many forest fires failed to come into being as a result? Likewise for unrealized possible dependent beings. How many times did you not copulate yesterday? And how many possible dependent beings did you deny existence to as a consequence (and remember to include possible twins, and so on)? In Chapter 2 of my *Negation and Non-Being*, I argue that we do have adequate extensional criteria of identity for unrealized possible individuals, but it is too long a story to be told here. And, moreover, it is not necessary to do so, since Rowe drops this extra explanatory demand when he presents his argument.

When Rowe formulates his argument against the possibility of giving an internalistic explanation for the existence of set A, he switches to yet another set of explanatory demands that require us to explain why A has now and always had members rather than never having had any members at all. His argument is presented first in terms of the exactly parallel case of attempting to explain the existence of the infinite set M of men in terms of the causal efficacy of the members of M. He construes "Why does M exist?" as "Why is it that M has now and always had members rather than never having had any members at all?" (155). His argument against the possibility of explaining the latter solely in terms of the causal efficacy of men is this:

> Surely we have not learned the answer to this question when we have learned that there always have been members of M and that each member's existence is explained by the causal efficacy of some other member. (155)

Rowe does not tell us the name of the malady that afflicts such an internalistic explanation of M, but I take it that it is supposed to be viciously circular. Neither does he tell us exactly why the proffered explanation of M is viciously circular, probably because he thought it too obvious to require further explanation and justification. It will turn out that far from being obvious, it is highly dubious that a noncircular explanation cannot be given; but before we turn to this task, it will be helpful to pinpoint the exact part of Rowe's explanatory demands that supposedly cannot be given a noncircular internalistic explanation.

According to his least demanding account of what it is to explain the existence of the set of dependent beings, A, it is required that we explain each of the following two facts:

C. A has the members it does; and

D. A has any members at all, that is, that there exists at least one member of A.

According to the more demanding account that figures in his vicious circularity argument, it is required that we explain each of these three facts:

E. There now exists a member of A;

F. There always have existed members of A; and

D. There exists at least one dependent being.

It will be shown that Rowe's argument against the possibility of giving a noncircular explanation of A's existence really concerns or ought to concern fact D alone, and thus it does not matter whether he operates with the weak or strong set of explanatory demands.

Noncircular internalistic explanations can be given for C, E, and F. Such an explanation for C consists in the infinitely many explanations for each and every dependent being in terms of the causal efficacy of some other dependent being. When Rowe says that the question "Why is it that A has now and always had members rather than never having had any members at all?" is not adequately answered by the explanation "that there always have been members of A and that each member's existence is explained by the causal efficacy of some other member," he is not clearly locating the exact source of the difficulty, that being to explain D. He wrongly makes it appear that noncircular internalistic explanations cannot be given for E and F.

That this can be done is shown by the following noncircular internalistic explanations for F and E. For F,

17. If at any time t there exists a dependent being d, then at some earlier time t' there exists another dependent being d' who causes the existence of d;

18. There now exists a dependent being d, that is, a member of A; therefore,

F. There always have existed members of A.

For E,

19. If at any time t there exists a dependent being d, then at some later time t' there exists another dependent being d' whose existence is caused by d;

20. There exists a dependent being d at some time t that is earlier than now; therefore,

E. There now exists a member of A.

The propositions that occur in the explanans of these two explanations are such that no one of them alone entails the explanandum, thereby avoiding any charge of vicious circularity.

The general fact version

It would seem that it is D alone that is recalcitrant to internalistic explanation. This holds whether or not A has a finite or infinite number of members. Imagine that A has a finite number of members due to there being a circle of causes in the manner previously envisioned. There will still be a D-type fact about the set of dependent beings to the effect that it contains at least one existent member. And it is this fact that supposedly cannot be given a noncircular internalistic explanation.

Given that it is only explanatory demand D that cannot be met noncircularly if all beings are dependent, we can give the following formulation of Rowe's "true" argument, in which the main and subsidiary arguments are combined in the way in which we already did for Clarke.

The combined general fact version

6. There exists at least one being [existential-fact premise];

1. Every individual is either a dependent or independent being [PSR$_1$];

2. Either every being is dependent or there exists an independent being [from 1 by logical equivalence];

7. Every being is a dependent being [assumption for indirect proof];

D. There exists at least one dependent being [from 6 and 7];

21. There is an explanation for the fact that there exists at least one dependent being [from 1 and D by universal instantiation];

22. The explanation for the fact that there exists at least one dependent being is in terms of the causal efficacy of either a dependent or an independent being [from 1 and 21];

23. The explanation for the fact that there exists at least one dependent being is not in terms of the causal efficacy of an independent being [from 7];

24. The explanation for the fact that there exists at least one dependent being cannot be in terms of the causal efficacy of a dependent being [premise];

25. There is no explanation for the fact that there exists at least one dependent being [from 22 to 24 by modus tollens and DeMorgan theorem];

26. There both is and is not an explanation for the fact that there exists at least one dependent being [from 21 and 25 by conjunction];

16. It is false that every being is a dependent being [from 7, D, and 21 to 26 by indirect proof];

4. There exists an independent being [from 2 and 16 by disjunctive syllogism]; and

5. There exists a necessary being [from 4 by definition of an *independent being*].

There is a difficulty with this argument that probably has not escaped the careful reader's attention. The version of the PSR that is given in premise 1, since it quantifies over *individuals*, does not properly mesh with the *general existential fact* D, for which an explanation is demanded in premise 21. To close this gap, we can replace 1 with a version of the PSR that applies to *facts*, namely,

1'. There is an explanation for every fact[15] (to be called PSR_2).

When the combined formulations of the concrete-aggregate and general fact versions are compared, it becomes quite manifest that the distinction between them is over their respective explanatory demands, for the former it being that

10. There is an explanation for the existence of this infinite succession of dependent beings,

and for the latter that

21. There is an explanation for the fact that there exists at least one dependent being.

Just as the controversial premise in the combined concrete-aggregate formulation was

13. The explanation for the existence of this infinite succession of dependent beings cannot be in terms of the causal efficacy of a dependent being;

the controversial premise in this combined argument is

24. The explanation for the fact that there exists at least one dependent being cannot be in terms of the causal efficacy of a dependent being.

We have already considered Clarke's vicious circularity objection to the possibility of explaining the existence of the infinite succession of dependent beings in terms of the causal efficacy of a dependent being and found it to have some merit, but it is not obvious that there is any vicious circularity in explaining the fact that there exists at least one dependent being in this way. Rowe's sketchily presented vicious circularity argument against this possibility needs further probing. Two objections against this argument will be considered: First, it rests on an unacceptable set of explanatory requirements; and, second, even in terms of these requirements, a noncircular explanation can be given for fact D.

While Rowe never explicitly states the requirements for an explanation, he seems to require of an explanation that its explanans (i) entails the explanandum and (ii) has no proposition that alone does. Requirement (i) is too strong, because it precludes inductive-statistical explanations; but this will not concern us. It is (ii) that is at the core of Rowe's vicious circularity argument, but it also is too strong, facing counterexamples in mathematical and personal explanations. Each step in a mathematical proof of a theorem alone entails it, since the other steps in the deduction are all necessary; but the explanation is not vitiated on this count. A perfectly good personal explanation for why my arm went up is that I raised it, or for why there exists at least one dependent being that God willed that there be. Herein we have an explanans composed of a single proposition that alone entails the explanandum. These are decisive counterexamples to the Humean thesis that in an adequate causal explanation, the proposition reporting the cause must not entail the proposition reporting the effect. Requirement (ii) would appear to rest on a hasty generalization from the case of Hempelian deductive-nomological type explanations in which it is required that no statement of a particular fact alone entail the explanandum, since it would render the covering law(s) otiose in the deduction.[16]

It might be retorted that my explanation of my arm's rising is elliptical, for I endeavored (tried, and so on) to raise my arm; and there are causal laws that say roughly that whenever someone endeavors in this manner to raise their arm in such circumstances, their arm goes up. Herein the statement of the cause does not entail the statement of the effect. This full-blown explanation imputes to me the belief that my intentional actions are causally determined; but I do not have this belief. Furthermore, this sort of covering-law explanation could have no application to the explanation of D in terms of God's will, since the connection between God's will and its effects is certified by the conceptual truth that he is omnipotent rather than by some contingent causal law connecting God's endeavorings with their worldly effects.

Even if requirements (i) and (ii) are accepted, counterexamples can be given to Rowe's claim that it is impossible to give a noncircular formal explanation of D in terms of dependent beings. The following is an example of just such an explanation:

27. Fred exists;
28. Fred is a dependent being; therefore,
D. There exists at least one dependent being.

It might be countered that 27 and 28 each alone entails D, since each is expressed by a sentence containing a proper name of a dependent being. But by this reasoning, it also would follow that each alone entails that there exists at least one fireman, if Fred should happen to be a fireman! Being a dependent being (as well as being a fireman) need not be included in the sense of the proper name "Fred." And this is how the name "Fred" is to be understood in my above explanation. Some might find a special problem with 28, since they think that it has existential import and thereby entails that Fred exists, with the result that it alone entails D. But there is no reason why 28 must be interpreted in this way.

Certainly we can predicate a property of an individual without committing ourselves to its existence, as in "Santa Claus is a man." This is how 28 is to be read. Maybe it would be clearer if it were replaced by

28'. For any x, if x is identical with Fred, then x is a dependent being.

Even if my explanation is not formally circular, it might be felt to fail as an explanation on the ground that it does not give any cause for D. This can be rectified as follows:

29. Fred endeavored to create a dependent being;
30. If Fred were to endeavor to create a dependent being, he would succeed; therefore,
D. There exists at least one dependent being,

in which the proper name "Fred" again denotes a dependent being, thereby explaining D in terms of the causal efficacy of a dependent being.

It might be objected that 29 violates (ii) because it alone entails D. If Fred endeavors to do X, he brings about or agent-determines his act of endeavoring, from which it follows that there exists at least one dependent being, his act of endeavoring. This objection is not decisive because of the murky nature of agent determination.

Even if my two "explanations" of D, and for sure the first one, do not fail on formal grounds since they satisfy (i) and (ii), they still might fail on pragmatic grounds. The pragmatic aspect of explanation has to do with the basic fact that an explanation is an attempt to answer some person's why-question and thereby must be geared to their knowledge, beliefs, skills, interests, and purposes. It is this pragmatic aspect of explanation that accounts for why an explanatory context is nonextensional; as well as the fact that explanation is not closed under deduction, that is, an explanation of p does not explain every proposition that p entails, the reason being that the person to whom the explanation is directed might be ignorant of the entailment, just as he might be ignorant of the fact that $X = Y$ and thus be satisfied by an explanation of why X is F but not find it adequate as an explanation of why Y is F. Putnam's account of why the physicist's description of the microstructure of a round peg and a square hole on a board is not an explanation of the fact that the peg doesn't go in the hole rests on such pragmatic considerations concerning the knowledge and skill of the person to whom the explanation is directed.[17] Most people are not knowledgeable and quick enough to derive the macrodescription of the peg and hole from the microdescription, even though it is entailed by the latter.

Granted that there are these pragmatic requirements for a successful explanation, in exactly what way are my two explanations of D pragmatically deficient?[18] Let us say that an explanation is *pragmatically circular* if the person to whom it is addressed is in an epistemic situation that precludes his being able to know some proposition in the explanans without knowing the explanandum. I imagine that all ordinary human beings are in epistemological circumstances that make it impossible for us to know one or more of the propositions in the analysans of my two explanations of D without knowing D.

In respect to the second explanation, it is very dubious that we could know that

30. If Fred were to endeavor to create a dependent being, he would succeed

without knowing that some dependent being exists and thereby knowing D. If 30 resembles an F-conditional in having a consequent that is not determined by its antecedent, we cannot know it since we are not possessed of some mysterious faculty of "middle knowledge." We can know a subjunctive like 30 only if there is some nomic connection between its antecedent and conclusion and we have observed past cases of Fred's successfully creating dependent beings, thereby knowing of certain individual beings, namely, the ones created by Fred in the past, that they are dependent beings. And since we know certain singular propositions that predicate being a dependent being of some individual, we know D as well, since D is entailed by such a singular proposition in virtue of the principle of existential generalization. We must assume that the person to whom the second, as well as the first, explanation is directed reasons in accordance with this principle; otherwise the explanation could not work for him since it must appeal to this principle in deducing its explanandum from its explanans.

The first explanation also seems to suffer from pragmatic circularity. It is hard to imagine how beings in our epistemic circumstances could know

28. Fred is a dependent being

without knowing D. The problem gets down to whether we could know 28 without knowing that Fred exists. One way we could get to know 28 is by observing Fred's coming into existence through the causal efficacy of some other being, but this involves our knowing that Fred exists. Another way we could learn that 28 is true is by finding out that Fred is a fictional or mythical being who is described in some story as a dependent being; but, again, this involves knowing that some being is dependent, since we know that the story itself is such a dependent being, since being created by its author(s). Although I am sure that my two explanations are pragmatically deficient, I am not confident that I have correctly brought out the manner in which they are, and I must leave it to my philosophical superiors to do a better job than I have been able to do.

So far we have tried with dubious success to undermine the combined general fact version of the cosmological argument by finding an internalistic explanation for D in terms of a dependent being. But a more effective way of criticizing the argument is to show that

22. The explanation for the fact that there exists at least one dependent being is in terms of the causal efficacy of either a dependent or an independent being

does not, as claimed by this argument, follow from the conjunction of

1. Every individual is either a dependent or independent being; and
21. There is an explanation for the fact that there exists at least one dependent being.

The strategy is to find some possible explanation for the fact D that does not invoke any dependent being or *causally efficacious* independent being. Let us call such an explanation of D an "atheistic explanation." We are permitting an atheistic explanation to make use of independent beings provided that they are not capable of being causal explainers, examples of which are numbers, properties, and so on. Plainly, 22 is incompatible with the possibility of such an atheistic explanation of D.

Rowe shows that he is aware of this strategy for attacking 22, for he considers the possibility of giving some kind of atheistic explanation for why D is necessary. Such an explanation would also explain why D is true since we philosophers – the people to whom the explanation is directed – are aware that a necessary proposition is true. After correctly faulting Clarke for inferring from the proposition that every dependent being has the possibility of not existing that it is possible that no dependent being exist, Rowe presents an argument of his own for the nonnecessity of D based upon God's omnipotence that avoids Clarke's de re–de dicto confusion.

The premises of Rowe's argument are that it is possible that God exists and that it is necessary that if God exists, God can bring it about that no dependent beings exist (166). While his argument is valid, its second premise is question-begging, provided that God's omnipotence is restricted, as it ought to be, to that which it is logically consistent for God to bring about. If it should turn out to be necessary that there exists at least one dependent being, then not even an omnipotent being could bring it about that none exist. Two arguments will now be presented for D being necessary. The premises from which the necessity of D is deduced must each be necessary, and there are grounds for doubting that they are.

For instance, each argument contains the PSR as a premise, and the PSR hardly seems necessary. But even if each premise is only possible, provided that the premises are compossible and entail D, it suffices to establish that, pace Rowe's 22, it is possible to have an atheistic explanation for D. Thus, an atheistic explanation need not worry about whether the PSR is necessary, only that it is true in some possible world, and certainly we'll grant at least this much.

The necessity of time argument

31. It is necessary that time exists [premise];
32. It is necessary that if time exists there exist empirical beings [premise];
33. It is necessary that there exists at least one empirical being [from 31 and 32];
34. It is necessary that every being is either an independent or dependent being [PSR₁];
35. It is necessary that no empirical being is an independent being [premise];
36. It is necessary that every empirical being is a dependent being [from 34 and 35]; and
37. It is necessary that there exists at least one dependent being [from 33 and 36].

Serious challenges can be made to both 31 and 32, as well as 34, but the latter issue will not concern us for the previously stated reason. Two sorts of objections might be raised against 31. While all but some mystics and mystically inclined metaphysicians would grant that time is real, many would deny that it is necessary. Arguments for the latter can be found in Kant's *Transcendental Aesthetic*. I have developed a very different argument for its necessity in my *Negation and Non-Being* based upon the need for a spatiotemporal receptacle of a topologically and metrically amorphous nature to serve as the ground for the possibility of forms being instantiated and, moreover, being multiply instantiated, space and time herein serving as the ultimate ground of individuation of qualitatively similar empirical particulars. The basic underlying metaphysical intuition is that possibility is grounded in actuality. It is conceptually necessary that the Platonic forms exist. They specify possibilities for existence, and it is necessary that there are these possibilities. But such possibilities are possibilities for the instantiation of a form, and this requires a realm in which such instantiations could take place. And what could this be but space-time. There are many who are not convinced by these arguments, but the only important issue is whether it is at least possible that time exists, and about this there should be no argument, unless it can be presented *very* quickly, that is, in no time at all.

It might be objected that 31 refers to an independent being – time – since there is an ontological argument of sorts, such as my above *Timaeus*-inspired argument for its existence. But an atheistic explanation of D is allowed to invoke an independent being, provided it is not capable of being a causal agent. And remember, neither time can wither nor custom stale! If 31 is recast, as some think it must be, so that it is only contingently true that time exists, the explanation invokes a being that is neither an independent nor a dependent being, since time itself cannot cause anything. While it might be reasonable to define an atheistic explanation of D so that it is permitted to use individuals that are neither dependent nor independent beings, there would be a clash with 34–PSR$_1$. This requires that the necessity of time employ a more restricted version of PSR$_1$, but I do not think that it is very difficult to find a version that will do the trick.

The most serious difficulty concerns 32's attempt to ground an ontological claim on empirical considerations. Since it is not possible for us to identify times except by reference to the empirical particulars that exist in time, time itself could not exist without such particulars. Even though 32 has been accepted by such luminaries as Plato, Aristotle, and St. Augustine, to mention just a few, I find it dubious. And if 32 isn't acceptable, neither are its weaker cousins that claim only that it is contingently true or possibly true, for the only reason we could have for accepting these weaker claims is that it is a necessary conceptual truth that time could not exist without empirical particulars.

The argument from negation

38. It is necessary that every being is either an independent or dependent being [PSR$_1$];

39. It is necessary that every contingent being is a dependent being [from 38];

40. It is necessary that for every contingent being x, if it is a fact that x exists, there is an explanation of this fact, and if x does not exist, there is an explanation of this negative fact [a version of the PSR];

41. It is necessary that an explanation for the fact that a contingent being does not exist be in terms of some existent contingent being(s) whose properties logically preclude its existence [premise];

42. It is necessary that some contingent beings exist [from 41]; and

43. It is necessary that at least one dependent being exist [from 39 and 42].

What this argument amounts to is an ontological argument for the existence of a world of contingent or dependent beings. It is borrowed from Bergson's account of nothingness in *Creative Evolution* and was advanced by him for the expressed purpose of precluding the need to invoke necessary, timeless abstracta – Platonic forms – in explaining why there is something rather than nothing.[19] Again, we need not worry about the modal status of the different versions of the PSR that appear in 38 and 40, only that they are at least possible. Furthermore, there is no question about this being an atheistic explanation of D, since it invokes no independent beings at all, not even causally inefficacious ones.

Premise 41 is the vulnerable spot in the argument, and objections to it cannot be sidestepped by downgrading it to a contingent or possible truth, since the only grounds for accepting the weaker versions of 40 is that 40 is a conceptual truth. This premise is based upon the "incompatibility" theory of negation and involves an application of it to negative existentials. The incompatibility theory claims that every negative fact is logically entailed by some positive fact(s). This theory satisfies a deep rational longing to be able completely to describe the world in wholly positive terms; for once every true proposition is listed, every negative fact about the world can be deduced from them, which was Wittgenstein's ideal in the *Tractatus*. Negation, although ineliminable, is redundant.[20] To understand fully why an object lacks some positive property, we must know what positive property of the object is logically incompatible with the excluded property. For instance, the reason why the table is not red is that it is blue. The "otherness" analysis of negative proposition, which is advanced by Plato in the *Sophist*, merely informs us that every positive property of the table is other than redness; but this does not adequately explain the positive ground for this exclusion, leaving us with ultimate, brute, negative facts.

The incompatibility theory probably isn't true, since we seem able to conceive of the incredible odorless man – a man who lacks any odor without this being entailed by any of his positive properties – or, as some might prefer, the fabulous tasteless woman. But our concern is not with whether this theory is true, only with whether it correctly articulates what constitutes an intellectually satisfying explanation of a negative fact. By the same reasoning, a rationally satisfying explanation of a general negative existential fact, for instance, that there are no hippogriffs, will present a conjunction of positive facts along with a Porky-the-Pig-type fact to the effect that "da, da, da, da that's all folks," for instance, X is a pig and Y is a hammer and so on, and every existent being is identical with either X or Y and so on. Without such existent objects as X and Y and their positive sortal properties that are logically incompatible with hippogriffness, there would be no satisfactory explanation of why these beasts fail to make it into existence. It might be retorted by the theist that the positive fact that explains the failure of hippogriffs to exist could be that God willed that they not exist. How rationally satisfying we find such an explanation will depend upon our assessment of the overall adequacy of theistic explanations of worldly facts. And about this philosophers disagree.

The ontological disproof argument

This argument attempts to prove only that it is possible that there is an atheistic explanation for D, not that there necessarily is; but this suffices to refute the combined general fact version's attempt to *deduce* from the assumption that every being is dependent that there is no explanation for D. It goes as follows:

1'. There is an explanation for every fact [PSR$_2$];

D. There exists at least one dependent being [assumption for conditional proof];

21. There is an explanation for the fact that there exists at least one dependent being [from 1 and D by universal instantiation];

44. The explanation for the fact that there exists at least one dependent being is either an atheistic one or in terms of the causal efficacy of an independent being [premise];

45. It is logically impossible that there exists an independent being capable of causally explaining the fact that there exists at least one dependent being [premise];

46. The explanation for the fact that there exists at least one dependent being cannot be in terms of the causal efficacy of an independent being [from 45];

47. The explanation for the fact that there exists at least one dependent being is an atheistic one [from 44 and 46 by disjunctive syllogism];

48. If there exists at least one dependent being, then the explanation for the fact that there exists at least one dependent being is an atheistic one [from D, 21, and 44–47 by conditional proof];

49. It is possible that there exists at least one dependent being [premise]; and

50. It is possible that the explanation for the fact that there exists at least one dependent being is an atheistic one [from 48 and 49 by theorem of modal logic [$L(p \supset q)$ and Mp] $\supset Mq$].

No one has ever given this argument. It is not due to its lacking validity or its premises being mutually inconsistent but rather because they make strange bedfellows. The philosopher who is rationalistic (i.e., gullible) enough to swallow PSR$_2$ will go all the way and also countenance the possibility of there being a successful ontological argument for the existence of God or a being very much like God, and thereby would not accept 45, which denies the possibility of such an argument. The cosmological arguer is committed to the denial of 45 and will rightly demand an argument for it. I have already issued a promissory note for this argument that will be cashed at the end of this chapter.

This completes the critical evaluation of Rowe's general existential fact version of the cosmological argument, the results of which can now be summarized. There were two ways in which Rowe's general existential fact could be explained without reference to the causal efficacy of an independent being. The first was an internalistic explanation in terms of some dependent being. Rowe's vicious circularity argument against this being possible was challenged by two possible explanations of this sort for D; and, though they were not defective on formal grounds, they appeared pragmatically deficient. The second was in terms of three atheistic explanations or arguments for D, those being the arguments from the necessity of time, the incompatibility theory of negation, and the ontological disproof. Each was found to contain highly mooted philosophical premises. Many philosophers will find one or more of these arguments attractive, due to their philosophical intuitions predisposing them toward their premises. This sociological fact about the philosophical profession does not refute Rowe's cosmological argument, but it does give us an incentive to seek a version that will be subject to fewer philosophical challenges. The next version achieves this.

THE WORLD BOOK VERSION

It is surprising that this version has never been given before; for, in addition to being more simple and less controversial than either the concrete-aggregate or general existential fact versions, it better realizes the desiderata that were given at the outset of this chapter. A world book is a maximal, compossible set of propositions that serves to define a given possible world, being all the propositions that would be true if that world were to be actualized. There is a one to one correlation between possible worlds and world books. We could even think of a possible world as identical with its world book. Necessarily, one and only one possible world has absolute actuality, even if it be one in which every contingent proposition is false, and therefore one and only one world book contains propositions each of which is true simpliciter or absolutely. It was the burden of Chapter 5 to establish this against Lewis's ontological parity thesis.

While our radical limitations in knowledge preclude our knowing which world book is the true one, we know for sure that some one book alone is absolutely true. The world book version of the cosmological argument begins with this unassailable fact. Call that unique world book B and the possible world it corresponds to or is identical with W. B is the big conjunction, containing not only all of the contingent propositions, such as all the atomic and lawlike propositions, true in W, but all of the necessary propositions as well.[21] If God exists in W there will be propositions in the big conjunction that assert God's existence and describe his creative activity.

While the world book version begins with the existential fact consisting of the conjunction of all the propositions in B, it does not direct its explanatory demand at this big conjunction but instead at a depleted conjunction, B', that is derived from it by dropping out all of its conjuncts that are either necessary or entail that God exists. There are two reasons for directing the explanatory demand at this depleted conjunction. First, it avoids the horrendous problem of what constitutes an explanation of a necessary proposition, for instance, some fact about linguistic use or an essential property of a Platonic entity and the like. Second, it escapes the possibility of giving an internalistic explanation in terms of the conjuncts themselves. If God were to exist in *W, B* would contain such God-entailing propositions as that God has willed that all of the propositions in *B'* be true together, thereby explaining the conjunction formed from the propositions in *B'*. And this internalistic explanation of the *B'*-derived conjunction, in conjunction with whatever internalistic explanation might be offered for the necessary propositions in *B* (e.g., the Platonic or linguistic account), might be thought together to constitute an internalistic explanation of the big conjunction formed from *B*, thereby pulling the rug from under the explanatory argument that attempts to show that it is impossible for there to be an internalistic explanation of this big conjunction.

The question is whether the explanatory argument succeeds when directed at showing the impossibility of giving an internalistic explanation for the *B'*-derived conjunction. Let us imagine that this conjunction contains the contingent propositions *p* and *q* and *r*, some of which are atomic and others lawlike. It would appear that it is impossible to explain the conjunction (*p* and *q* and *r*) in terms of its conjuncts. Even if each and every member of this conjunction had an internalistic explanation, for instance, *p* is explained in terms of *q*, *q* in terms of *r*, and *r* in terms of *p*, this would not constitute an explanation for the fact that they are all true together, due to the nonagglomerative nature of explanation. Even though the several internalistic explanations of *p*, *q*, and *r* do not constitute an explanation of their conjunction, might it not be the case that some member of this conjunction explains the entire conjunction? I don't see how this is possible. Suppose it were conjunct *p* that performed this explanatory task; conjunct p would have to explain, among other things, each and every conjunct and thereby would have to explain itself. But this it cannot do, since it is only a contingent proposition. Herein we face what seems to be an irresolvably vicious circularity of explanation. My imagination is quite limited, and I might have overlooked some foxy way of giving an internalistic explanation of B'; however, our prima facie intuitions are against this being possible, and thereby I place the onus on those who think it can be done. I await my next letter from Phil Quinn telling me that my intuitions are not shared by the maintenance people at Notre Dame on this issue.

All that remains is the PSR component of the world book version, and it is obvious what form it will take, namely, that of PSR_2 requiring that *every* fact, including truth-functional ones, have an explanation. Thus, in the name of PSR_2, there must be an explanation for a B'-derived conjunction. And since the explanatory argument has already established that it cannot be an internalistic one, it must be in terms of the causal efficacy of some independent being who is very much like God.

Some general objections

Our critical evaluations of the different versions of the cosmological argument have mostly been confined to an assessment of their relative strengths and weakness, with the world book version emerging as the most attractive of the lot; but there are several objections that apply to all of them that have not yet been considered. And we now turn to this final task so as to reach an absolute evaluation of them.

Denial of the PSR. This is the obvious way of cutting off at the pass any version of the cosmological argument: refuse to grant, even as a contingent truth, the version of the PSR that it requires – PSR_2 in the case of the world book and general existential fact versions and PSR_1 in that of the concrete-aggregate version.

The cosmological arguer's response to this objection should be to recast her argument so that its conclusion no longer is that there is in fact a theistic-type explanation for the existential fact in question in terms of the causal efficacy of an independent being but that this is the only possible explanation of this fact. If there is to be an explanation for this existential fact, it must be the theistic one. If successful, this argument would have a very important and startling result – that only God can satisfy our rational longing to have a really intellectually satisfying explanation of the universe. All along this has been the real goal of the cosmological argument. Furthermore, if this conditional version of the cosmological argument works, it can be urged that we ought to accept the theistic explanation by the principle that anything is better than nothing or, even better, by the currently fashionable principle of inference to the best explanation. The critic will respond that these principles do not hold when the only available or best explanation is a bad one.

Regressiveness of a theistic explanation. It will be recalled that the aim of the cosmological argument was to shut up precocious brats by putting an end to their regress of why-questions. The point of this objection is that the cosmological argument fails to do this because it must employ in its explanation of the existential fact in question some contingent proposition, such as that God or the independent being willed that this be a fact; and, since this proposition is not a self-explainer, it is a legitimate subject of a why-question. "Why did God will that way?" The Spinozisitic theist can respond that this proposition is necessary, because God was not free to make any creative choice but this one. But few theists find this way out of the regress of explanations attractive, since, in addition to denying free will to God, it entails that there is only one possible world, given that it is necessary that God exists.

Fortunately, there is a less drastic way for the theist to block the regress of why-questions – argue along Libertarian lines that a free act is not a legitimate subject of an explanatory demand. According to the intuitions of the Libertarian, a free choice cannot have a sufficient event-cause and thereby cannot be causally explained, though the agent can make her choice intelligible by giving reasons for it. Thus, the proper response to the child's request to explain what caused God's creative choice is, "Shut up! It was done freely." Whereas the fact that God exists supposedly can be explained by deducing his existence from his essence, God's creative decision admits of no explanation whatever and thereby is a suitable place at which to stop the regress of explanations. The sort of theistic explanation that a cosmological argument offers for its initial existential fact could be called, in contradistinction to a scientific explanation, a "final explanation," in that each proposition in its explanans is either self-explained via some ontological argument or requires no explanation on conceptual grounds.

The ontological disproof. Each of the above three cosmological arguments had a different existential fact for which it demanded an explanation, but in each case the conclusion was drawn that there exists a necessary being that is the cause of the fact in question – that the universe or the infinite succession of dependent beings exists, that D is true, and that the B'-derived conjunction is true. Several arguments will now be given for their conclusions being impossible. The underlying strategy in each of these arguments is to show that the necessary being referred to in their conclusion is an unsurpassably great being – a being that is both maximally excellent, that is, essentially (omnipotent, omniscient, omnibenevolent, providential, etc.), and necessarily existent. Appeal will then be made to the Chapter 6 argument for it being logically impossible that there exist an unsurpassably great being based on there being properties, such as being a morally unjustified evil or a world in which all free persons always freely go wrong, that are both strongly incompatible with having unsurpassable greatness (i.e., if either has the possibility of instantiation the other does not) and intuitively more likely candidates for the possibility of instantiation than is having unsurpassable greatness. My arguments will be directed against the concrete-aggregate version, but they can be deployed with equal effectiveness against the other versions.

The first argument is an ad hominem one, since it does not demonstrate that it is absolutely impossible that there exist a necessary being who determines the existence of the universe, and the like, only that it is impossible relative to the propositions that the cosmological arguer is committed to accepting, namely, that this necessary being is the God of traditional theism. It was Clarke himself who went on to argue in the second stage of his cosmological argument in the *Demonstration* that this necessary being has all of the essential omniproperties of the God of traditional Western theism, that is, maximal excellence.

The argument begins with the conclusion of the concrete-aggregate argument as an assumption for indirect proof:

51. There exists a necessary being, N, who determines that the universe or the infinite succession of dependent beings exists [assumption for indirect proof];

52. N is a maximally excellent being [granted, even argued for, by cosmological arguer];

53. N has necessary existence [from 51];

54. N is an unsurpassably great being [from 52 and 53 by definition of unsurpassable greatness];

55. It is conceptually impossible that there exists an unsurpassably great being [proven by argument in Chapter 6];

56. N does not exist [from 54 and 55 by universal instantiation];

57. N exists [from 51];

58. N both does and does not exist [from 56 and 57 by conjunction]; and

59. It is not the case that there exists a necessary being, N, that determines that the universe and the like exists [from 51 to 58 by indirect proof].

There is another path that leads from

51. There exists a necessary being, N, who determines that the universe, and the like, exists

to

54. N is an unsurpassably great being

that appeals to an assumption that is more plausible in its own right than is

52. N is a maximally excellent being.

It holds that N is a universe determiner not just in the actual world but in any world in which N exists:

60. In every world in which N exists, N determines that the universe exists [premise].

Basically, this is applying the Chapter 4 principle of sovereign type-invariance to N.[22] This seems a reasonable extension of this principle, for any necessarily existent being that is a universe determiner in one world should perform this function in every world. It would be extremely anomalous to allow it to be a universe determiner in one world but not in another in which it exists, prompting unanswerable questions as to what caused it to lose its job, how it could lose its job given that it has such wonderous properties as being necessarily existent, and so on. The next step in the derivation of 54 from 51 is the quite plausible assumption, obviously acceptable to the cosmological arguer, as well as Anselm's Fool opponent, that it is at least possible that there exists a maximally excellent being capable of completely and solely determining that the universe exists. Since a being is capable of doing something only if it does it in some possible world, this entails

61. There is a possible world, W, in which there exists a maximally excellent being, E, who completely and solely determines that the universe exists [granted by both Fool and cosmological arguer].

Since N is necessarily existent, it follows that

62. *N* exists in *W* [from 51].

But from 62 in conjunction with 60 it follows that

63. *N* determines in *W* that the universe exists.

From 61 and 63 it follows that

64. *N* is numerically one and the same being as *E* in *W*,

the reason being that, since *E* is the complete and sole universe determiner in *W*, any being who is a universe determiner in *W* is identical with *E*. Since *N* is identical with *E*, a maximally excellent being, in virtue of Leibniz's Law, it follows that

65. *N* is maximally excellent in *W*.

Because maximal excellence is an essential property and *N* has necessary existence, it follows that

66. In the actual world, *N* is both maximally excellent and necessarily existent,

and thus

54. *N* is (in the actual world) an unsurpassably great being [by definition of unsurpassable greatness].

And from here the argument proceeds to deduce a contradiction by appeal to the argument in Chapter 6.

My two arguments against the possibility of 51 constitute ontological disproofs of the existence of the very sort of being whose existence is asserted in the conclusion of every version of the cosmological argument, thereby showing that these arguments are radically defective. These ontological disproofs, however, do not pinpoint the defective spot in these arguments. Hopefully, some guidance for accomplishing this task has been supplied by the critical analyses of these arguments that have been given in this chapter.

Chapter 8

Religious-experience arguments

Throughout history, in almost every society, persons have claimed to experience God or some ultimate reality in the same sort of immediate way that they experience physical objects through their senses. Their experiences have been quite diverse, running the gamut from extrovertive and introvertive mystical experiences of some underlying unity into which the experient is totally or partially incorporated to numinous experiences and direct experiences of God's presence as a very powerful, loving, nonhuman person who shows concern for the well-being of the experient. Different descriptions are given of the apparent object of their experiences – God, one's personal *purusha*, Brahman, the eternal one, the undifferentiated unity, and the like. In spite of these different characterizations, the subjects agree in taking the object of their experience to be the ultimate reality, the really real, and, most important, are convinced that man's greatest possible good consists in achieving a direct, experiential contact or union with this reality. For these reasons, I shall call all these experiences "religious experiences," even though they are not taken to be such by everyone who has them.

I shall duck the thorny issue of whether there is a common phenomenological content to all or most of these experiences, at least the unitive ones, that supposedly gets interpreted differently by mystics in diverse cultures, as well as the larger problem of whether the phenomenological–interpretative and observation–theoretical language distinctions are viable. While I am in basic agreement with the twentieth-century "mystical ecumenicalists" – Underhill, Otto, Stace, Suzuki, Merton, and N. Smart – who accept these dualisms and find a common phenomenological content, it will not be necessary for me to defend their views against their contemporary critics, such as R. C. Zaehner and Steven Katz. I will assume that these distinctions are viable relative to our epistemic circumstances – the manner in which we experience the world and process information. Our perception of something as a chair involves a minimal amount of theoretical interpretation, if any, but our perception of a track in a Wilson cloud chamber as a movement of an electron involves a highly theoretically based inference. Similarly, our experience of an undifferentiated unity or a personal, loving presence is relatively noninferential as contrasted with our perception of an evil as a test set for us by God or of a sunset as an expression of God's love. The latter involve causal inferences that make use of a theological theory concerning the relation between God and the world.

My concern is with those religious experiences that are the analogue to the relatively theory-free, noninferential sensory perceivings-as, such as seeing something as a desk. They could be called "recognitional," as contrasted with "inferential," perceivings-as. Sensory experiences of visions and voices as God-caused, therefore, will not be considered. My concern, rather, is with nonsensory experiences that their subjects take to be "direct" or noninferential experiences of God, the eternal one, and the like. Furthermore, if any of these religious experiences are such that they do not get ontologized by their subjects, as is alleged to be the case with some Buddhist mystical experiences, due to a total obliteration of any subject–object distinction, they will fall outside the purview of my discussion. My concern is only with those that are taken by their subjects to be of some objective reality that transcends consciousness and exists independently of being experienced.

The underlying question of this chapter is whether these religious experiences constitute evidence for reality being as it appears to the experients. If they do constitute evidence or epistemic justification for believing that there is such an objective reality, they will serve as the basis for a good argument for the existence of God or this highest reality:

A. Religious experiences occur;
B. Religious experiences constitute evidence for the existence of their apparent object, God and the like; therefore,
C. There is evidence that God and the like exist.

To have this sort of evidential status, these experiences must not only be veridical but cognitive as well. A type of experience could be veridical without being cognitive. It could qualify as veridical in virtue of the apparent object of the experience causing the experience in the "right way," but not count as cognitive since it does not constitute evidence or warrant for believing that this object exists and is as it appears to be in the experience. Even if we were to have a good argument for the veridicality of religious experiences, for instance, based on a successful ontological or cosmological argument and the analytic truth that God would not allow us to be duped on a large scale by experiences that seemed to be veridical perceptions of him, it still would not show these experiences to be cognitive, since they *alone* would not constitute a basis for our gaining knowledge of some objective reality. A cognitive faculty should stand on its own two epistemological feet. It will be argued that religious experiences, although possibly veridical, could not be cognitive. Even if it were possible that their apparent object exist and be the right sort of cause of the experience, we could never know on the basis of these experiences either that this object exists or that the experience is caused in the "right way" by it. I shall go on to argue that a religious experience also could not qualify as a veridical perception of an objective reality, even if its apparent object were to exist and be the cause of the experience.

If a type of experience *E* is cognitive, then the occurrence of an *E*-type experience counts as evidence for the existence of its intentional accusative, *even for those who have not had this experience or even any E-type experiences*. It was for this reason that propositions B and C in the former argument did not relativize their claims about the evidential status of religious experiences to the people who have them. That a cognitive experience's evidential status is not person-relative is a fundamental conceptual requirement for an experience having cognitive status, a point that is often missed by those who defend the cognitivity of religious experiences. William James, in his assessment of the cognitivity of mystical experiences in the concluding section of *The Varieties of Religious Experience*, violated this epistemic counterpart to the moral principle of universalizability when he wrote, "Mystical states, when well developed, usually are, *and have the right to be*, absolutely authoritative over the individuals to whom they come" (my italics). But, he adds, "no authority emanates from them which should make it a duty for those who stand outside of them to accept their revelations uncritically." This makes it look as if the occurrence of mystical experiences constitutes evidence for their veridicality for those who have them but not for those who do not, which clearly violates the requirement that a cognitive experience's status as evidential is observer-neutral. No doubt those who have mystical experiences will be caused to believe in what they seem to reveal, whereas no such causal compulsion will operate on the nonmystic, but this is a psychological issue and of no epistemological interest. Further, mystics will be more certain of the occurrence of mystical experiences than nonmystics, but this makes no difference to the evidential status of mystical experiences, only to the certainty of their occurrence.

What argument can be given for the cognitivity, as opposed to the veridicality, of religious experiences of the sort under consideration? Every argument that I know of is based on an analogy with sense experience and is a special instance of this general argument, to be called the "analogical argument for cognitivity":

1. Religious experiences are analogous to sense experiences;
2. Sense experiences are cognitive; therefore,
3. Religious experiences are cognitive.

Why should religious experiences have to ride the coattails of sense experience in their quest for epistemic respectability? It is due to two factors. First, sense experiences are a paradigm of cognitivity or knowledge-yielding experiences, unlike religious experiences, whose credentials have been perennially challenged. Second, we are clearer about the conceptual lay of the land in regard to the former than the latter. As William Alston, one of the leading defenders of the cognitivity of religious experiences, has said, "It seems reasonable to take principles which are well established with respect to sense-perception, an area where we pretty much know what to say under a given set of conditions, and extend them to the discussion of purported direct experiences of God, an area where it is not at all clear what one should say."[1] Thus, the most likely way to establish the cognitivity of religious experiences is to show that they are sufficiently analogous to sense experiences, those paradigms of cognitive experiences. William Wainwright, another leading proponent of the analogical argument for cognitivity, is quite right when he says that "the analogy (or lack of it) between mystical experience and sense experience appears, then, to be critically important both to those who ascribe cognitive value to mystical experience and to those who refuse to do so."[2]

While few will venture to challenge premise 2, for this leads to complete scepticism, a serious problem arises in respect to 1, the analogical premise. How close must the analogy be to support the inference of 3 from 1 and 2? There is no agreed upon answer to this question among the proponents of the different versions of the analogical argument, since these arguments fill out the analogical premise in different ways, some giving a very thin, high-level analogy that holds only that both kinds of experiences form the basis of ongoing language games, and others a more thoroughgoing analogy that claims similarity in the sort of checks and tests or defeating conditions that apply to both. The problem of how close the analogy must be is very acute, since everything is like everything else in some respect; for instance, any two entities share the property of being self-identical. This, I take it, was the point a burly Canadian good-old-boy truck driver, Bob, made when he responded to my question about what it is like driving his monstrous sixteen wheeler by saying that "it was just aboot like anything else you do, just aboot like drinking a glass of beer; you just sit back and do it without making a big fuss." I was tempted to ask Bob if he was contemplating writing a book about Zen and the art of truck driving, but I know he would have replied that "Zen is just aboot like anything else," which, by the way, would be an excellent one-sentence summary of the Zen vision.

The analogical premise must specify not any old analogy between religious and sense experiences, for instance, that both are among Bob's favorite type of experiences, but one that is relevant to their cognitivity. But, even with this restriction, there is no decision procedure for determining how close the analogy must be for it to be reasonable to infer 3 from 1 and 2. The best that can be done is to consider the different versions of the analogical argument and, for each of them, explore in detail and depth all of the *relevant* analogies and disanalogies, with the hope that once this is accomplished it will become reasonably clear what is the right judgment to pass. I hope to show that the various analogies are very thin and that the disanalogies are very extensive and deep, thereby destroying the different versions of the analogical argument. I know that this will leave Bob unmoved; but, hopefully, not all of my readers are imbibing a Molson, as they say "This book is just aboot like every other book."

The results of my discussion will have widespread interest, since they can be applied to several other nonsensory faculties that are claimed to be cognitive on the basis of an analogy with sense experience, most notably Plato's faculty of intellectual intuition and Moore's faculty of moral intuition, both of which are described in perceptual terms. The fate of all these nonsensory faculties of "perception" are intertwined such that if my polemic against the cognitivity of religious experience succeeds, it works equally well mutatis mutandis against these other nonsensory "perceptual" faculties. "Catch one of them and you catch all of them!"

We shall begin with the weakest version of the argument from analogy and then progress to ever stronger versions. The weakest version is based on a very thin analogy between religious and sense experience. In its thinnest form it holds only that both serve as the basis on which objective existential claims are made within different ongoing language games, such a game being a normatively rule-governed human practice of using language. No further similarity is claimed, but in the stronger versions the analogy gets filled in further so that in both games there are checks and tests or defeating conditions for these claims, and, in the strongest versions, that these tests are similar.

The weakest version will be called "language-game fideism," since it derives from Wittgenstein's language-game approach to religion in his *Lectures and Conversations on Aesthetics, Psychology and Religious Belief*. There are several different versions of language-game fideism, all of which can find some basis in Wittgenstein's writings. There are the cognitive and noncognitive versions, the former viewing the religious language game as involving truth claims for which epistemic justification can be given, the latter as involving nothing more than the expression of attitudes toward life, basic values, convictions, and the like. The latter version admits of a further distinction between descriptive and revisionary accounts. Philosophers like Hare, Phillips, Hudson, and Malcolm and Winch in some of their pronouncements, have claimed that the religious language game that we actually play is noncognitive, whereas others, like Braithwaite and Schmidt, accept that the actual game is cognitive but propose, so as to avoid a clash with science, that we revise it so that its sentences no longer play a fact-stating role but instead play an evocative and evincing role. We shall not bother with either of the two versions of noncognitive language-game fideism, though it should be noted that both are atrocious. The descriptive version radically misdescribes the actual enterprise of religion, and the revisionary account, if actually implemented, would result in the death of religion. There is no doubt that religious believers, including Kierkegaard, think they are saying things that are literally true about God and his relation to creation; their activities of attempting to commune with God would make no sense without such beliefs, for we do not think of ourselves as entering into a personal relationship, especially one of love, with a nonexistent person. Even the star of *Harvey* thought the big white rabbit to be real.

In the weakest version of cognitive language-game fideism, the analogy between sense and religious experiences consists in nothing more than both types of experiences serving within their respective language games as an epistemic warrant or justification for making an existential claim to the effect that the apparent object of the experience really exists. William Alston describes a version of such fideism, of which the following is a modified account.[3]

The first thing that must be done is to give some criterion for individuating language games, since this version of fideism depends upon religious and sense experiences occurring within *different* language games. A language game is individuated by the part of its ontology – what it is about or refers to – that has its categoreal nature defined by the rules of the game. Each language game has epistemological autonomy in that it has its own principles of rationality and justification, especially in regard to the unique part of its ontology. Language games can overlap in their ontologies, categories, and epistemology. Whether a type of experience counts as cognitive is relative to a language game. An of-O-type experience – an experience that has O as its apparent object or intentional accusative – counts as cognitive relative to language game L just in case: (a) The vast majority of the L-players upon having an of-O-type experience assert or believe that they are having an experience of an objectively existent O or that there exists an objective O and agree that it is correct to do so; and (b) L contains a noninductively derived rule of presumptive inference that if one has an of-O-type experience, then one probably has an experience of an objective O or there exists an objective O.[4] The a priori presumptive inference rule of (b) is grounded in the agreement in "language-entry" assertions described in (a), an of-*O*-type experience serving as both the occasion and the justification for asserting that one experiences an objective *O* or that *O* objectively exists.

This version of fideism winds up by pointing out that religious experiences count as cognitive relative to the language games played within various religious traditions. In these extant games, the having of an of-God (undifferentiated unity, etc.) -type experience serves as both the occasion and the a priori-based justification for the language-entry assertion that one experiences an objectively existent God (undifferentiated unity, etc.) or that God objectively exists. This version ends with the Greatest Story Ever Told, that "the language game is played."

Alston applies this fideist account not only to direct, nonsensory experiences of God's presence but also to sensory experiences of some worldly item as God-caused – what was previously called an "inferential perceiving-as." Herein I think he misdescribes the Christian language game. He says that "one learns to see good and ill fortune as blessings of God or as trials sent by God to test us or to provide the occasion for moral and spiritual growth."[5] Thus, one learns to respond to an evil by making the language-entry assertion or believing that it is a test sent by God. Since this assertion entails that God exists, it follows that evil, by virtue of the a priori presumptive inference rule that applies to it within the Christian language game, counts as evidence for the existence of God!

What could be a more radical distortion of this game, at least as played by Phil Quinn's "intellectually sophisticated adults in our culture,"[6] in which evil tries rather than confirms one's faith. Alston's "seeing-as" language-entry assertions involve a theoretically based inference to God as the cause of some worldly item. They are not the recognitional sort of seeing-as, which alone are our concern, and thus we shall not pursue the problem further.

Alston is unable to embrace this extreme version of fideism because it grates against his deep realist intuitions. He objects that an assertion is true by virtue of reality's being the way it is asserted to be. But, pace Alston, the correspondence theory of truth leaves fideism untouched, since it can be incorporated into every language game. The religious experience language game can hold that the assertion that there exists an Eternal One (God, etc.) is true by virtue of there existing an Eternal One (God, etc.). The correspondence theory is the willing tool of a language game's assertibility principles.

The obvious and decisive objection to extreme language-game fideism is that it is based on too thin an analogy, one that would impress only Bob. It does not enable us to infer the cognitivity of religious experience from the admitted cognitivity of sense experience; for, whereas the existential claims based upon sense experience have only a prima facie warrant, since subject to a battery of interconnected tests and checks, there are no defeating conditions for existential claims based upon religious experience. Whatever the experient takes to be the case on the basis of his religious experience really is the case. Because there are no tests for the veridicality of his experience, there is no basis for drawing the distinction between his actually perceiving God and it just seeming to him as if he is perceiving God. By not providing for any chance of being wrong, the analogy fails to make religious experience relevantly similar to sense experiences, for which the veridical–unveridical distinction holds.

An even more devastating objection to extreme language-game fideism is that its religious experience language game is not actually played. It is only a figment of my imagination that I have introduced as a foil by which to bring into clear relief less severe versions of fideism that are to follow. The religious experience language game we actually play allows for the possibility of error, because it contains tests for the existential claims based on religious experiences. Such experiences give only a prima facie epistemic justification for the former due to the existence of these defeating conditions.

LANGUAGE-GAME FIDEISM WITH ANY OLD TESTS

The crucial question is how close the analogy must be between the sort of tests and checks that enter into the religious and sense experience language games for the analogical argument to work. Let us begin with an analogical argument based upon the thinnest analogy between them, namely, that each game contains some test for the veridicality of an existential claim based upon its respective experience.

This imputes considerable epistemological autonomy to these games, each having its own distinctive criteria of rationality and epistemic justification, and thereby achieves the fideistic end of protecting religion from science.[7] This comes close to embracing a multivocalist theory of meaning according to which "cognitive," "knowledge," "veridical," "rationality," "justification," and "objective existence" have a different meaning in a religious context or language game than they have in a scientific or ordinary fact-stating one. An example of such a multivocalist-based defense of the cognitivity of religious experiences is Walter Stace's claim that such experiences, although not qualifying as objective by ordinary sensory-based standards, are objective in the sense of being "trans-subjective." Herein he seems to hold that there is in the mystical context a different and equally legitimate sense of "objective," along with the other related terms, to the ordinary, sensory-based one.

This version of fideism, although superior to the extreme form, is still unacceptable. In the first place, it misdescribes the religious language game. The players are not willing to say that their religious experiences provide them with *knowledge* of an *objective reality* but in a different sense of "knowledge" and "objective reality" from their ordinary, sensory-based one; for this would be to award the booby prize to their game. Admittedly, a proposition that predicates objective reality or existence of a table has categoreally different entailments than does one that predicates objective reality of God or the undifferentiated unity; but these differences are due not to any difference in the meaning of "objective reality" in the two propositions but a difference in the categoreal nature of the subjects of predication. Similarly, "and" is univocal in "Tables and chairs exist" and "Minds and sensations exist," in spite of the radical differences in the categoreal kind of propositions they entail.

Furthermore, the religious-experience language game does not have the sort of self-containment and epistemological autonomy that is imputed to it by this version of fideism. This game is a part of the larger religious language game, which employs many of the same principles of deductive and inductive logic as does the sensory-based physical object language in science and everyday life. The claim that God exists is not justified solely by appeal to religious experience but also by inductive-type arguments, as well as ontological and cosmological ones employing principles of deductive logic. For the "intellectually sophisticated adults in our culture" who participate in the religious language game, the proposition that God exists is not basic in Plantinga's sense, since they are willing to give various sorts of epistemic justifications for it.

In general, the use of "language game" to characterize the different ways in which we use language is misleading, since it makes it look as if different uses of language enjoy the sort of self-sufficiency and insularity that different games do. But this is a myth. There is only one big language game of which different so-called language games are interconnected parts. The religious-experience language game, as well as the larger religious language game, is part and parcel of the physical-world one, sharing many of its basic concepts concerning cognitivity, knowledge, existence, and warranted assertibility. Pace Wittgenstein, the theist and atheist really do believe incompatible propositions when one asserts and the other denies that there is a Last Judgment.

The most devastating objection, however, to this version of fideism is that it not only could, but actually does, justify far too much. By not requiring that the checks and tests for the veridicality of religious experience be significantly similar in cognitively relevant respects to those that enter into the sense-experience language game, it requires us to count as cognitive those religious experiences that occur within a cultist, religious-experience language game, in which the only test or check is based upon what the cult leader says. For instance, if a member of the PTL wants to find out if she has had a veridical religious experience, she simply telephones Jim Bakker, whatever he says settling the matter. While this is an exaggeration of the PTL game, it is not of some of the other cultist games, which, sad to say, actually are played and played with a vengeance. That this version of fideism is committed to saying that these cultist religious experiences count as cognitive shows that there is something radically wrong with this account of cognitivty. Anyone who doesn't agree should be horsewhipped.

It might be urged against my cultist counterexamples to language-game fideism with any old tests that they can be ruled out on the grounds that there are good independent reasons for rejecting their outputs, for instance, that they clash with the outputs of logic, science, or our deepest and most widely shared moral convictions. But we can avail ourselves of merely possible counterexamples to this version of fideism, such as a possible PTL language game in which Bakker and his followers are paragons of virtue and do not say anything that clashes with science and the like. The point is that even in such counterfactual circumstances, we would not want to count their epistemic practice, based upon the edicts issued by Bakker being decisive, as cognitive.

Another difficulty is that there are a multiplicity of different religious-experience language games, each with its own tests for veridicality – its own holy scriptures, holy men, and paradigmatic religious experiences. A religious experience could count as veridical relative to the tests provided by one of these games or religious traditions but not another, which, in fact, is the case. Whether this failure among players of religious-experience language games to agree about the proper methods for determining veridicality is destructive of their claims of cognitivity for their experiences will be discussed later, since this problem arises even for versions of the analogical argument that require that the tests for religious and sense experience be analogous. And we now turn to such versions.

LANGUAGE-GAME FIDEISM
WITH ANALOGOUS TESTS

This version of fideism has found four very able defenders in recent years – William Alston, Gary Gutting, Richard Swinburne, and William Wainwright. All can be viewed as responding to C. B. Martin's charge that "there are no tests agreed upon to establish genuine experience of God and distinguish it decisively from the ungenuine"[8] by showing that there are not only checks and tests for the veridicality of religious experiences but ones that are analogous in cognitively relevant respects to those for sense experiences. There are only minor, in-house differences between them that will be noted in passing.

All four begin with an a priori presumptive inference rule, subject to defeating conditions, linking how things perceptually seem with how they really are that applies to sense experiences and then argue by analogy that it should also hold for religious experiences. The rule must be a priori because in both cases any attempt to justify its adoption or establish the reliability of the doxastic practice of making existential claims on the basis of the type of experience in question will suffer from vicious circularity.[9] This is just as true of the doxastic practice of forming beliefs about physical objects on the basis of sense experience as it is of the doxastic practice of forming beliefs about God on the basis of religious experiences. Given that we must appeal to sense experiences to establish that a given sense experience or sense experience in general is veridical, fairness, what Alston calls "parity,"[10] requires that we do not demand that the veridicality of a given religious experience or religious experience in general be established by appeal to experiences other than religious ones. If we are willing to accept a circular justification in one case so as to escape scepticism, we should be willing to do so in the other. It would not only violate the principle of parity but also be an unwarranted display of chauvinism for us to demand that the reliability of the religious-experience doxastic practice be established by appeal to sense experience. This would be as unfair and chauvinistic as requiring that the sense-experience doxastic practice be justified by appeal to religious experience.

That the two doxastic practices of belief formation are to be accorded parity is justified by showing that they are analogous in cognitively relevant respects, especially in regard to both containing their own checks and tests. Some give the analogy up front, while others present it in the manner of rearguard action, first challenging someone to produce a disanalogy that would justify our not extending the a priori rule of presumptive inference to religious experiences and then neutralizing any proferred disanalogy. For Richard Swinburne this rule takes the form of his principle of credulity: "If it seems (epistemically) to S that x is present," that is, S believes on the basis of her experience that x is present, "that is good reason for S to believe that it is so, in the absence of special considerations" that defeat the claim.[11] Gary Gutting argues (convincingly) that this principle is too strong and builds his analogical argument on the weaker rule that if it seems to a subject that x is present, then there is "significant but not sufficient evidence" that x is present, hereby departing from Swinburne, who takes it to be sufficient in the absence of canceling conditions. This is one of those minor in-house disputes that need not detain us. For William Alston, the presumptive inference rule, as applied to religious experiences, takes this form: "The experience . . . of God provides prima facie epistemic justification for beliefs about what God is doing or how God is 'situated' *vis-à-vis* one at the moment."[12]

Before getting down to an in-depth comparison of the tests involved in the sense- and religious-experience language games, it should be pointed out that we are being imposed on at the very outset in being asked to countenance the latter as a separate language game or doxastic practice. Alston holds that a language game or "a doxastic practice will typically operate on certain basic assumptions that cannot be justified within the practice but rather serve as presuppositions of any exercise thereof."[13] Sense experience certainly is constitutive of the language game or doxastic practice in which claims are made about the existence and properties of physical objects. Such claims must ultimately rest upon sense experience; and it is a presupposition, not justifiable without circularity within this practice, that such experiences generally are veridical. Doubt this presupposition and you cannot engage in the practice. Disanalogously, claims about the existence and nature of God need not, and typically are not, based upon religious experience, and thus religious experiences are not constitutive of the religious language game. There are many believing participants in the religious language game who make claims about the existence and nature of God who have not themselves had religious experiences and, moreover, do not use the religious experiences of others as a means of anchoring their reference of the name "God," but instead do so via the use of descriptions of God's hard-and soft-core properties, to use the distinctions from Chapter 1. Religious experiences are not constitutive of any doxastic practice, but instead are an inessential part of the encompassing religious language game.

Alston disagrees and offers the following causal theory of the reference of "God," in which the referent of "God" initially is pinned down via religious experiences with subsequent members of the religious community picking up the referent from their predecessors, ultimately terminating in these seminal "baptismal" bestowals of the name:

In the Judaeo-Christian community we take ourselves to be worshipping, and otherwise referring to, "the God of Abraham, Isaac, and Israel", i.e. the being who appeared to such worthies of our tradition, revealed Himself to them, made convenants with them, and so on. If it should turn out that it was actually Satan, rather than the creator of the heavens and the earth, with whom they were in effective contact, would we not have to admit that our religion, including the referential practices involved, is built on sand, or worse (muck, slime), and that we are a Satan-worshipping community, for all our bandying about of descriptions that fit the only true God?[14]

I have consulted a wide variety of religious believers, and all of them answer Alston's rhetorical question in the negative. I do not doubt that there are Orthodox Jews and Christian Fundamentalists whose religious language game fits Alston's causal theory of reference, but it certainly does not properly describe the religious language game of Phil Quinn's "intellectualy sophisticated adults in our culture," many of whom are ignorant of which Biblical dignitaries were alleged to have had religious experiences, and thus cannot be picking up the referent of "God" from them and who, moreover, would not accept the characterization of themselves as devil worshippers or LSD worshipers, if it should turn out to be the case that the experiences of these dignitaries were caused by the devil or LSD. I feel sorry for Alston's type of believers; they must tremble every time they open their copy of the *National Enquirer* for fear that they will come upon a headline that reads "Anthropologists Discover that Ancient Israelites Were Acid-Heads." Another fundamental inadequacy in Alston's causal theory of reference for "God" is that it cannot account for how two persons who use "God" can be coreferrers even if God does not exist. As argued in Chapter 1, our use of "God" allows for such a case of intentional identity.

In spite of these misgivings about there being a separate religious-experience doxastic practice or language game, we will grant that there is for the sake of argument and will now get on with our main task of exploring the analogies and disanalogies between the tests for the two practices. We will begin with a brief overview of the various tests and checks for the veridicality of sense experience, hereafter "sensory tests" for short, mainly as seen by the analogical arguers, and then see how our four analogical arguers attempt to show that for a sufficient number of them, there is a sufficiently similar mystical analogue.

SENSORY TESTS

1. *Logical consistency*. Are the sensory-based claims of the subject logically consistent?
2. *Empirical consistency*. Are they consistent with well-established empirical facts?
3. *Existence of apparent object*. Are there good arguments either for or against the existence of the apparent object of the sense experience?
4. *Reliability of subject*. Does the subject have a good track record in his past perceptual claims?
5. *Agreement*. Do the sense experiences had by others under normal or standard conditions agree with the subject's?
6. *Continuity between contents*. Does the content of the experience stand in the right sort of lawlike relations to those of the vast majority of the subject's preceding and succeeding experiences?
7. *Prediction*. Can future sense experiences of the subject and others be predicted on the basis of the assumption that the experience is veridical?
8. *Proper position*. Was the subject properly located in space and time so as to have been able to perceive the apparent object of his sense experiences?
9. *Physiological state of subject*. Was the subject's sensory faculty in good working order?
10. *Psychological state of subject*. Did the subject have any psychological impediments to his being able to perceive adequately, for instance, phobias, prejudices, or the like?
11. *Causal requirement*. Did the apparent object cause the experiences in the right way?

The analogical arguer takes these tests to form a "cluster" in that no one of them is either necessary or sufficient for veridicality, but satisfaction of a sufficient number is such. Such vagueness, double vagueness in fact, should not surprise us *if* we are dealing with a cluster concept.

Before proceeding further, I would like to drop tests 1–4 from further consideration. Test 4 obviously is parasitic upon the others, since the subject's past perceptual claims must have their veridicality determined by them. Tests 1–3 have very little positive probative force, both individually and collectively, serving a primarily eliminative function. The logical consistency test is not really a test but a sine qua non for being a fit subject for testing. That the apparent accusative of a sense experience is logically and empirically consistent, or even that it is existent, does almost nothing toward increasing the probability of the experience's veridicality, since most unveridical sense experiences, for instance, dreams, have an intentional accusative that satisfies these conditions. Furthermore, in regard to the religious-experience analogue to 3, the existence of the apparent object would have to be established either by an argument that is not based upon religious experiences, in which case it would be relevant only to the veridicality of the experience but not its cognitivity, as previously indicated, or by appeal to other religious experiences, in which case appeal is made to one of the other tests, such as agreement, thereby rendering this test parasitic upon other ones.

In eliminating tests 1–3 from further consideration, I am really doing the defender of the cognitivity of religious experiences, at least of the mystical sort, a favor, since there is serious doubt that they satisfy them. Their descriptions are often either contradictory or in conflict with our best-established empirical beliefs, such as that there exists a multiplicity of distinct objects and events in space and time. Wainwright has argued skillfully in defense of the logical and empirical consistency of mystical claims. Basically, what he does is to give watered-down reconstructions of these claims so that they are neither contradictory nor in opposition to empirical claims, but instead are making claims about a reality that is numerically distinct from any empirical reality, God or the undifferentiated unity being distinct from the physical world. Wainwright's thesis does not square with the claims of nature mysticism or cosmic consciousness, since these experiences seem to have the same apparent object as do sense experiences, namely, nature. Furthermore, if God or the undifferentiated unity is numerically distinct from the physical world, it belies the claim of the monistic mystic that there is only the One.

Wainwright claims that, in respect to mystical experiences, a sufficient number of analogues to the sensory tests can be found within various religious communities and offers the tests employed by the Catholic mystical tradition as an example: (1) the subject's moral improvement as a result of the experience, (2) the morally beneficial effects the experience has on others, (3) the depth of the mystic's description, (4) the concurrence of the mystical report with the holy scriptures and revealed truths of Catholicism, (5) resemblance of the experience with paradigmatic mystical experiences within the Catholic tradition, and (6) pronouncements of authorities and holy men on the experience's veridicality. These tests are tailored to theistic mystical experiences and need to be modified slightly for monistic experiences. Tests (1) and (2) – the moral tests – will have to be altered to take note of the fact that it is not a loving personal being that is the apparent object but an impersonal undifferentiated unity. Accordingly, they will require good spiritual rather than moral consequences for the subject and others.[15] Tests (1)–(3) are instances of the prediction test and (5) the agreement test, with the added provision that some member of the agreement set is paradigmatic. Supposedly, his privileged status, as well as the privileged epistemic status accorded to certain scriptures and men in (4) and (6), respectively, are to be justified by appeal to either other mystical experiences or arguments not based on religious experience. If it is the latter, tests (4) and (6), although relevant to the veridicality of the experience being tested, contribute nothing in support of its status as cognitive, that is, as a warrant for a knowledge claim.

William James, in his discussion of mysticism in *Varieties of Religious Experience,* employed something like tests (1)–(3). As a physician and psychologist he was well aware of the darker side of mystical experiences, that many were diabolical rather than benevolent in their effects on the subject and others. He claimed that the veridicality of mystical experiences must be determined not on the basis of their "medical" cause but on the goodness of their effects. "To pass a spiritual judgment upon these states," he writes, "we must not content ourselves with superficial medical talk, but inquire into their fruits for life."

Gutting also works with a trimmed down version of (1)–(6). He is concerned with a nonmystical theistic experience involving a nonsensory perception of a very powerful, loving, nonhuman person who is concerned with our well-being. All his tests are predictability ones based on the further experiences the subject and others can expect if the of-God experience is veridical: "(1) Those who have had such experiences once would be likely to have them again; (2) other individuals will be found to have had similar experiences; (3) those having such experiences will find themselves aided in their endeavors to lead morally better lives."[16] Gutting's (2) and (3) are virtually identical with Wainwright's (1) and (2). His test (2) also is an agreement test of sorts.

Alston, in defending the "objectivity" or cognitivity of the Christian version of the religious-experience language game, first points out that (a) the language game, along with the form of life that it involves, has proven itself viable over time and (b) no assertion warranted by the rules of a sophisticated version of this game contradicts anything that is warrantedly assertible within other language games we play. He then goes on to argue that (c) religious experiences, as a group, cohere together in a way analogous to that in which sense experiences, as a group, cohere together. In each case the experiences are connected together in a way that is to be expected, given the categoreal nature of the apparent object of the experiences. "The behavior of God, as revealed in the

Christian language-game, is in line, roughly speaking, with what one could reasonably expect from the categoreal features of God, as depicted within this language-game."[17] He appeals to something like the previous tests of Wainwright, Gutting, and James based upon the moral and spiritual growth of the subject, as well as that of agreement. "The Christian life, or, in the present parlance, seriously playing the Christian language-game, is self-justifying and self-fulfilling."[18] And, in a later paper, he says, "Given standard theistic conceptions and beliefs, it is reasonable to expect that prolonged communion, perceptual and otherwise, with God would lead to an increasing sanctity of character and a more Christlike mode of life, ceteris paribus."[19] Herein there is an appeal to a religious experience analogue to the sensory agreement and prediction tests, the claim being that the religious-experience language game is internally consistent because things happen by and large in a manner that is explicable in terms of the categoreal nature of the entities within the game's unique ontology.

Swinburne, who presents a rearguard-action version of the analogical argument, does not speak of tests but instead of defeating conditions – conditions that lower the probability of the experience being veridical and thereby its being subject to his earlier mentioned principle of credulity. A defeating condition is a flunked test. He begins by listing the defeating conditions for a sense experience: The subject or conditions under which the apparent perception were made are of a sort that have proven to be unreliable; other observers in like conditions disagree with the subject's perceptual claim; the experience was not caused in the right way by its apparent object. It is then argued that religious experiences, specifically direct perceptions of God's presence, do not flunk enough of these tests so as not to be subject to the principle of credulity, and thereby qualify as cognitive. As we shall see below, his defeating conditions incorporate all of the sensory tests, save for 9 and 10.[20]

With this overview completed, it can now be considered how good an analogical case has been made out by these four authors. It will be argued that their analogies between religious- and sense-experience tests are weak and that they become even weaker, approaching the vanishing point, when we replace the above cluster view of the sensory tests with a more adequate organic view.

That the agreement test applies in analogous ways to both sense and mystical experiences was asserted by C. D. Broad:

> When there is a nucleus of agreement between the experiences of men in different places, times, and traditions, and when they all tend to put much the same kind of interpretation on the cognitive content of these experiences, it is reasonable to ascribe this agreement to their all being in contact with a certain objective aspect of reality *unless* there be some positive reason to think otherwise. . . . I think it would be inconsistent to treat the experiences of religious mystics on different principles. So far as they agree they should be provisionally accepted as veridical unless there be some positive ground for thinking that they are not.[21]

Subsequent writers have shown, however, that the application of the agreement test to mystical and religious experiences is not as straightforward as Broad suggested. The agreement or disagreement of other observers is relevant only if their observations are made under so-called normal or standard conditions. We have a pretty good idea of what they are for sense experience. Their mystical or religious analogues vary from one mystical or religious tradition to another but usually involve asceticism, meditation, breathing exercises, and the like.

So far the analogy looks fairly tight, but, as Wainwright points out, it falters because mystics (i) count as confirmatory mystical experiences that occur without following the prescribed "mystical way" and (ii) do not count failure to have a mystical experience under the prescribed conditions as disconfirmatory. The evidential asymmetry in (ii) is especially disturbing, since it makes the mystical use of the agreement test look like a "heads I win, tails you lose" sort of con game.

The same holds mutatis mutandis for direct perceptions of God's presence.

There is an even more serious problem for the religious agreement test. The application of this test to sense experience requires, as Swinburne points out, that we "know what sense-organs and training you need, and how attentive you need to be to perceive the object in question."[22] The trouble is that we can specify none of these things with respect to religious experiences. Whereas we have tests for when one's sensory faculties are not in proper working condition and when the context of perception is not normal or standard, there are no analogous tests for when one's faculty of religious intuition or the circumstances are not normal. And since the notion of a normal observer and normal conditions has no application to religious experience, neither will tests 8–10, since their requirements of a physiologically and psychologically normal observer properly stationed in space and time are parts of the normal or proper conditions requirement. And since these tests, along with the agreement test, lack religious analogues, this greatly weakens the analogical case for cognitivity.

It might be objected that we do have *some* idea of the psychological and moral conditions that facilitate having a mystical or religious experience, such as the previously mentioned features of the mystical way – asceticism and so on. This may be true, but it is irrelevant to the determination of the veridicality of a religious experience. Such causal knowledge as we have pertains to the occurrence of a psychological occurrence or state – the having of an of-God-type experience – and not to its veridicality.

In summary, it is highly dubious that there is a religious-experience analogue to the sensory agreement test, and for reasons that also call into question whether there are religious-experience analogues to the proper-conditions tests 8–10. But the analogical arguer has not yet run out of tests. There still remain tests 6, 7, and 11, and the question of whether they have religious-experience analogues that might suffice for their analogical argument.

The continuity-between-contents and prediction tests over-lap. The latter, unlike the former, is not confined to the sub-ject's experiences nor does it require that there be strict nomic connections between the content of the experience to be tested and those of the predicted experiences. Since the ap-parent object of a religious experience, be it God or the undif-ferentiated unity, is not one object among others in a nomi-cally determined system, the continuity-between-contents test cannot apply to it. But maybe probabilistic predictions can be made about how and when this object will reveal itself and what sort of impact it will make upon the subject and others.

Wainwright, Alston, and Gutting make the morally good consequences of the theistic religious experience central in their deployment of the prediction test to such experiences. We saw that James appealed to the same test in order to distinguish between veridical mystical experiences and their unveridical diabolical counterparts. In some of his unguarded remarks, James endorsed a happiness criterion of truth in general – true propositions being those that bear beneficial consequences for their believers. One might raise against the good-moral-consequences criterion for the veridicality of of-God experiences the standard objection to this criterion of truth – happiness has nothing to do with truth or veridicality. Whatever force this objection might have against James's pragmatism, it has no application to the theistic religious experience's good-moral-consequences criterion, for in the case of the latter there is a conceptual or categoreal link between the nature of the apparent object of such an experi-ence and good moral consequences. Since God is essentially good, it is probable that those who have a veridical experi-ence of him will benefit morally and spiritually. The morally beneficial consequences of the experience are not confirma-tory qua good consequences (as a crude pragmatism might hold) but qua being a fulfillment of a categoreally based prediction.

It would be asking too much to require that precise predic-tions be made of the occurrence of of-God experiences. God's nature precludes this. What is disturbing is that it is not even clear that any probabilistic estimates at all can be made. Swinburne holds that "if there is a God, there is a greater probability that men will have such experiences."[23] But on the basic assumption of theism, it is not clear that the opposite is not the case. Theistic mystical experiences are often so overpowering that they psychologically necessitate the subject to believe in God. Such a belief, however, goes counter to the theist's view that God wants man freely (in the Libertarian sense) to elect to believe in him. This point would have even greater force against Gutting's claim that "those who have had" veridical of-God experiences "once would be likely to have them again."[24] This really would be going too far toward usurping a person's free will.

It could be objected that I have mislocated the point at which freedom is supposed to enter in for the theist. The theists who stress the importance of our freedom to choose faith in God would not suppose that one is free to either perceive or not perceive something (once one is in a position to do so), God included. Furthermore, significant freedom enters the picture in terms of our efforts to have experiential contact with God by following the prescribed mystical way. Thus, we exercise our free will in the manner in which we pursue this way, not in our believing or not believing in what our religious experience apparently reveals. But this response from the theist fails to give us significant freedom to believe or not believe in the veridicality of one of our religious experiences. And, as a result, God, by choosing to cause a person to have an of-God experience, renders them unable to do other than believe that he exists. This gives a very different version of our freedom to have faith in God from the one commonly advanced by theists.

It is not even clear that, as Swinburne claims, "there are no grounds for supposing that if there is a God, the atheist would have experience of him," thereby hoping to block application of the principle of credulity to atheistic experiences of it seeming (epistemic) that God is not there.[25] The atheist is far more in need of God's grace than is the person who is already launched along the path of faith. Thus, the atheist would seem more likely to have an of-God experience if God exists than would the believer, especially since the atheist's disbelief would help to offset the potentially freedom-canceling impact of the experience. I am not, of course, sincere in these probabilistic pronouncements, but merely wish to show how little basis there is for making any probabilistic estimates at all in this area. This radical unpredictability stands in marked contrast with the familiar sort of probabilistic predictions that are made within quantum and thermodynamic theory, as well as of the free actions of persons, even the Libertarian admitting that free actions are predictable for the most part. Again, we find a cognitively relevant disanalogy between the tests for sense and religious experience, this time pertaining to the prediction test rather than the agreement test.

Because the religious-experience prediction test is so liberal, it should not surprise us that all sorts of bizarre experiences that obviously are not cognitive pass it. In this connection let us recall Gutting's tripartite test for the objectivity or cognitivity of an of-God experience,

(1) those who have had such experiences once would be likely to have them again;
(2) other individuals will be found to have had similar experiences;
(3) those having such experiences will find themselves aided in their endeavors to lead morally better lives.

Consider the experience of an orgasm. Most of us consider this a paradigm of a subjective experience, an experience that has a cognate accusative, "orgasming" being perspicuous for "experiencing an orgasm." But this experience satisfies all three of Gutting's predictive requirements:

(1) Those who have had orgasms once would be likely to have them again;
(2) other individuals will be found to have had similar experiences;

311

(3) those who have orgasms find themselves aided in their endeavors to lead sexually better lives.

in which "sexually better lives" replaces "morally better lives" in (3) so as to match the nature of the accusative. Obviously, Gutting's criteria for an objective or cognitive experience let in too much, since we don't want to say that people who have an orgasm that satisfies Gutting's criteria experience or merge with the Big O (and I don't mean Oscar Robertson), some kind of objective reality that has as its main function to produce orgasms in people, sometimes employing ordinary persons as its causal intermediaries, thank God!

Alston's attempt in "The Christian Language-Game" to spell out the conditions under which a language game is "objective" or "in touch with reality" also lets in too much. His tripartite criterion requires: (A) The language game is played successfully in that the form of life it involves has proven viable, (B) no assertion warranted by the rules of the game contradicts anything that is warrantedly assertible within other language games we play, and (C) the game is internally consistent because things happen by and large in a manner that is explicable in terms of the categoreal nature of the entities within the game's ontology. Condition C, as pointed out, incorporates the prediction test.

We all take the experience of pain to be a paradigm of a subjective experience, one in which the accusative does not exist independently of its being experienced and is not common to different subjects of experience. We accept the cognate accusative (adverbial) analysis of "X feels a pain" into "X pains" ("X feels painfully"). But the language game in which we report our pains satisfies Alston's conditions (A)–(C) for a language game being objective: (A) The game is played, its form of life in which we aid and commiserate with people in distress having proven to be very valuable, (B) the language-entry assertions warranted within this game, for instance, "I feel a pain," do not contradict those warranted by any other game we play, and (C) the game is internally consistent, for instance, people who utter avowals of pain usually take steps

to eliminate their pain and try to avoid pain, and we can predict under what conditions persons will feel pain. But we
don't want to say that the pain language game is "objective";
for while there no doubt are pains – occurrences of paining –
there are no objectively existent pains, that is, pains or pain-
ings that exist independently of their being experienced and
are common objects of the experiences of different persons.
Pains are nothing but certain psychological states or processes. Thus, the fact that the religious language game satisfies conditions (A)–(C) does not establish that of-God
experiences are objective. While there are of-God-type psychological states or experiences, they may take a cognate
rather than an objective accusative. And unless of-God experiences are objective, they do not qualify as cognitive, since a
cognitive experience is one on the basis of which we gain
knowledge of some objective reality. Much more needs to be
said about the objectivity of religious experiences. It will turn
out that the really decisive disanalogy between religious and
sense experiences concerns the concept of a veridical objective experience.

One might try to block my counterexamples to the Gutting
and Alston criteria for the objectivity or cognitivity of a kind
of experience by restricting these criteria to kinds of experiences that are either putatively perceptual or such that the
apparent object of the experience would be objective if real.
The latter restriction would be no help, since pains and other
types of subjective experiences have apparent objects that
are real (there really are pains) but not objective in the sense
of being mind independent and a common object of the
experiences of different persons. Such restrictions, furthermore, are viciously regressive, since people, especially philosophers, often disagree about whether a certain type of
experience is putatively perceptual or such that its apparent
object is objective if real at all. Alston and Wainwright, for
example, think that religious experiences are putatively perceptual, but I view them as being only psychological, that is,
as taking cognate rather than objective accusatives. Moore
took sense experiences to have objective accusatives, but C. J.

Ducasse and Wilfrid Sellars thought their accusatives to be only cognate. What is needed is a criterion for distinguishing between cognate and objective accusatives so that these disputes can be settled. The criteria of Gutting and Alston are of no help in this regard. Surface grammar and ordinary language are inadequate, for there are some verbs that obviously take a cognate accusative but for which there is no corresponding verb or adverb for its grammatical accusative. For instance, whereas we can convert "Jones played a trill" into "Jones trilled" we cannot convert "Jones played a sonata" into "Jones sonataed," since ordinary language lacks such a verb. But obviously the latter, like the former, takes a cognate accusative. It is the aim of this chapter to supply just such a criterion of objectivity and thus for a verb taking an objective rather than a cognate accusative.

Having found the religious-experience prediction test to be inadequate, there remains only the caused-in-the-right-way test to consider. While everyone would agree that veridical religious experiences must be caused in some way by their intentional accusative, we find the defenders of their cognitivity in sharp disagreement over whether it can have a natural cause and, if so, whether it can be any kind of natural cause. At one extreme we find those like Stace with his principle of causal indifference, who hold that it makes no difference how a mystical experience is caused. Swinburne also places no restrictions on how an of-God experience is caused:

> But if there is a God, he is omnipresent and all causal processes only operate because he sustains them. Hence any causal processes at all which bring about my experience will have God among their causes, and any experience of him will be of him as present at a place where he is.[26]

Wainwright agrees. "If theism is true," the causal requirement condition "is met by theistic experiences, since God is a cause of everything that exists."[27] God, however, is essentially benevolent, and thereby would not cause an of-God experience in a devious or ignoble way. Swinburne confounds the true proposition that it is impossible for God to cause an of-God experience in the wrong way with the false proposition that it is impossible for an of-God experience to be caused in the wrong way, that is, a way that would preclude it having God as its cause. Many have felt that an of-God experience that was caused by ingestion of LSD or unconscious sexual desires could not be veridical.[28]

At the other extreme we find someone like Wayne Proudfoot who claims that by definition a mystical experience, like a miracle, cannot have a natural cause.[29] This use of "mystical experience" is not only eccentric but also perverse, since it blurs the veridical–unveridical distinction. Certainly the very same phenomenological-intentional state that is realized in a veridical mystical experience could be realized in an unveridical one. Alston once claimed that a veridical religious experience could not have a sufficient natural cause.[30] Instead of making it true by definition, as does Proudfoot, he presented this argument: God must be at least a necessary cause of a veridical religious experience, but if there were to be a sufficient natural cause of it, that is, a natural cause comprised of every necessary cause of it, God, not being a natural entity, would not be among them. This argument fails because, as seen in Chapter 4, causation can reach through a proximate sufficient cause; for instance, my hiring of an assassin who then commits the murder and my hand moving the stick that moves the stone are necessary causes respectively of the murder and the moving of the stone. If I were not to have done what I did, the effect would not have occurred. This shows that an event can be causally necessary for a given event even though there intervenes between them a causally sufficient event. It would seem, then, that a veridical religious experience can have a sufficient natural cause, provided it is consistent with the nature of the experience's apparent object to allow such a cause.

The problem is how it could be determined that a religious experience is caused in the right way by its apparent object. There is a significant disanalogy between how this is determined for sense and religious experiences, which is not objectionably chauvinistic by making sense experiences the measure of all things, that renders it dubious that there is a religious experience analogue to the caused-in-the-right-way test. Whereas we can determine on the basis of sense experience that a given sense experience is caused in the right way by its apparent object, we cannot determine on the basis of religious experience alone that a given religious experience is caused in the right way by its apparent object. Wainwright was quite right when he said,

> One cannot determine whether the [caused-in-the-right-way] condition is met independently of metaphysical and theological considerations. The practical value of an appeal to this consideration is therefore limited.[31]

To determine that a religious experience is caused in the right way by its apparent object, we require an argument that is not based on religious experience for the existence of this object and a theological theory concerning how it is related to experiences of it.[32]

But why can't we have an argument based upon religious experiences for the existence of the apparent object of a given religious experience and its bearing the right sort of causal relation to the experience? There can be such an argument only if religious experiences count as cognitive. But they can count as cognitive only if they are subject to similar tests to those that sense experiences are. And it has already been shown that this is not the case. Sensory tests 6 and 8–10 had no religious-experience analogues at all, while tests 5 and 7 were found to have at best quite weak analogues. The mystical analogues to the agreement and prediction tests are further undermined by the diversity of different doxastic practices for basing existential claims on religious experiences, since each has its own revealed truths, holy scriptures, paradigmatic religious experiences, holy men, authorities, and conception of what constitutes desirable moral and spiritual growth. Circumstances that count as confirmatory of a given religious experience's veridicality relative to one of these practices are not relative to another. Even if I have somewhat overstated the diversity between the religious-experience doxastic practices of the great extant religions, there still is no analogous diversity of doxastic practices for basing claims about physical objects on sense experience that differ among themselves as to what counts as confirmatory and disconfirmatory of a given sense experience being verid-ical.[33] This is a cognitively invidious disanalogy that should destroy the requirement to extend the presumptive inference rule from the sense experience to the religious-experience doxastic practice in the name of the principle of parity. There should be parity in their treatment only if they are sufficiently analogous. Equals should be treated equally but not unequals.

For these reasons, the case for the cognitivity of religious experiences based on language-game fideism with analogous tests is quite unconvincing. None of the objections that have so far been made has escaped its defenders. We shall now consider their rebuttals to my objections. After showing that they have little force, the "big disanalogy" – the really deci-sive one – between the two doxastic practices or language games will be given.

THE ANALOGICAL-ARGUER'S RESPONSE

The major objection to countenancing a religious-experience analogue to the sensory agreement test was that the former, unlike the latter, involved evidential asymmetry, as well as an inability to specify what constitutes a normal observer and standard circumstances. Swinburne, Wainwright, and Alston have a response to it.

Swinburne does not think that the problems of evidential asymmetry and the inapplicability of the normal-conditions requirement can be rendered completely harmless. They pose a problem all right but only a small one:

If we do not know what experience would count against some perceptual claim (because we do not know which observers could have been expected to have had an experience apparently of *s* if *s* had been there), that somewhat lessens the evidential force of an apparent perception – but only somewhat. This is because in that case we cannot have the confirming evidence of failure to find evidence which counts against the claim.[34]

The basis of Swinburne's "somewhat lessens the evidential force of" is obscure. But this slight concession on Swinburne's part hides the seriousness of the challenge posed for the analogical argument by evidential asymmetry. The in-principle impossibility of disconfirming the veridicality of a religious experience by appeal to the testimony of other observers, rather than just lessening the probability of its veridicality, calls into question the very applicability of the agreement test to it. If religious experiences cannot flunk the agreement test, then the test is not applicable to them. And this is a far more serious matter than a mere lessening of the probability that such an experience is veridical. Swinburne seems to have forgotten that he is supposed to be justifying the extension of the principle of credulity to religious experiences on the ground that they are sufficiently analogous to sense experiences, especially in regard to their respective defeating conditions. For this purpose, it is not sufficient to show that religious experiences cannot flunk some test that sense experiences can, for this is to admit that this test does not apply to religious experiences, thereby undermining his analogical argument. The same considerations hold for the admitted impossibility of religious experiences running afoul of the proper-conditions tests 8–10, since such tests are not even applicable to them, thereby further undermining the analogical premise of this argument.

Wainwright and Alston admit these disanalogies but try to neutralize them by claiming that they are due to a difference in the categoreal nature of the apparent object of sense and religious experience. God is an infinite being who freely bestows his grace upon people according to no discernible law or rule when he causes them to have a direct perception of him, unlike physical objects that operate according to deterministic laws and therefore admit of fairly rigorous predictions of their behavior. This explains why the agreement and prediction tests will not apply to religious experiences in the same way that they do to sense experience. The mystical tests, says Wainwright, although they must be "similar" to the sensory tests so as to sustain the analogical argument, are allowed to differ in their "nature" because of the difference in the natures of the apparent objects of mystical and sense experiences. In one breath he says that mystical tests are "similar to the tests which we employ in ordinary perceptual cases to determine whether an apparent perception of an object is a genuine perception of it" and in the other that "the nature of the tests is not much alike."[35]

There are two difficulties with this response. First, to explain why the tests for sense and religious experiences are not analogous is not to explain away the disanalogies; and these disanalogies are devastating to the analogical argument. This fundamental oversight also infects Alston's way of responding not only to this disanalogy but to others as well. For example, he responds to the claim that physical objects and God are disanalogous because only the former can be picked out by phenomenal qualities with a good news–bad news joke, though he does not realize it as such. He begins by saying that the existence of this disanalogy is "the bad news," but then goes on to say, after he has explained why there is this disanalogy in terms of the categoreal difference between the nature of physical objects and God, that the "good news is that it explains why we would be in a position of almost complete ignorance here even if there are basic phenomenal qualities that make up the phenomenal character of divine appearances."[36] This is like the doctor saying, "I've got good news and bad news; the bad news is that you will die of an untreatable cancer within six months and the good news is that we know the reason why you have cancer." That there are these disanalogies destroys the analogical argument, and in giving a conceptual explanation of them, Alston is unwittingly doing the job of the critic of this argument. To paraphrase Butler, everything is what it is, no matter why it is what it is.

There is another way in which Alston attempts to neutralize the disanalogy based upon evidential asymmetry by appeal to the categoreal nature of the apparent objects:

> But a more specific objection is that we have set things up so that facts about the occurrence of religious experience are allowed to count only as positive evidence. About this I will say the following. (1) This is true. Since we cannot hope to anticipate the patterns of the divine operation, God's nonrevelation at any point cannot count as evidence against His existence, but whenever He does reveal Himself that is a mark in his favor. (2) But *I* didn't set it up this way. This "set-up" is deeply imbedded in the Christian . . . conception of God. Now if the features of that concept responsible for this asymmetry were developed in order to protect the scheme from disconfirmation, this would be highly suspicious. But, and this is the crucial point, the complete blend of positive and negative theology that we have in this language-game developed, I believe, from quite other roots. Hence the evidential asymmetry is a consequence of integral features of the language-game that were basically a response to other demands.[37]

Why should the motivation behind a doctrine that falls prey to evidential asymmetry be relevant to excusing it from the charge of fraudulence? The con game of "heads I win, tails you lose" is objectionable as a dishonest game even if its rules were formulated not for the purpose of separating suckers from their money but instead from some lofty Spinozisitic necessitarian principle that denies the reality of chance. But the fact that the author's intention in creating a game of "chance" that involves no chance is of this sort makes it no less of a con game.

Another difficulty with the Wainwright response is that there is a tension, if not a downright inconsistency, in the claim that the tests are similar, but different in nature. If the tests do not have to be similar in nature, Wainwright's analogical argument degenerates into a version of the previously discredited language game fideism with any old tests. Herein we see Wainwright fluctuating between a univocalist account of cognitivity (the tests are similar) and a multivocalist one (the tests differ in nature).[38] The tests must be similar to support his analogical argument, but they must also be dissimilar in nature due to the categoreal difference between the apparent objects of mystical and sense experiences.[39]

There is a similar tension, if not inconsistency, in Alston's work. It is between his demands, on the one hand, for parity of treatment of the religious- and sense-experience doxastic practices and, on the other, that we not be chauvinistic, that we not uphold the epistemological principles of one practice as a standard by which to judge the adequacy of others. Alston's demand for parity of treatment of the two practices is based on the claim that the religious-experience doxastic practice is sufficiently analogous to the sense-experience doxastic practice so as to be subject to all of the cognitive rights and privileges thereunto appertaining to the latter. In saying that he "wants to explore and defend the idea that the experience . . . of God plays an epistemic role with respect to beliefs about God importantly analogous to that played by sense perception with respect to beliefs about the physical world,"[40] Alston is espousing the analogical argument and thereby accepting the version of chauvinism that attributes a special sort of paradigmatic status to the sense-experience doxastic practice, such that a doxastic practice of basing beliefs on experiences counts as cognitive only if it "exhibits the same generic structure as the former."[41] This requires that its tests be analogous to those of the sense-experience doxastic practice, although they need not be in terms of sense experiences, which would be an objectionable type of chauvinism. Therefore, it would be most inconsistent of him to charge an objector with being an objectionable chauvinist when it is claimed that the religious-experience doxastic practice fails to count as cognitive because its tests are quite disanalogous to those of the sense-experience doxastic practice. Alston, at this point, might try to fudge the issue in the way in which Wainwright did when he claimed that the tests of the two practices are "similar" yet different in "nature." He could say that the tests exhibit the same "generic" or "basic" structure but still are disanalogous in all the respects that have been pointed out. But this is the same as the Wainwright position, one that only Bob would find unobjectionable. Both authors begin by professing a version of language game fideism with analogous tests but, when pressured by significant disanalogies, make an unannounced retreat to language game fideism with any old tests.

Alston also attempts to neutralize the challenge posed by the disagreement among different religious traditions over the correct tests, which supposedly has no analogue in the sense-experience doxastic practice, thereby rendering it an invidious disanalogy because it undermines the analogical argument. His first response is to claim that experientially based disagreement among people undermines the reliability of their doxastic practices of belief formation only if they share a common set of tests or overriders. Since this isn't the case in the disagreements among people within different world religions, their experientially based disagreements do not undermine the reliability of their respective practices:

> Since . . . each of the major world religions involves (at least one) distinct doxastic practice, with its own way of going from experiential input to beliefs formulated in terms of that scheme, and its own system of overriders, the competitors lack the kind of common procedure for settling disputes that is available to the participants in a shared doxastic practice. Here, in contrast to the intra-doxastic practice cases, my adversary and I do not lack something that we know perfectly well how to go about getting. Hence the sting is taken out of the inability of each of us to show that he is in an epistemically superior position.[42]

Again, we find Alston committing the fallacy of thinking that if he can give a categoreally based explanation for a disanalogy between the religious- and sense-experience doxastic practices, it renders the disanalogy harmless. This should be

called the "Alston fallacy." He unwittingly is giving us another good news–bad news joke. What he fails to see is that
this disanalogy concerning a shared set of tests or overriders
undermines his analogical argument, with its analogical-
based justification for according parity of treatment to the
two practices, in particular for extending the presumptive
inference rule of the latter to the former. We rightly doubt the
cognitivity of religious experiences, in part, because those
who make claims based on such experiences cannot agree
among themselves what are the proper tests for their veridicality, for which there is no analogue in the sense-experience
doxastic practice.

Alston has a second way of neutralizing the diversity of
tests disanalogy that is presented in two stages. The first
argues that there are *actual* cases in science in which there is
a comparable disagreement over which tests are applicable
without detriment to the epistemic legitimacy of the rival
scientific practices. He gives the example of the dispute between behaviorists and psychoanalysts over the nature and
proper treatment of neurosis:

> Here we are not so ready, or should not be so ready, to judge
> that it is irrational for the psychoanalyst to continue to form
> clinical beliefs in the way he does without having non-circular
> reasons for supposing that his method of forming clinical
> diagnoses is a reliable one. Since we are at a loss to specify
> what such non-circular reasons would look like even if the
> method is reliable, we should not regard the practitioner as
> irrational for lacking such reasons.[43]

He next imagines a *counterfactual* situation in which there
is a diversity of sense-experience doxastic practices that are
analogous to the diversity of the religious doxastic practices.
These competing sense-experience doxastic practices "construe what is presented in visual perception in a radically
different way."[44] In one the apparent object is described in
Whiteheadian terms as a continuous succession of actual
occasions, in another as an Aristotelian substance, and in yet

another as a Cartesian indefinitely extended medium that is more or less concentrated at various points. These "alternatives . . . give rise to difficulties for the rationality of engaging in the sense-experience doxastic practice that are quite parallel to those arising from the actual diversity of religions for the rationality of engaging in the Christian doxastic practice."[45] In each of these analogous cases, the people can "justifiably engage" in their doxastic practice despite not being able to show its epistemic superiority to its competitors. "It may seem strange that such incompatible positions could be justified for different people, but this is just a special case of the general point that incompatible propositions can be justified for different people if what they have to go on is suitably different."[46]

In the first place, it must be pointed out that what is at issue is not whether one may "justifiably engage" in the religious doxastic practice or whether it is "rational" to do so, for there can be pragmatic reasons for doing so, as we shall see in the next chapter. What is at issue is whether the practice is a knowledge-yielding or cognitive one.

Second, both the actual and counterfactual examples of rival doxastic practices are irrelevant to the point at issue, since they are not doxastic practices for forming experientially based beliefs. They involve instead the activity of formulating scientific or philosophical theories to explain certain empirical facts that are common to the rival theories. These rival practices are incommensurable exactly because they accept the same empirical facts. There is no disagreement among their practitioners about the existential language-entry assertions that are to be made on the basis of sense experience, nor over the tests for determining their veridicality; and, thereby, these cases are not analogous to the disagreement among rival religious-experience doxastic practices, in which the disagreements concern both the correct language-entry responses to religious experience inputs and the test for determining their veridicality.

The Aristotelian, Cartesian, and Whiteheadian, for example, do participate in the same sense-experience doxastic practice. They make the same physical object assertions when subject to the same sensory input. Where they disagree is over the way in which such assertions are to be analyzed. Even Berkeley, who thought physical objects were congeries of ideas in different minds, insisted that it was correct to say that we perceive tables, chairs, and the like. He was not challenging our ordinary doxastic practice of asserting physical object propositions on the basis of sense experience but instead offering a philosophical analysis of what these propositions mean. The same is true for the other philosophers in question. Thus, their disagreement is over the correct philosophical analysis of physical object propositions. Whether their activity of philosophical analysis is a cognitive one is a can of worms that will be left unopened, but, it might be noted, one does not have to be a Richard Rorty to view their failure to agree upon the proper method to employ in doing philosophy as calling into question its cognitivity.

Alston's analogy with the dispute between behaviorists and psychoanalysts over the nature and genesis of neurosis fails for the same basic reason, the dispute now concerning the proper scientific rather than philosophical theory to adopt. Again, we find considerable agreement in the sensory-based language-entry assertions of the rival theorists concerning when there is a case of neurosis, such as someone who is a compulsive hand washer or is unable to walk across an open area.[47] Without such agreement about the empirical facts, their theories would not be incommensurate theories. They offer different theories about the cause and cure of these agreed upon neuroses. And, most important, they are in basic agreement about the tests that are relevant to resolving their disagreement. That Freudians have been lax if not unconscionable about putting their theories to empirical test and have been too quick to take certain clinical data as confirmatory of their causal theories of the etymology of neuroses does not show that they disagree with their behaviorist rivals over the proper tests. We must distinguish between the methods and tests that inform the scientific doxastic practice, the ones that are actually accepted by scientific practitioners, and the correctness with which some practitioners follow them. Another can of worms that I will leave unopened concerns whether psychoanalysis, as Ricoeur and Habermas claim, is not to be viewed as a scientific theory at all. For a thorough discussion of these issues one can do no better than to read Adolf Grunbaum's monumental *The Foundations of Psychoanalysis*.

"NEARER MY GOD TO THEE"

The conclusion to be drawn is that language-game fideism with analogous tests is in serious difficulty and that the responses to the various disanalogies that challenge it by the doxastic practice theorists or language-game fideists do little to neutralize them. But the case is even worse for this version of fideism that has been made out so far. We have yet to unearth a deep disanalogy between sense and religious experience that will totally destroy the analogical premise of its analogical argument. This "big disanalogy" will prove to be the shipwreck of this defense of cognitivity, a time for Alston, Gutting, Swinburne, and Wainwright to join their fellow analogical arguers on the deck for a few heart-felt choruses of "Nearer My God to Thee," though Bob, I know, will be unimpressed, remaining below deck sipping a Lablatt's, his last words being "This is just aboot like any other shipwreck."

Necessarily, any cognitive perception is a veridical perception of an objective reality. It now will be argued that it is conceptually impossible for there to be a veridical perception of God (the undifferentiated unity, etc.), from which it follows by modus tollens that it is impossible that there be a cognitive religious experience. My argument for this is an analogical one that, like those for the cognitivity of religious experiences, takes sense experience to be the paradigmatic member of the analogy. A veridical sense perception must have an object that is able to exist when not actually perceived and be the common object of different sense perceptions. For this to be possible, the object must be housed in a space and time that includes both the object and perceiver. It then is shown that there is no religious experience analogue to this concept of objective existence, there being no analogous dimensions to space and time in which God, along with the perceiver, is housed and which can be invoked to make sense of God existing when not actually perceived and being the common object of different religious experiences. Because of this big disanalogy, God is categoreally unsuited to serve as the object of a veridical perception, whether sensory or nonsensory.

In arguing that it is impossible for there to be a veridical religious experience of an objective reality, I am not engaging in an objectionable form of chauvinism by requiring that the sort of objective existence enjoyed by the objects of veridical sense experiences, physical objects, hold for all objective existents. I am happy to grant that there are objective realities that do not occupy space and/or time nor any analogous dimensions, such as the denizens of Plato's nonspatiotemporal heaven; and God might very well be among these objectively existent abstract entities. What is impossible is that there be a veridical *perception* of one of them, even of the intellectual sort described by Plato in the *Phaedrus*, according to which we "see" them with our mind's eye as we might see bigger-than-life Macy Day Parade balloons – "Look, coming up Broadway, is triangularity and behind it is the Idea of the Good in itself." Only those who have veridically "perceived" them are fit to be philosopher-kings. It is notorious that would-be philosopher-kings disagree among themselves as to the nature of these "balloons" and the proper methods for correctly apprehending them, which parallels the disagreements between different religious-experience doxastic practices as to the true nature of the object of these experiences and the correct methods and tests for gaining a veridical perception of it. "Catch one of them and you catch all of them!"

So far we have been working with the analogical arguer's view of the sensory tests as forming a cluster, such that some of them might have a religious experience analogue and others not. This is a fundamentally mistaken view of these tests.

327

Tests 5–11 are an organic unity of conceptually interrelated tests that presuppose the same concept of a veridical sense perception of an objective reality, namely, that of a common space-time in which the subjects and objects of veridical sense experiences causally interact in a mostly deterministic manner and that permits these objects to exist when not actually perceived and be common objects of different perceptions, as well as to be individuated by their positions in space-time.

The agreement test's requirement that the different observations be made under normal or standard conditions, which encompasses the requirements of tests 8–10 that the observer be physiologically and psychologically normal and properly positioned in space and time, are fillings in for the caused-in-the-right-way requirement of test 11. Our concept of the sort of objective reality that is the object of a veridical sense experience supplies an explanation of the fact of agreement under standard conditions in terms of a common cause – an object or event that is the initial member of the several causal chains that terminate in these different experiences. The notion of a common cause also underlies tests 6 and 7, which thereby are branches of the same conceptual trunk as these other tests. This common cause is also invoked to account for the lawlike continuity between the contents of a single person's successive sense experiences as well as the coherence between the way in which different observers are perceptually appeared to at their different spatiotemporal perspectives. Thus, tests 5–11 all involve the same worldview – that of a common space-time receptacle in which the objective accusatives of veridical sense experiences are the common causes of the nomic-type coherence among the sense experiences of the differently positioned perceivers.[48]

The ultimate ground of individuation for the objective empirical particulars in this worldview is supplied by space and time, it being a necessary truth that no two empirical individuals of the same kind spatiotemporally coincide. It is the space-time receptacle that creates the possibility of there being counterexamples to the principle of the identity of indiscernibles when restricted to fully general or descriptive properties. Any such property admits of the possibility of multiple instantiations at different regions in this receptacle. And this in turn creates the possibility of distinguishing between numerically and qualitatively identical particulars. And as a consequence we are able to distinguish between perceptions that are of numerically one and the same particular and those of particulars that are only qualitatively similar. In the latter case there are noncoincident particulars that are hooked up with different perceptions via different causal chains.[49]

Before completing my analogical argument by demonstrating that none of the features of this worldview of objective empirical particulars could have any analogue in regard to religious experience, I will attempt to enrich and deepen our understanding of this view by showing why its objective particulars must be housed in both space and time. While no one would question the need for a temporal dimension, some would deny that objective particulars of this kind *must* be located in space as well. A persuasive case for this not being necessary has been made out by P. F. Strawson in his highly original and imaginative chapter on "Sounds" in *Individuals*. Through a detailed criticism of his effort I hope to show that such particulars must be located in space as well as time.

The question whether objective empirical particulars must be in space is given an epistemic twist by Strawson in terms of his general principle that we cannot have a concept of a certain type of individual unless we have experientially grounded criteria of identity for individuals of that type. Accordingly, it turns into the question of whether criteria of identity for objective empirical particulars could be formulated in terms of sense experiences that are not representative of things as being in space.[50] He puts aside visual experiences, since they seem to be representative of space, at least two-dimensional space. Kinaesthetic and tactual experiences also seem to be representative of space, and there can be no doubt that in combination they are. Olfactory and gustatory experiences, neither alone nor in conjunction, are representative of space, but Strawson chooses not to work with them since he thinks there is little hope of establishing the possibility of a world of objective smells or tastes.

It is auditory experience that he thinks holds out the best chance for success. He argues, convincingly in my opinion, that auditory experiences *alone* are not representative of space. Our ability to locate a sound in space on the basis of an auditory experience is dependent (in some way that is left unspecified) upon correlations between auditory experiences and other kinds of experiences of a visual, kinaesthetic, or tactual sort. This ability often depends upon having knowledge of a sound's cause, but such knowledge is not based upon auditory experiences alone.

It is Strawson's aim to show that criteria for objective sound particulars can be formulated exclusively in terms of auditory experiences, thus establishing the logical possibility of there being a no-space world composed of objective sounds. These sounds would resemble commonsensical sounds in that both can occur when not actually heard. (A tree that falls in a forest devoid of sentient beings does make a loud noise, unless it falls into a snow bank or pile of leaves.) They differ from commonsensical sounds only in not being in space.

According to Strawson our purely auditory criteria of identity for objective sound particulars must enable us, first, to distinguish numerically between sounds, even in cases in which sounds are qualitatively the same, and, second, to re-identify sounds, even in cases in which there has been a lapse in our perception of them. The latter is crucial to our ascription of a mind-independent status to the sounds of the no-space world. No mere regularity in uninterrupted auditory experiences would suffice. If we were continually to hear a repetition of an A–B–C–D sequence of sounds, we would be able to distinguish numerically between an occurrence of one A-type sound and an earlier or later occurrence of this same type of sound, but we would have no grounds for holding that these sequences of sounds could occur even when not actually heard.

To make sense of a sound occurring when unperceived, the no-space world of sounds must be given some dimension analogous to space so that we can say where a sound is when it fails to be heard. "We must have a dimension other than the temporal in which to house the at present unheard sensory particulars, if we are to give a satisfactory sense to the idea of their existing now unperceived, and hence to the idea of reidentification of particulars in a purely auditory world."[51] This would make the no-space world of sounds analogous to our ordinary spatial world for which

> the crucial idea is that of a spatial system of objects, through which oneself, another object, moves, but which extends beyond the limits of one's observation at any moment. . . . This idea obviously supplies the necessary non-temporal dimension for, so to speak, the housing of the objects which are held to exist continuously, though unobserved.[52]

The necessity for a nontemporal dimension in which unperceived sounds are housed can be established in a way that Strawson does not explicitly consider, although he says things that suggest it. This consists in showing a fatal flaw in the most likely way of making out a case for the logical possibility of there being objective sound particulars that occur only in the dimension of time, this consisting in the application of a well-founded inductive generalization to a case in which there is a gap in perception. It works in the following way.

Let us suppose that on n number of occasions an A–B–C–D sequence of sounds is heard and no sound of any one of these types is ever heard except in such a sequence. This observed regularity justifies the inductive generalization that every A–B sequence of sounds is followed by a C–D sequence. On occasion $n+1$, an A–B–E–D sequence is heard rather than an A–B–C–D sequence. The question is whether C occurred on this occasion even though not actually heard. It is claimed that our above inductive generalization justifies an affirmative answer, and thereby a case has been made out for the possibility of sounds existing unperceived even though not housed in any nontemporal dimension analogous to space.

The obvious rebuttal to this argument is that the $n+1$ occasion, the one one which sequence A–B–E–D was heard, constitutes a counterinstance to the inductive generalization that every A–B sequence is followed by a C–D sequence. How might this seeming counterinstance be neutralized? There are two ways in which seeming counterinstances to empirical generalizations are met. It will be seen that neither is of any avail in this case.

The first way is to show that a perceptual error occurred: On occasion $n+1$, C was misheard as E, or the observer only thought she heard E, it being C that was really heard. We can determine that a perceptual error occurred only if we have criteria for determining what objectively is the case. But it is just such criteria that are lacking in the above case: We cannot appeal to the empirical generalization that every occurrence of A–B is followed by C–D to establish that a perceptual error occurred on occasion $n+1$ since this would render the "empirical" generalization unfalsifiable by experience. It is this generalization that is supposed to give us a criterion for determining what objectively is the case, but it seems to face a counterinstance.

The second way of meeting a seeming counterexample is to show that the observer was not in a *position* to observe what was there to be perceived; for instance, she or the object had moved away, she was looking in the wrong direction, her view was blocked, and the like. The fact that on some occasion I saw a burning log and later saw ashes in place of this log does not refute the generalization that a log burns down continuously into ashes, provided that I had moved away in the interim or had my view of the log blocked, or the like. It is apparent that all of these explanations invoke a spatial dimension in which are housed coexistent objects, one of which is an observer capable of moving in relation to these other objects. Since the above no-space world contains no nontemporal dimension that houses coexistent sounds, this sort of explanation cannot be offered. Without such a dimension, there is no way our inductive generalization can be saved from the seeming counterinstance.

If the above line of reasoning is correct, it bears out Strawson's claim that a no-space world of objective sounds must contain some nontemporal dimension in which coexistent sounds are housed. But for exactly what features of space must analogues be found in this nontemporal dimension? According to Strawson it is not simply that of distance, so that one sound can be said to move nearer to another or be further away from one sound than it is from another, but that of an observer, who is one sound among others and can move in relation to these other sounds. This would make the analogy with the way in which material objects fill space rather precise in that the observer is a material object or at least has a body that is one object among others and can move in relation to these objects. This would enable us to dispose of the seeming counterinstance on occasion $n+1$ by saying that the observer – the hearer – had moved away from the place in the nontemporal dimension at which sound C occurred and therefore wasn't properly positioned to hear C, which is a species of the second way of meeting a seeming counterinstance to an empirical generalization.

The problem is how we can derive from the properties of a sound alone a nontemporal dimension having the above analogous features to space. There are three properties of sound: pitch, volume, and timbre. Only pitch and volume determine a serial ordering, and either of them could be selected to determine this dimension. Strawson elects to work with pitch, no doubt because there are rich spatial metaphors concerning pitch; for instance, we speak of the pitch of one note as being closer to that of another than it is to that of some third note, of one note becoming closer in pitch to another, of higher and lower pitches. Such analogies between pitch and space will be familiar to students of the Schillinger system of musical composition in which melodies are represented on graphs.

Strawson concocts the following description of a possible sound world in which pitch alone determines the nontemporal dimension in which objective sound particulars are housed. Auditory experience contains a sound, called the "master sound," which is unique in its timbre and continuity. The sound varies in pitch, and when it is at certain pitches other sounds are heard, some of which have the kind of unity possessed by a musical composition. For instance, at pitch level L of the master sound, a unitary musical composition M is heard, while at level L' a different composition M' is heard. When the master sound remains at L, composition M can be heard in its entirety, as well as repetitions of it. As the master sound gradually moves up or down in pitch from L, there is a gradual decrease in the volume of M, and as its pitch approaches close to L, there is an increase in the volume of M.

The master sound serves as the surrogate in the sound world for the body of the observer in the spatial world, its pitch being the position from which the observer hears other sounds, and changes in its pitch representing her change of position in the pitch dimension. This can serve as an explanation of why certain sound sequences cannot be heard at certain pitches of the master sound, that is, at certain positions in the pitch dimension. In saying that the pitch of the master sound gives the position of the observer, we do not mean to impute self-consciousness to her.[53] It is we, the storytellers, who talk about her position and change of position, not the observer who does.

The sounds or sound sequences that are heard at the different pitch levels of the master sound qualify as objective particulars because there are criteria for reidentifying them when they are not continuously heard, as well as for distinguishing between qualitative and numerical identity within the pitch dimension itself and not just within the time dimension. Imagine a case in which the master sound is at pitch-level L and M is being heard:

Then suppose the master-sound changes fairly rapidly in pitch to level L' and back again to L; and then M is heard once more, a few bars having been missed. Then the sound-

334

particular now being heard is reidentified as the same particular instance of M. If during the same time, the master-sound had changed not from L to L' and back again to L, but from L to L'', then even though M may be heard once more, a few bars having been missed, it is not the same particular instance of M that is now heard, but a different instance.[54]

In the final sentence Strawson commits himself to the possibility of the principle of the identity of indiscernibles being counterexampled within the pitch dimension, which is to say that we can draw the distinction between qualitative and numerical identity within this dimension. Just as the same purely descriptive property can be instanced at two or more places in space at the same time, the same sound universal or pattern of universals can be instanced at two or more places (pitches) in the pitch dimension at the same time.

There is a minor flaw in Strawson's account. It is clear that there is a need for some kind of clock. This comes out in his claim that the same particular instance of M is heard only if the master sound changes "fairly rapidly" from L to L' and back again. He has not provided the observer with any way of determining when such a change occurs rapidly enough. This difficulty can be circumvented by imagining a Jimmy Durante-type of observer who has his own inner clock or standard of temporal congruence that is marked by his continual hearing of "boop-boop-bee-doop."

Has Strawson's ingenious account of his wonderful world of sounds shown that there could be objective empirical particulars that are not in space? Two different kinds of arguments will be advanced to show that he has not. The first challenges Strawson's unstated assumption that there are exclusively auditory criteria of identity for sounds in virtue of which it can be determined both when a sound persists and when it is distinct from some coexistent sound. The second is based upon there being crucial conceptual disanalogies between the way in which physical individuals occupy space and the way in which sounds occupy the pitch dimension that renders the latter dimension logically incapable of housing objective particulars.

Strawson's account assumes that we have purely auditory criteria for the persistence of a sound as well as for distinguishing between coexistent sounds. This is quite dubious. What criteria we have are not only imprecise but also seem to require a reference to the causal source of a sound, and thus invoke knowledge that is not gained from auditory experience alone. If we have a continuous and phenomenologically invariant auditory experience, do we hear numerically one and the same sound particular throughout this time? The only way of answering this question is by reference to the causal source of our auditory experience. At the old Savoy Ballroom, there was a large bandstand on which two bands could be seated. The music went on continuously; when one band stopped playing, the other immediately began to play. I remember once hearing Count Basie's band playing the "Two O'Clock Jump," and when they ended with a sustained chord, without any perceptible break, Cootie Williams's band began to play this chord. On this occasion I heard two phenomenologically similar sounds, the first of which was produced by Basie's band and the second by Williams's. My criteria of identity are based on the causal source of my auditory experience, but obviously my knowledge of such causes is not based on auditory experience alone.

A similar problem arises for sustained auditory experience in which there is phenomenological alteration. Strawson assumes that the master sound persists even though it changes in its pitch. But this is gratuitous since we have no criteria for a sound's persisting that are independent of its causal source. The glissando we hear remains one and the same sound particular throughout if it is produced by someone sliding his finger up a violin or a guitar string. But the glissando would be composed of numerically distinct successive sounds if it were instead produced by a very rapid playing of a chromatic scale on a piano.

It is also dubious that there are purely auditory criteria for distinguishing between simultaneously heard sounds. It would seem that our ability to distinguish between the notes of a heard chord ultimately depends on our knowledge of some nonauditory feature of the situation in which it is produced. If this be so, Strawson has no right to assume that the master sound is numerically distinct from the sounds that are alleged to accompany it at its different pitches.

I suspect that the reason Strawson failed to see the dependency of our criteria of identity for sounds upon their causal source is that he leaned too heavily upon the radio analogy by which he first introduced the master sound. The master sound is said to be analogous to "the persistent whistle, of varying pitch, which, in a wireless set in need of repair, sometimes accompanies the programmes we listen to."[55] The way in which we hear different sound sequences at different pitch levels of the master sound is compared to gradually "tuning-out one station and tuning-in another. . . . Only . . . instead of a tuning-knob being gradually turned, we have the gradual alteration in the pitch of the master sound."[56] Our ability to distinguish between the persistent whistle and the programs that accompany it, as well as to distinguish between different programs, is based on knowledge of how these sounds are produced.

The preceding arguments against Strawson's wonderful world of sounds are not decisive because our criteria of identity for sounds are so imprecise. Some arguments based upon *crucial* conceptual disanalogies between space and the pitch dimension will now be advanced. And they are decisive. What will make these disanalogies crucial is that they concern the very grounds of individuation for objective empirical particulars.

The first crucial disanalogy to be argued for is that whereas it is possible for the identity of indiscernibles, when restricted to purely descriptive properties, to be counterexampled within the spatial dimension(s), it is not possible for it to be counterexampled within the pitch dimension. In other words, the distinction between qualitative and numerical identity has a possible application within the spatial dimension(s) but not within the pitch dimension. Strawson would deny that there is this disanalogy. In the lengthy quotation cited, he claims that if M is heard at pitch-level L of the master sound, which then changes to pitch-level L'' at which M is heard "it is not the same particular instance of M that is now heard, but a different instance." Although these two tokenings of the sound-type M are qualitatively identical, they are numerically distinct because they occur at different places (i.e., pitches) in the pitch dimension. It will be illuminating to see why there could not be any such use of the distinction between qualitative and numerical identity within the pitch dimension.

The tokening of M at L is supposed to be diverse from that at L'' because they occur at different positions in the pitch dimension, which would make the grounds of individuation for sounds quite analogous to that for coexistent spatial individuals. But whereas Strawson tells us how to determine the position in this dimension of the master sound, he says nothing about how we are to determine the position of a non-master sound.[57] If the position of the master sound at any given time is to be determined by its pitch, we should expect the same to hold true for all sounds. Since, *ex hypothesi*, the tokenings of M at L and L'' have *all* their purely descriptive properties in common, they have the same pitch (or are in the same key), and thereby are at the same position. If we should persist in holding that, nevertheless, there are two tokenings of M, we would be working with a principle of individuation for sounds that is radically disanalogous to that for spatial individuals, for which it is necessarily true that sortally similar diverse individuals are not spatiotemporally coincident.

Even if we were to hold that only the master sound's position is determined by its own pitch, the position of every other sound being determined by the pitch level of the master sound from which it is heard, the principle of the identity of indiscernibles still could not be counterexampled within the pitch dimension. The tokenings of M are supposed to constitute a counterexample to this principle. Although they have all their purely descriptive properties in common, they nevertheless are diverse because they occupy different positions, this being due to their being heard at different pitch levels of the master sound. They do not, however, have all their purely descriptive properties in common, since they have different relational properties; one has the property of being heard at pitch-level L of the master sound while the other had, instead, the property of being heard at pitch-level L''. It is not only the master sound that can be tokened only once within the pitch dimension, but every sound type as well.

The disanalogy between a spatial dimension and the pitch dimension consisting in the principle of the identity of indiscernibles being capable of counterexample within the former alone is a consequence of an even more fundamental conceptual disanalogy between the two. The pitch dimension, unlike a spatial dimension, is an empirically determined dimension in that its parts or positions are generated or determined by differences in the empirical properties, namely, pitches, they instantiate. In other words, the principle of the identity of indiscernibles is necessarily true of positions in the pitch dimension but not of places in space. Whereas diverse positions in the pitch dimension cannot have all their purely descriptive properties in common, diverse places in space could, for instance, the places occupied by two qualitatively indiscernibles discs. This, of course, is not to say that diverse places never differ in their properties, for one place might have the property of being occupied by a disc and another place not have this relational property. Since the principle of the identity of indiscernibles is not necessarily true of the parts of space, it is not necessarily true of the objective particulars in space.

This more fundamental disanalogy between space and the pitch dimension explains why only the former can account for the ultimate grounds of individuation of coexistent objective empirical particulars. To account for the ultimate grounds of the diversity between such particulars, we must invoke some realm or dimension(s) within which they can simultaneously occupy different positions. If this realm is an empirically determined one, the positions in it are themselves objective empirical particulars; for instance, the positions in the pitch dimension are not universals – pitch types – but objective particulars that instantiate these types. But then we will have failed to account for the grounds of individuation of these objective particulars. Obviously, we are launched on a vicious infinite regress if we try to account for their individuation in terms of their occupying different positions in some other empirically determined dimension(s). Since the space of the receptacle is not an empirically determined realm, being nothing but pure extension, it can serve as the ground of individuation of objective empirical particulars. This is in substantial agreement with Plato's somewhat poetical account of the receptacle:

> Hence that which is to receive in itself all kinds must be free from all characters . . . that which is duly to receive over its whole extent and many times over all the likenesses of the intelligible and eternal things ought in its own nature to be free of all the characters. For this reason, then, the mother and Receptacle of what has come to be visible and otherwise sensible must not be called earth or air or fire or water, nor any of their compounds or components.[58]

This completes my account of the concept of an objective *empirical* particular, that is, one that is a suitable object of a veridical sense experience. Hopefully, it was established that for such an object to be capable of existing when not perceived and being a common object of different perceptions, as well as being individuated in a way that makes room for a distinction between numerical and qualitative identity, it had to occupy both space and time. It will now be argued that none of these features of the concept of an objective empirical particular have any religious-experience analogues, thereby completing my analogical argument.

Whereas it is necessary that the apparent object of a veridical sense experience must be housed in the dimensions of space and time, there are no analogous dimensions in which the apparent object of a religious experience could be housed. The apparent object of a unitive religious experience, the undifferentiated unity, obviously, does not occupy any analogous dimensions to these; and, although God could, and as argued in the first three chapters ought, to be conceived as in time, he does not occupy any analogous dimension to space, such that we could be said to draw nearer or further from God in this dimension. "Nearer My God to Thee" is a metaphor.

Because these objects are nondimensional, they will be disanalogous to empirical particulars in several important respects. First, they will have radically different grounds of individuation. Whereas empirical particulars are individuated by their position in nonempirical dimensions, they are not. They are individuated instead by their properties – those that they have both essentially and uniquely across worlds – in a way that satisfies the principle of the identity of indiscernibles. As a result, the numerical–qualitative identity distinction has no application to them. That their grounds of individuation, in virtue of their nondimensionality, are so radically disanalogous to those for the objects of veridical sense experiences does not disqualify them as objective particulars, but it does disqualify experiences of them as veridical *perceptions* of objective particulars. I am not being chauvinistic about the concept of objective existence.

Another invidious consequence of their nondimensionality is that no analogous explanation can be given for how they can exist unperceived and be common objects of different perceptions to that which was previously given for empirical particulars. Whereas we could explain our failure to perceive an empirical particular, as well as our perceiving numerically one and the same empirical particular, in terms of our relationship to it in some nonempirical dimension, no such analogous explanation can be offered for our failure to perceive God and the like, or our perceiving numerically one and the same God. This means that it is impossible in principle to distinguish between, for example, mystical experiences that are of numerically one and the same undifferentiated unity and the like and those that are of merely qualitatively similar ones. Stace's argument for the numerical identity of the pure souls of different mystics clearly reveals this. He argues that the undifferentiated unities experienced by different mystics in introvertive mystical experiences are *qualitatively* indiscernible. He then infers, by appeal to the principle of the identity of indiscernibles, that they are *numerically* identical. This is the "deep" it-is-time-to-start-singing-hymns disanalogy.

Similarly, how is Gutting going to decide when two religious experiences of a very powerful and loving nonhuman person had by two people at one time or by one person at two different times are of numerically one and the same being or only qualitatively similar ones? People in our epistemic circumstances – we human beings – are not able to vouchsafe the uniqueness of the object by its phenomenological traits. To know that one is experiencing God, and not just any old very powerful, loving, nonhuman person, of which there could be several, it is necessary to know that it completely and *solely* determines every feature of the world. But this requires knowing the negative fact that there does not exist any being other than it that determines any of these features. Swinburne, who restricts his principle of credulity to positive-seeming experiences,[59] thereby winds up being inconsistent when he applies it to of-God experience since they are, in part, negative for this reason.

A third consequence of the dimensionality disanalogy is that whereas the worldview into which empirical particulars enter offers an explanation for the organic unity of the sensory tests, there is no analogous view into which the apparent object of religious experiences enters that explains how the various religious-experience analogues to these tests (assuming that there are any!) are interconnected. It was the common cause theory, based upon a receptacle that houses both objects and subjects of sense experience in a mostly nomically determined system, that ultimately explained why tests 5–11 worked together in harness, but no such explanation can be given for the interconnection of religious-experience tests. They form a mere heap, with no rhyme or reason why they should go together and serve to mutually reinforce each other. No doubt Alston will be ready to explain away this disanalogy, as well as the preceding ones, in terms of the categoreal differences between God and empirical particulars, but it would be just another instance of the Alston fallacy.

Summation. The case for religious experiences being cognitive is exceedingly weak, and thus they cannot serve as an epistemological or truth-directed reason for believing that God exists. Even though it is impossible to have a veridical *religious experience,* that is, nonsensory *perception* of God, it does not follow that an of-God-type experience could not be caused by God in the right way and thereby qualify as some kind of *nonperceptual* apprehension of God. It just wouldn't be analogous enough to a veridical sense experience so as to qualify either as a veridical perception of God or as evidence or epistemic warrant for believing in the existence of its apparent object. Because we lack a *truth-directed* reason for believing in the existence of the apparent object of these experiences – God – it does not follow that there could be no reason for accepting them as revelations of an objective reality; for there are, in addition to truth-directed reasons, pragmatic ones concerning the benefits of so believing. To trust such experiences as objective revelations might prove to be of the greatest possible benefit to the experient, enabling him to live a richer and more meaningful life. The prediction test, as applied to religious experiences, concerned the moral and spiritual growth of the experient; and, if it should be the case that such desirable growth occurs only if the experient trusts his experience as an objective revelation, then he might have a valid pragmatic reason for so believing. This is the topic that will be our concern in the next chapter.

Chapter 9

Pragmatic arguments

So far only epistemological or truth-directed reasons have been considered for believing that God exists. It is now time to consider pragmatic reasons based on the desirable consequences of belief. There is the big question, which will not be considered, of whether individuals, as well as society at large, are better off having religious faith. While religion and the faith it inspires has a mixed track record, having been among the causes of man's greatest and basest deeds, we have no way of determining whether things overall would have gone, or will go, better with it than without it. My interest, however, is not with questions of empirical fact but with the conditional question "If overall there were to be desirable consequences of believing that God exists, would that justify, that is, constitute a sufficient reason for, one's believing?"

The desirable consequences can take different forms and thereby serve as the basis for different types of pragmatic argument. They can be *prudentially* desirable if they satisfy the needs, wants, or interests of the believer. Or they might be desirable on *moral* grounds either by enabling us to engage in the practice of morality, that is, following moral rules even when doing so sacrifices our own self-interest, or making the believer and/or her society morally better. Kant's moral argument for believing is an example of the former: The demands of morality to follow the categorical imperative make sense only if we assume that there exists a God who will bring it about that those who do so are rewarded with happiness, something that rarely happens in this life. Because this justification of faith takes us so deeply into the nature of morality, it will not be possible to consider it in this book, nor am I up to tackling it. Given that it is rational or reasonable to promote one's own interests as well as those of morality, both sorts of consequences can serve as a justification or sufficient reason for believing.[1] Pragmatic arguments from prudence will be discussed first, then those from morality.

PRAGMATIC ARGUMENTS FROM PRUDENCE

The most influential of the prudential-type pragmatic arguments for faith is Pascal's "wager" in his *Pensées*. His wager begins with this piece of negative theology: "If there is a God he is infinitely incomprehensible, since having neither parts nor limits, he has no proportion to us: we are then, incapable of knowing either what he is, or whether he is." Because God is infinite and we are finite, we can know neither that he exists nor what he is like.[2] Not all negative theologians would agree with the former; as we saw in Chapter 6, Anselm thought that he could use a largely negative conception of God as a being than which a greater *cannot* be conceived as the basis for a successful ontological argument.

That we cannot know *what* God is like seems inconsistent with his wager's claims about how God will treat believers and nonbelievers in respect to rewards and punishments. We could call these claims "linkage propositions" since they concern how God is related to the created world, especially its free persons. What is offered for our belief in the wager is not the bare proposition that God exists but an entire creed that includes these linkage propositions reporting how God will respond to various free deeds on our part. Obviously, Pascal is not being true to his initial severe version of negative theology. Maybe the best way to interpret his negative theology is that we cannot know in this life, short of a mystical experience, God's true *positive* nature or essence. The linkage propositions do not describe this but only some of his relational properties.

Strictly speaking, the option that is offered to us in the wager is not to believe that God exists, along with other propositions in the Christian creed, but to do everything in our power to self-induce such a belief. Pascal recognizes that belief is not, to use later terminology, a basic action, something that we can do at will, and instead claims that it can be self-induced by various basic actions. Pascal suggests that we learn how to do this by imitating the outward actions of those who cured themselves of disbelief. "Follow their course, then, from its beginning; it consisted in doing all things as if they believed in them, in using holy water, in having masses said, etc." Pascal's causal recipe does not require us to act hypocritically, since we are enjoined only to act as if we believed, not to pretend to believe. Pascal is probably right that if we become an active member of a religious community of believers, we shall wind up believers. For the sake of brevity, in what follows I shall speak of choosing to believe, when what is meant is choosing to perform those actions that are likely to induce belief.

He also says that we must make a choice. "Yes, but you must wager." He does not explain why one cannot place no bet at all, such as one might do at a racetrack when they place no wager at all on a given race. His reason, no doubt, is based on the nature of the linkage propositions in the Christian creed, namely, that in terms of afterlife payoffs, God treats the agnostic the same way he treats the atheist. Thus, to make no choice at all and thereby wind up an agnostic has the same consequences as if one chose to disbelieve.

Depending on how the linkage propositions are filled in, we get different versions of the wager. In one way, God rewards all and only believers with an unending life of infinite felicity in a Christian-type heaven, the big utility, agnostics and atheists merely ceasing to exist upon death. In another he also assigns agnostics and atheists to an endless existence in hell – the big disutility. And, in a third, which is not an extant version of Christianity, he punishes with hell all agnostics and atheists, believers merely ceasing to exist upon death. The first is the best-possible case version, the third

346

Pragmatic arguments from prudence

the worst-possible case version, and the second the combined version. Some have claimed that the third and second versions rest on a linkage proposition that is incompatible with God's goodness – that he would endlessly torture nonbelievers. Even if this is so, there still remains the best-possible case version, which is the version that can be used for wimps who cannot get themselves to worship and adore a Charles Bronson-type deity.[3]

These three versions spell out what is to be gained and lost by the wagerer on the different possible outcomes of the available options, namely, to believe or not to believe that God exists. But payoffs are only one factor in determining what is the smart bet; otherwise one would always bet on the longshot. The probability of the different outcomes must also be taken into consideration. In accordance with his doctrine of God's total epistemological inaccessibility, Pascal makes the a priori assumption that "the chance of gain and loss are equal." The probability that God exists is taken to be .5. What Pascal is doing in effect is to render probability considerations otiose in his wager.

Since the probability of winning and losing are the same, Pascal holds that one should bet solely on the basis of the utility or payoff of the different outcomes. When the probability of winning and losing a wager are equal, one should bet on the basis of payoffs – the odds. If you bet on God, that is, get yourself to believe that God exists and follow the requisite religious course of life, and win, there is an infinite payoff according to the best possible case and combined versions, while if you lose there is only at best a finite loss, some sacrifice of worldly pleasures and advantage. However, if you bet against God and win, there is only a finite gain at best consisting in not being hampered in seeking your worldly interest by the restrictiveness of the Christian way of life, while, if you lose, on the first version your loss or gain is finite, and on the second and third versions the loss is infinite. If we are to bet solely on the ground of self-interest, we should bet on the existence of God, since, as Pascal puts it, we are risking a single life – our worldly life – with an equal chance of gaining an infinity of otherworldly lives. It would be like betting that a true coin will come up heads when we win an infinite number of dollars if it does and lose only one dollar if it doesn't. Thus, it is prudentially rational to believe that God exists, since doing so advances one's own self-interest. Let us call this version the "wager sans probability."

Some very bad objections have been made to this version. One holds that it is internally inconsistent, because, according to its own conception of God, God would not reward with heaven someone who believed in him for only pruden-tial reasons. Rather, he would take great delight in assigning such selfishly motivated individuals to hell. The proper reply is that Pascal is not advocating that the person who chooses to believe wind up with a prudentially motivated belief, only that, given her presently fallen nature, she must be so ini-tially motivated. What the person attempts to do by getting herself to believe is in effect to change her character, her net-work of values and motivations, so that she will eventually wind up with a nonprudentially based belief in God. God should judge someone on the basis of how she winds up, not how she began. Thus, there is no internal inconsistency.

Some have objected that the first (third) version of the wager is an instance of the best (worst) possible case fallacy. Since the only possible way to realize (avoid) the best (worst) possible outcome is to believe that God exists, we ought to believe that God exists. In many cases this mode of reasoning is fallacious. For example, if it is urged that since there is some possibility, however small, that if we engage in recom-binant DNA experiments, we will realize the worst possible outcome – the extinction of life – we ought not to engage in such research.[4] What is fallacious about this argument is that it is based only on considerations of the utility of the different possible outcomes, not their expected utility, in which the expected utility of the outcome of some option is the product of its utility, as determined by the chooser, and the probabil-ity of it being realized if this option is selected. Pascal, how-ever, is not committing this fallacy; for, while he can grant that we ought to work with expected utilities rather than just utilities when probabilities can be assigned to the different possible outcomes, his negative theology entails that no such probability assignments can be made in respect to the existence of God and thereby to the different possible outcomes in his wager. Thus, we cannot do other than to work with considerations of utility alone.

This reply does not end the matter, for the critic can charge that Pascal has no right to make the a priori assumption that the probability that God exists is .50. Pace his negative theology, it might be claimed that the amount and kind of evil we find in the world renders it highly improbable that God exists. To meet these objections the following "rational choice wager" can be given:

1. It is logically possible that God, as conceived of by the Christian creed, exists;

2. The probability that God, so conceived, exists is greater than zero [from 1];

3. It is prudentially rational for a person to choose that option among those open to her that will maximize her expected gain, in which the expected gain of a given option is the sum of the expected utilities of its possible outcomes [premise];

4. Believing that this God exists maximizes one's expected gain [based on the Christian creed]; and

5. It is prudentially rational for a person to choose to believe that this God exists [from 3 and 4].

There is nothing to argue with in regard to 3, since it does not make the bold claim that the *only* rational choice for a person to make is the one that she thinks will maximize her expected gain, as would be claimed by contemporary rational choice theorists. Step 4 holds on the best and worst possible case versions of the wager, as well as the combined version. On the former there is an infinite utility, an infinitely long life of infinite happiness, realized when one's bet on God is won, and since the probability of realizing this outcome is greater than zero (is a number n such that $0 < n \leq 1$), it follows that the expected utility of this outcome, along with the expected gain of the option to believe that God exists, is infinite, given that the product of an infinite number and any number greater than zero is infinity. The expected gain for the option of not believing that God exists must be only finite at best, since the expected utility of winning one's bet against the existence of God is finite, given that it has a finite utility and a probability of $1 - n$. Similar considerations hold mutatis mutandis for the other two versions.

There are decisive objections to this rational choice wager, some of which also apply to the wager sans probability. In the first place, from the fact that it is logically possible that God exists, it does not follow that the product of the probability of his existence and an infinite number is infinite. In a fair lottery with a denumerable infinity of tickets, for each ticket it is true that it is logically possible that it will win, but the probability of its doing so is infinitesimal, and the product of an infinitesimal and an infinite number is itself infinitesimal. Thus, the expected gain of buying any ticket is not infinite but infinitesimal. There is at least a denumerable infinity of logically possible deities who reward and punish believers in the manner described by the three versions of the wager. For instance, there is the logically possible deity who rewards with infinite felicity all and only those who believe in him and step on only one sidewalk crack in the course of their life, as well as the two-crack deity, the three-crack deity, and so on ad infinitum. And similarly for the other two versions.

It might be urged that it is still prudentially rational to bet on one of these rewarding and/or punishing deities, since, by doing so, one assures that it is logically possible that one will realize the big utility and/or logically impossible that one realize the big disutility. The same response can be made on behalf of the wager sans probability version when it is confronted with the infinitely-many-deities objection. The problem is that among the logical possibilities is that there exists the antitheistic deity – the one who rewards with the big utility all and only those who believe in no theistic God and/or punishes all and only those who believe in some theistic God.

The only way of dealing with the problem posed by the infinitely many possible deities, as well as the possibility of the antitheistic God, is to resort to epistemological consider-ations that give favored status to some member or finite number of members of the former. This way out is not avail-able to Pascal, given his negative theology, but there is no reason why the defender of a wager argument must accept his negative theology.[5] If we come out with a finite number of theistic Gods with equally good epistemic credentials, the prudential thing to do is to bet on any one of them or as many of them as you can consistently bet on or combine into a higher synthesis, thereby becoming the "religious hustler" who spends the weekend racing around town attending as many different religious services as possible, producing a higher synthesis when possible by, for example, not eating pork on Fridays. The expected gain on any of these finitely many theistic options is infinite, since now the probability of winning is no longer infinitesimal, while that of nonbelief is only finite. And, if it should turn out that the probability that one of these theistic Gods exists is greater than that for any of the others, it would be reasonable to supplement rational choice theory with the ad hoc proviso that when two or more options have infinite expected utilities, the rational thing is to choose the one that has the highest probability of realizing the big utility (and/or avoiding the big disutility).[6] I will not comment on whether one of these deities is in fact in an epistemically privileged position, especially since no conclu-sion was reached in my discussion in Chapters 1–8 of the epistemological reasons for believing or disbelieving in the God of Western theism.

The epistemologically reinforced version of the wager is not without difficulties. First, Pascal is being presumptuous in filling in our utility assignments for the different possible outcomes. As Richard Swinburne correctly pointed out, "Pascal assumed that all men would evaluate in the same way as he the various outcomes. But in fact, rightly or wrongly, men will put different values from each other on the different outcomes."[7] Pascal seems to be assuming that because the afterlife in a Christian heaven is one of infinite bliss or happiness without end that all of us will assign it an infinite utility, but we can imagine Humphrey Bogart responding to this by saying, "Listen, Blaise, there are other things in life than infinite bliss, like doing right by a pal."

Many people, in particular, would reject the value he places on our worldly life vis-à-vis an eternal life of infinite bliss in a Christian heaven. He states that in opting to believe we risk losing only the finite – this worldly life – with the equal chance to gain an "infinity of life infinitely happy." He holds that "when there is the finite to hazard in a play where the chances of gain and loss are equal, and the infinite to gain" one has to be irrational not to play. Consider an existentialist who believes that the most important thing, that which has the highest utility assignment in his scheme of values, is that he lives this worldly life, the only one that he knows for sure he has, as authentically as possible. If he squanders this life by living in a manner that is not expressive of his true self, he risks losing everything. The loss, given his pecking order, is an "infinite" one, that is, the totality. It must be remembered in this connection that there is no neat correlation between the payoffs of the various outcomes and the utility that will be placed upon them by different persons. For instance, if a person has only two dollars and needs it to secure food so as to survive, she might well refuse to gamble this sum even if she has an equal chance to win an infinite or as-large-as-you-please number of dollars. This person would not give the highest or infinite utility assignment to the winning outcome but would give the lowest possible utility assignment to the losing outcome. My own ethical intuitions accord with the existentialist's in this matter. People morally ought not to live their worldly lives in a way that they deem inauthentic, no matter what possibilities it might open up for other worldly gains or benefits.

The question, then, is whether the worldly life required of those who accept the wager is an authentic one. For some it is and for others not. There are those free spirits who think that they would not be true to themselves if they were to adopt the authoritarian orientation that is required of an active, believing member of most of the world's leading religions. The restrictions that this would entail in regard to how they must think, feel, and act would be anathema to them.

On the other hand, there are those for whom the religious way of life is authentic and self-fulfilling. They are the sort who would want to pursue this religious way of life even if it did not lead on to the big afterlife payoff. They agree with Pascal that "you will gain by it in this life." In the great extant religions of the world, which are the only live or practically possible religious options for the vast majority of people, worldly means and afterlife ends are of a piece, forming an integral unity. In Christianity, for example, heavenly existence is just a more intense and refined version of the worldly religious life in which one's relation to God, since not encumbered by the body, is an unceasing beatific or mystic vision of his true positive nature. Only people who find the Christian way of life attractive would find an unending survival in a Christian heaven especially valuable. Their reason, accordingly, for believing that God exists is not a pragmatic one based on its being a means to some desirable end, but that they want to be people of faith, the religious way of life having an intrinsic value for them.

Thus, Pascal's wager is not really a wager, since the people who will accept it do not see themselves as *gambling* at all. According to their scheme of preferences, they are not *risking* something finite, their worldly life, for the chance of gaining some infinite otherworldly reward, since the religious way of life is the one that has the greatest value for them. Pascal's "wager" turns out to be nothing but a pep talk to those who suffer from a kind of weakness of will. They find the religious way of life attractive (and thereby the afterlife to which it supposedly leads) but can't get themselves to make the requisite commitment because of counteracting traits of their present character. They are in the same situation as those who want to change their character but finds it difficult because they must overcome the counterbalancing force of formed habits. They need a pep talk so that they can strengthen and make dominant their second-order intentions to change their first-order motivations and reasons for acting.

Not only is there an integral unity to the means–ends relationships described by the linkage propositions of the creeds of the great religions, there ought to be such a unity. It was pointed out that for the wager to work it was necessary to limit the field of entrants to at least a finite number of theistic deities. It was suggested that this might be accomplished by appeal to pragmatic considerations. But the requirement that the this-worldly-means and the-otherworldly-ends form an integral unity also is a way of narrowing the field, since many of the logically possible theistic creeds do not satisfy it. For instance, the one-crack-deity creed does not, since it enjoins us to follow a worldly life in which we step on just one sidewalk crack in the course of our life as a means to gaining entrance into a Chirstian-type heaven. Herein means and ends fall apart; the connection between them is a purely accidental one that is secured by the causal efficacy of an external agent. Anyone who followed such a creed would be acting in a totally irrational manner, and not just because of any lack of adequate epistemological support for it. A lot more will be said about this integral unity requirement when we discuss moral justifications of faith, to which we now turn.

PRAGMATIC ARGUMENTS FROM MORALITY

According to this mode of pragmatic justification of faith, one could have a sufficient reason for believing if doing so were to promote the cause of morality by rendering the believer and/or her society morally better. It could be contended, for example, that if the subject of a religious experience develops in a morally desirable manner as a result of her accepting the experience as an objective revelation, thereby believing that God exists, she is justified in believing that God exists. Since some moral good results from her so believing, she has at least a prima facie moral justification for her belief, even though, as argued in the previous chapter, she does not have adequate epistemic warrant for it. The onus is on the naysayer to show that there are defeating conditions, namely, that by so believing, our believer brings about some moral evil that outweighs the moral good that is realized.

W. K. Clifford would contend that the good our believer realizes by her epistemically unsupported belief is out-weighed by the evil that results from her allowing herself to have such a belief. He holds that "it is wrong always, every-where, and for anyone, to believe anything upon insufficient evidence."[8] Let us call this "Clifford's principle." His argu-ment for it is based on an act-utilitarian moral theory, al-though it is not explicitly stated. His basic contention is that while such a belief might maximize utility in the short run, in the long run its overall consequences are horrendous. The reason is that by allowing ourselves one such belief, however seemingly trivial and harmless, we become infected with an incurable case of credulity and dishonesty that will eventu-ally infect the entire community, with disastrous long-range consequences. The following quotations, which for maxi-mum effect should be read aloud while "Pomp and Circum-stance" is played in the background, defend this "plague theory" of epistemically unwarranted belief:

> Our words, our phrases, our forms and processes and modes of thought, are common property, fashioned and perfected from age to age; an heirloom which every succeeding genera-tion inherits as a precious deposit and a sacred trust to be handed on to the next one, not unchanged but enlarged and purified, with some clear marks of its proper handiwork. Into this, for good or ill, is woven every belief of every man who has speech of his fellows. An awful privilege, and an awful responsibility, that we should help to create the world in which posterity will live.[9]

> Whoso would deserve well of his fellows in this matter will guard the purity of his belief with a very fanaticism of jealous care, lest at any time it should rest on an unworthy object, and catch a stain which can never be wiped away.[10]

That duty is to guard ourselves from such beliefs as from a pestilence, which may shortly master our own body and then spread to the rest of the town. What would be thought of one who, for the sake of a sweet fruit, should deliberately run the risk of bringing a plague upon his family and his neighbours?[11]

In like manner, if I let myself believe anything on insufficient evidence, there may be no great harm done by the mere belief; it may be true after all, or I may never have occasion to exhibit it in outward acts. But I cannot help doing this great wrong towards Man, that I make myself credulous. The danger to society is not merely that it should believe wrong things, though that is great enough; but that it should become credulous, and lose the habit of testing things and inquiring into them; for then it must sink back into savagery.[12]

The credulous man is father to the liar and the cheat; he lives in the bosom of this his family, and it is no marvel if he should become even as they are. So closely are our duties knit together, that whoso shall keep the whole law, and yet offend in one point, he is guilty of all.[13]

I assume that ten minutes have passed and that the reader has just begun to pull back together again after rolling around on the floor in hysterical convulsions. But my purpose in presenting this series of quotations is not just to entertain but to protect myself against the charge of creating a strawman by attributing the plague theory of epistemically unwarranted belief to Clifford. Like many an act utilitarian trying to fend off a desert-island unkept-promise counterexample, Clifford has greatly exaggerated the deleterious consequences of allowing ourselves even a single epistemically unwarranted belief, however trivial and disconnected from the workaday world. To put it mildly, his plague theory has very dubious empirical credentials. It would be most unnecessary for the United States to mount a "Just Say No to Epistemically Unwarranted Beliefs" campaign. Imagine the TV commercials that Clifford would make for it: We see little Johnny happy in his totally unfounded belief that the Yankees will win the World Series followed by a grown-up Johnny, now the "liar and the cheat," who is a PR nan for Exxon assuring the nation that everything possible is being done to clean up the oil spill, and then we see some super-straight farm family in Iowa who, immediately upon hearing this spiel, travels to downtown Ames to hustle phony Rolex watches.

That Clifford's principle is not supportable by act utilitarianism does not show it is false. Counterexamples, however, can be given to it consisting of cases in which people, in virtue of entering into a trust relationship, have a moral duty to trust each other and therefore to believe certain things about others regardless of whether they have adequate epistemic support for these beliefs. For instance, spouses have such a moral duty to trust each other and believe in the faithfulness of the other person, even if their belief is not supported by the results of an empirical inquiry; they even have a duty not to perform such an inquiry. To perform it is already to stand outside of the special relationship. I believe that family members have a similar moral duty in regard to their beliefs about each other.

While Clifford's principle faces such trust-relationship counterexamples, an epistemically unwarranted belief that God exists is not among them; and thus it is open to Clifford to restrict his universal principle in such a way that it will not apply to trust-relationship cases but will apply to all other cases of belief. William James in "The Will to Believe" produces counterexamples even to this restricted version of Clifford's principle, the most exciting of which is an epistemically unwarranted belief that God exists. His intent, however, is not just to produce counterexamples but to spell out the necessary and sufficient conditions under which one has a moral right to believe without adequate epistemic justification.

These necessary and sufficient conditions will be marshaled by James to mount a pragmatic argument from morality for epistemically unfounded faith. It is a substitution instance of the following argument form:

6. Doing X helps to bring about Y;
7. It is morally desirable that Y; therefore,
8. One has a prima facie moral permission to do X.

Notice that the moral permission in 8 is only prima facie, since it faces possible defeating conditions. It is desirable that I keep my promises, and my giving a revolver to someone whom I promised a revolver to brings it about that I keep my promise. But I have only a prima facie permission to hand over the revolver, since this person could have gone insane since I made my promise and would use the gun to kill an innocent person. Our duty not to do that which will result in an innocent person being killed takes precedence over our moral duty and/or permission to keep our promise.

James's pragmatic argument from morality plugs into this argument form as follows:

6'. By believing that God exists, I help to bring it about that I and/or my society become morally better;
7'. It is morally desirable that I and/or my society become morally better; therefore,
8'. I have a prima facie moral permission to believe that God exists.

Notice that the conclusion is weaker than might appear necessary, but it will suffice for James's purpose of countering Clifford's moral prohibition against epistemically unfounded belief under any circumstances, save for those that occur within a trust relationship. It will be seen that there are several possible defeating conditions for the prima facie moral permission in 8' that James did not consider.

We shall now follow in detail the route James takes in developing his counterexamples to Clifford's principle, even in its restricted form, and the set of necessary and sufficient conditions for the moral right to belief without adequate epistemic support that fall out of them. Since all of these examples involve what James calls a "genuine option" to believe, we must begin with his account of a genuine option.

He begins by offering two definitions. We are "to give the name of *hypothesis* to anything that may be proposed to our belief and to call the decision between two hypotheses an *option.*"[14] James's choice of "hypothesis" to characterize the object of a decision is unfortunate, for not all options involve a decision between hypotheses in the sense of choosing one of them as a working hypothesis or, more dubiously, to believe one of them. We need a more generic term to characterize the object of choice, and I suggest that we use "Proposition," understood in the sense of a proposal. This term will be written with a capital "P" so as to distinguish it from that which refers to what is the bearer of a truth-value; the latter will be written as "proposition" with a lower case "p." A proposal is best described by a predicate infinitive – "to *F*" – rather than by a noun "that"-clause. My terminology begs no question against James, since it leaves it open whether among the Propositions that could be subject to our choice is to believe some proposition (or hypothesis).

A *genuine option* is one that is *live, momentous,* and *forced.* "A *living* option is one in which both hypotheses [Propositions according to my terminology] are live ones" (WB 3) in the sense that each is a "real possibility to him to whom it is proposed" (WB 2).

An option is momentous when it is either unique (it's your only chance to do what is proposed) or significant (whether or not you elect to do what is proposed will vitally affect your future life). It should be clear from what is required for an option to be live and momentous that a genuine option must be relativized to a person at a time, since what is living or momentous can vary from person to person and from one time in a person's life to another. This relativization of a genuine option to a person at a time will become important when we devise a way out of a difficulty in James's argument.

James's account of when an option is forced is unclear. After offering some examples of unforced options, he says that in a forced option "there is no standing place outside of the alternative" (WB 3). This rather unhelpful remark is followed by the puzzling sentence "Every dilemma based on a complete logical disjunction, with no possibility of not choosing, is an option of this forced kind." What is puzzling about

this is that even when we have an option between Propositions that are mutually exclusive and exhaustive – to do *F* or
not to do *F* – it is not clear why we are forced to *choose* one of
them. Why can't we refrain from choosing either alternative?
Judging by some of the things James later says about forced
options, the basis of a forced option is that if one does not
choose one of the Propositions, then, given the circumstances that obtain, one winds up doing what the other Proposition proposes, even when one does not actually choose to
do the latter. We could call the Proposition in a forced option
that becomes actual if no choice at all is made the "negative
alternative," the other the "positive alternative." We put in
the qualification "in the circumstances that obtain" so as to
preclude the positive alternative becoming actualized when
not chosen. The option to join Dr. Nansen's expedition, to
use James's example, is not forced if we will wind up joining
the expedition regardless of what choice is made, as would
be the case if the good Dr. Nansen were to shanghai us.

At the outset, all of James's examples of options, including
genuine ones, involve a decision between proposed *actions*,
that is, pieces of intentional behavior. He next attempts to
show that there can be a genuine option to believe a proposition. He has a rebuttal to the objection that there cannot be
such an option since belief is not an action – something we
can do intentionally, at will, voluntarily, and the like. This
problem will be considered later, and for the time being we
shall assume that there is no problem about choosing to
believe.

A genuine option to believe must also be forced, live, and
momentous. An agent *A*, at a time *T*, has a genuine option to
believe or not to believe a proposition *p* just in case:

9. The circumstances are such that if *A* does not choose to
believe *p*, she will not believe *p*;
10. To believe *p* and to not believe *p* are each real possibilities for *A* at *T*; and
11. Whether or not *A* believes *p* will vitally affect her future life.

Condition 9 says that only if A chooses to believe p will she wind up believing p: Not only does she not already believe p, no external power such as a hypnotist or mad surgeon will "shanghai" her into believing p. Condition 10 requires that A have an open mind about the truth of p. Condition 11 can be satisfied only if it is assumed that what A believes concerning the truth of p will have important consequences in her future, this requiring that her belief concerning p be determinative of her behavior.

Although James does not explicitly state this, a case of a genuine option to believe a proposition is a necessary but not a sufficient condition for a counterexample to Clifford's principle. The needed additional conditions can be gleaned from what James says, as well as from his examples, which will be discussed later. The first condition which must be added is

12. It is impossible at T for A to decide on epistemological grounds the truth of p.

Here the impossibility can be of the *in-practice* or *in-principle* sort. This is strongly suggested by these remarks:

> Our passional nature not only lawfully may, but must decide an option between propositions, whenever it is a genuine option that cannot by its nature be decided on intellectual grounds. (WB 11)

> *In concreto*, the freedom to believe can only cover living options which the intellect of the individual cannot by itself resolve.[15] (WB 29)

The following sort of possible counterexample to Clifford's principle, involving a genuine option to believe, is ruled out by 12. Imagine that at T one of the sons of the Rosenbergs has a genuine option to believe or not to believe that his parents were not guilty of espionage: He is undecided about the truth of this proposition; his belief option is forced; and what he believes will determine much of his future behavior, for instance, how he relates to people and institutions. Even if we assume that at T he has no evidence one way or the other for this proposition, 12 still precludes his being morally justified in choosing to believe what he wants, since its truth can *in practice* be determined at T by empirical inquiry – checking records and traces, examining witnesses, and so on. And this prohibition holds regardless of how beneficial the consequences of believing this proposition might be. James is far from the "cheap pragmatist" that he is depicted as being by Russell and others, for he holds that we are never free to shirk our responsibility to investigate a question in a thorough, scientific manner when it is amenable to such an investigation. In fact, James goes too far with Clifford's principle, since he fails to note that trust-relationship cases are a counterexample to it.

Another requirement that James seems to place on a counterexample is that

13. It is within the power of A to help make p true (or false).

The textual support for this additional requirement, which, it will turn out, is not needed, is this:

> There are, then, cases where a fact cannot come at all unless a preliminary faith exists in its coming. And where faith in a fact can help create the fact, that would be an insane logic which should say that faith running ahead of scientific evidence is the "lowest kind of immorality" into which a thinking being can fall. (WB 25)

> In truths dependent on our personal action, then, faith based on desire is certainly a lawful and possibly indispensable thing. (WB 25)

Condition 13, in conjunction with the conceptual truth that causation cannot go backward, entails that p must be about the future. The Rosenberg case also fails to meet this requirement; for nothing that is done at T or at a later time can bring it about or prevent it from being the case that the Rosenbergs committed espionage prior to T as defined by the pre-T laws.

Pragmatic arguments from morality

There is one further necessary condition that imbues James's discussion, especially his examples, namely,

14. It is morally desirable that p be true.

Since A is supposed to be *morally* justified in choosing to believe p so that she can help to make p true, it must be that it is morally desirable that p be the case, thereby fitting the earlier argument form.

It is James's contention that any case that satisfies conditions 9–14 above constitutes a counterexample to Clifford's principle. Such a case will be called a "special genuine option to believe" so as to distinguish it from a "genuine option to believe," which need satisfy only the first three of the six conditions. It now will be shown that James's counterexamples are in fact special genuine options to believe.

His first case is the option to believe or not to believe the proposition that you will like me:

> Whether you do or not depends, in countless instances, on whether I meet you half-way, I am willing to assume that you must like me, and show you trust and expectation. The previous faith on my part in your liking's existence is in such cases what makes your liking come. But if I stand aloof, and refuse to budge an inch until I have objective evidence, until you shall have done something apt . . . ten to one your liking never comes. (WB 24)

Yet another case involves the special genuine option to believe that God exists. First, James gives a pragmatic analysis of this proposition. He finds a pragmatic common denominator for all religions in these two propositions:

> First . . . the best things are the more eternal things . . . the things in the universe that throw the last stone . . . and say the final word.
> The second affirmation of religion is that we are better off even now if we believe her first affirmation to be true. (WB 25–6)

363

We shall consider only the first affirmation as constituting the religious hypothesis, the second affirmation being not a tenet of any religion but rather a proposition about the dynamics of religious faith, such as might be made by a social scientist or an apologist for religious faith.

The first affirmation, basically, seems to say:

R. Good will win out over evil in the long run.

This seems to be what is meant by the "the best things . . . throw the last stone . . . say the final word." The idea is that the universe is morally good in that, in spite of its undeniable evils, it will have a morally good outcome, a just and good order eventually will come to prevail, *if* we make the requisite moral effort. There are forces within the universe that will support our most noble moral efforts so that they will come to a successful denouement. There are interesting affinities between James's theology and later process theologies.

It remains to be shown how each of these options constitutes a special genuine option to believe. Condition 14 is satisfied in both cases, since, supposedly, it is good that good win out over evil in the long run and that you like me. Condition 13 is satisfied, since the agent has some power to help make these propositions true, although the extent of her power differs radically in the two cases. She can do little to make the former true, no matter how altruistically she acts, but her actions are almost the sole determinant of the truth of the latter. This difference results in a difference in the way 12 is satisfied in the two cases. In both cases I cannot have evidence for the proposition *before* I choose to believe it, but *after* I choose to believe that you will like me I have good evidence that you will, since I then know that I shall act in a friendly way and that this is very likely to succeed. However, *after* the agent chooses to believe *R*, she still has virtually no evidence for it. Thus, in the you-will-like-me case, the agent does not wind up having an epistemically unjustified belief, and thereby there is no counterexample to Clifford's principle. But it does violate the spirit if not the letter of it, since

it also means to proscribe choosing or getting yourself to believe without epistemic justification.

There is a further reason for thinking that the you-will-like-
me case fails to satisfy 12. I could have good inductive evidence that I am likable, and this could constitute adequate
justification for believing that you will like me. But James can
respond that whether you will like me hinges on what I
choose to believe in this matter (since what I believe determines how I act toward you), and I cannot know what I shall
choose before I choose. The latter is a conceptual truth and
does not rest on James's dubious Libertarian doctrine that
choice is acausal and thus unpredictable.

It only remains to be shown that both cases involve a genuine option to believe, thereby satisfying all six conditions.
We can cook the circumstances so that failure to choose the
positive option results in the actualization of the negative
option – not believing the proposition in question. Not everyone will find it a live option to believe R, but this poses no
difficulty since we can follow James in restricting ourselves to
those for whom it is live:

> If we are to discuss the question at all, it must involve a living
> option. If for any of you religion be a hypothesis that cannot,
> by any living possibility be true, then you need go no farther.
> I speak to the "saving remnant" alone. (WB 26)

It is over the momentousness of the options that serious
problems arise. The momentousness of a belief option depends not on the momentousness of what the proposition
forecasts but the momentousness of the agent's believing or
not believing it. While R predicts something of great importance to most people, it is not obvious that it is of great
importance to the agent's future life whether or not she
believes it; for, it could be claimed, she can behave altruistically even if she does not actually believe R, just as I can act
in a friendly manner even if I suspend belief in the proposition that you will like me. Because belief does not seem to

determine action, what I believe in these matters need not have any future behavioral consequences; and, as a result, the belief options are not momentous.[16]

James has a ready response to this difficulty:

> Since belief is measured by action, he who forbids us to believe religion to be true, necessarily also forbids us to act as we should if we did believe it to be true. The whole defence of religious faith hinges upon action. If the action required or inspired by the religious hypothesis is in no way different from that dictated by the naturalistic hypothesis, then religious faith is a pure superfluity, better pruned away, and controversy about its legitimacy is a piece of idle trifling, unworthy of serious minds. (WB 29–30)

James even goes so far as to claim that there is no behavioral difference between suspending belief in R and actually disbelieving it:

> We cannot escape the issue by remaining sceptical and waiting for more light, because, although we do avoid error in that way *if religion be untrue*, we lose the good, *if it be true*, just as certainly as if we positively disbelieve. (WB 26)

> When I look at the religious question as it really puts itself to concrete men, and when I think of all the possibilities which both practically and theoretically it involves, then this command that we shall put a stopper on our heart, instincts, and courage, and *wait* – acting of course meanwhile more or less as if religion were *not* true – till doomsday, or till such time as our intellect and senses working together may have raked in evidence enough – this command, I say, seems to me the queerest idol ever manufactured in the philosophical cave. (WB 29–30)

These three quotations make clear that although James does not commit himself to a behavioral analysis of belief, he does commit himself at a minimum to the doctrine that there is a one-to-one correspondence between beliefs and sets of actions and/or dispositions to act. For any proposition p, if and only if a person believes p will she perform or be disposed to perform actions $A_1 \ldots A_n$.

Unfortunately, this one-to-one correspondence doctrine is patently false, for one can try to make a proposition p true without antecedently believing p; for instance, our agent might suspend belief, neither believing nor disbelieving p, but attempt to make p true because she believes that it is morally desirable for p to become true. Often when a person has the power to make p true and believes it will become true, she becomes overconfident and does not sufficiently exercise herself in trying to make it true. We could even imagine a kamikaze-type person who actually disbelieves p but nevertheless does everything she can to make it true. It is obvious that there is no one-to-one correspondence between beliefs and actions. Human psychology is quite varied. In response to James's demand that the "action required or inspired by the religious hypothesis" must be "different from that dictated by the naturalistic hypothesis" we could have the behavioral difference in some specific case consist only in the believer of R having the disposition to say yes when asked whether she believes R.[17]

This objection to James looks more formidable than it really is. James creates a needless problem for himself when he says that "since belief is measured by action, he who forbids *us* to believe religion to be true, necessarily also forbids *us* to act as we should if *we* did believe it to be true" (my italics). It is the use of the universal "us" and "we" that commits him to the false one-to-one correspondence doctrine. Since a special genuine option is relative to a person at a time, he does not have to commit himself to a universal correlation between a belief in R and a set of actions. He could instead restrict himself to some specific person about whom it is an empirical fact that if and only if she actually believes R, will she perform or be disposed to perform good-making actions. It is obvious that there not only could be, but actually are, persons who are so constituted psychologically that they cannot try to make a proposition true unless they believe in advance that their efforts will succeed and thus that the proposition is true. Accordingly, we must add to the six preceding conditions this new one:

15. *A* knows that she will act so as to help make *p* true if and only if she believes in advance that *p* is true.

The reason why it is required that the agent know this fact about herself is that it must be possible for the agent, as well as other people, to morally justify her choosing to believe an epistemically unsupported proposition if we are to have a counterexample to Clifford's principle.[18]

There still remains the objection that it is conceptually impossible for there to be an option to believe a proposition since we cannot believe at will, voluntarily, intentionally, and so on. James's response consists in an argument for the empirical proposition that "our non-intellectual nature does influence our convictions" (WB 11). This is a flowers-that-bloom-in-the-spring response, since this psychological truth has nothing to do with the case. Granted that there are non-rational causes of an emotional and passional sort for all our beliefs, how is this supposed to show that we can choose to believe? If anything, it proves the contrary, since we cannot control our passions and emotions at will.

It is surprising that James did not deploy his theory of the will from *The Principles of Psychology* to meet the belief-is-not-an-action objection. By an intentional act of attention or concentration we can get ourselves to be conscious in a certain way. Once we are conscious of what a proposition *p* reports with sufficient intensity over a long enough time, we will have acquired the belief that *p*, since "our belief and attention are the same fact."[19] Following Spinoza, James argued that if an infant were to be conscious of nothing but the image of a candle, this would amount to a belief in the existence of this candle.

Many would find this account of belief unacceptable and thus would reject any attempt to deflect the belief-is-not-an-action objection that appealed to it. What, then, is the proper response to this objection? In the first place, its claim that it

is *conceptually* impossible to believe at will should be challenged. To be sure, it would be very queer to speak of believing at will, voluntarily, on purpose, carefully, and so on, but
that might be due, not to such talk violating any rule of
language, but our never having had the occasion to so speak
since we haven't yet learned the knack of controlling our
beliefs at will. At one time in history it might have sounded
equally queer to speak of controlling the frequency of our
brain waves at will but now that we have learned the knack
through biofeedback training such talk is unobjectionable.
Possibly something similar could happen in regard to our
learning how to control our beliefs at will.

For the purpose of constructing a moral justification of
epistemically unsupported belief, James need not involve
himself in the issue of whether belief is, or could be, a basic
action. He can avail himself of Pascal's strategy of holding
that there is a causal recipe consisting of basic actions by
which belief can be self-induced, in particular the belief that
God exists. Although James and Pascal have radically different conceptions of God, they agree that in principle we cannot have an adequate epistemic justification for belief in God.
Therefore, the methods that our causal recipes for self-inducing faith prescribe are nonrational ones, for instance, "taking
the holy water, having masses said," and the like, as opposed
to examination of arguments and evidence. James's claim
that all of our beliefs are caused, at least in part, by nonrational factors can be viewed as a justification for nonrationally
self-inducing a belief in p when rational methods can be of no
avail.

It should now be clear what must be done to protect James
against the belief-is-not-an-action objection. His special genuine option for A at T to believe or not to believe p must be
changed to a special genuine option for A at T to try by
nonrational means to get herself to believe p or not to try this.
The latter will have to satisfy the same seven conditions for a
special genuine option to believe, with the exception of the
first three, which are modified to account for the difference
in the objects of choice:

9'. The circumstances are such that if A does not choose to try to get herself to believe p, she will not believe p;

10'. To try to get herself to believe p and not to do this are each real possibilities for A at T;

11'. Whether or not A tries to get herself to believe p will vitally affect her future life;

12. It is impossible at T for A to decide on epistemological grounds the truth of p;

13. It is within the power of A to help make p true (or false);

14. It is morally desirable that p be true; and

15. A knows that she will act so as to help make p true if and only if she believes in advance that p is true.

Let us call an option that satisfies these conditions a "special genuine option to self-induce a belief."

It is not only James's sufficient and necessary conditions for a counterexample to Clifford's principle that must be reconstructed in this manner so as to get around the belief-is-not-an-action objection, but this principle as well. If I cannot believe at will, there cannot be a moral imperative enjoining me not to believe without adequate epistemic justification. The principle, accordingly, must be revised to say that it is morally wrong under any circumstances to induce an epistemically unwarranted belief.

Since our concern is with whether one can be morally permitted (or justified) to believe or get oneself to believe that God exists when lacking adequate epistemic support, we must consider whether a person who satisfies all seven of the conditions for having a special genuine option to self-induce a belief in R is morally permitted to do so. It is not difficult to imagine a person who is so psychologically constituted that she satisfies all of these conditions. To simplify matters, let us imagine that there is available to her a belief-in-R inducing pill, this being representative of any nonrational method for self-inducing a belief in R, which are the only methods that can be of any avail, given that R is a prediction of what will come to pass in the indefinite future.

It is clear that James would say that in these circumstances our agent is morally permitted (or has a moral justification) to take the pill, since by doing so she brings about something morally desirable, namely, that she acts in an altruistic or good-making fashion.[20] Herein he is plugging into the previous valid argument form, according to which our agent has a prima facie moral permission to do that which helps to bring about something that is morally desirable. It will be argued at some length that there are defeating conditions for her prima facie moral permission to take the pill, that by taking the pill under those circumstances, she brings about an evil that outweighs the good she promotes. But first it will be shown that to accord her such permission violates the moral principle of universalizability.

The moral principle of universalizability states that if it is morally permissible (required, forbidden) for X to do Y in circumstances C, then it is morally permissible (required, forbidden) for anyone to do Y in circumstances C. Let us imagine two persons, A and A', who are exactly alike save for one feature of their psychology. A, being short of courage, will not act so as to help make R true unless she first believes that R will become true, whereas this is not true of A', the psychologically stronger member of the pair. It thereby turns out that A, but not A', is morally permitted to take the belief-in-R inducing pill. And this seems to violate the principle of universalizability. The reply is that their circumstances are not the same since A satisfies condition 15 while A' does not. But is this a morally relevant feature of the circumstances? I think not. It seems wrong to accord a moral privilege to someone but not to another on the grounds that the former is a psychologically weaker person. This question of moral permission must not be confused with the quite different question of whether it is morally permissible to give the weaker member of the pair more help and consideration than the stronger one, to which the answer is yes.

My argument that the good realized by taking the pill is outweighed by the evil that results makes use of a highly normative concept of personhood, according to which freedom of the will is essential. After I have developed this concept, it will be utilized for the purpose of showing why, on balance, it is immoral to take the pill, thereby canceling the prima facie moral permission to do so.

It is my firm moral conviction that there is an absolute value to personhood. (If the reader is unable to go this far, I trust that he at least will grant that it has a very great value, which will suffice for my argument.) This means the following:

P. It is always wrong to bring it about that a person becomes less than or less of a person or that a potential person becomes something less than a person.

Before pointing out what it is to be a person and what is involved in treating someone as a person, it must be noted that neither capital punishment nor abortion is ruled out by P. In killing a fetus one does not bring it about that an individual who is potentially a person becomes something less than a person, for one simply terminates this individual's existence. As both Kant and Hegel have correctly argued, the administration of capital punishment under certain conditions involves treating the criminal as a person. Robert Brandom has pointed out to me a resemblance between P and the Christian doctrine of the absolute value of the soul. Martyrdom is not ruled out, for the martyr loses her life but not her soul: The person who is executed by the state loses his life but does not become something less than a person, since, assuming there is no survival of death, he does not become anything at all. P also does not rule out treating *human beings* paternalistically, for not all human beings qualify as persons. In some cases the justification for so treating them is that it helps them develop into persons.

What, then, is it to be a person? This is a normative question, and according to my moral convictions a necessary and sufficient condition for personhood is having free will. To have free will is to behave as a morally responsible agent. I shall explicate the latter notion in terms of the moral responsibility game, the playing of which is a necessary and sufficient condition for being a person.

This game is determined by two kinds of rules, ontological and sociological. The former specify the conditions under which a person is morally responsible for an action, the latter what is involved in treating someone as a morally responsible agent. The ontological rules must be given first, since to treat someone as a person (i.e., as a morally responsible agent) is to view their actions as satisfying these rules. While the ontological rules have this priority in the order of analysis, there is, as Annette Baier has shown me, a psychological sense in which the sociological rules have priority in that by treating individuals as persons, we help to bring it about that their actions satisfy the ontological rules.

The first ontological rule states:

R_1. A player is morally responsible for an act only if he could have avoided doing it.

For the purpose of my argument, I need not commit myself to any particular analysis of "could have avoided." In Chapter 4 I tried to refute Lockean objections to R_1 and will not discuss the issue again.

Although no analysis will be offered of R_1, some necessary conditions for moral responsibility can be spelled out in terms of the following rules:

R_2. A player is morally responsible for an act only if he did it as a rational agent.

R_3. A player performs an action F as a rational agent only if:

(a) he knows what he is doing;

(b) he has good reasons for doing F;

(c) his reasons are at least a necessary cause of his doing F; and

(d) he has no reasons that are both necessary causes of his doing F and not good reasons for doing F.

While it is reasonable to make rational agency a necessary condition for moral responsibility, R_3 needs further explanation and justification, especially since some of its conditions are mooted.

Condition (a) is unproblematic, but (b) is not. A reason r is a *good reason* for an agent A to do an action F just in case it is true both that A is justified in accepting r (even if r is in fact false) and r is logically relevant to his doing F (even if r is not *the* best reason). The concept of a good reason is a part of our normative concept of a rational agent. There are some sorts of things that a rational agent would not believe (only a madman would believe that sort of thing!), as well as some sorts of motives, intentions, and purposes that no one could have and be a rational agent. The concept of insanity is in part a normative one.

Some examples will help. My reasons for reaching for a glass of water are that I desire a drink and believe that there is a glass of water in front of me and that water quenches thirst. These constitute good reasons for my actions in that I am justified in accepting them and they are logically relevant. If, instead, my reasons were that I desired to prevent the "heat death" of the universe and believed that there is a glass of water in front of me and that drinking water causes entropy to decrease, my reasons would not be good, since I have no justification for the latter belief reason. If, instead, my reason were that I believed that the sky is blue, my reasons again would not be good, this time because my belief reason, although justified, is logically irrelevant.

Let us consider some possible counterexamples to (b). A person pinches someone and when asked why she did it replies "For no reason at all." This is the same as saying "Because I wanted to." But this gives a logically relevant reason, namely, that she enjoys pinching people and believed that there was a pinchable subject in front of her. By telling us what sorts of things she enjoys and desires, she tells us a lot about what kind of person she is. Another possible counterexample is the case of weakness of the will. The incontinent person should be held morally responsible for his action since he fails to act on what he considers to be the best or proper reason. But the incontinent person, at the time he acts, does have a good reason, namely, self-interest, even though at other times he judges that moral reasons should take priority over those of self-interest. To be a good reason is not to be *the* best reason or even a morally acceptable reason.

While conditions (c) and (d) permit a reason to be a cause, no attempt is made to assimilate the concept of a cause to that of a reason or vice versa, which would be wrong-headed, since reasons and causes play different logical roles. These conditions only point out that a rational action must be caused in a certain way, and the rationale for these conditions can best be seen by considering cases that run afoul of them.

Consider first a case in which a person's reasons (e.g., his desires, wants, intentions, and beliefs) for doing *F*, although constituting good reasons for his doing *F*, are not necessary causes for his doing *F*. Chapter 4 considered such a case, that of the conscious puppet, Pinnochio, who, by coincidence, with good reason endeavored to move his limbs just when Stromboli caused them to move by pulling on some wire. This is a case of causal overdetermination, and since Pinnochio's reasons are not necessary causes of his actions, he is not morally responsible for these actions.

Notice that (c) is consistent with the identity thesis; for, if my desires, wants, intentions, and beliefs are identical with various neurophysiological states and events, then if the latter are necessary causes of my actions, so are the former by Leibniz's law of the indiscernibility of identicals. Furthermore, (c) allows there to be causes for a rational act other than the agent's reasons; for instance, neurophysiological events that are numerically distinct from these reasons.

The need for condition (d), which rules out any reason cause, whether necessary or not, among the causes of a rational act that is not a good reason, can be seen from this case. I intentionally reach out for the glass of water, but among the reason causes are the above good reasons plus my belief that Verdi wrote *Ernani*. Since the latter is not a good reason for my action, being logically irrelevant, it destroys the rationality of my action.

That a rational act must be caused in a certain way, which is what R_2 and R_3 require, has interesting analogies with

causal theories of memory and perception. In recent literature there are many examples of seeming memories (perceptions) that do not count as a memory (perception) because
the causal chain linking them with their apparent object is
not of the right sort, being too kinky. We can imagine similar
types of science fiction fantasies in which a person has good
reasons for her action but ones that are not linked with her
action by the right sort of causal chain.

Now for the sociological rules. The first of these specifies
how one can opt into the moral responsibility game.

R_4. One opts into the game by declaring that one wants to
be held morally responsible for one's actions by the other
players or by being willing to hold them and be held by them
to be morally responsible.

Rarely does one opt into the game by uttering some explicit
performatory sentence, such as "I hereby declare that I want
to be held morally responsible for my actions." Rather, one
becomes of age and just finds oneself playing the game by
holding others morally responsible and in turn being willing,
at least on some occasions, to be held morally responsible
by them.

Since one can be held to be morally responsible only by
another person, R_4 has the logical consequence that

R_5. A player must hold the other players to be morally
responsible for their actions.

It should be apparent why the principle of reciprocity applies
here. Since a necessary condition of personhood is being held
morally responsible and only a person can be held or hold one
morally responsible, I must invest the other game players
with personhood by holding them morally responsible so that
they in return can invest me with personhood by holding me
morally responsible. A consequence of rules R_4 and R_5 is that
no one can be a person except in the society of other persons.

The next group of rules specify what is involved in treating
someone as a morally responsible agent. The first of these
rules is

R_6. To treat someone as being morally responsible for an action requires that her action be viewed as satisfying the requirements specified in rules R_2 and R_3.

A consequence of R_2 is that we cannot treat someone as a morally responsible agent unless we treat her as a rational agent. The requirements for treating someone as a rational agent can be derived from R_3. Since R_3 requires that a rational agent have good reasons for her actions that are causally operative in the appropriate way, it should follow that we cannot treat someone as a rational agent if we either deny that her reasons for acting are good or induce her to perform an action without her having good reasons for it. Thus, we get these rules:

R_7. To treat someone as a rational agent requires that her reasons for performing an action not be dismissed or undermined.

R_8. To treat someone as a rational agent requires that she not be induced or caused to perform an action for which she lacks a good reason.

R_7 forbids us to say of a rational agent's professed reasons for acting that they are not the real reasons, a mere coverup or rationalization by her "conscious" mind for the true "unconscious" reasons. We are all too familiar with these devices for explaining away, undermining, someone's professed reasons. However, R_7 does permit us to *supplement* a rational agent's reasons and to offer causal explanations, for instance, neurophysiological ones, that do not make use of her professed reasons.

If I were to induce someone to perform an action without her having good reasons at the time she acts, I would bring it about the she fails to act as a rational agent. This, certainly, is not to treat her as a rational agent. Notice that R_8 does not entail the further rule: To treat someone as a rational agent requires that only rational methods be used to induce her to perform an action. Later it will be shown that someone can be induced by nonrational methods to perform an action for which she has good reasons.

There is nothing in R_7 or R_8, or any of the other rules of the game, nor even in principle P itself, that rules out treating a *human being* as a nonperson. But to treat someone in a way that violates a rule of the game must be justified by ample evidence that she cannot act in a way that satisfies the ontological rules R_1–R_3. It could even be a former game player that gets so treated. This indicates a need for a further rule specifying how a player can be eliminated from the game:

R_9. A player may be eliminated from the game by the other players when there is good evidence that her behavior cannot satisfy the requirements specified in rules R_1–R_3.

There are less radical moves than total elimination from the game. A player could be viewed as lacking moral responsibility for some but not all kinds of act for which she was formerly held morally responsible. As a consequence, there is a need for a restricted version of R_9:

R_{10}. A player may no longer be held morally responsible by the other players for a kind of action F when there is good evidence that she cannot perform F-type actions in a way that satisfies the requirements specified in rules R_1–R_3.

Rules R_9 and R_{10} bring out some important features of our concept of a person. R_9 shows that it is a phasal property (i.e., one that can apply to an individual at some but not all times in that individual's history), R_{10} that it admits of degrees, one's degree of personhood depending upon the number and different kinds of action for which one can be held morally responsible.

The reader may wonder why R_9 and R_{10} do not allow for reflexive instances – self-elimination from the game or self-restriction on degree of personhood. It is because I basically agree with Sartre's dictum that the one thing we are not free to do is to give up our own freedom.[21] When rendered in terms of rules of the game it becomes

R_{11}. No player can opt out of the game;

R_{12}. No player can request that other players no longer hold her morally responsible for actions of kind F.

There can be no voluntary commitment. An interesting consequence of these rules is that it can never be part of our justification for treating a former game player as a nonperson that she has consented to such treatment, which does not mean that we cannot have justification.

These rules are controversial and thereby require some defense. To some it might seem odd that we can opt into but not out of the moral responsibility game. The reply to this is that there is nothing absurd about certain kinds of noncancelable contracts and compacts. A more serious objection is that I can have exactly the same justification for eliminating myself from the game as for eliminating another player. The justification for my eliminating a person from the game is that I have good empirical evidence that her behavior fails to satisfy the ontological rules, but I can have exactly the same such evidence for my own behavior failing to satisfy these rules.

The answer to this objection will consist in establishing first, although there is no epistemic asymmetry between an agent and observer in regard to the agent's *past* actions, there is in regard to her *future* actions; and, second, this epistemic asymmetry results in a justificatory asymmetry between the elimination of oneself and others from the game, since eliminating someone from the game concerns her future behavior.

Let us call someone an agent in respect to an action if she does this action intentionally. It is obvious that the very same kind of evidence that can be appealed to by an observer to justify his claim to know what some agent did in the *past* can be appealed to by the agent in support of her claim to know that she did this. But this evidential symmetry between agent and observer does not hold for the agent's *future* actions in virtue of the following conceptual truth: It is impossible for an agent to know in advance of her forming an intention to do some action (which could coincide with her beginning to do it) that she will do that action. A special case of this is it is conceptually impossible for an agent to deliberate and at the same time know what she will decide to do.[22] An observer, however, faces no such conceptual bars from knowing in advance what an agent will choose or intentionally do. The inductive argument that she can give to support her knowledge claim can be of no avail to the agent who has yet to make up her mind; for, to try to decide what to do is not to try to inductively infer what someone will choose do.[23] Deciding is not predicting. A decision, unlike a prediction, is not justified by appeal to an inductive argument but by giving good reasons for bringing about what one has decided to do.

It remains to be shown that this *epistemic* asymmetry between agent and observer in respect to the agent's future actions results in a *justificatory* asymmetry between first- and third-person elimination from the game. As pointed out, a necessary part of the justification for eliminating a player from the game is possession of good empirical evidence that this player's *past* actions did not satisfy the requirements of the ontological rules. A player can have such evidence in regard to her own past actions. So far there is no asymmetry. However, there is a prospective dimension to eliminating someone from the game, since it results in her not being held morally responsible for her *future* actions. Obviously, this requires justification in the form of a good inductive argument that her future actions will not satisfy the ontological rules. But, in accordance with the stated epistemic asymmetry between agent and observer, the agent who has yet to decide how to act in the future cannot then use any such inductive argument to support her claim to know how she will act in the future, since she cannot know in advance of her decision how she will decide to act. Whether or not the agent acts in a morally responsible way in the future – in a way that satisfies the ontological rules – depends, at least in part, upon what choices she will make. Thus, in advance of these choices, she is conceptually barred from knowing what she will do, although she faces no such bar from knowing in advance on inductive grounds the choices and intentional behavior of others. Therefore, if a person were to opt out of the game, she would have to justify this move by appeal to inductive knowledge of her future lack of moral responsibility; but it is exactly this sort of inductive knowledge that she cannot have in advance of her decisions regarding her future conduct.[24] So far only R_{11} has been defended, but it should be apparent that exactly the same sort of argument can be given in support of R_{12}, which only deals with a more restricted case of opting out of being held morally responsible.

This completes my rather sketchy analysis of personhood in terms of playing the moral responsibility game. If I treat a person in a way that violates a rule of the game, I impugn her personhood, since to be a person is to play this game. Thereby, I violate P, the absolute (or very great) value of personhood. It can be shown that to take the belief-in-R inducing pill is to treat myself in violation of the rules of the game: And this is sufficiently immoral so as to defeat the good that might be realized by taking the pill. But first I would like to dispose of a bad-personhood-based argument.

The agent's moral justification for taking the belief-in-R inducing pill is that this constitutes a sufficient and necessary condition for her acting altruistically in the future. But, the argument points out, this results in her future altruistic actions failing to satisfy R_1, since she cannot avoid acting altruistically. This involves a loss of or radical restriction upon her personhood, which violates P. Thus, it is immoral for her to take the pill.

This argument lacks force because it rests on the dubious premise of causal incompatibilism. Even if causal incompatibilism is granted, the argument can be answered. One way is to assume that the agent can take a pill that negates the effects of the belief-in-R inducing pill. Thereby she is not permanently locked in on a future of altruistic acts, since she has it within her power to reverse the effects of this pill by taking an antidote pill. Another strategy is to hold that a belief in R is only a necessary cause of the agent acting altruistically. This would in no way weaken the force of the Jamesian argument for her being morally permitted to take the pill.

Now for a good-personhood-based argument based on A's violating P by taking the pill. According to James's argument, our hypothesized agent is supposed to be morally permitted to take the belief-in-R inducing pill, since her belief in R, given the proposition 15-type fact about her psychological makeup, is at least a necessary condition of her acting altruistically so as to help make R true. First it must be established that A's belief in R constitutes part of her reasons for acting altruistically, that is, so as to help make R true.

When a *rational* agent's belief is part of the cause of her action, this belief constitutes part of her reasons for this action. A must be considered to be a *rational* agent for the following reasons: (1) A is supposed to be morally permitted to take the belief-in-R inducing pill; (2) but only a person can be morally permitted to do something; therefore, (3) A is a person; (4) a necessary condition for being a person is playing the moral responsibility game; (5) a necessary condition for playing the game is that a player's actions satisfy ontological rule R_2 requiring that she act as a *rational* agent; therefore, (6) A is a rational agent. Since A is a rational agent and her belief in R is part of the cause of her acting altruistically, it follows that her belief in R constitutes part of her reasons for acting altruistically.

It should be obvious that A's belief in R fails on both counts to be a good reason for her acting altruistically. First, A, *ex hypothesi*, lacks any epistemic justification for R. Second, and more important, R is logically irrelevant as a justification for her acting altruistically so as to make R true. It would be absurd to give as one's reason for acting so as to make a proposition true that it is in fact true or will turn out to be true. It would be crazy to work to bring about an economic depression because one believes that an economic depression will occur. But this is exactly the sort of logically irrelevant reason that A has for acting so as to help make R true. A logically relevant reason for so acting would be that it is morally desirable that R become true. That one's reasons for acting be logically relevant is a variant on the cited requirement that an acceptable prudential justification for doing X so as to bring about Y involves an integral unity between X, the means, and Y, the end. Thus, A violates her personhood by taking the belief-in-R inducing pill, since she causes herself to perform actions for which she lacks good reasons.

How serious is this moral transgression against P? Is it serious enough to defeat our agents prima facie moral permission to take the pill based on the good that will result from doing so? If we take P to be an absolute moral rule, the answer is yes. Even if we do not go so far as to accord an absolute value to personhood, and thereby an absolute status to P, a case can be made out for an affirmative answer, provided we are willing to grant that there is very great value to personhood, and thereby that it takes a very powerful justification to act in a way that violates P. The case goes as follows.

Given the very extensive nature of the actions and dispositions caused by taking the pill and the extent to which they are constitutive of A's character and personality, she in effect opts out of the moral responsibility game, which violates R_{11}. By taking the pill she causes most of her future actions to fail to satisfy the R_3 requirement of rational agency, since she will not have good reasons for these actions.[25] We can, of course, modify the case so that the future behavior that is caused by her taking the pill is not so extensive, thereby allowing A still to be a game player in respect to some of her actions. Nevertheless, she would still violate P, since by constricting the range of her rational, and therefore morally responsible, behavior, she lessens her degree of personhood. She makes herself less of, if not less than, a person. This violates P, and thereby is a very serious moral transgression, even if P is not accorded absolute status. Thus, there appear to be sufficient defeating conditions for A's prima facie moral permission to take the pill when she has a special genuine option to self-induce a belief in R; and, thereby, James's argument for a person in such circumstances being morally justified in self-inducing an epistemically unjustified belief in R fails. In general, James has failed to show that one can have a *sufficient* moral reason for self-inducing an epistemically unsupported belief.[26]

The battle is not over yet, since by a slight revision in the conditions of James's special genuine option to self-induce a belief, a more defensible moral justification of faith can be constructed. According to the former it is numerically one and the same proposition that the agent can help to make true and that, given her psychological makeup, she must first believe before she will work to make it true. A more interesting option results if the latter proposition is distinct from the former. This results in this revised version of James's argument in which propositions p and q are distinct:

9′. The circumstances are such that if A does not choose to try to get herself to believe p, she will not believe p;

10′. To try to get herself to believe p and not to do this are each real possibilities for A at T;

11′. Whether or not A tries to get herself to believe p will vitally affect her future life;

12. It is impossible at T for A to decide on epistemological grounds the truth of p;

13′. It is within the power of A to help make q true (or false);

14′. It is morally desirable that q be true; and

15′. A knows that she will act so as to help make q true if and only if she believes in advance that p is true.

Before using this revised version of James's argument to morally justify someone's acquiring an epistemically unwarranted belief that God exists, a further condition will be added to it so as to get around a devastating objection to the justification based on the case of the special genuine option to self-induce a belief having to do with its rendering the agent a nonrational agent in virtue of giving her a logically irrelevant reason for her "desirable" action.

Let p be the proposition that two dinosaurs were rutting on this very spot five million years ago and q be the proposition R. Let us assume that A at T is so psychologically constituted that she can act so as to help make R true only if she first believes p. According to the revised version of James's argument, A is morally permitted to take the belief-in-p inducing pill, since this brings it about that she will behave in a morally desirable manner. Obviously, her belief in p is not a logically relevant reason for her subsequent efforts to help make R true, and thereby she brings it about that she becomes less than or less of a person, for the reasons already given. And since she thereby violates P, this constitutes a defeating condition of her prima facie moral permission to take the pill.

To protect the revised version of James's argument from the logically irrelevant-reason-type of counterexample, the following condition must be added:

16. The belief in p is a logically relevant reason for trying to make q true.

This also meets the desideratum of means and end forming an integral unity. The connection between means and end should not rest on some purely accidental, external factor, such as the psychological quirks of the agent.

Let us now see how this revised version of James's argument, with the additional condition 16, can be used to give a moral justification for acquiring an epistemically unwarranted belief that God exists, understood in the orthodox way, rather than in terms of James's phony substitute for it, R.[27] There are many people who are so psychologically constituted that they can act so as to help make R true only if they first believe that theism is true. Let us use "G" as a generic name for a theistic creed, such as the Christian one, according to which God, an absolutely perfect being, is the creator of and sovereign over the universe and also the rewarder of morally good persons. The latter linkage proposition is very important in their system of motivation, since they can't get themselves to sacrifice their own interest unless they believe there is some reward for doing so. By getting themselves to believe G, which they will have to do by some nonrational method since we are assuming that we could not have adequate epistemological warrant for G, they help to bring about something morally desirable, namely, that they act in a good-making fashion so as to help make R become true. Herein their belief in G is a logically relevant

385

reason for their acting so as to make R true, since it is prudentially rational for one to maximize his own self-interest.
Therefore, these people seem to be morally permitted to take
the belief-in-G inducing pill, since doing so helps to bring
about something morally desirable and there are no apparent
defeating conditions.

There is an oddity to this moral defense of faith – that there
are moral reasons for certain people, namely, those whose
psychology fits 15', acting prudentially by taking the pill.
This creates the problem of who can give this defense. The
concerned persons, being prudentially motivated, cannot
consistently give moral reasons, based on the moral desir-
ability of their future good-making actions, for their taking
the pill. It would have to be some third person who gives this
moral justification of their prudentially motivated act of taking of the pill. Whether this justificatory asymmetry between
third persons and the concerned persons is vicious is a
mooted issue that will not be further pursued, being better
left in the hands of the Derek Parfits.

An even more serious worry is whether the moral defense
of faith based on the revised version of James's argument,
like that based on the special genuine option to self-induce a
belief, violates the moral principle of universalizability.
Again, it turns out that someone's moral permission to perform some action, that of nonrationally inducing an epistemically unwarranted belief, depends on her psychological
quirks, whether she satisfies the psychological requirements
specified in 15'. Is this a morally relevant feature of the circumstance? I think that it is no more morally relevant than is
the fact that the agent suffers from cowardice and thereby
cannot try to make something come to pass without prior
belief that she will succeed, though I have no powerful argument to support my intuition in either case. It seems wrong
that a prudentially motivated person (or one lacking in self-
confidence) should have moral permission to do something
that a morally motivated person (or one possessed of self-
confidence) is denied. Why should the more highly principled
person (or stronger person) be morally penalized in this way?

This completes my critical evaluation of pragmatic arguments, both from prudence and morality, for having faith. While grounds were given for doubting that any of them succeed, no knockout was scored. At best some nasty cuts were opened that might lead to a TKO. That no decisive result was reached should come as no surprise, since, as Aristotle pointed out, one cannot expect the same sort of conclusive results in reasoning about normative issues as can be had in other areas.

EPILOGUE

The skeptical outcome of my discussion of pragmatic arguments for faith dovetails with the sceptical outcome of my earlier discussions of epistemological arguments for faith. Since I completely eschewed inductive arguments, no definite conclusion can be drawn regarding the rationality of faith. Only the hypothetical conclusion can be drawn that *if* the only available arguments were the epistemological and pragmatic arguments examined before, faith would lack any rational justification. Such an outcome would be welcomed by a wide range of Kierkegaardian types who completely eschew any attempt to give an "objective" justification of faith. I resonate to their view of faith as a subjective passion that outstrips our reason.

Notes

INTRODUCTION

1. For the seminal discussion, see Peter T. Geach, "Intentional Identity," *Journal of Philosophy* 64 (1967), pp. 627–32.
2. Belonging to the same religious community must not be construed as necessary but only as part of a sufficient condition for two users of "God" to be coreferers, since some person outside a given religious community, such as an anthropologist or philosopher writing about the God referred to by the members of this community, can refer to the same God as do the members of this community. These descriptive and critical uses of "God" are secondary, since they are parasitic upon the uses of "God" by members of an established religious community.

CHAPTER 1

1. For an insightful discussion of this point, see Peter Geach, *Providence and Evil* (Cambridge University Press, 1977).
2. Clement Dore, "Plantinga on the Free Will Defense," *Review of Metaphysics* 24 (1971), p. 692.
3. St. Anselm gave this sort of argument for God's noncompositeness in *Monologion* chap. 17. He implicitly assumed that an individual is composed of the properties she instantiates, but this assumption, unlike the assumption that the individual is composed of her different instancings of various properties, is dubious and thereby undercuts this motivation for the doctrine of the divine simplicity.

4. Eleonore Stump and Norman Kretzmann, "Absolute Simplicity," *Faith and Philosophy* 2 (1985), pp. 356–7.
5. Ibid., p. 357.
6. Ibid., pp. 379–80.
7. William Mann, "Simplicity and Properties: A Reply to Morris," *Religious Studies* 22 (1986), p. 352.
8. It will not do, as Leibniz is sometimes interpreted as doing, to say that God is not essentially benevolent in this sense but instead essentially freely chooses to follow the principle of perfection. If he freely chooses to follow this principle, in some possible situation in which he exists he does not so choose; but if he essentially freely chooses to follow this principle, then in no possible situation in which he exists does he not choose to follow it.
9. The pickle the Leibnizian God is in is quite different from that of Buridan's anorexic ass, in which there is a choice between equally good alternatives. The latter, but not the former, can be solved by allowing a benevolent being to make an arbitrary choice between equally good alternatives when there is a good reason to choose one of them. In the former case God would have to choose the lesser of the alternatives available to him.

CHAPTER 2

1. All quotations are from Saint Augustine, *Confessions*, trans. E. B. Pusey (Literary Guild of America, Chicago, 1948). Numerals in parentheses indicate sections of Book 11.
2. The exceptions to this are terminal events that are the beginning or end of a state or process, but such terminal events are conceptually dependent upon the temporally elongated states and processes that they bound.
3. The reader is reminded of the qualification in note 2 concerning so-called terminal events and moments of time.
4. Eleonore Stump and Norman Kretzmann, "Eternity," *Journal of Philosophy* 78 (1981), p. 432.
5. Ibid., p. 444.
6. Ibid., p. 446.
7. William Alston's "Divine–Human Dialogue and the Nature of God," *Faith and Philosophy* 2 (1985), pp. 5–20, presents a clear and forceful defense of this position.
8. Stump and Kretzmann, "Eternity," p. 452.

CHAPTER 3

1. By the use of the plural ending on "propositions," it is being assumed that successive tokenings of the same A-sentence with the same meaning express different A-propositions. This way of speaking squares better with ordinary usage concerning when people say the same thing than does the Aristotelian–scholastic–Lukasiewicz–Prior stipulation according to which such tokenings always express the same proposition, though one that can change in truth-value over time. If I successively tokened "It is now t_7," I would not be said to have said the same thing – expressed the same proposition – on each occasion. In fact, I would be said to have changed in regard to what I believe, which shows that my successive tokenings express different and incompatible propositions. Further, if I said at one time "Jones is now seated" and at a later time "Jones is not now seated," I would not be thought to be denying what I formerly said. For a full discussion of this, as well as other intricacies and subtleties concerning A-propositions, see chapter 2 of my *Language of Time* (Routledge & Kegan Paul, London, 1968).

2. A. N. Prior, "The Formalities of Omniscience," *Philosophy* (1962), pp. 114–29. These arguments are repeated by A. Kenny in "Divine Foreknowledge and Human Freedom," in *Aquinas: A Collection of Critical Essays,* ed. A. Kenny (Anchor Books, New York, 1969), pp. 255–70. Both articles are reprinted in *Readings in the Philosophy of Religion,* ed. B. Brody (Prentice-Hall, Engelwood Cliffs, N.J., 1974). Future references are to the pagination in the Brody volume, since it is more widely available than the Kenny.

3. A. N. Prior, "Thank Goodness That's Over," *Philosophy* (1959), p. 17.

4. Prior, "The Formalities of Omniscience," p. 415.

5. Prior's use of "there are" should be replaced by "there could be," since if it were always raining, as is possible, then every tokening of "It is now raining" would in fact express a true proposition.

6. There is another argument for 4 in Prior's "The Formalities of Omniscience" in which it is made to appear that the mere fact that a timeless being's knowing cannot be located in time bars the being from being omniscient, in fact, from knowing any-

thing at all. "It seems an extraordinary way of affirming God's omniscience if a person when asked what God knows now, must say 'Nothing', and when asked what He knew yesterday, must again say 'Nothing', and must yet again say 'Nothing' when asked what God will know tomorrow" (p. 416). This rhetorical flourish derives its effectiveness from the fact that since most of the time we are not talking about a timeless being we might forget that we are doing so on this occasion. Since such a being is extraordinary, it should not surprise us that what we must say about it is extraordinary.

7. Geach, *Providence and Evil*, p. 40.

8. See Hector-Neri Castaneda, " 'He': A Study in the Logic of Self-consciousness," *Ratio* 8 (1966), pp. 130–57; idem, "Indicators and Quasi-indicators," *American Philosophical Quarterly* 4 (1967), pp. 85–100; idem,"On the Phenomeno-Logic of the I," *Proceedings of the XIVth International Congress for Philosophy*, vol. 3, pp. 260–6; idem, "On the Logic of Attributions of Self Knowledge to Others," *Journal of Philosophy* 65 (1968), pp. 439–56; idem, "On the Philosophical Foundations of the Theory of Communication: Reference," *Midwestern Studies in Philosophy* 2(1977), pp. 165–90; and idem, "Perception, Belief, and the Structure of Physical Objects and Consciousness," *Synthese* 35 (1977), pp. 285–351.

9. The same claim is implicit in the attempt by Stump and Kretzmann in "Eternity" to refute the omniscience-immutability argument by appeal to a nontemporal type of simultaneity relation, called "ET-simultaneity," in which a timelessly eternal God stands to every event in time. In virtue of having this relation to a given event, God is able to observe it "as temporally present" (p. 439). He "knows what is actually happening as it is happening" (p. 457). There is the same ambiguity in these claims as in Geach's in regard to how we are to interpret the temporal indexical references within the *oratio obliqua* construction; and, again, if premise 4 is to be challenged, we must interpret them as expressing both the speaker's and God's indexical reference.

10. Robert Coburn, "Professor Malcolm on God," *Australasian Journal of Philosophy* 41 (1963), pp. 155–6.

11. For a helpful account of God's timeless causation, see W. E. Mann, "Simplicity and Immutability in God," *International Philosophical Quarterly* 23 (1983), pp. 267–76.

12. Stump and Kretzmann, "Eternity," p. 435.
13. Ibid., p. 439.
14. Nelson Pike, *God and Timelessness* (Schocken Books, New York, 1970), p. 90.
15. The coreporting thesis is the brainchild of Michelle Beer. See her "Temporal Indexicals and the Passage of Time," *Philosophical Quarterly* 38 (1988), pp. 158–64.
16. John Perry, "Frege on Demonstratives," *Philosophical Review* 86 (1977), pp. 474–97, and idem, "The Problem of the Essential Indexical," *Nous* 13 (1979), pp. 3–22. Views similar to Perry's are to be found in the writings of Tyler Burge, Joseph Almog, and Jeremy Butterfield, to mention only a few.
17. Perry, "The Problem of the Essential Indexical," p. 16.
18. Perry, "Frege on Demonstratives," pp. 481–2.
19. For a fuller treatment of these problems, see my article "Propositions, Judgments, Sentences, and Statements," in *Encyclopedia of Philosophy*, ed. P. Edwards (Collier-Macmillan, New York, 1967), pp. 494–505.
20. He does this in Hector-Neri Castaneda, "Omniscience and Indexical Reference," *Journal of Philosophy* 64 (1967), pp. 203–10. Norman Kretzmann's article, "Omniscience and Immutability," appeared in the same journal one year earlier. Both articles have been reprinted in *Readings in the Philosophy of Religion*, ed. Brody, and all future references are to the pagination in this book.
21. Kretzmann, "Omniscience and Immutability," p. 366.
22. Castaneda, "Omniscience and Indexical Reference," p. 378. I have changed Castaneda's numbering of this proposition from "(4a)" to "6" so as to fit the format of my chapter and similarly for his other numbered propositions.
23. Ibid., p. 381. In what follows the qualification "(or would know)" will be dropped since, as will be seen, it is not needed.
24. Ibid.
25. Ibid.
26. In correspondence Castaneda has expressed his wholehearted approval of this amendment, since it was his intention all along to refute the timeless version of the omniscience-immutability argument.
27. A good discussion of this is to be found in Robert Carr-Wiggin, "God's Omnipotence and Immutability," *The Thomist* 48 (1984), pp. 44–51.

CHAPTER 4

1. H. J. McCloskey, "God and Evil," *Philosophical Quarterly* 10 (1960), p. 97.
2. Ibid., p. 105.
3. Ibid., p. 112.
4. J. L. Mackie, "Evil and Omnipotence," *Mind* 64 (1955), p. 1. This article is reprinted in *Readings in the Philosophy of Religion*, ed. Brody. Future references will be to the pagination in this book.
5. Mackie, "Evil and Omnipotence," p. 160. Mackie, like McCloskey, has a short memory span, for at the end of his article he creates a bogus paradox of omnipotence that requires of an omnipotent being that he be able to create free creatures whose wills are so free that not even he can control them, resulting in there being something that he cannot do – control the free will of these creatures. What Mackie fails to notice is that the latter act description is contradictory according to the Libertarian intuitions of the theist and thus is not something that an omnipotent being must be able to do, given the restricted 5_1 definition of "omnipotence" that he accepts in the earlier part of his discussion. His paradox of omnipotence, far from being an important new discovery, is only a variant on the timeworn paradox of the stone discussed in Chapter 1, being based on the same abuse of our concept of omnipotence.
6. Ibid., p. 161.
7. Ibid., p. 163.
8. Ibid., pp. 163–4. My italics.
9. In fairness to Mackie it must be stressed that at the time he wrote, no adequate formulation of the FWD had yet been given and that Mackie was instrumental in eliciting these more adequate formulations.
10. Mackie, "Evil and Omnipotence," p. 164.
11. This point is well made by Terence Penelhum in "Divine Goodness and the Problem of Evil," *Religious Studies* 2 (1967), pp. 95–107.
12. Nelson Pike gives this response on behalf of the theist in "Hume on Evil," *Philosophical Review* 72 (1963), pp. 180–97.
13. Penelhum argues effectively for this in "Divine Goodness."

14. Not all theists accept this. Robert M. Adams, in "Must God Create the Best?" *Philosophical Review* 81 (1972), pp. 317–22, argues against it, claiming that God's grace permits him to create less perfect people than he might have. I am convinced that his view is based on a misinvocation of the traditional doctrine of grace but will not argue for it here.

15. The exception is McCloskey, "God and Evil," p. 114, who writes as follows: "The real alternative is, on the one hand, rational agents with free wills making many bad and some good decisions on rational and non-rational grounds, and 'rational' agents predestined always 'to choose' the right things for the right reasons – that is, if the language of automata must be used, rational automata. Predestination does not imply the absence of rationality in all senses of that term. God, were he omnipotent, could preordain the decisions and reasons upon which they were based; and such a mode of existence would seem to be in itself a worthy mode of existence, and one preferable to an existence with free will, irrationality and evil." The proper response to McCloskey is not to challenge his moral intuitions, though I would want to, but to point out that they are not those of the theist. And since it is the internal consistency of theism that is at issue, it should be the theist's values that are operative.

16. Alvin Plantinga, "The Free Will Defence," in *Philosophy in America*, ed. Max Black (Cornell University Press, Ithaca, N.Y., 1965). This article is reprinted in *Readings in the Philosophy of Religion*, ed. Brody; all future references to it will be cited in the text of this chapter (as will be the case for all references to Plantinga's publications) and will refer to the pagination in this volume.

17. Alvin Plantinga, *God and Other Minds* (Cornell University Press, Ithaca, N.Y., 1967); idem, *The Nature of Necessity* (Oxford University Press, Oxford, 1975); idem, *God, Freedom, and Evil* (Harper, New York, 1974), pp. 7–64; and idem, "Self-Profile," in *Alvin Plantinga*, ed. James Tomberlin and Peter van Inwagen (Reidel, Dordrecht, 1985).

18. This objection is forcefully made by Antony Flew, "Divine Omnipotence and Human Freedom," in *New Essays in Philosophical Theology*, ed. A. Flew and A. MacIntyre (SCM Press, London, 1955), pp. 150, 151, 153.

19. In GFE (pp. 31–2) Plantinga aludes to an argument against causal compatibilism in which it is pointed out that if an action is causally determined then the conjunction of an earlier state of affairs, which is not preventable by the agent at the time of the action, with certain causal laws makes it causally impossible for him to do otherwise. But this hardly refutes causal compatibilism, since the compatibilist thinks a person could have acted otherwise even when it was not causally possible to do so. An interesting argument could be developed from Plantinga's remarks if it were added that the agent cannot prevent the causal laws in question from holding. Thus, two things that he cannot individually prevent together entail that he perform the action in question; and, supposedly, this has the consequence that he cannot prevent doing the action and thus does not do it freely. This unpreventability argument winds up begging the question, for the compatibilist believes that a person can act otherwise than she is causally determined to act and thereby believes that she can prevent the causal laws from holding. Also, it is dubious whether being unpreventable is closed under deduction.

20. Others of similar opinion are Antony Flew, "Compatibilism, Free Will and God," *Philosophy* 48 (1973), pp. 237–8; Richard L. Purtill, "Flew and the Free Will Defense," *Religious Studies* 13 (1977), pp. 477–83; and J. E. Barnhart, "Theodicy and the Free Will Defense: Response to Plantinga and Flew," *Religious Studies* 13 (1977), pp. 439–53.

21. R. E. Hobart (Dickenson Miller), in his classic formulation of causal compatibilism, "Free-Will as Involving Determinism and Inconceivable Without It," *Mind* 43 (1934), pp. 1–27, writes, "In proportion as an act of volition starts of itself without cause it is exactly so far as the freedom of the individual is concerned, as if it had been thrown into his mind from without – suggested to him by a freakish demon." Another prominent causal compatibilist, A. J. Ayer, in his *Philosophical Essays* (Macmillan Press; London, 1959), p. 275, concurs: "Either it is an accident that I choose as I do or it is not. If it is an accident, then it is merely a matter of chance that I did not choose otherwise; and if it is merely a matter of chance that I did not choose otherwise, it is surely irrational to hold me morally responsible for choosing as I did. But if it is not an accident that I choose to do one thing rather than another, then pre-

sumably there is some causal explanation of my choice: and in that case we are led back to determinism."

22. Mackie, "Evil and Omnipotence," p. 165.

23. Flew, "Compatibilism," p. 238, raises a verificationist-type objection to Libertarianism and thereby to the FWD to the effect that there is no way empirically to determine when an act is free, since its cause is a nonobservable self. But Libertarians from Kant to Campbell were not suggesting that the penal code be formulated in terms of their kind of free acts: that would be disastrous because of the admittedly unverifiable nature of such acts. Their point, rather, was that we can consistently think of ourselves and others as performing such acts and that this is required if we are to be coparticipants in the moral responsibility game. For Flew's objection to touch them, he would have to show that necessarily whatever is conceivable is verifiable. And I do not think he can show this.

24. Plantinga adds that if the atheologian does not grant the viability of this conception, then the real objection to theism is based not on evil but on the unviability of this conception of God. "And if he insists that the theistic conception is impossible just because it involves the idea of a person who is free but not causally determined, then his real quarrel with theism is not that God's existence is incompatible with that of evil; it is instead that God's existence is impossible simpliciter" (SP 47). This overlooks the value of an atheologian's having more than one argument against the existence of God; for while it is true that any one of them, if successful, would do the job, each is subject to some doubt, and thus there is value in having converging independent arguments.

25. The minor exception is Flew, "Compatibilism," p. 243, who, in spite of being a professed "ordinary language" type of philosopher, makes the wildly counterintuitive claim that "there can be no ultimate and fundamental contradiction in suggesting that another man, or God, might, by direct physiological manipulations, ensure that someone performs whatever actions that other man, or God, determines; and that the actions of this creature would nevertheless be genuine actions, such that it could always be truly said that he could have done otherwise than he did."

26. Plantinga, for the most part, leaves room for my strategy, for he usually treats being causally determined as only one

among other sufficient conditions for an action not being free, among which he recognizes being supernaturally determined by God's will. The exception to this is his careless remark that "if compatibilism is correct, the FWD fails" (SP 45). Herein he fails to realize that there are sufficient conditions for an action not being free other than its being causally determined.

27. Mackie, "Evil and Omnipotence," pp. 164–5. Mackie errs, as we shall soon see, in his wild claim that according to the FWD "second order evils are logically necessary accompaniments of freedom," but his objection is independent of this incorrect portrayal.

28. This account is the same as O_3 in Chapter 1 and is adopted by Plantinga.

29. Plantinga uses the more specific term "human"; but no harm is done by working with the more generic, non-species-specific notion of a person. Plantinga also confines moral evil to what is wrought by human beings, while throughout this chapter the more generic notion of a moral evil as one freely wrought by a person has been used.

30. In SP Plantinga calls them "counterfactuals of freedom," which is inaccurate terminology, since not all of them have counter-to-fact antecedents. It is especially strange that he should give as an example of a "counterfactual of freedom" "If Eve were free to take the apple, then she would have freely done so." What's the matter – don't theists believe in the Bible any more? In the future I will substitute "F-conditional" for "counterfactual of freedom" when I quote Plantinga.

31. I didn't realize, until I reread this chapter, just how apt my abbreviational terminology is.

32. As we shall see, in SP Plantinga hints at a different version of the FWD based on a weaker account of omniscience in which God's excuse is the Reagan one of ignorance.

33. Robert M. Adams, "Middle Knowledge and the Problem of Evil," *American Philosophical Quarterly* 14 (1977), pp. 109–17.

34. This is not how Plantinga defines "strongly actualize," but as we shall see, it is how he should have.

35. "Prior" can mean either prior in time or prior in the order of explanation or determination, depending on whether we are conceiving of God as having, respectively, omnitemporal or timeless eternality. That F-conditionals have the truth-values they do helps to explain or determine God's creative decision,

regardless of whether God's decision occurs in time. I would hope that the polemic against God's having timeless eternality in Chapters 2 and 3 has convinced the reader; but knowing that philosophy is philosophy, I want to formulate my argument so that it does not presuppose that God has omnitemporal eternality.

36. William Wainwright, "Freedom and Omnipotence," *Nous* 2 (1968), pp. 293–301.
37. Ibid., p. 301.
38. This analogy is elaborately developed in Nelson Pike, "Plantinga on Free Will and Evil," *Religious Studies* 15 (1979), pp. 449–73. Another theological compatibilist attack on Plantinga can be found in James E. Tomberlin and Frank McGuinness, "God, Evil, and the Free Will Defense," *Religious Studies* 13 (1977), pp. 455–75.
39. For readers who are too young to remember, Gabby Hayes was an ugly version of Willie Nelson, if such a thing is possible, who always played the hero's sidekick in the old Roy Rogers Westerns.
40. Pike fails to see this because he gets misled by his analogy into confounding possible with concrete persons, often speaking of the former as *having*, rather than *containing*, dispositions to perform various actions. For example, "The actual mouse," which corresponds to John Wayne in my rodeo version of his mice analogy, "came already assembled – all God did was allow it to be" by opening the door of the cage containing it (p. 460). Pike's "emanation" account of the instantiation relation is a piece of mystical mischief that further fudges the numerical distinction between possible persons and their instantiator.
41. Adams, "Middle Knowledge," p. 109.
42. Ibid., p. 117.
43. The just-in-the-nick-of-time objection is raised by our indefatigable theological compatibilist Nelson Pike, who writes: "Surely a being of this sort could create a world containing creatures who freely do what is right but in which no creature succeeds in performing actions (perhaps even choosing actions) that are morally pernicious. In cases where a morally wrong action could be expected to result in the suffering and sorrow of other people, it would seem that interference on God's part would, in fact, be morally required" (pp. 470–1).

44. Clement Dore persuasively presents this argument in chapter 5 of his book, *God, Suffering, and Solipsism* (Macmillan, New York, 1989).
45. Joel Feinberg endorses Locke's counterexample in his *Doing and Deserving* (Princeton University Press, Princeton, N.J., 1970), p. 185.
46. Nelson Pike gives an excellent account of such cases in his "Over-Power and God's Responsibility for Evil," in *The Nature and Existence of God*, ed. A. Freddoso (Notre Dame University Press, Notre Dame, Ind., 1983).
47. For a helpful discussion of this see Feinberg, *Doing and Deserving*.
48. Again it is Pike who is the objector. He points out that the result of God's creating free persons without having middle knowledge "might be a world containing creatures who perform no morally right actions at all. In fact, the result might even be worse–a world containing creatures whose every morally significant action is wrong and is such as to produce an amount of suffering that would boggle even the most calloused imagination. What should we say of a being who would risk actualizing a world of this description simply on the chance that it *might* contain a balance of morally right action over morally wrong action? 'Perfectly good'? Hardly. 'Reckless' would be more to the point" ("Plantinga on Free Will and Evil," pp. 455–6).
49. A wrong move for the theist to make in meeting this objection is to argue that God did not take a very big risk, because, although he lacked middle knowledge, at least he knew that it was probable that his creation of free persons would result in a favorable balance of moral good over moral evil. The probabilities of what would result from the instantiation of the antecedents of F-conditionals must be determined a priori, since there are no actual prior cases to which God could appeal. And I do not see any way in which it could be determined a priori that this desirable outcome has a probability greater than .5.
50. Adams, "Middle Knowledge," p. 110.
51. Were someone to deny thesis I on the grounds of a warranted assertibility theory of truth, I would object that truth and warranted assertability are not the same thing and prove my case by pointing out that while there are brands of cigarettes

named "True" and "Fact," there never was and never will be one named "Warrantedly Assertable," for no one would buy it, not even John Dewey.

52. Adams, "Middle Knowledge," p. 112.

53. Ibid., p. 117.

54. Adams gives a penetrating critique of such analyses in his essay.

55. In this connection the reader is reminded of proposition 55 – that it is impossible that an agent deliberate while knowing what decision she will make – or of an event for which her decision is a causally necessary condition.

CHAPTER 5

1. David Lewis, *On the Plurality of Worlds* (Blackwell Publisher, Oxford, 1986), p. 2.

2. For Lewis, the Kantian thesis that necessarily all times (spaces) are temporally (spatially) related holds intra- but not interworld.

3. Lewis, *On the Plurality of Worlds*, p. 93.

4. Ibid. Lewis adds that "the 'actual at' relation between worlds is simply identity."

5. Ibid., p. 2.

6. Lewis, *Counterfactuals* (Harvard University Press, Cambridge, Mass., 1973), p. 183. This chapter is reprinted in *The Possible and the Actual*, ed. Michael Loux (Cornell University Press, Ithaca, N.Y., 1973), pp. 182–9. Future references are to the pagination in the latter volume. That Lewis commits a category mistake in conjoining this definition with his insistence that worlds are maximal spatiotemporal aggregates is noted by Robert Stalnaker, "Possible Worlds," *Nous* 10 (1976), pp. 65–75, and Peter van Inwagen, "Indexicality and Actuality," *Philosophical Review* 89 (1980), pp. 403–26.

7. Lewis asserts that other worlds are no more abstract or linguistic entities than is the actual world in *On the Plurality of Worlds*: "But worlds, as I understand them, are *not* like stories or story-tellers. They are like this world; and this world is no story, not even a true story" (p. 7, n. 3).

8. This argument from the indexicality of actuality is not Lewis's only argument for actuality being world relative. There is also

an elaborate cost–benefit argument of the inference-to-the-best-explanation sort to the effect that a systematic analysis of a number of concepts, including modality, causality, propositions, and properties, fares better under his theory of extreme modal realism than under any rival one that takes a possible world to be either a linguistic entity or an ersatz abstract entity such as a maximal compossible set of properties, propositions, or states of affairs. This argument forms the substance of chapters 1 and 3 of *On the Plurality of Worlds*. Space will not permit consideration of this argument, and thus Lewis's case for extreme modal realism can survive the demise of the argument from the indexicality of actuality.

9. van Inwagen "Indexicality and Actuality," p. 407.
10. See Lewis, *Counterfactuals*, p. 185.
11. David Lewis, "Anselm and Actuality," *Nous* 4 (1970), pp. 175–88; reprinted, with added postscripts, in idem, *Philosophical Papers* (Oxford University Press, New York, 1983), vol. 1.
12. See Lewis, *On the Plurality of Worlds*, pp. 92–3, and *Counterfactuals*, p. 86.
13. Lewis, "Anselm and Actuality," pp. 184–5. My italics.
14. Ibid., p. 185.
15. Robert M. Adams, "Theories of Actuality," *Nous* 8 (1974), pp. 211–31; reprinted in *The Possible and the Actual*, ed. Loux, p. 205. Future references are to the pagination in the latter.
16. This point seems to be missed by the charges of inconsistency raised by Michael Loux in his introduction to *The Possible and the Actual*, p. 47, and William Lycan in "The Trouble with Possible Worlds," in ibid., p. 289.
17. Lewis, "Anselm and Actuality," pp. 186–7.
18. Lewis, *On the Plurality of Worlds*, p. 94.
19. Lewis, *Counterfactuals*, p. 185.
20. Adams, "Theories of Actuality," p. 195. Lewis responds in *On the Plurality of Worlds*, p. 125.
21. Allen Hazen, in "One of the Truths about Actuality," *Analysis* 39 (1977), p. 3, denies that there is any connection between them: "Semantically, logically, the indexical theory is the truth. This does not answer the metaphysical question about the nature of possible worlds; it is a metaphysical question."
22. Lewis, "Anselm and Actuality," pp. 186–7.
23. Ibid., pp. 184–5.
24. Ibid., p. 185.

25. This is the analogy that Lewis himself uses. It makes no difference to the argument if the analogy is drawn with some other indexical term. It might seem to some that the analogy is closer if it is drawn to "here," since a possible world is a place. This is wrong: A world, i.e., a maximal spatiotemporal aggregate, although it contains places, is not itself a place.
26. See Lewis's postscript to "Anselm and Actuality" in his *Philosophical Papers*, p. 22, as well as "Anselm and Actuality," p. 185, and *On the Plurality of Worlds*, p. 94.
27. Lewis, *On the Plurality of Worlds*, p. 94.
28. The following discussion builds upon van Inwagen, "Indexicality and Actuality," pp. 418–19, from which I learned a great deal.
29. For a fuller discussion of these problems, the reader is referred to the account of A-propositions in Chapter 3.
30. Lewis fails to see the need to relativize truth to a world, as is done in 9', when he says that " 'This is the actual world' *is* true whenever uttered in any possible world" (my italics; "Anselm and Actuality," p. 186).
31. van Inwagen explores this strategy in "Indexicality and Actuality," p. 422.
32. Lewis, "Anselm and Actuality," p. 188. A similar remark is made, but in an inaccurate way, in *Counterfactuals*: "My indexical theory of actuality exactly mirrors a less controversial doctrine about time. Our present time is only one time among others. We call it alone present not because it differs in kind from all the rest, but because it is the time we inhabit" (p. 184). But we do not inhabit just one time (although we might inhabit only one world if counterpart theory is true). That we inhabit more than one time is true whether we conceive of ourselves as enduring substances or bundles of successive person-stages.
33. My discussion here is indebted to Adams, "Theories of Actuality," esp. p. 160.
34. A parallel problem plagues a simple property theory of being now or the present according to which "X is now" is analyzed into "X has the property of nowness," in which the latter means "X now has the property of nowness." An examination of McTaggart's vicious infinite regress argument against any individual being present is instructive in this connection.

CHAPTER 6

1. I do not claim that my use of "abstract entity" is the "official" or even the most common one in the history of philosophy. What is not a mere terminological point is whether an abstract entity in my sense is capable of causal agency and serving as the accusative of propositional attitudes. Peter van Inwagen, in a very penetrating article, "Ontological Arguments," *Nous* 11 (1977), denies that nonspatiotemporal entities such as "numbers, properties, propositions, sentence-types, sets" can be objects of "love, hate, worship . . . fear" (p. 380). This seems wrong, since a noun "that"-clause can properly serve as the accusative of a propositional attitude verb; e.g., I can fear that John is using drugs. But no spatiotemporal location can be assigned to that John is using drugs. St. Thomas loved God, and yet he thought of God as being nonspatiotemporal. Whether an abstract being can be a causal agent is more controversial, but plainly Anselm and the other medieval theists thought that God was both nonspatiotemporal and capable of timelessly bringing about effects in time.

2. Ross's version is put forth with great elaboration in his *Philosophical Theology* (Bobbs-Merrill, New York, 1969), pp. 173–81.

3. For a fuller discussion of this kind of explanation, see chapter 2 of my *Negation and Non-Being, American Philosophical Quarterly*, monograph no. 10 (1976).

4. *St. Anselm's Proslogion*, trans. M. J. Charlesworth (Notre Dame University Press, Notre Dame, Ind., 1979), pp. 169–71.

5. "M," "L," and "−" are monadic operators that abbreviate, respectively, "it is logically possible that," "it is logically necessary that," and "it is not the case that."

6. Norman Malcolm, "Anselm's Ontological Argument," *Philosophical Review* 69 (1960), p. 48.

7. Ibid.

8. Ibid., pp. 49–50.

9. Ibid., p. 48.

10. Malcolm's failure to note that such language games are actually played is due to a failure to take ordinary usage seriously, which is surprising in an "ordinary language" philosopher. For example, in support of his timeless conception of God he appeals to the Ninetieth Psalm: "Before the mountains were

brought forth, or ever thou hadst formed the earth and the world, even from everlasting to everlasting, thou art God" (ibid., pp. 55–6). This is the conception not of a timeless but of an omnitemporal Deity. For a good critique of Malcolm on this point see Pike's *God and Timelessness*, pp. 183–4.

11. Malcolm's first argument does not, because its premise 29 says that it is impossible that God have duration. An omnitemporal God, although he can neither begin nor end, does have duration and thereby does not satisfy this premise.

12. *St. Anselm's Proslogion*, trans. Charlesworth, p. 117.

13. In "Anselm and Actuality," David Lewis interprets Anselm, incorrectly in my opinion, as requiring only the psychological possibility of existence, but he retracts this interpretation in his later postscript to this essay in his *Philosophical Papers*, vol. 1.

14. I have updated Malcolm's example from "Anselm and Actuality," p. 45. Lewis claims that if persons A and B were to include the same properties on their list of desirable properties for a secretary of defense, save for A alone including being existent, "any persons who satisfied A's description would *necessarily* satisfy B's description and *vice versa!*" Malcolm must be wrong, because if there were to be a merely mythical or fictional secretary of defense who satisfied B's description, he still would not satisfy A's.

15. My critique closely follows that of Lewis in "Anselm and Actuality."

16. This is a somewhat simplified version of Plantinga's argument.

17. Plantinga, *The Nature of Necessity*, p. 218.

18. This type of example is deployed against Plantinga's ontological argument by W. Tooley in "Plantinga's Defence of the Ontological Argument," *Mind* 90 (1981), pp. 422–8. See also Patrick Grim, "Plantinga's God and Other Monstrosities," *Religious Studies* 15 (1979), pp. 91–7, for further examples of problematic properties that are supposed to satisfy conditions (i) and (ii).

CHAPTER 7

1. For an excellent survey and devastating criticisms of such scientifically rooted cosmological arguments, see Adolf Grunbaum, "The Pseudo-Problem of Creation in Physical Cosmol-

ogy," *Philosophy of Science* 56 (1989), pp. 373–94, and its sequel, "Pseudo-Creation of the Big Bang," *Nature* 344 (1990), pp. 821–2.

2. Richard Taylor, *Metaphysics*, 2d ed. (Prentice-Hall, Englewood Cliffs, N.J., 1974), p. 105. The Leibniz quotation is from *Leibniz Selections*, ed. P. Wiener (Scribner, New York, 1951), p. 346.

3. I have availed myself of William Rowe's mounting of both the main and subsidiary arguments in his *Cosmological Argument* (Princeton University Press, Princeton, N.J., 1975). All subsequent references to this book are cited in the text of this chapter.

4. Some causal loops occasion special difficulties. For example, a person gains knowledge of how to build a time machine from a conversation with his future self, who has traveled back in time in order to impart this knowledge to him; and his future self's knowledge is due to his remembering (a causal process) what he heard when he was the earlier self. Herein there is an extra problem concerning how this knowledge was derived. But such extra difficulties are not endemic to every case of a closed causal loop.

5. That Clarke must make this existential assumption, as well as assume PSR_1, clearly brings out the a posteriori status of his argument. In Part 9 of the *Dialogues Concerning Natural Religion*, Hume characterizes an argument that obviously is Clarke's as being "a priori." William Rowe, in correspondence, suggested that the meanings of "a priori" and "a posteriori" were different in Clarke's time than they are now. These were not, as they are for us, epistemologically based distinctions, but rather concerned whether we are inferring a cause from its effect or vice versa. This issue is discussed in James P. Ferguson, *The Philosophy of Samuel Clarke and Its Critics* (Vantage Press, New York, 1974), pp. 11–21.

6. The text of the debate is reprinted under the title "The Existence of God: A Debate between Bertrand Russell and Father F. C. Copleston," in *The Existence of God*, ed. John Hick (Collier–Macmillan, London, 1964), p. 175.

7. Ibid.

8. Paul Edwards, "The Cosmological Argument," *Rationalist Annual* 1959 (Pemberton, London); reprinted in *Readings in the Philosophy of Religion*, ed. Brody. The quotation is from p. 78 of the latter.

9. Michael Slote, "Selective Necessity and the Free-Will Problem," *Journal of Philosophy* 79 (1982), pp. 5–24. I lean heavily on this excellent article in my criticisms of the HE principle.

10. Wesley Salmon, *Scientific Explanation and the Causal Structure of the World* (Princeton University Press, Princeton, N.J., 1984), p. 158. Farther down on this page he says: "The principle of the common cause states, roughly, that when apparent coincidences occur that are too improbable to be attributed to chance, they can be explained by reference to a common causal antecedent."

11. I am indebted to William Wainwright for pointing out these variants in a letter to me.

12. For an argument in support of this see chapter 5 of my *Language of Time*.

13. Rowe thinks his version superior to the one based upon a concrete aggregate because it completely escapes the objections to the latter that there is no such individual or, as Rowe would have it, "concrete entity" and that it admits of an internalistic explanation on the basis of the HE principle. These advantages are illusory, if the above-mentioned rebuttals of these objections are correct.

14. Rowe anachronistically reads his interpretation back into Clarke. Not only does the text not support this interpretation, the concept of a set as an abstract entity was not available to eighteenth-century thinkers, not coming upon the scene until the following century. Some of the things Rowe says indicate that he was aware that Clarke conceived of the succession as a concrete aggregate. "But having treated the world as the collection of existing things . . . Clarke proceeds to view it as an existing thing subject to the very PSR that applies to its members" (p. 147). And referring to Clarke and other eighteenth-century proponents of the cosmological argument, Rowe says that they "never saw clearly that the infinite collection of dependent beings is not itself a dependent being" (p. 146). Since a set is not a dependent being, it would seem that they did not take the collection to be a set. What is true is that Clarke, *in addition* to demanding an explanation for the concrete aggregate composed of the totality of dependent beings, *also* demanded an explanation for why there exists any dependent beings at all, which is the very explanatory demand that Rowe ultimately settles upon. In the

Demonstration Clarke asks, "What is it that has from eternity determined such a succession of [dependent beings] to exist, *rather than that from eternity there should never have existed anything at all?*" (my italics). Herein Clarke is demanding an explanation both for why this infinite succession of dependent beings exists and for why there exists at least one dependent being, which is Rowe's explanatory demand.

15. Rowe is well aware of this difficulty with his argument and explores many different ways of revising the PSR so that it will apply to fact D. He continues his discussion in "Rationalistic Theology and Some Principles of Explanation," *Faith and Philosophy* 4 (1984), pp. 357–69. It turns out to be a very difficult thing to do, and I will not go into the issue here.

16. For a discussion of this problem, see Carl G. Hempel, *Aspects of Scientific Explanation* (Free Press, New York, 1965), pp. 293–5.

17. Hilary Putnam, "Reductionism and the Nature of Psychology," *Cognition* 2 (1973), pp. 131–46; reprinted in *Mind Design*, ed. J. Haugeland (MIT Press, Cambridge, Mass., 1981).

18. For an interesting discussion of pragmatically deficient cosmological arguments, see Michael B. Burke, "Hume and Edwards on Why Is There Something Rather Than Nothing," *Australasian Journal of Philosophy* 62 (1984), pp. 355–62. Unfortunately, Burke accepts at face value the HE principle: "I certainly agree with Hume that to explain the existence of each member of a collection of twenty particles is to explain the existence of the 'whole twenty' " (p. 360).

19. For a full exposition of Bergson's theory, see my "Bergson's Analysis of the Concept of Nothing," *Modern Schoolman* 51 (1974), pp. 269–300.

20. For full details, see my *Negation and Non-Being*.

21. There will be considerable complexity in *B*, since an infinite series can be generated by applying certain truth-functional operations to any set of propositions, but there need not be anything vicious about this; and if it should turn out to be so, a requirement can be made that *W* be in conjunctive normal form.

22. This principle, *P*, in a somewhat simplified form, states: If in one world God determines whether a certain type of entity exists, then in every world in which God exists he determines whether this type of entity exists.

CHAPTER 8

1. William Alston, "Psychoanalytic Theory and Theistic Belief," in *Faith and the Philosophers*, ed. J. Hick (St. Martin's Press, New York, 1964), pp. 89–90.
2. William Wainwright, *Mysticism* (University of Wisconsin Press, Madison, 1981), p. 82.
3. William Alston, "The Christian Language-Game," in *The Autonomy of Religious Belief*, ed. F. Crosson (Notre Dame University Press, Notre Dame, Ind., 1981), pp. 128–62.
4. Alston includes the existence of defeating conditions or tests, but I am dropping this requirement since I want to start with the weakest version of the analogical argument for the cognitivity of religious experiences.
5. Alston, "The Christian Language-Game," p. 143.
6. Quinn's excellent "In Search of the Foundations of Theism," *Faith and Philosophy* 2 (1985), pp. 469–86, raises objections to taking the proposition that God exists as basic that parallel some of the objections that I shall make to fideism.
7. Wittgenstein's claim that religious reasoning "is an entirely different kind of reasoning" seems to impute epistemological autonomy to the religious language game and serves as the basis for his claim that the nonbeliever who denies that there will be a Last Judgment does not contradict the theist who believes there will be. See his *Lectures and Conversations on Aesthetics, Psychology and Religious Belief*, ed. C. Barrett (University of California Press, Berkeley, 1967), pp. 53, 58.
8. C. B. Martin, "A Religious Way of Knowing," in *New Essays in Philosophical Theology*, ed. A. Flew and A. MacIntyre (SCM Press, London, 1955).
9. For a thorough discussion of this issue, see William Alston, "Epistemic Circularity," *Philosophy and Phenomenological Research* 47 (1986), pp. 1–30.
10. See William Alston, "Perceiving God," *Journal of Philosophy* 83 (1986), pp. 655–65, for a discussion of this point. Alston overlooks a respect in which the two practices are asymmetrical. Whereas the tests for the veridicality of a sense experience are based solely on other sense experiences, those for the veridicality of a religious experience are not based solely on other religious experiences, since the latter are based on what we

hear other members of the religious community say about their religious experiences, what we *see* inscribed in certain "holy" books, etc. This will become clearer as we consider these tests.

11. Richard Swinburne, *The Existence of God* (Clarendon Press, Oxford, 1979), p. 260.

12. William Alston, "Religious Diversity and Perceptual Knowledge of God," *Faith and Philosophy* 4 (1988), p. 434.

13. Ibid., p. 435.

14. William Alston, "Referring to God," *Philosophy of Religion* 24 (1988), p. 121.

15. Herein Wainwright is siding with Zaehner against Suzuki, Stace, and Merton as to whether theistic and monistic mystical experiences are phenomenologically different, and as indicated earlier, this is an issue I want to avoid.

16. Gary Gutting, *Religious Belief and Religious Skepticism* (Notre Dame University Press, Notre Dame, Ind., 1982), pp. 149–50.

17. Alston, "The Christian Language-Game," p. 159.

18. Ibid., p. 161.

19. William Alston, "The Perception of God," *Philosophical Topics* 16 (1988), p. 50.

20. Swinburne applies his analysis to every type of of-God experience, including perceiving worldly items as God-caused. Like Alston, he makes too strong a claim on behalf of the latter: "That God is at work is no inference for these men but what seems (epistemically) to be happening" (p. 253). This makes it appear as if these are recognitional seeing-as experiences and are occasions for nontheoretically based language-entry assertions; but as shown earlier, the Quinn-type game players are willing to give inductive backing to their assertion that the sunset, for example, is an expression of God's love, which entails that it is God-caused.

21. C. D. Broad, *Religion, Philosophy and Psychical Research* (Harcourt, Brace, New York, 1953), p. 197.

22. Swinburne, *The Existence of God*, p. 262.

23. Ibid.

24. Gutting, *Religious Belief*, p. 255.

25. Swinburne, *The Existence of God*, p. 255.

26. Ibid., p. 270. The qualification "where he is" is puzzling, since a theistic religious experience is not of an embodied or spatially located being; and this is so even if God were to have (accidentally) the whole world as his body.

27. Wainwright, *Mysticism*, p. 130.
28. For insightful accounts of the manner in which the Catholic tradition dealt with the problem of deviously or ignobly caused mystical experiences, see Nelson Pike, "On Mystic Visions as Sources of Knowledge," and George Mavrodes, "Deceptive Mystical Experiences," both in *Mysticism and Philosophical Analysis,* ed. S. Katz (Oxford University Press, New York, 1978).
29. Wayne Proudfoot, *Religious Experience* (University of California Press, Los Angeles, 1985), p. 139.
30. Alston, "Psychoanalytic Theory." His later writings are more in agreement with Wainwright's and Swinburne's on the issue of whether a veridical religious experience can have a natural cause.
31. Wainwright, *Mysticism*, p. 131.
32. This is in substantial agreement with the "cognitive-wallop" theory of mystical experiences of John of the Cross, according to which they are not a source of propositional knowledge but instead serve to deepen our understanding of truths that are gained by nonmystical means. For a good account of this theory, see Nelson Pike, "John of the Cross on the Epistemic Value of Mystic Visions," in *Rationality, Religious Belief, and Moral Commitment,* ed. R. Audi and W. Wainwright (Cornell University Press, Ithaca, N.Y., 1986), pp. 15–37.
33. There is an aspect of the problem of religious diversity in addition to that of a diversity of incompatible tests among different religious traditions; it concerns the fact that the apparent object of religious experiences is described differently by experients within these different traditions. Hospers and Flew were too quick to impugn the cognitivity of religious experiences on this ground; for the experients either could have been describing one and the same reality in different ways or could have been describing numerically distinct realities, God, nirvana, etc., being numerically distinct objective realities. The latter is not very plausible, since all of the experients purport to be describing some highest, ultimate reality, and there cannot be more than one such reality.
34. Swinburne, *The Existence of God*, p. 275.
35. Wainwright, *Mysticism*, pp. 87–8.
36. Alston, "The Perception of God," p. 42.
37. Alston, "The Christian Language-Game," p. 161.

38. Peter Moore gives an analogical argument that is also ambiguous between a language-game fideism with any old tests and a language-game fideism with analogous tests, because it does not place sufficiently strong requirements on what counts as a "similar" or, in his case, "equivalent" test. "Where the objective validity . . . of any form of non-mystical experience is in doubt, recourse can be had to a variety of tests and checking procedures, although these do not always settle doubts or disputes. But mystics too have their own equivalents of such tests and checking procedures for the assessment of mystical experience. These are comprised on the one hand in the advice and instructions given by mystics concerning the ethical, ascetical, and technical pre-conditions of mystical experience and on the other hand in the detailed moral and psychological criteria used in mystical traditions to determine the authenticity and value of mystical states and revelations" ("Mystical Experience, Mystical Doctrine, Mystical Technique," in *Mysticism and Philosophical Analysis*, ed. Katz, p. 126).

39. It is interesting that although Wainwright defends the analogical argument on the basis of analogous tests, he is not willing to rest his case for the cognitivity of religious experience on it. In *Mysticism*, p. 102, he claims that even if it were not to work, due to religious and sense experience being radically dissimilar, religious experience could still qualify as cognitive in Stace's "trans-subjective" sense. This would be to retreat to the sort of multivocalist account that underlies extreme language-game fideism – a very unattractive position. It should be pointed out that there is no inconsistency in Wainwright espousing at one and the same time both extreme language-game fideism and the analogical argument based on analogous tests, this paralleling the point made on p. 1 of this book that one can both espouse fideism and give arguments for God's existence. However, philosophers, like trapeze artists, usually eschew such safety nets, since they take away from the bravura of their performance.

40. Alston, "Perceiving God," p. 655.
41. Alston, "The Perception of God," p. 27.
42. Alston, "Religious Diversity," p. 443.
43. Ibid.
44. Ibid., p. 444.
45. Ibid., p. 445.

46. Ibid.
47. No doubt their language-entry assertions involve some theoretical elements, but they are common to both their theories.
48. I want to avoid committing myself on the vexing question whether the apparent object of a veridical sense experience must be a necessary, sufficient, necessary and sufficient, or just plain old cause of the experience. I favor the last, since I believe that what is necessary is that the object be *a* cause or part of the cause of the experience in the right way. Our worldview's notion of causal nexi gives us some start on this notion, as P. F. Strawson has pointed out ("Causation in Perception," in *Freedom and Resentment* [Methuen, London, 1974]), in terms of tautologies concerning perceptual perspectives and the masking of one object by another; but an essential part of this commonsense view is that it is open to expansion and revision, as Grice has remarked, in the light of scientific advancement. Determining what is the right sort of causal connection between object and experience, therefore, might have to await the coming of the scientific millennium.
49. The material in this paragraph is extensively developed and defended in chapter 2 of my *Negation and Non-Being*.
50. The sense of *objective particular* that I am working with is weaker than the one employed by Strawson. For him an objective particular must not only be capable of existing when not actually perceived but also be distinguishable by a subject of experience from her own states of consciousness, which is to require self-consciousness on the part of this subject. Whether the possibility of self-consciousness depends on the representation of objects as being in space will not be considered. Strawson's answer to this question is indecisive, since he thinks that our concept of the self is not sufficiently precise.
51. Strawson, *Individuals* (Anchor Books, New York, 1963), p. 67.
52. Ibid., p. 66.
53. See note 49.
54. Strawson, *Individuals*, p. 70.
55. Ibid., p. 68.
56. Ibid., p. 69.
57. This oversight infects Jonathan Bennett's reconstruction of Strawson's sound world in his *Kant's Analytic* (Cambridge University Press, 1966), p. 37. For an insightful discussion of Strawson's sound world, see M. R. Ayers, "Perception and

Action," in *Knowledge and Necessity*, Royal Institute of Philosophy Lectures, vol. 3 (1968–9) (London, 1970).

58. Plato, *Timaeus*, 50E–51. Quoted from F. M. Cornford, *Plato's Cosmology* (Humanities Press, New York, 1952).

59. "The principle is so phrased that how things seem positively to be is evidence of how they are, but how things seem *not* to be is not such evidence" (Swinburne, *The Existence of God*, p. 254).

CHAPTER 9

1. There is also the pragmatic argument, sketched in the final paragraph of the preceding chapter, based upon the spiritual benefits to the person who believes her religious experience is an objective revelation, but we will not consider it since everything that will be said about the moral-development pragmatic argument can be extended to it.

2. This is a bit quick, since our finitude has not precluded us from gaining an understanding of infinity in mathematics. It doesn't take one to know one.

3. For a more complete account, see Nicholas Rescher, *Pascal's Wager: A Study of Practical Reasoning in Theology* (Notre Dame University Press, Notre Dame, Ind., 1985).

4. Stephen P. Stitch raises this objection to Pascal in his "Recombinant DNA Debate," *Philosophy and Public Affairs* 7 (1978), pp. 187–205.

5. Not even Pascal himself adhered to this negative theology, for in later portions of the *Pensées* he marshals historical evidence in favor of the reliability of the Bible, thereby according a privileged epistemic status to Christianity. For a discussion of this, see Thomas V. Morris, "Pascalian Wagering," *Canadian Journal of Philosophy* 16 (1986), pp. 437–54.

6. This is the policy advocated by William G. Lycan and George N. Schlesinger in their "You Bet Your Life: Pascal's Wager Defended," in *Reason and Responsibility*, 6th ed., ed. J. Feinberg (Wadsworth, Belmont, 1988), pp. 82–90.

7. Richard Swinburne, "The Christian Wager," *Religious Studies* 4 (1969), p. 221.

8. W. K. Clifford, "The Ethics of Belief," in *Lectures and Essays* (Macmillan Press, London, 1879); reprinted in *Readings in*

the *Philosophy of Religion*, ed. Brody. All references are to the pagination in the latter (p. 240).

9. Ibid., p. 244.
10. Ibid., p. 245.
11. Ibid.
12. Ibid., p. 246.
13. Ibid.
14. William James, "The Will to Believe," in *The Will to Believe and Other Essays* (Longmans, Green, New York, 1897), p. 2 (hereafter WB). All subsequent references to James's essay are cited in the text of this chapter.
15. By "lawfully may" and have "the freedom" to believe James means "is morally permitted." He also says that we have a "right" to believe (WB 29).
16. Surprisingly, James thinks that this problem concerns the forcedness of the options. Either he is confused here or our earlier exposition of a forced option is incorrect. Because of his unclarity on this issue, it is not clear which disjunct is true.
17. One wonders how James's doctrine of a one-to-one correspondence between beliefs and actions would behavioristically distinguish between a belief in R and a belief in the normative proposition that it is good for R to be true.
18. James claims that one acts *courageously* in choosing to believe an epistemically unjustified proposition. But it turns out that only a moral weakling – someone who cannot act unless she believes that she will succeed – can be the subject of a special genuine option to believe!
19. William James, *The Principles of Psychology* (Holt, New York, 1910), vol. 2, p. 322.
20. The "prima facie" qualification is an anachronistic sophistication of James's position but, as we shall see, a necessary one since the permission is only defeasible.
21. This is set out in a most sketchy fashion in Jean Paul Sartre, *Existentialism* (Philosophical Library, New York, 1947). However, I totally reject Sartre's more radical thesis that we are morally responsible for *everything* we do, other than being born: "Man is condemned to be free. Condemned, because he did not create himself, yet in other respects is free; because, once thrown into the world, he is responsible for everything he does." Such strict liability would make the ontological rules pointless.

22. These conceptual truths need tidying up along the lines spelled out in chapter 5 of my *Language of Time.*

23. This asymmetry between agent and observer is made possible by the fact that the premises of the inductive argument *permit* but do not make *mandatory* the drawing of the conclusion, as Teddy Seidenfeld pointed out to me.

24. That we are not permitted to opt out of the moral responsibility game does not entail that a game player must believe that she is free (whether or not she is), but only that she must act as if she is free, which she does by playing the game. This includes her willingness to make this performatory utterance: "I hereby ask you to hold me morally responsible for my actions." This has an imperatival illocutionary force and does not logically or pragmatically entail "I believe that I shall behave in a morally responsible way in the future," any more than "I command you to shut the window" entails "I believe that the window will be shut."

25. *When* she performs these future altruistic actions, she lacks good reasons for doing them, and thereby does not qualify *at that time* as either a rational agent or morally responsible; however, *at the time she takes the pill* she is morally responsible for both taking the pill and these future altruistic actions that result from it. This shows that an agent's moral responsibility for a given act must be relativized to a time within her life. If I intentionally take a drug to bring it about that at a time T in the future I become a mental basket case, I am responsible at T for both taking the drug and my future state of mental incapacitation. But subsequent to T, I am no longer morally responsible for these things.

26. Nothing that has been said so far entails that one is never morally justified in self-inducing a belief by nonrational methods. In fact, I can imagine cases in which one has a sufficient moral reason to do so. Consider a case in which A has adequate epistemic grounds for believing a proposition p but for psychological reasons is unable to believe it; and A can successfully perform some morally desirable action only if she first believes p. Imagine, to use Nancy Davis's favorite example, a diamond cutter who cannot successfully cut a certain diamond unless she first believes that she is capable of doing so. She has ample inductive evidence from her past successes that she is capable of doing so but because of a lack of

416

self-confidence does not believe she is. Certainly, she is morally justified in availing herself of nonrational methods for self-inducing this epistemically warranted belief, since this helps to bring about some desirable outcome.

27. James's reasons for eschewing good, old-time theism in favor of R run deep in his theory of meaning and truth. He was led to embrace this pale substitute because of his extremely narrow phenomenological empiricism.

Index

Index

Index

Index

Locke, 152, 159, 373
logical atomism, 2
logical positivism, 2, 201
Lukasiewicz, Jan, 62, 175
Lycan, William, 402 n16, 414 n6

McCloskey, H. J., 98–9, 108–9, 395 n15
McGuinness, Frank, 399 n38
Mackie, John, 99–109, 114, 118, 120, 123–4
McTaggart's argument for the unreality of time, 403 n34
Malcolm, Norman, 205, 208–16, 221
manichaeanism, 37
Mann, William, 27–9, 392 n11
Martin, C. B., 298
Mavrodes, George, 411 n28
means–ends relationship
  as an integral unity, 354, 382, 385
Merton, Thomas, 286, 410 n15
middle knowledge, see God, divine perfections of
Molina, 116, 149, 170
Moore, G. E., 290, 313
Moore, Peter, 412 n38
Morris, Thomas, 414 n5
mysticism, 47–55, 69, 216, 271, 285–6, 288, 303–4, 315, 410 n15
  as ineffable, 49–51

negation
  incompatibility theory of, 273–5
negative events, 260

objectivity, 311–4, 326–40; see also religious experience, objectivity of
omnipotence, see God, divine perfections of
ominscience, see God, divine perfections of
ontological arguments, Chapter 6, 2, 54, 238, 273, 345
  Anselm's version, 202, 217–24
  from God's abstractness, 202, 212–17
  from God's unpreventability (the Scotus–Ross version), 202–5
  Plantinga's version based on necessary existence, 202, 218, 224–7, 231, 233–5
ontological disproofs, 227–37, 238–9, 275–6, 281–4
ordinary language philosophy, 2
Otto, Rudolf, 286

Parfit, Derek, 386
Pascal, 220, 345–53, 369; see also Pascal's Wager

Pascal's Wager, 2, 344–54
Penelhum, Terence, 109, 394 nn11 and 13
Perry, John, 75–82, 88
persons, 92–3 371–2,376, 378, 382
  as morally responsible, 93, 372–82
  rationality of, 373–5, 377, 382
Phillips, D. Z., 291
Pike, Nelson, 71–4, 147, 153, 393 n14, 394 n12, 399 nn38, 40, and 43, 400 nn46 and 48, 404 n10, 411 nn28 and 32
Plantinga, Alvin, 2, 111, 113–69, 171–3, 176, 224–34, 296
Plato, 24, 34, 47, 81, 95, 109, 126, 171, 202, 272, 273–4, 278, 290, 327, 340
Plotinus, 40
possible persons, 125–38, 143–4, 148, 154, 160, 162–4, 166–8, 171–76; see also possible worlds
possible worlds, 112, 125–6, 180–1, 183, 401 n8
  accessibility relations between, 226–7
pragmatic theory of truth, 309, 362, 400 n51
propositional attitudes, 61–4, 81, 83–5, 96, 187–8, 196
propositions, 62, 75, 171
  identity of 61–2, 73–4
Prior, A. N., 60–2
Proudfoot, Wayne, 315
psychoanalysis, 323, 325–6
Purtill, Richard, 396 n20
Putnam, Hilary, 6, 268

quasi-indicators, 82–9, 187
questions-begging arguments, 213
Quine, W. V., 181
Quinn, Philip, 235, 279, 293, 301, 410 n20

rational choice theory, 348–51
Reagan, Ronald, 132
reference (see also God, reference to)
  casual theory of, 6–7, 10–1, 300–1
  descriptive theory of, 5, 8
  by rigid designators, 73–4, 188–93, 197
Reichenbach, Hans, 245
religious diversity, 297–8, 316, 322–5, 327
religious experience, Chapter 8, 286–7, 293
  as direct experience of God's presence, 285, 289, 300–1, 305, 342
  objectivity of, 326, 340–3
  tests for veridicality of, 298–300, 303–28, 342
religious experience arguments, Chapter 8
religious experience arguments, from analogy with sense experiences, 288

421

Index